ASTOUNDING SPACE THRILLS
ARGOSY SMITH AND THE CODEX RECKONING

WRITTEN AND ILLUSTRATED BY
STEVE CONLEY

THANKS

So many people provided generous support to *AST* over the years that no list could be complete. The names below are those people who Steve would simply kick himself for the next ten years if they weren't mentioned...

Britt Conley, Marty Baumann, Marc Nathan, Rick Veitch, Dave Sim, Jackie Estrada, Karon Flage, Batton Lash, Greg McElhatton, Jeff Alexander, Greg Bennett, Joel Pollack, Marcia Allass, Jennifer Contino, Tony Isabella, Scott Schreck, Barry Lyga, Michael Dean, Cliff Biggers, Jim McLauchlin, Stephen Blue, Carla "Speed' McNeil, Sam Tannous, Aaron Myers, John Gallagher, Steve Bissette, Jeff Smith, Chris Staros, Jamie Graham, Al Stolz, Matt Brady, Glen Folland, Mark Herr, Jon Cohen, Rich Henn, Michael Cohen, Mark Wheatley, Mike Zarlenga, Marv Wolfman, Craig Miller, Jim Valentino, Larry Marder, Anthony Bozzi, Harlan Ellison and Steranko.

Also thanks to Drew Struzan, Greg and Tim Hildebrandt, Kelly and Laura Freas, Dave Dorman, Ken Kelly, Frank Cho, Dave Gibbons, Rudy Nebres and especially Steranko for their artististic contributions and spectacular talent.

Thanks to the team at IDW including Chris Ryall, Ted Adams, and Justin Eisinger.

And special thanks to the fans and readers who kept Argosy Smith alive a lot longer than anyone expected.

Cover by **DREW STRUZAN**

Collection Edits by **JUSTIN EISINGER** & **LESLIE MANES**

Production by **NEIL UYETAKE**

IDW Publishing
Operations:
Moshe Berger, Chairman
Ted Adams, Chief Executive Officer
Greg Goldstein, Chief Operating Officer
Matthew Ruzicka, CPA, Chief Financial Officer
Alan Payne, VP of Sales
Lorelei Bunjes, Dir. of Digital Services
Marci Hubbard, Executive Assistant
Alonzo Simon, Shipping Manager

Editorial:
Chris Ryall, Publisher/Editor-in-Chief
Scott Dunbier, Editor, Special Projects
Andy Schmidt, Senior Editor
Justin Eisinger, Editor
Kris Oprisko, Editor/Foreign Lic.
Denton J. Tipton, Editor
Tom Waltz, Editor
Mariah Huehner, Assistant Editor

Design:
Robbie Robbins, EVP/Sr. Graphic Artist
Ben Templesmith, Artist/Designer
Neil Uyetake, Art Director
Chris Mowry, Graphic Artist
Amauri Osorio, Graphic Artist

978-1-60010-320-9

11 10 09 08   1 2 3 4

www.IDWpublishing.com

Foreword

"A few short years into the 21st century, the laws governing the universe change — time flows at a different angle, space folds against the grain and positive particles aren't so sure."

Racing against death. Living as fully as possible. Never giving up. Smiling 90% of the time. Clearly not sleeping much.

I really, really like Argosy Smith.

I know, I know. As his creator, I'm biased.

Ask most artists to look back on their work from ten years ago and they won't do it. It's too painful. Too embarassing. We tend to be our own harshest critics but as I look back on these stories and despite the growing pains of the artwork, I have only one reaction: what the hell was I thinking?

A hero who's supposed to die in the second issue? A 100-year-old sidekick? Efeldian fire poodles?

I think the best thing about these adventures is the go-for-broke nature of each one. Just like Argosy Smith racing the clock, the skeptic in me assumed that each issue of *Astounding Space Thrills* would be the last so I might as well jam as many weird, funny and off-the-wall ideas as I could into each issue. And I did that for 15 issues and 500 online comics strips.

When I set out to start *Astounding Space Thrills*, it was to create the kind of comics I wanted to read. Looking back from the safe distance of a decade, it turns out I did.

I hope you enjoy them as well!

— Steve Conley, 2008

STEVE CONLEY'S
ASTOUNDING
1
SPACE THRILLS
$2.95
FEATURING
ARGOSY SMITH
IN THE
CODEX
RECKONING

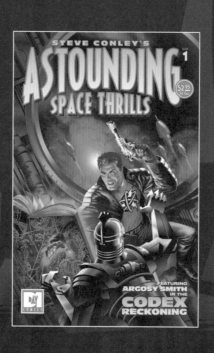

ASTOUNDING SPACE THRILLS #1
MAY 1998

COVER BY STERANKO AND STEVE CONLEY

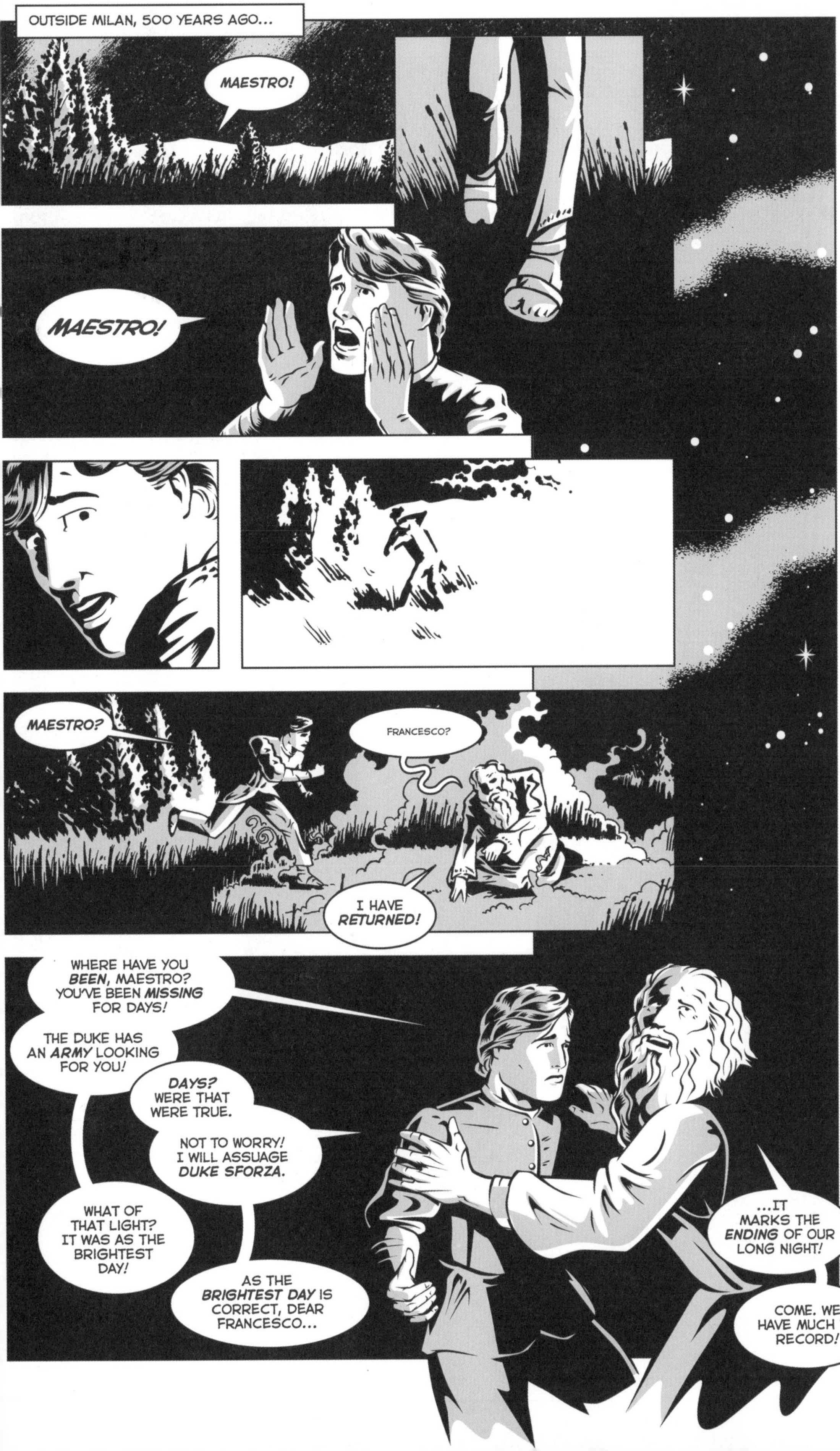

OUTSIDE MILAN, 500 YEARS AGO...
MAESTRO!
MAESTRO!
MAESTRO?
FRANCESCO?
I HAVE RETURNED!
WHERE HAVE YOU BEEN, MAESTRO? YOU'VE BEEN MISSING FOR DAYS!
THE DUKE HAS AN ARMY LOOKING FOR YOU!
DAYS? WERE THAT WERE TRUE.
NOT TO WORRY! I WILL ASSUAGE DUKE SFORZA.
WHAT OF THAT LIGHT? IT WAS AS THE BRIGHTEST DAY!
AS THE BRIGHTEST DAY IS CORRECT, DEAR FRANCESCO...
...IT MARKS THE ENDING OF OUR LONG NIGHT!
COME. WE HAVE MUCH TO RECORD!

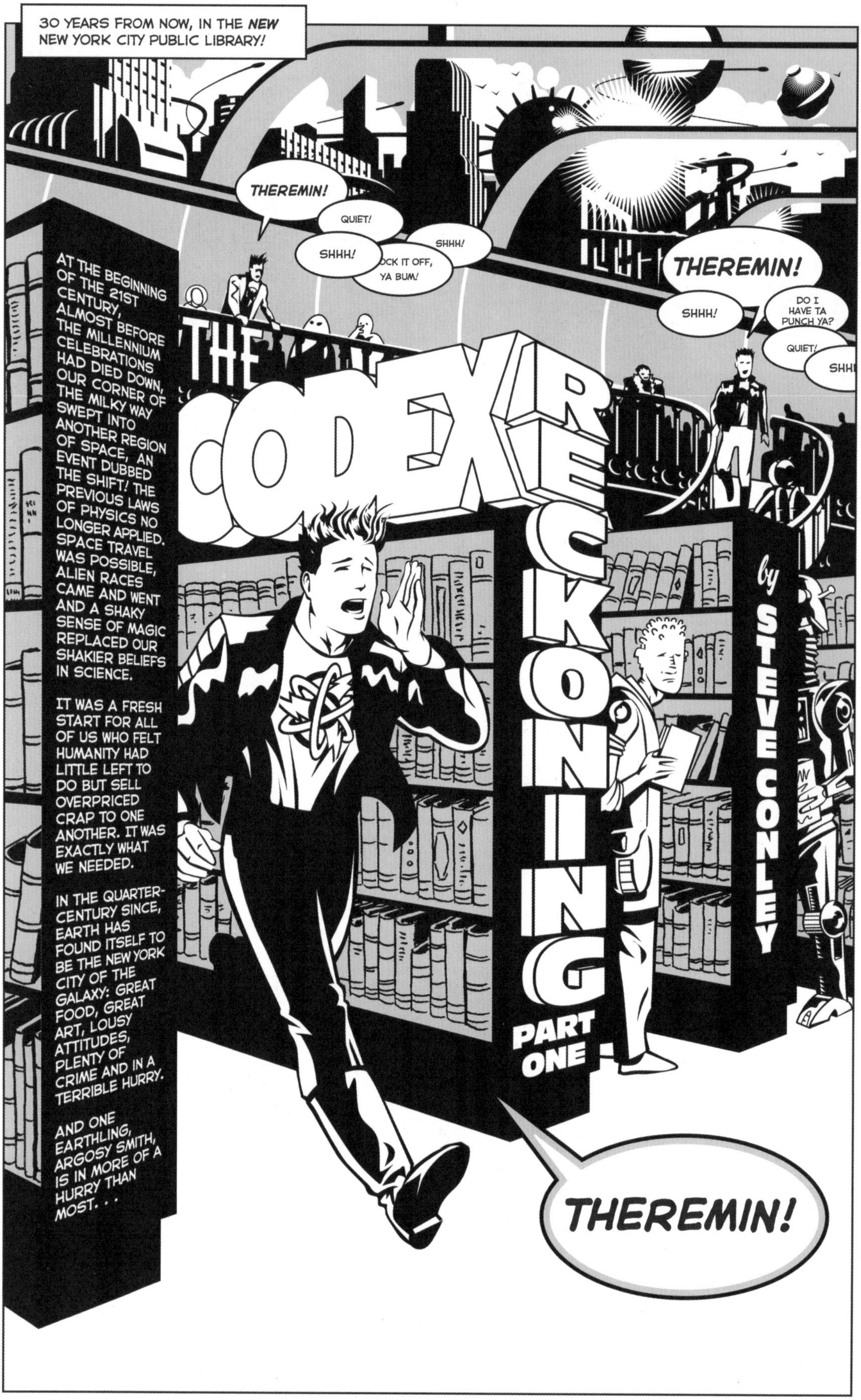
30 YEARS FROM NOW, IN THE *NEW* NEW YORK CITY PUBLIC LIBRARY!
AT THE BEGINNING OF THE 21ST CENTURY, ALMOST BEFORE THE MILLENNIUM CELEBRATIONS HAD DIED DOWN, OUR CORNER OF THE MILKY WAY SWEPT INTO ANOTHER REGION OF SPACE, AN EVENT DUBBED THE SHIFT! THE PREVIOUS LAWS OF PHYSICS NO LONGER APPLIED. SPACE TRAVEL WAS POSSIBLE, ALIEN RACES CAME AND WENT AND A SHAKY SENSE OF MAGIC REPLACED OUR SHAKIER BELIEFS IN SCIENCE.
IT WAS A FRESH START FOR ALL OF US WHO FELT HUMANITY HAD LITTLE LEFT TO DO BUT SELL OVERPRICED CRAP TO ONE ANOTHER. IT WAS EXACTLY WHAT WE NEEDED.
IN THE QUARTER-CENTURY SINCE, EARTH HAS FOUND ITSELF TO BE THE NEW YORK CITY OF THE GALAXY: GREAT FOOD, GREAT ART, LOUSY ATTITUDES, PLENTY OF CRIME AND IN A TERRIBLE HURRY.
AND ONE EARTHLING, ARGOSY SMITH, IS IN MORE OF A HURRY THAN MOST. . .
THEREMIN!
QUIET!
SHHH!
SHHH!
OCK IT OFF, YA BUM!
THEREMIN!
SHHH!
DO I HAVE TA PUNCH YA?
QUIET!
SHH
THE CODEX RECKONING
PART ONE
by STEVE CONLEY
THEREMIN!

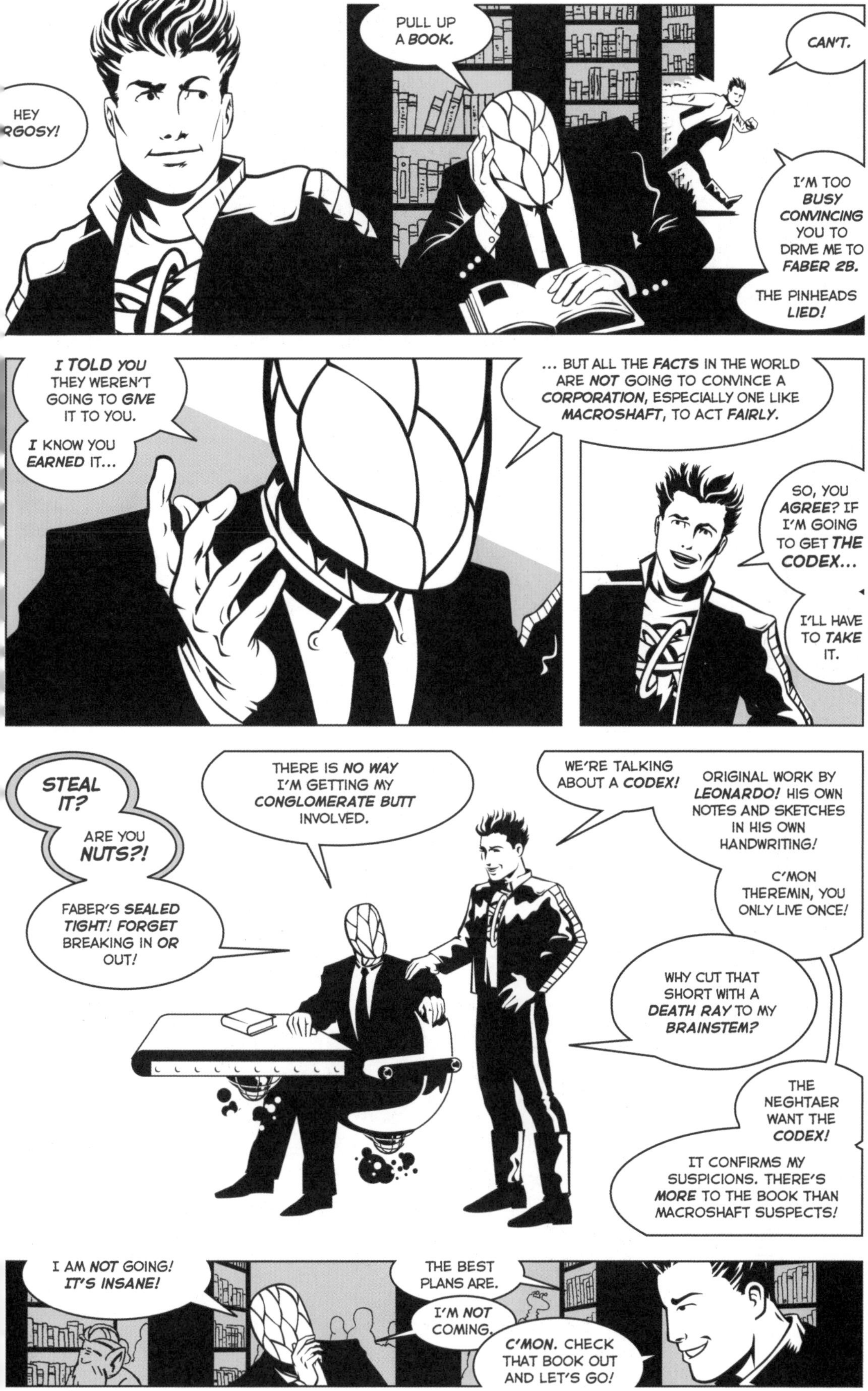

HEY
RGOSY!
PULL UP
A BOOK.
CAN'T.
I'M TOO BUSY CONVINCING YOU TO DRIVE ME TO FABER 2B.
THE PINHEADS LIED!
I TOLD YOU THEY WEREN'T GOING TO GIVE IT TO YOU.
I KNOW YOU EARNED IT...
... BUT ALL THE FACTS IN THE WORLD ARE NOT GOING TO CONVINCE A CORPORATION, ESPECIALLY ONE LIKE MACROSHAFT, TO ACT FAIRLY.
SO, YOU AGREE? IF I'M GOING TO GET THE CODEX...
I'LL HAVE TO TAKE IT.
STEAL IT?
ARE YOU NUTS?!
FABER'S SEALED TIGHT! FORGET BREAKING IN OR OUT!
THERE IS NO WAY I'M GETTING MY CONGLOMERATE BUTT INVOLVED.
WE'RE TALKING ABOUT A CODEX!
ORIGINAL WORK BY LEONARDO! HIS OWN NOTES AND SKETCHES IN HIS OWN HANDWRITING!
C'MON THEREMIN, YOU ONLY LIVE ONCE!
WHY CUT THAT SHORT WITH A DEATH RAY TO MY BRAINSTEM?
THE NEGHTAER WANT THE CODEX!
IT CONFIRMS MY SUSPICIONS. THERE'S MORE TO THE BOOK THAN MACROSHAFT SUSPECTS!
I AM NOT GOING! IT'S INSANE!
THE BEST PLANS ARE.
I'M NOT COMING.
C'MON. CHECK THAT BOOK OUT AND LET'S GO!

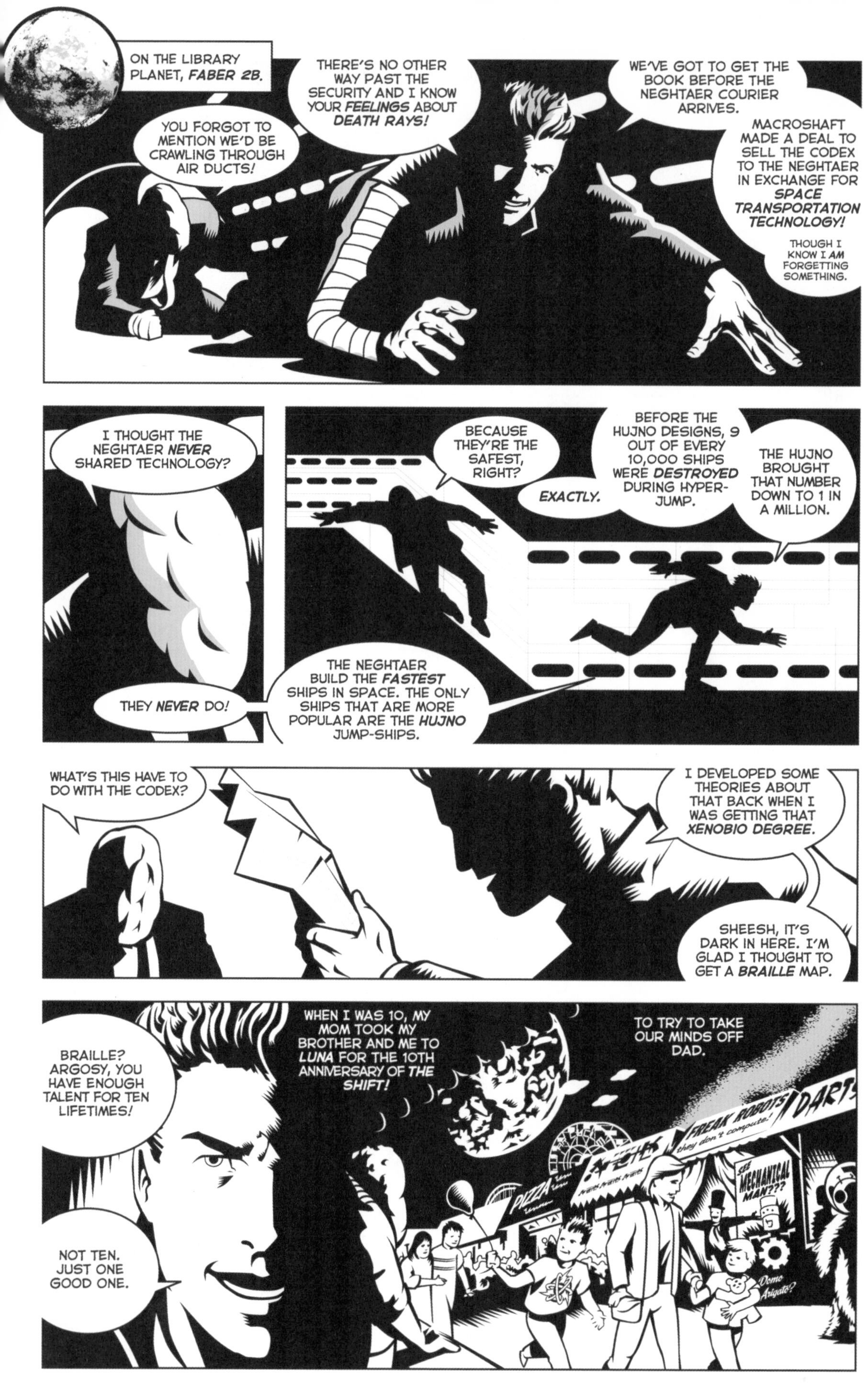
ON THE LIBRARY PLANET, *FABER 2B.*
YOU FORGOT TO MENTION WE'D BE CRAWLING THROUGH AIR DUCTS!
THERE'S NO OTHER WAY PAST THE SECURITY AND I KNOW YOUR *FEELINGS* ABOUT *DEATH RAYS!*
WE'VE GOT TO GET THE BOOK BEFORE THE NEGHTAER COURIER ARRIVES.
MACROSHAFT MADE A DEAL TO SELL THE CODEX TO THE NEGHTAER IN EXCHANGE FOR *SPACE TRANSPORTATION TECHNOLOGY!*
THOUGH I KNOW I *AM* FORGETTING SOMETHING.
I THOUGHT THE NEGHTAER *NEVER* SHARED TECHNOLOGY?
THEY *NEVER* DO!
THE NEGHTAER BUILD THE *FASTEST* SHIPS IN SPACE. THE ONLY SHIPS THAT ARE MORE POPULAR ARE THE *HUJNO* JUMP-SHIPS.
BECAUSE THEY'RE THE SAFEST, RIGHT?
EXACTLY.
BEFORE THE HUJNO DESIGNS, 9 OUT OF EVERY 10,000 SHIPS WERE *DESTROYED* DURING HYPER-JUMP.
THE HUJNO BROUGHT THAT NUMBER DOWN TO 1 IN A MILLION.
WHAT'S THIS HAVE TO DO WITH THE CODEX?
I DEVELOPED SOME THEORIES ABOUT THAT BACK WHEN I WAS GETTING THAT *XENOBIO DEGREE*.
SHEESH, IT'S DARK IN HERE. I'M GLAD I THOUGHT TO GET A *BRAILLE* MAP.
BRAILLE? ARGOSY, YOU HAVE ENOUGH TALENT FOR TEN LIFETIMES!
NOT TEN. JUST ONE GOOD ONE.
WHEN I WAS 10, MY MOM TOOK MY BROTHER AND ME TO *LUNA* FOR THE 10TH ANNIVERSARY OF *THE SHIFT!*
TO TRY TO TAKE OUR MINDS OFF DAD.
PIZZA
FREAK ROBOTS
they don't compute!
DARTS
SEE MECHANICAL MAN???
Domo Arigato?

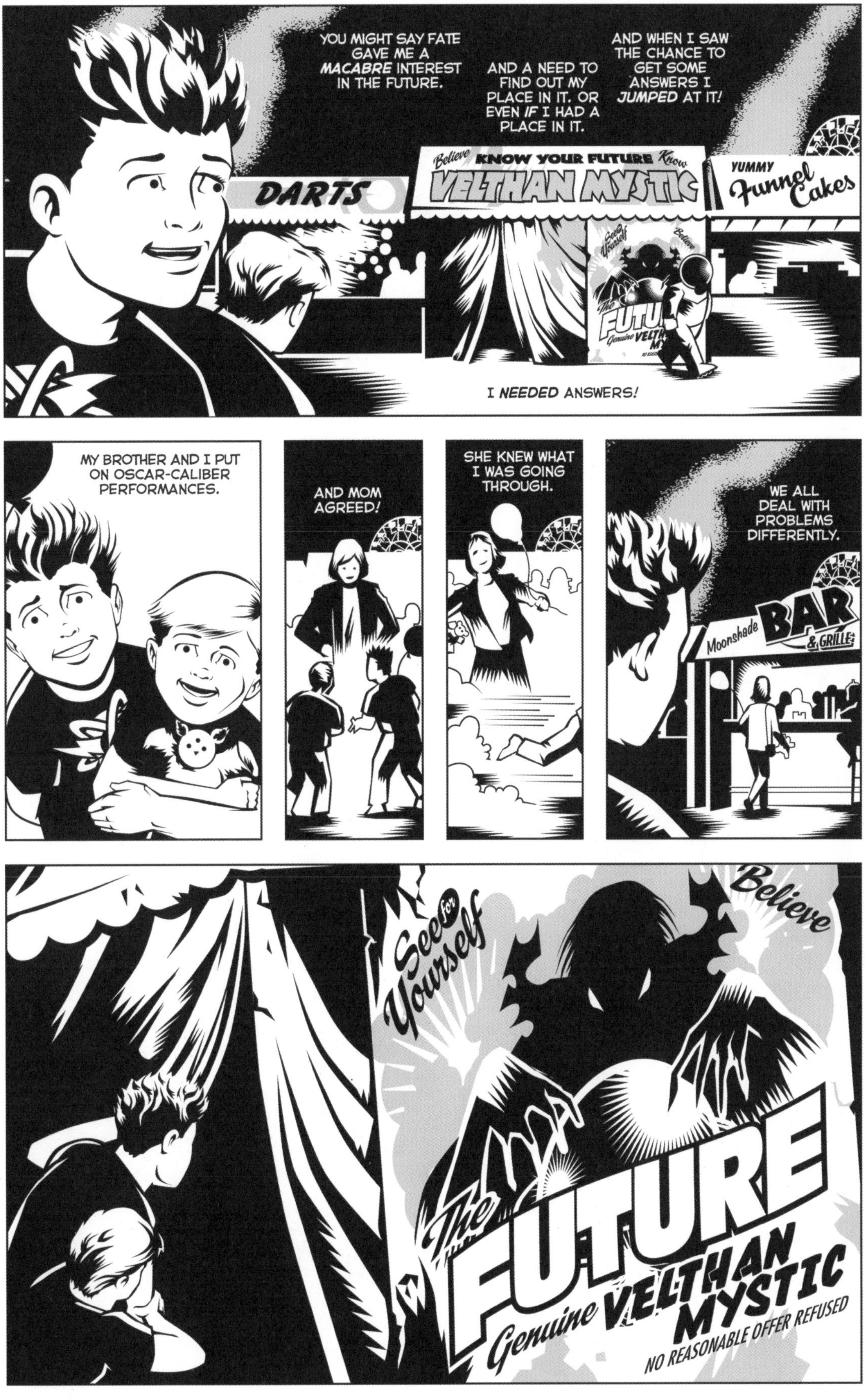

YOU MIGHT SAY FATE GAVE ME A *MACABRE* INTEREST IN THE FUTURE.
AND A NEED TO FIND OUT MY PLACE IN IT. OR EVEN *IF* I HAD A PLACE IN IT.
AND WHEN I SAW THE CHANCE TO GET SOME ANSWERS I *JUMPED* AT IT!
DARTS
Believe
KNOW YOUR FUTURE
Know
VELTHAN MYSTIC
YUMMY
Funnel Cakes
I *NEEDED* ANSWERS!
MY BROTHER AND I PUT ON OSCAR-CALIBER PERFORMANCES.
AND MOM AGREED!
SHE KNEW WHAT I WAS GOING THROUGH.
WE ALL DEAL WITH PROBLEMS DIFFERENTLY.
Moonshade BAR & GRILLE
See for Yourself
Believe
The FUTURE
Genuine VELTHAN MYSTIC
NO REASONABLE OFFER REFUSED

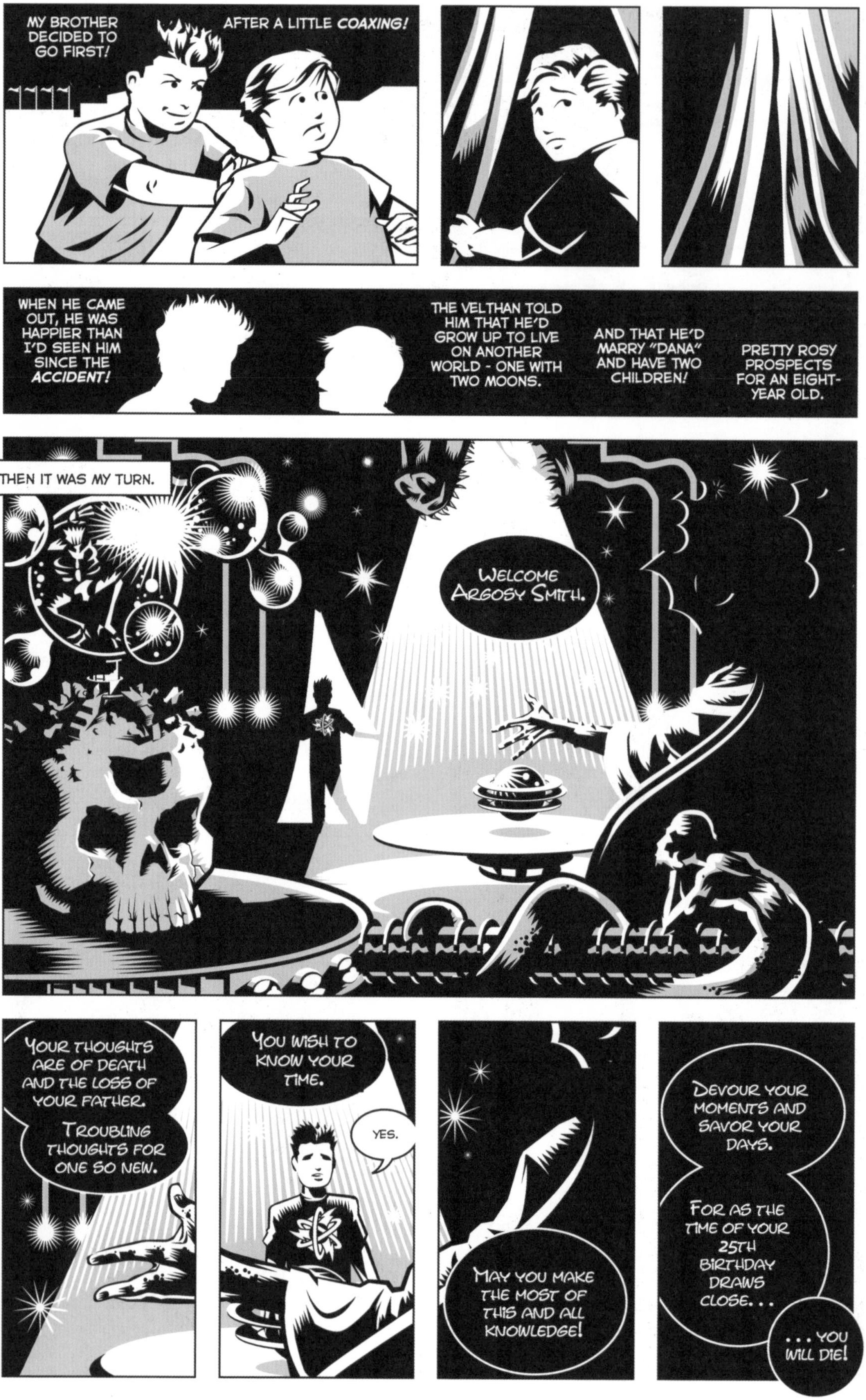
MY BROTHER DECIDED TO GO FIRST!
AFTER A LITTLE COAXING!
WHEN HE CAME OUT, HE WAS HAPPIER THAN I'D SEEN HIM SINCE THE ACCIDENT!
THE VELTHAN TOLD HIM THAT HE'D GROW UP TO LIVE ON ANOTHER WORLD - ONE WITH TWO MOONS.
AND THAT HE'D MARRY "DANA" AND HAVE TWO CHILDREN!
PRETTY ROSY PROSPECTS FOR AN EIGHT-YEAR OLD.
THEN IT WAS MY TURN.
WELCOME ARGOSY SMITH.
YOUR THOUGHTS ARE OF DEATH AND THE LOSS OF YOUR FATHER.
TROUBLING THOUGHTS FOR ONE SO NEW.
YOU WISH TO KNOW YOUR TIME.
YES.
MAY YOU MAKE THE MOST OF THIS AND ALL KNOWLEDGE!
DEVOUR YOUR MOMENTS AND SAVOR YOUR DAYS.
FOR AS THE TIME OF YOUR 25TH BIRTHDAY DRAWS CLOSE...
...YOU WILL DIE!

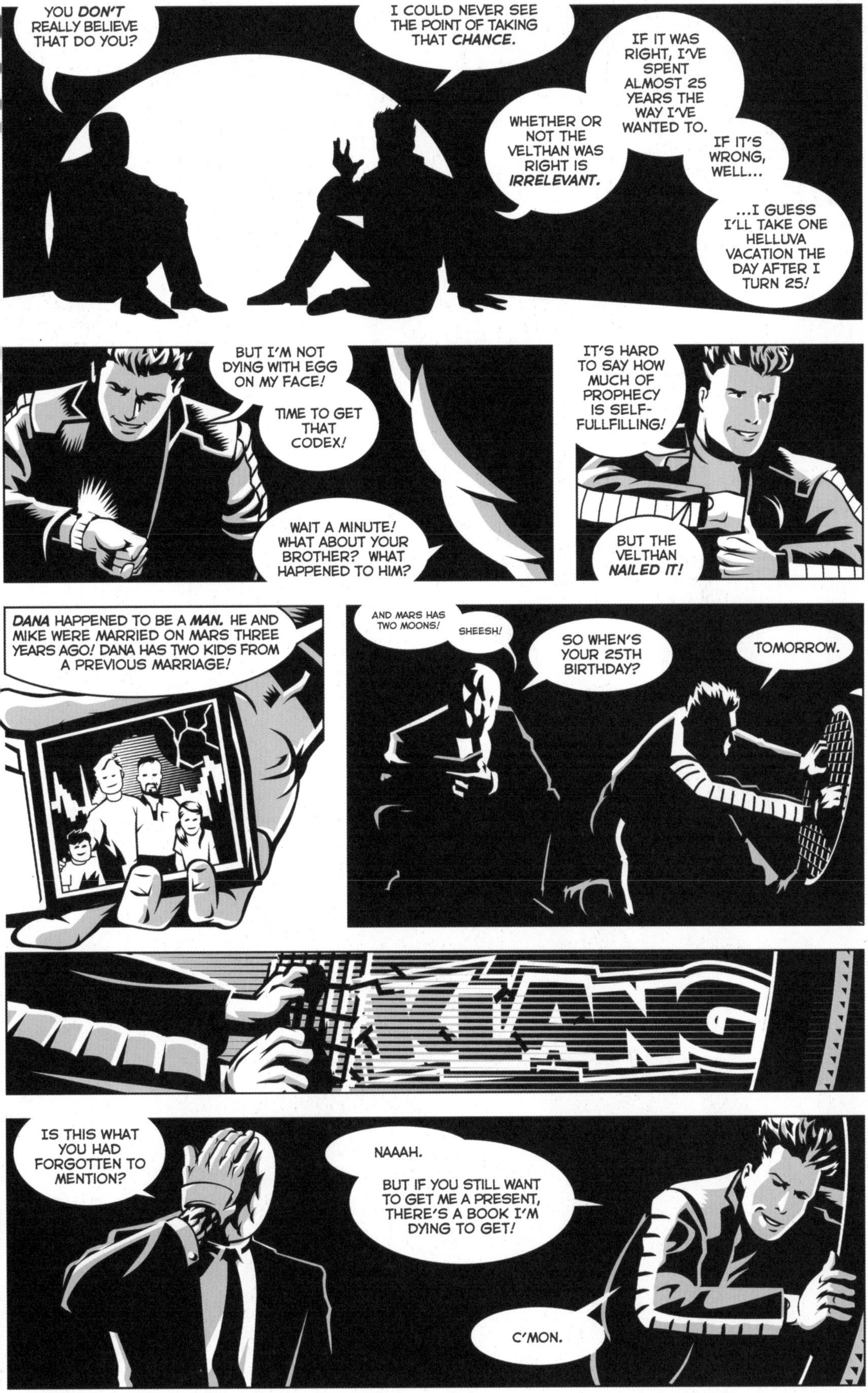
YOU DON'T REALLY BELIEVE THAT DO YOU?
I COULD NEVER SEE THE POINT OF TAKING THAT CHANCE.
WHETHER OR NOT THE VELTHAN WAS RIGHT IS IRRELEVANT.
IF IT WAS RIGHT, I'VE SPENT ALMOST 25 YEARS THE WAY I'VE WANTED TO.
IF IT'S WRONG, WELL...
...I GUESS I'LL TAKE ONE HELLUVA VACATION THE DAY AFTER I TURN 25!
BUT I'M NOT DYING WITH EGG ON MY FACE!
TIME TO GET THAT CODEX!
WAIT A MINUTE! WHAT ABOUT YOUR BROTHER? WHAT HAPPENED TO HIM?
IT'S HARD TO SAY HOW MUCH OF PROPHECY IS SELF-FULLFILLING!
BUT THE VELTHAN NAILED IT!
DANA HAPPENED TO BE A MAN. HE AND MIKE WERE MARRIED ON MARS THREE YEARS AGO! DANA HAS TWO KIDS FROM A PREVIOUS MARRIAGE!
AND MARS HAS TWO MOONS!
SHEESH!
SO WHEN'S YOUR 25TH BIRTHDAY?
TOMORROW.
KLANG
IS THIS WHAT YOU HAD FORGOTTEN TO MENTION?
NAAAH.
BUT IF YOU STILL WANT TO GET ME A PRESENT, THERE'S A BOOK I'M DYING TO GET!
C'MON.

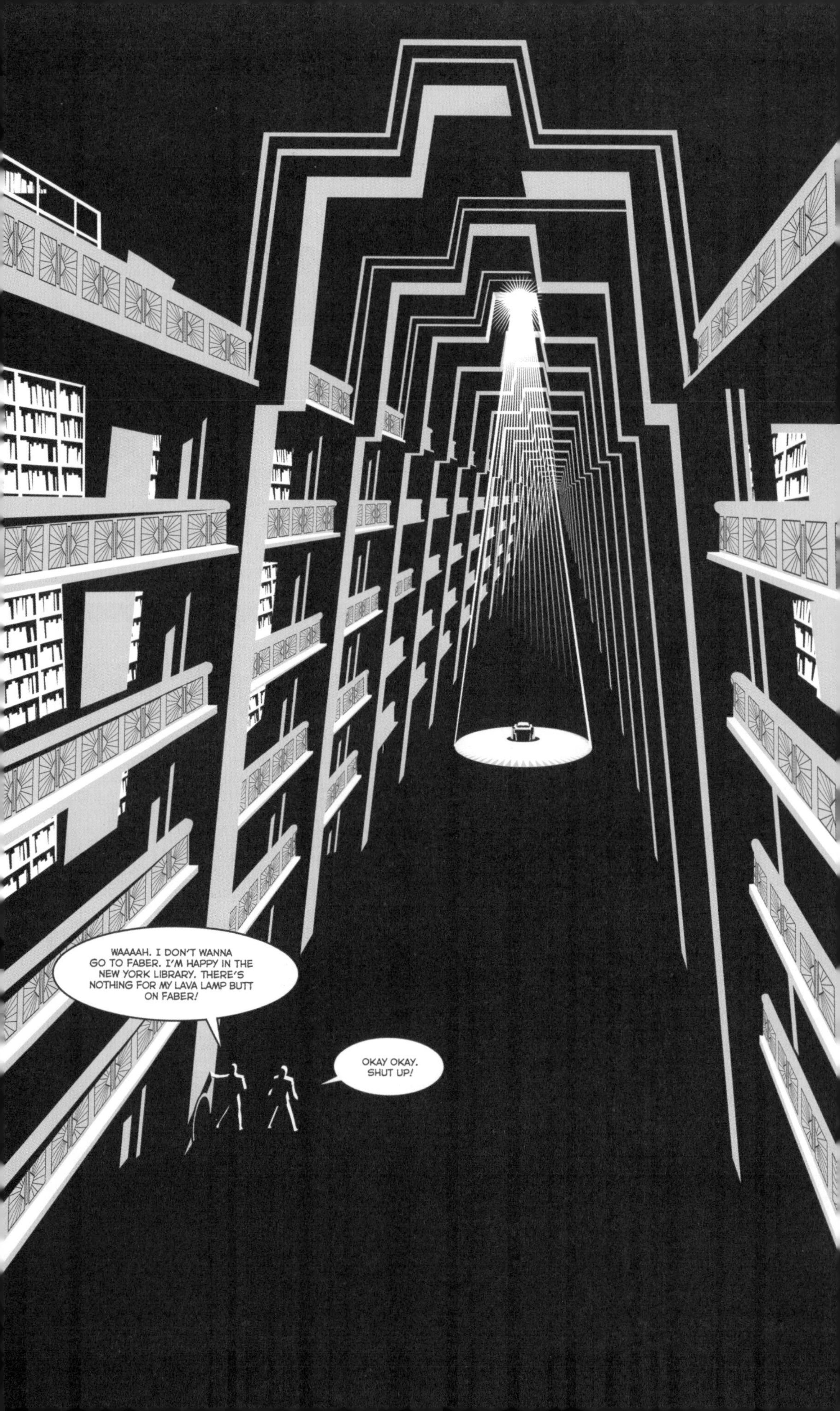

WAAAAH. I DON'T WANNA GO TO FABER. I'M HAPPY IN THE NEW YORK LIBRARY. THERE'S NOTHING FOR MY LAVA LAMP BUTT ON FABER!
OKAY OKAY. SHUT UP!

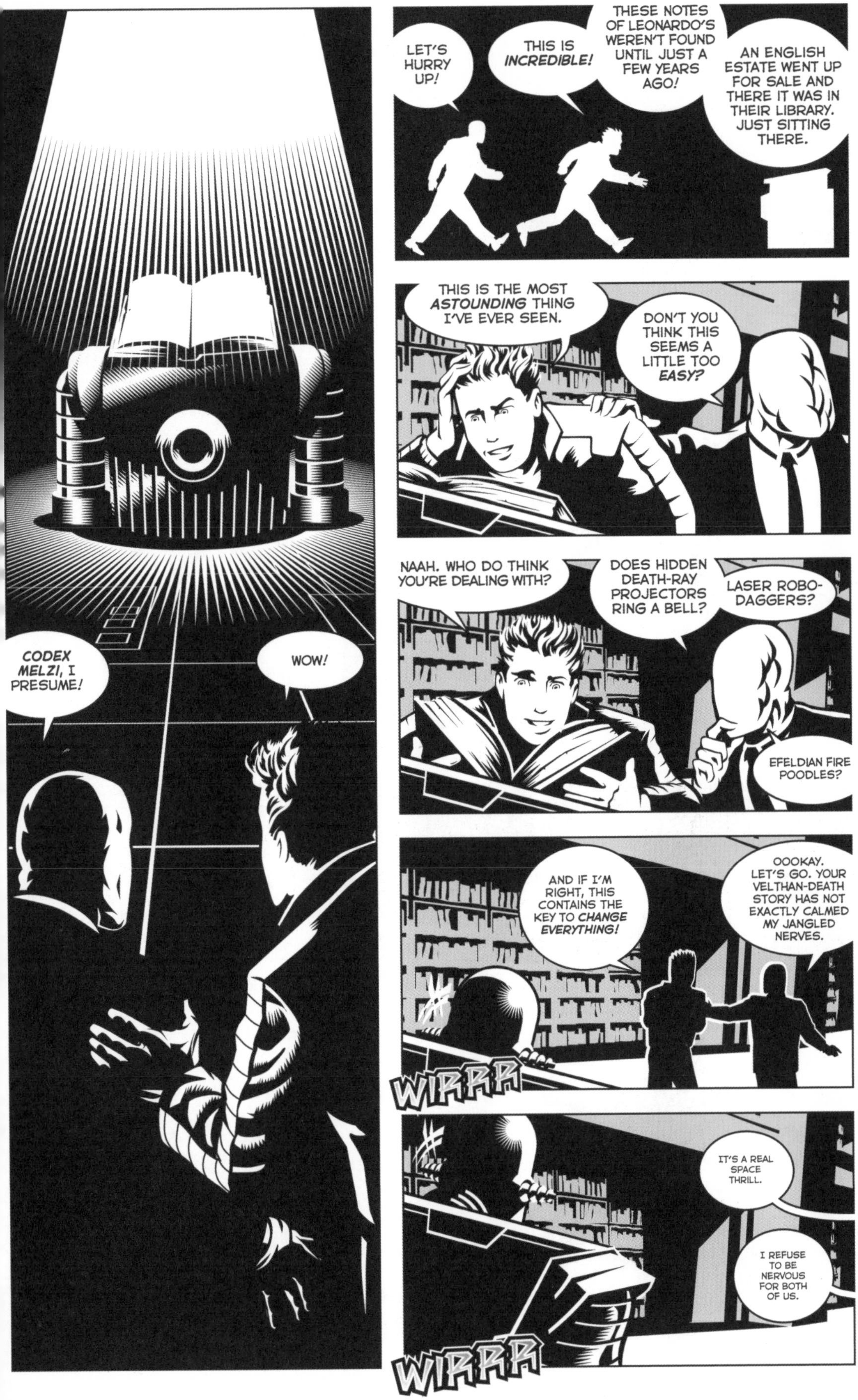
CODEX MELZI, I PRESUME!
WOW!
LET'S HURRY UP!
THIS IS INCREDIBLE!
THESE NOTES OF LEONARDO'S WEREN'T FOUND UNTIL JUST A FEW YEARS AGO!
AN ENGLISH ESTATE WENT UP FOR SALE AND THERE IT WAS IN THEIR LIBRARY. JUST SITTING THERE.
THIS IS THE MOST ASTOUNDING THING I'VE EVER SEEN.
DON'T YOU THINK THIS SEEMS A LITTLE TOO EASY?
NAAH. WHO DO THINK YOU'RE DEALING WITH?
DOES HIDDEN DEATH-RAY PROJECTORS RING A BELL?
LASER ROBO-DAGGERS?
EFELDIAN FIRE POODLES?
AND IF I'M RIGHT, THIS CONTAINS THE KEY TO CHANGE EVERYTHING!
OOOKAY. LET'S GO. YOUR VELTHAN-DEATH STORY HAS NOT EXACTLY CALMED MY JANGLED NERVES.
WIRRR
IT'S A REAL SPACE THRILL.
I REFUSE TO BE NERVOUS FOR BOTH OF US.
WIRRR

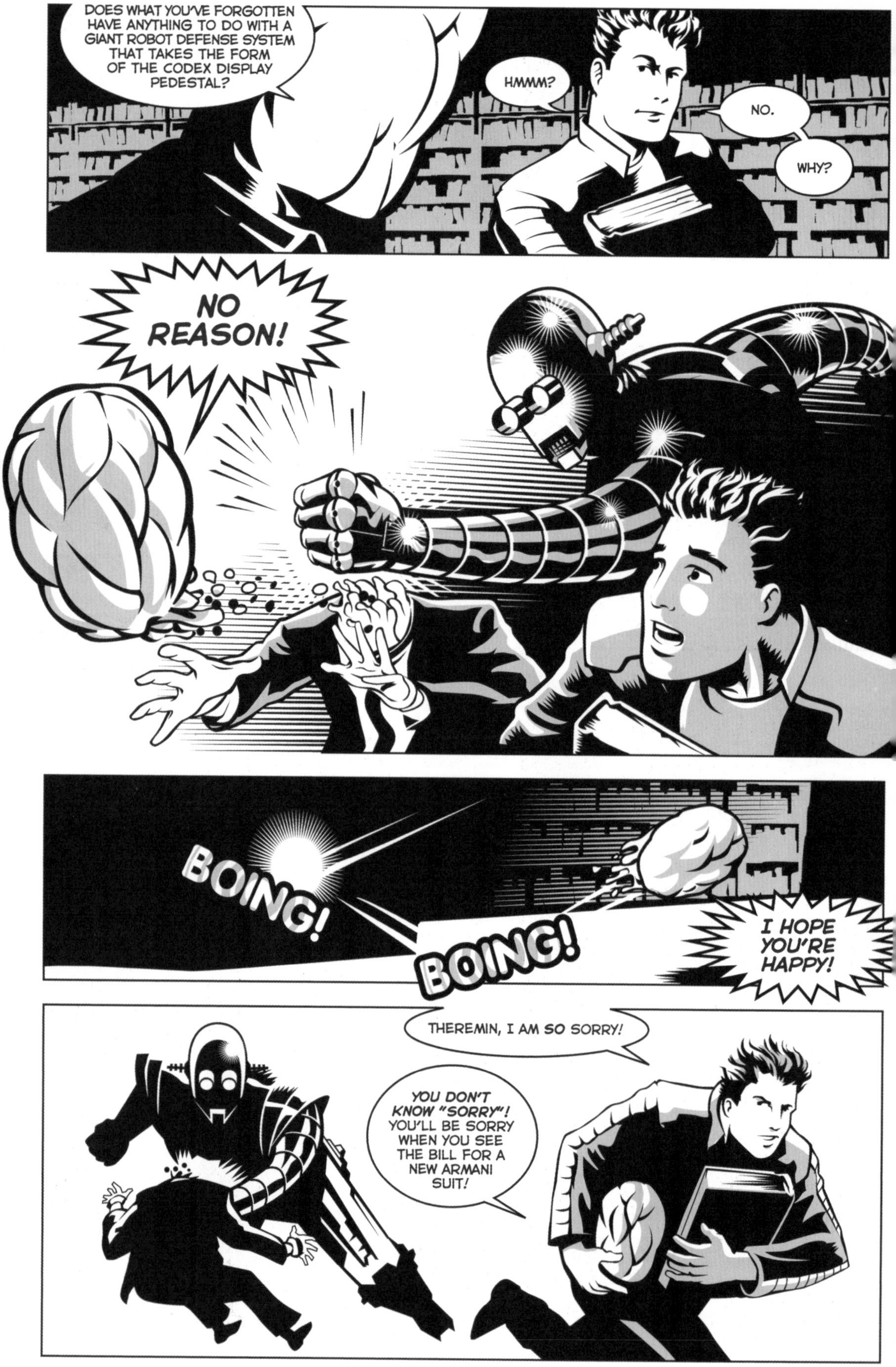
DOES WHAT YOU'VE FORGOTTEN HAVE ANYTHING TO DO WITH A GIANT ROBOT DEFENSE SYSTEM THAT TAKES THE FORM OF THE CODEX DISPLAY PEDESTAL?
HMMM?
NO.
WHY?
NO REASON!
BOING!
BOING!
I HOPE YOU'RE HAPPY!
THEREMIN, I AM SO SORRY!
YOU DON'T KNOW "SORRY"! YOU'LL BE SORRY WHEN YOU SEE THE BILL FOR A NEW ARMANI SUIT!

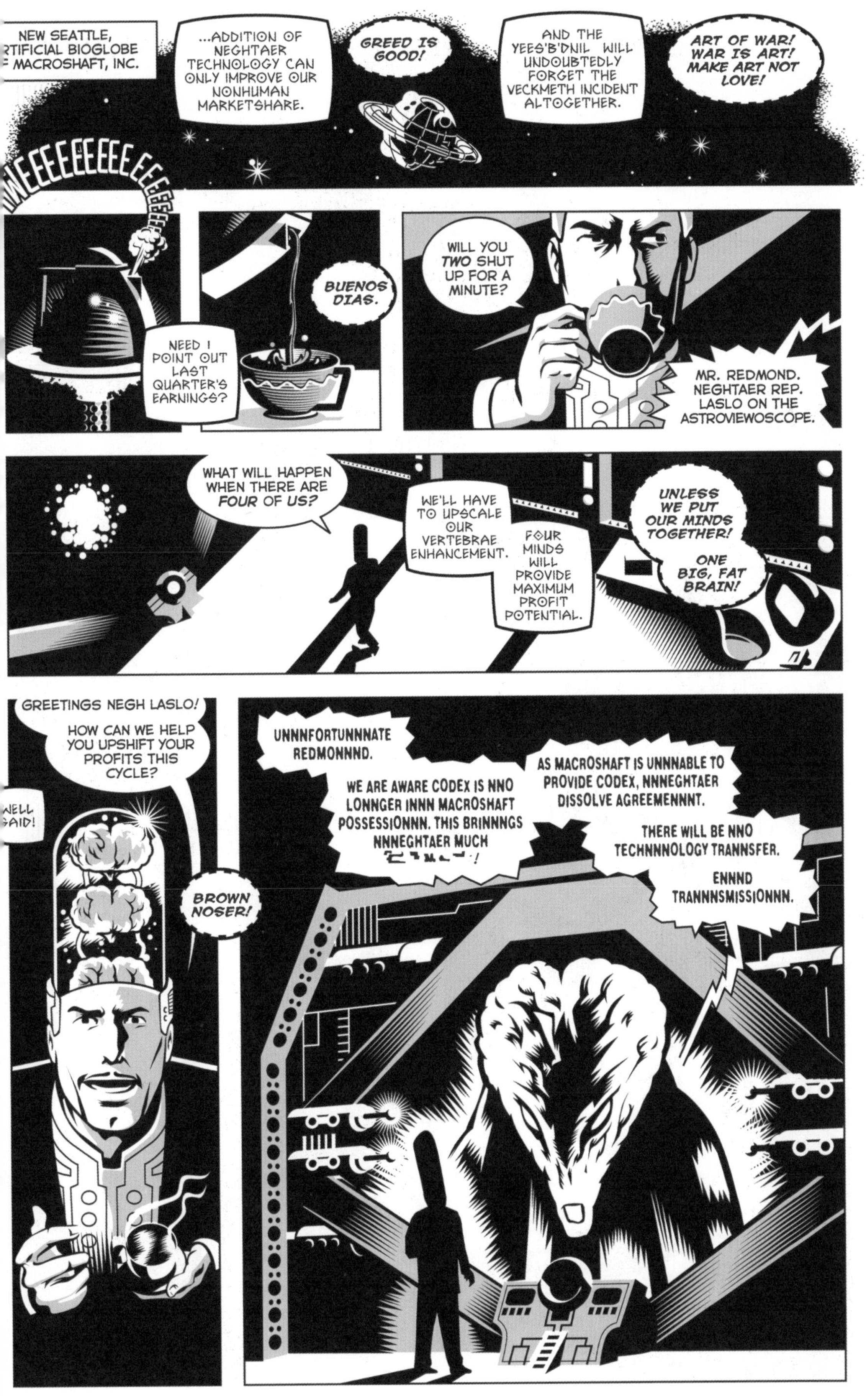
NEW SEATTLE, RTIFICIAL BIOGLOBE F MACROSHAFT, INC.
...ADDITION OF NEGHTAER TECHNOLOGY CAN ONLY IMPROVE OUR NONHUMAN MARKETSHARE.
GREED IS GOOD!
AND THE YEES'B'DNIL WILL UNDOUBTEDLY FORGET THE VECKMETH INCIDENT ALTOGETHER.
ART OF WAR! WAR IS ART! MAKE ART NOT LOVE!
WEEEEEEEEEEEEEEEEEE
NEED I POINT OUT LAST QUARTER'S EARNINGS?
BUENOS DIAS.
WILL YOU TWO SHUT UP FOR A MINUTE?
MR. REDMOND. NEGHTAER REP. LASLO ON THE ASTROVIEWOSCOPE.
WHAT WILL HAPPEN WHEN THERE ARE FOUR OF US?
WE'LL HAVE TO UPSCALE OUR VERTEBRAE ENHANCEMENT.
FOUR MINDS WILL PROVIDE MAXIMUM PROFIT POTENTIAL.
UNLESS WE PUT OUR MINDS TOGETHER!
ONE BIG, FAT BRAIN!
GREETINGS NEGH LASLO!
HOW CAN WE HELP YOU UPSHIFT YOUR PROFITS THIS CYCLE?
WELL SAID!
BROWN NOSER!
UNNNFORTUNNNATE REDMONNND.
WE ARE AWARE CODEX IS NNO LONNGER INNN MACROSHAFT POSSESSIONNN. THIS BRINNNGS NNNEGHTAER MUCH
AS MACROSHAFT IS UNNNABLE TO PROVIDE CODEX, NNNEGHTAER DISSOLVE AGREEMENNNT.
THERE WILL BE NNO TECHNNNOLOGY TRANNSFER.
ENNND TRANNNSMISSIONNN.

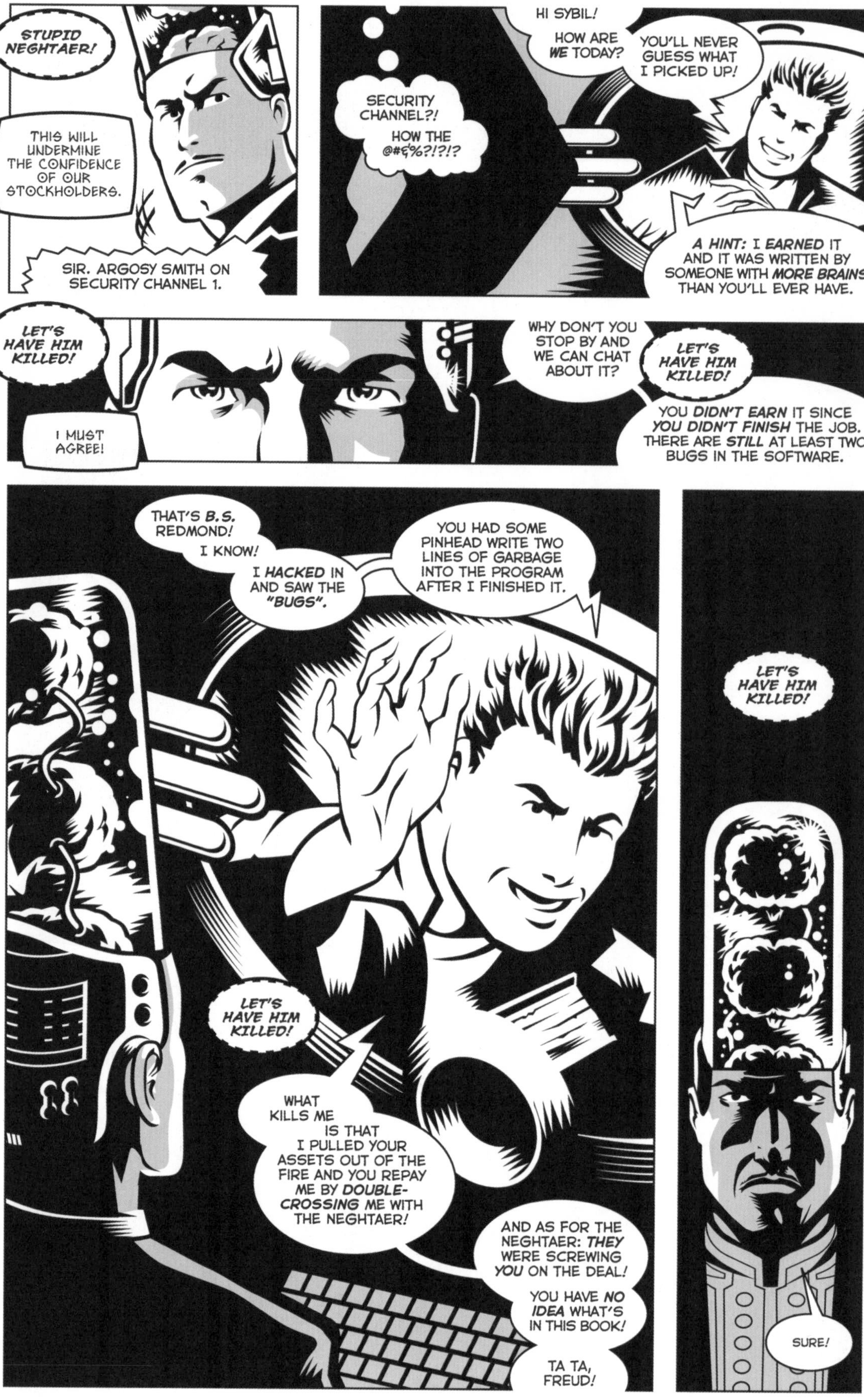
STUPID NEGHTAER!
THIS WILL UNDERMINE THE CONFIDENCE OF OUR STOCKHOLDERS.
SIR. ARGOSY SMITH ON SECURITY CHANNEL 1.
SECURITY CHANNEL?! HOW THE @#€%?!?!?
HI SYBIL!
HOW ARE WE TODAY?
YOU'LL NEVER GUESS WHAT I PICKED UP!
A HINT: I EARNED IT AND IT WAS WRITTEN BY SOMEONE WITH MORE BRAINS THAN YOU'LL EVER HAVE.
LET'S HAVE HIM KILLED!
I MUST AGREE!
WHY DON'T YOU STOP BY AND WE CAN CHAT ABOUT IT?
LET'S HAVE HIM KILLED!
YOU DIDN'T EARN IT SINCE YOU DIDN'T FINISH THE JOB. THERE ARE STILL AT LEAST TWO BUGS IN THE SOFTWARE.
THAT'S B.S. REDMOND!
I KNOW!
I HACKED IN AND SAW THE "BUGS".
YOU HAD SOME PINHEAD WRITE TWO LINES OF GARBAGE INTO THE PROGRAM AFTER I FINISHED IT.
LET'S HAVE HIM KILLED!
WHAT KILLS ME IS THAT I PULLED YOUR ASSETS OUT OF THE FIRE AND YOU REPAY ME BY DOUBLE-CROSSING ME WITH THE NEGHTAER!
AND AS FOR THE NEGHTAER: THEY WERE SCREWING YOU ON THE DEAL!
YOU HAVE NO IDEA WHAT'S IN THIS BOOK!
TA TA, FREUD!
LET'S HAVE HIM KILLED!
SURE!

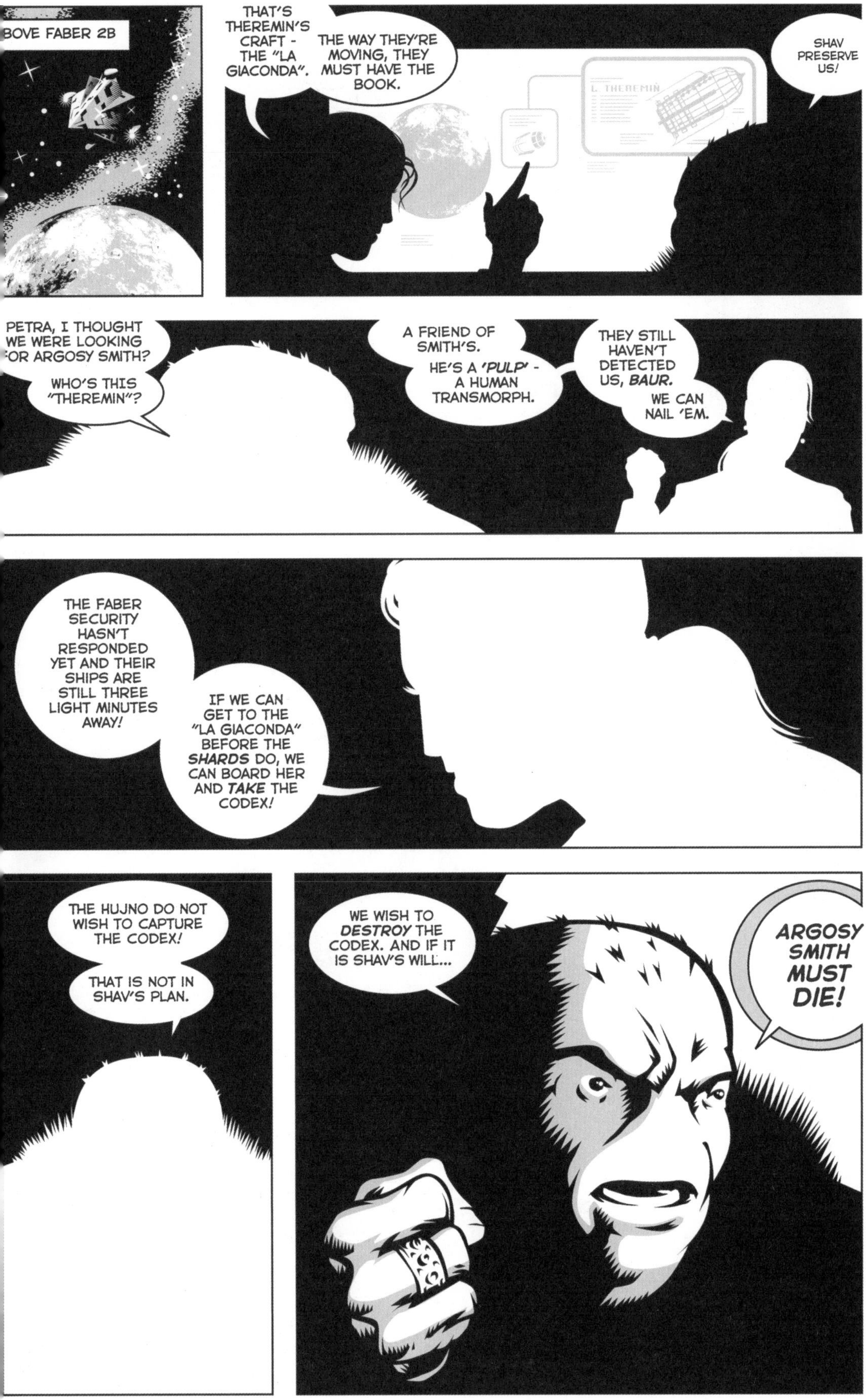
BOVE FABER 2B
THAT'S THEREMIN'S CRAFT - THE "LA GIACONDA".
THE WAY THEY'RE MOVING, THEY MUST HAVE THE BOOK.
SHAV PRESERVE US!
L. THEREMIN
PETRA, I THOUGHT WE WERE LOOKING FOR ARGOSY SMITH?
WHO'S THIS "THEREMIN"?
A FRIEND OF SMITH'S.
HE'S A *'PULP'* - A HUMAN TRANSMORPH.
THEY STILL HAVEN'T DETECTED US, *BAUR.*
WE CAN NAIL 'EM.
THE FABER SECURITY HASN'T RESPONDED YET AND THEIR SHIPS ARE STILL THREE LIGHT MINUTES AWAY!
IF WE CAN GET TO THE "LA GIACONDA" BEFORE THE *SHARDS* DO, WE CAN BOARD HER AND *TAKE* THE CODEX!
THE HUJNO DO NOT WISH TO CAPTURE THE CODEX!
THAT IS NOT IN SHAV'S PLAN.
WE WISH TO *DESTROY* THE CODEX. AND IF IT IS SHAV'S WILL...
ARGOSY SMITH MUST DIE!

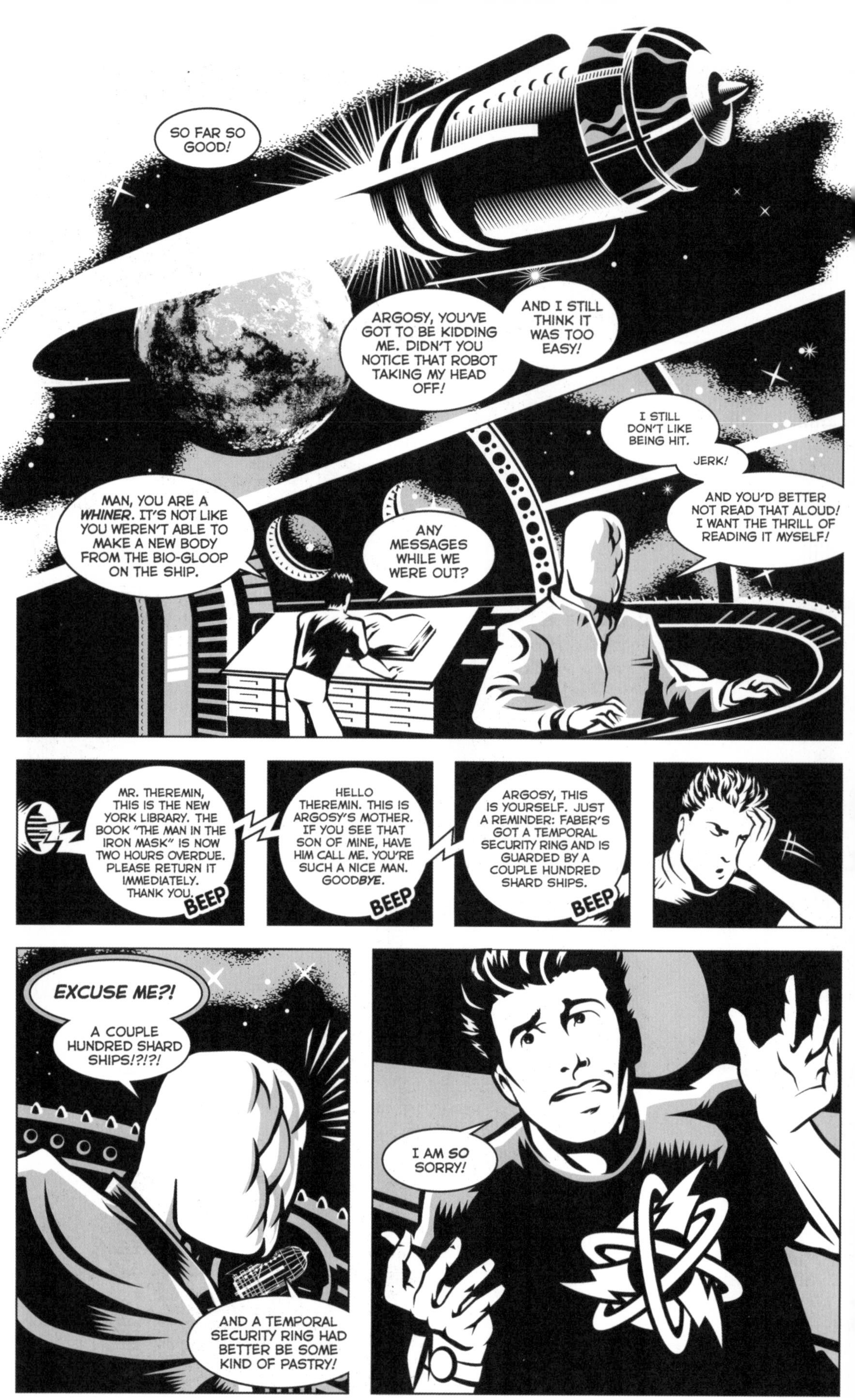

SO FAR SO GOOD!
ARGOSY, YOU'VE GOT TO BE KIDDING ME. DIDN'T YOU NOTICE THAT ROBOT TAKING MY HEAD OFF!
AND I STILL THINK IT WAS TOO EASY!
I STILL DON'T LIKE BEING HIT.
JERK!
MAN, YOU ARE A *WHINER*. IT'S NOT LIKE YOU WEREN'T ABLE TO MAKE A NEW BODY FROM THE BIO-GLOOP ON THE SHIP.
ANY MESSAGES WHILE WE WERE OUT?
AND YOU'D BETTER NOT READ THAT ALOUD! I WANT THE THRILL OF READING IT MYSELF!
MR. THEREMIN, THIS IS THE NEW YORK LIBRARY. THE BOOK "THE MAN IN THE IRON MASK" IS NOW TWO HOURS OVERDUE. PLEASE RETURN IT IMMEDIATELY. THANK YOU.
BEEP
HELLO THEREMIN. THIS IS ARGOSY'S MOTHER. IF YOU SEE THAT SON OF MINE, HAVE HIM CALL ME. YOU'RE SUCH A NICE MAN. GOOD*BYE*.
BEEP
ARGOSY, THIS IS YOURSELF. JUST A REMINDER: FABER'S GOT A TEMPORAL SECURITY RING AND IS GUARDED BY A COUPLE HUNDRED SHARD SHIPS.
BEEP
EXCUSE ME?!
A COUPLE HUNDRED SHARD SHIPS!?!?!
AND A TEMPORAL SECURITY RING HAD BETTER BE SOME KIND OF PASTRY!
I AM SO SORRY!

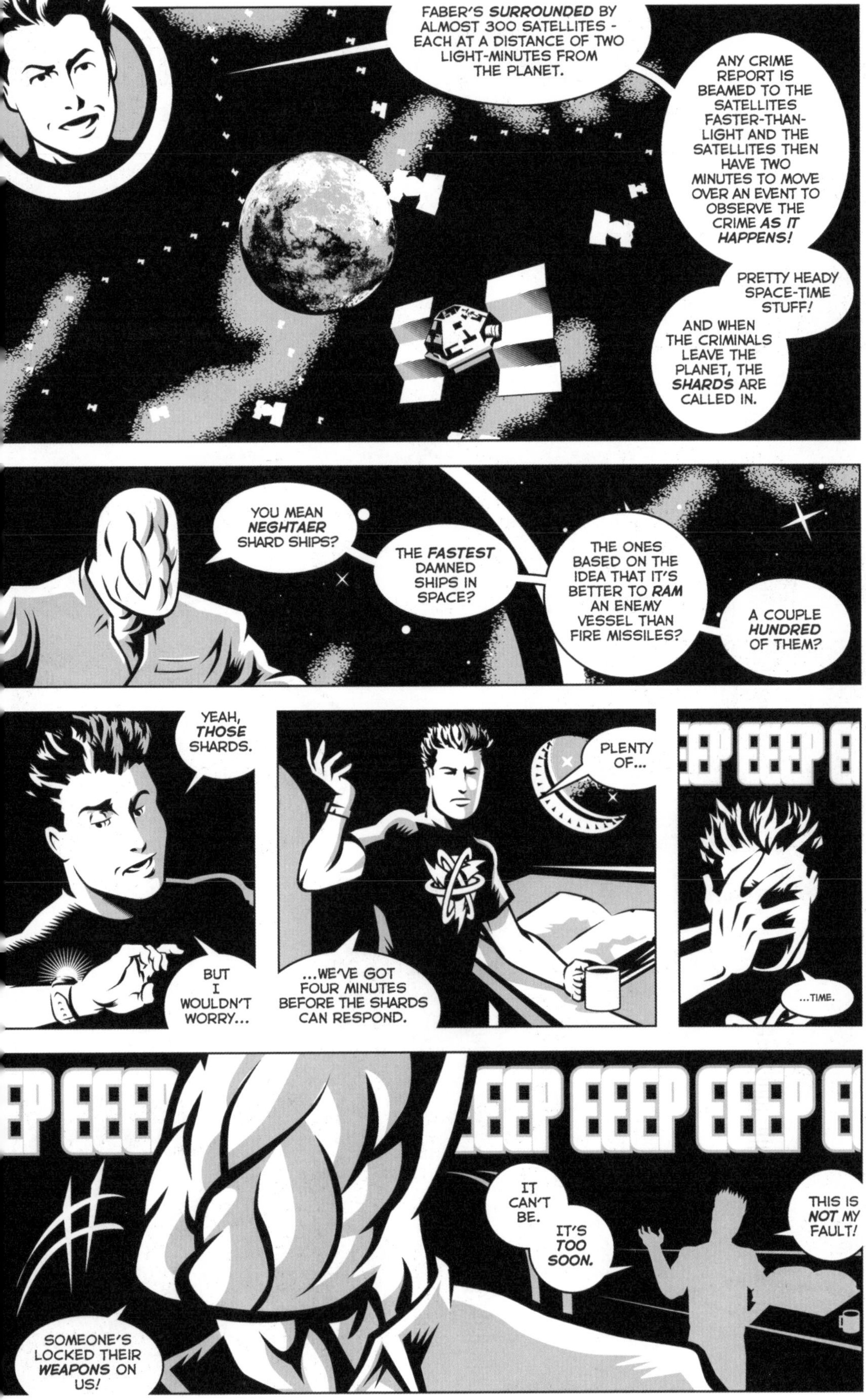
FABER'S *SURROUNDED* BY ALMOST 300 SATELLITES - EACH AT A DISTANCE OF TWO LIGHT-MINUTES FROM THE PLANET.
ANY CRIME REPORT IS BEAMED TO THE SATELLITES FASTER-THAN-LIGHT AND THE SATELLITES THEN HAVE TWO MINUTES TO MOVE OVER AN EVENT TO OBSERVE THE CRIME *AS IT HAPPENS!*
PRETTY HEADY SPACE-TIME STUFF!
AND WHEN THE CRIMINALS LEAVE THE PLANET, THE *SHARDS* ARE CALLED IN.
YOU MEAN *NEGHTAER* SHARD SHIPS?
THE *FASTEST* DAMNED SHIPS IN SPACE?
THE ONES BASED ON THE IDEA THAT IT'S BETTER TO *RAM* AN ENEMY VESSEL THAN FIRE MISSILES?
A COUPLE *HUNDRED* OF THEM?
YEAH, *THOSE* SHARDS.
BUT I WOULDN'T WORRY...
...WE'VE GOT FOUR MINUTES BEFORE THE SHARDS CAN RESPOND.
PLENTY OF...
EEP EEEP EEEP E
...TIME.
EP EEEP EEEP EEEP EEEP E
IT CAN'T BE.
IT'S *TOO SOON.*
THIS IS *NOT* MY FAULT!
SOMEONE'S LOCKED THEIR *WEAPONS* ON US!

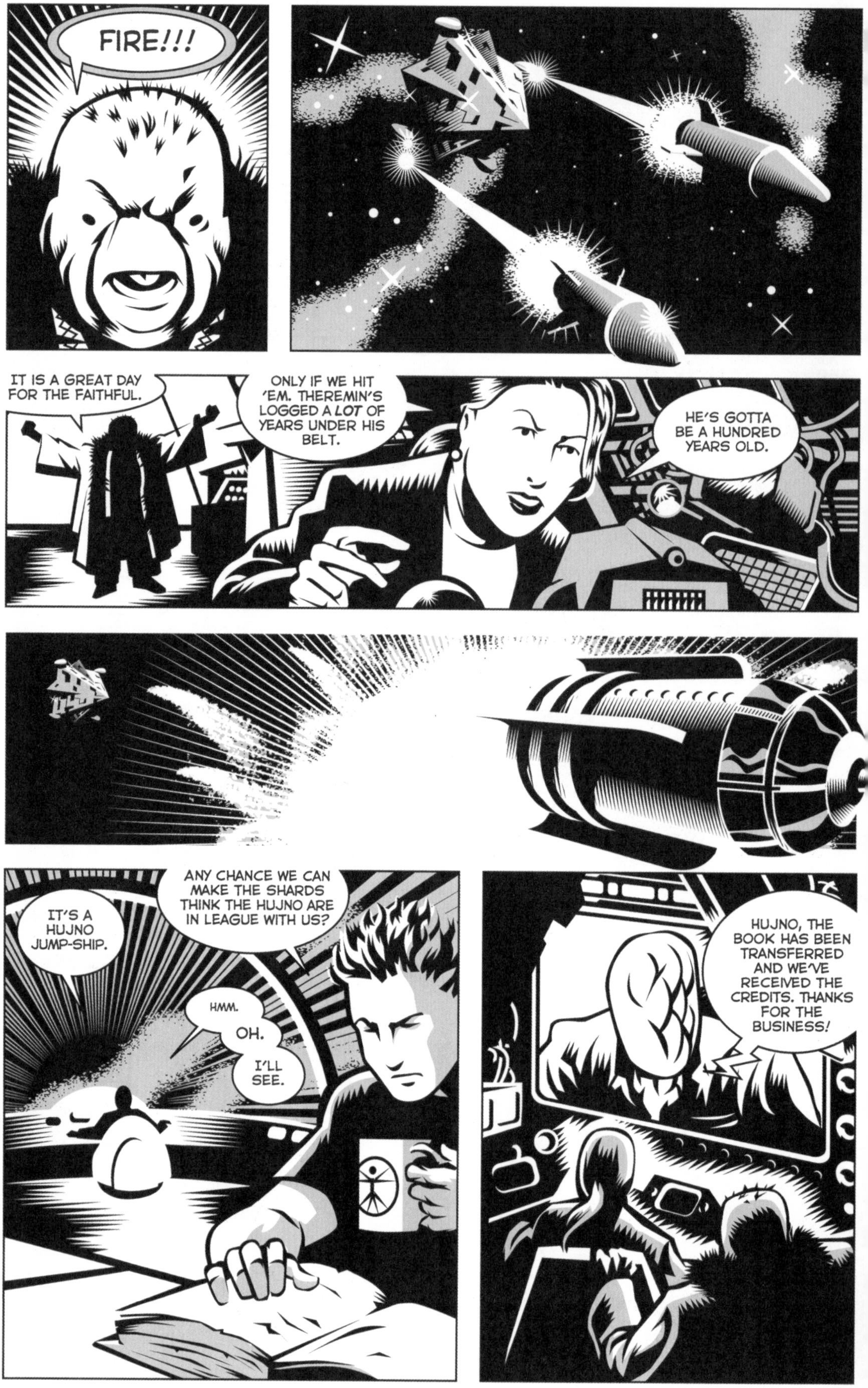
FIRE!!!
IT IS A GREAT DAY FOR THE FAITHFUL.
ONLY IF WE HIT 'EM. THEREMIN'S LOGGED A LOT OF YEARS UNDER HIS BELT.
HE'S GOTTA BE A HUNDRED YEARS OLD.
IT'S A HUJNO JUMP-SHIP.
ANY CHANCE WE CAN MAKE THE SHARDS THINK THE HUJNO ARE IN LEAGUE WITH US?
HMM.
OH.
I'LL SEE.
HUJNO, THE BOOK HAS BEEN TRANSFERRED AND WE'VE RECEIVED THE CREDITS. THANKS FOR THE BUSINESS!

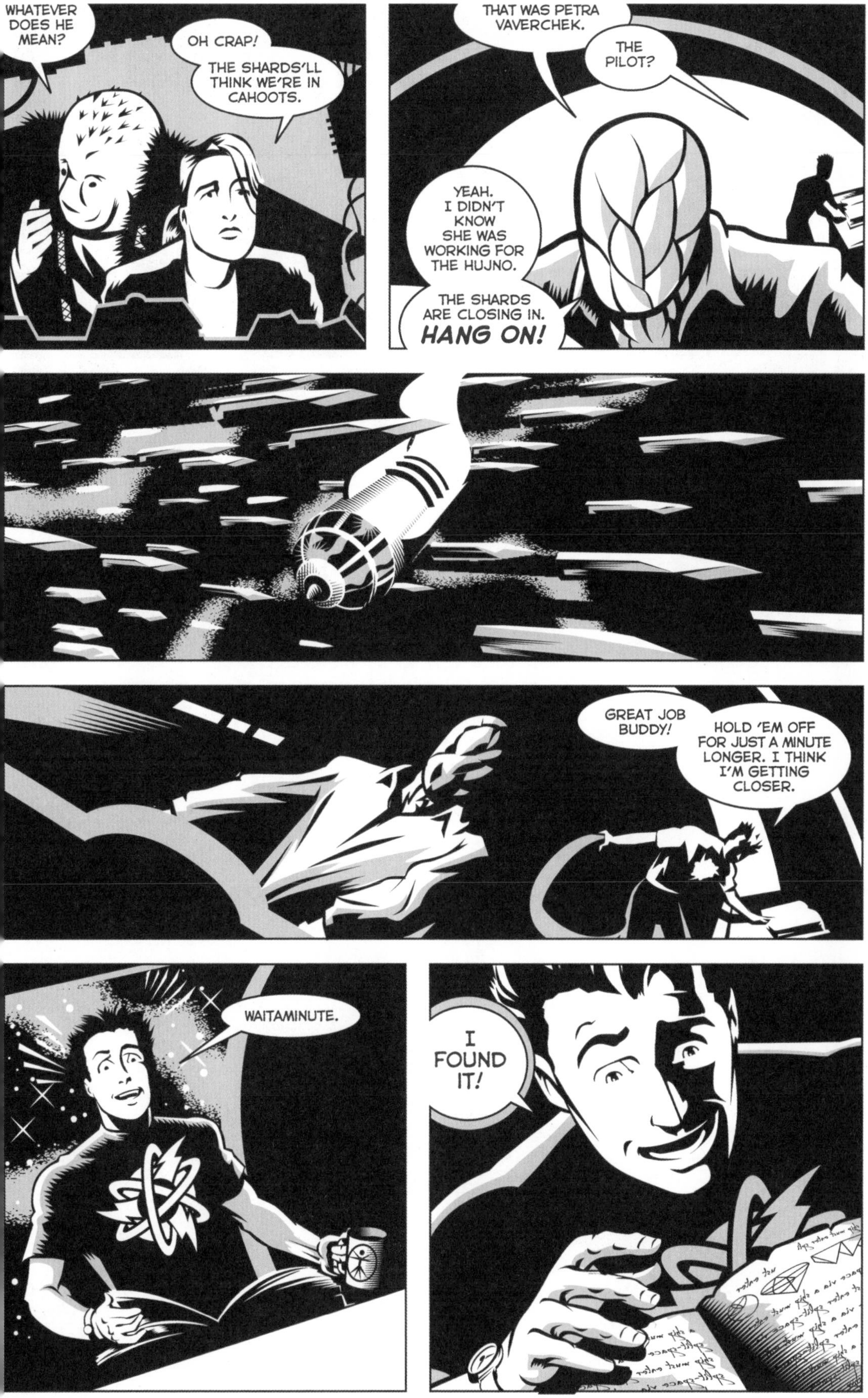
WHATEVER DOES HE MEAN?
OH CRAP!
THE SHARDS'LL THINK WE'RE IN CAHOOTS.
THAT WAS PETRA VAVERCHEK.
THE PILOT?
YEAH. I DIDN'T KNOW SHE WAS WORKING FOR THE HUJNO.
THE SHARDS ARE CLOSING IN. HANG ON!
GREAT JOB BUDDY!
HOLD 'EM OFF FOR JUST A MINUTE LONGER. I THINK I'M GETTING CLOSER.
WAITAMINUTE.
I FOUND IT!

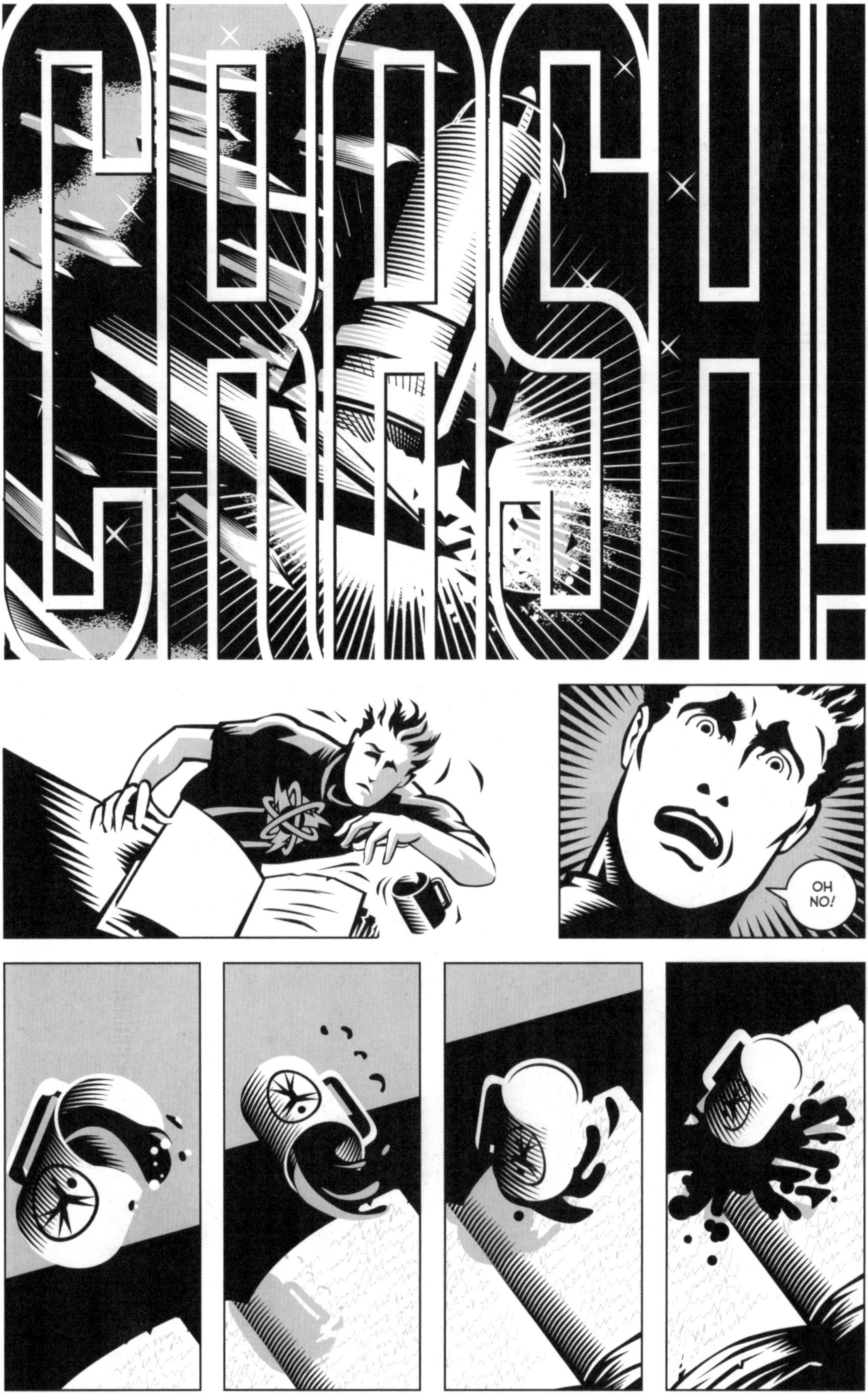
CRASH!
OH NO!

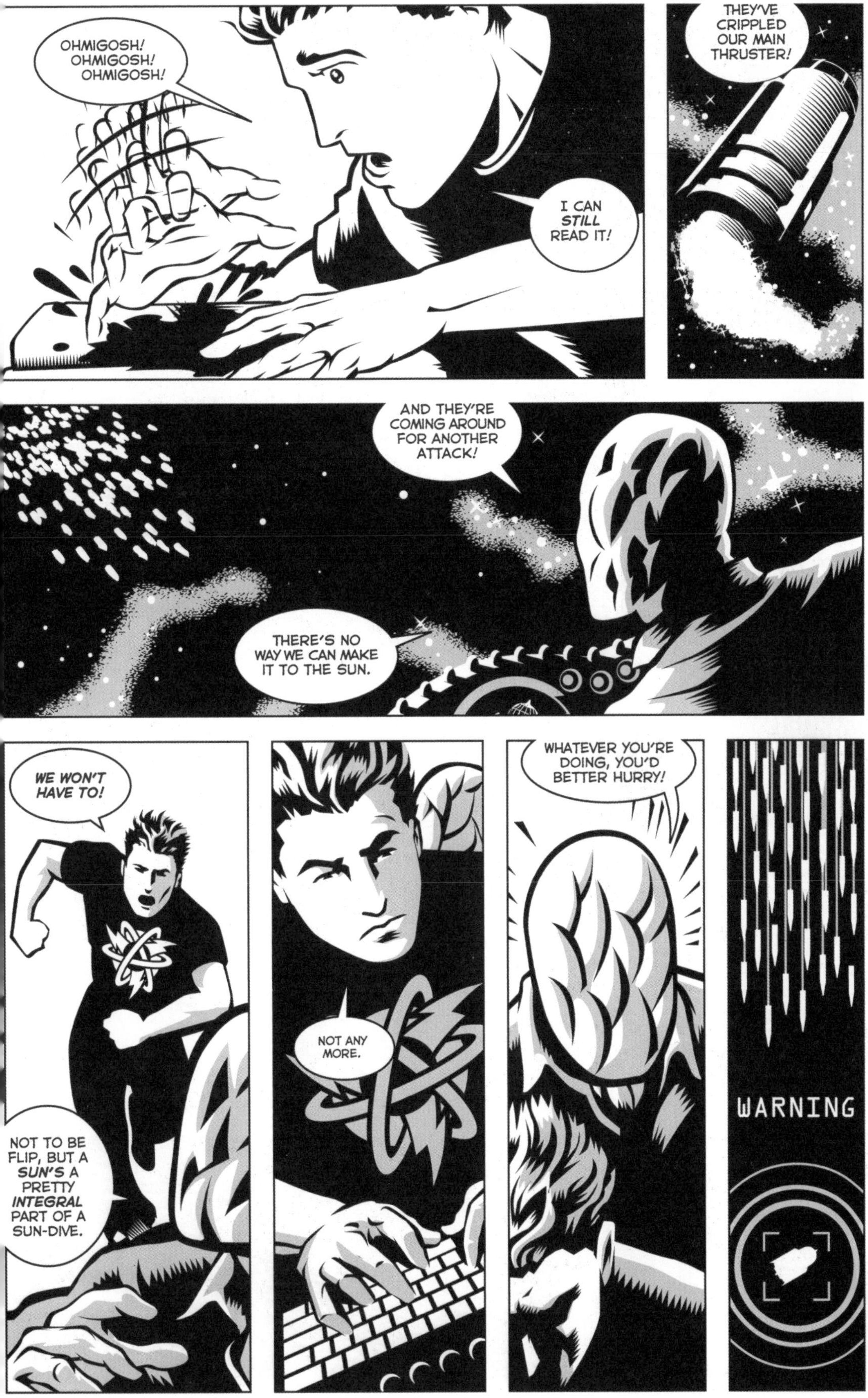
OHMIGOSH! OHMIGOSH! OHMIGOSH!
I CAN STILL READ IT!
THEY'VE CRIPPLED OUR MAIN THRUSTER!
AND THEY'RE COMING AROUND FOR ANOTHER ATTACK!
THERE'S NO WAY WE CAN MAKE IT TO THE SUN.
WE WON'T HAVE TO!
NOT TO BE FLIP, BUT A SUN'S A PRETTY INTEGRAL PART OF A SUN-DIVE.
NOT ANY MORE.
WHATEVER YOU'RE DOING, YOU'D BETTER HURRY!
WARNING

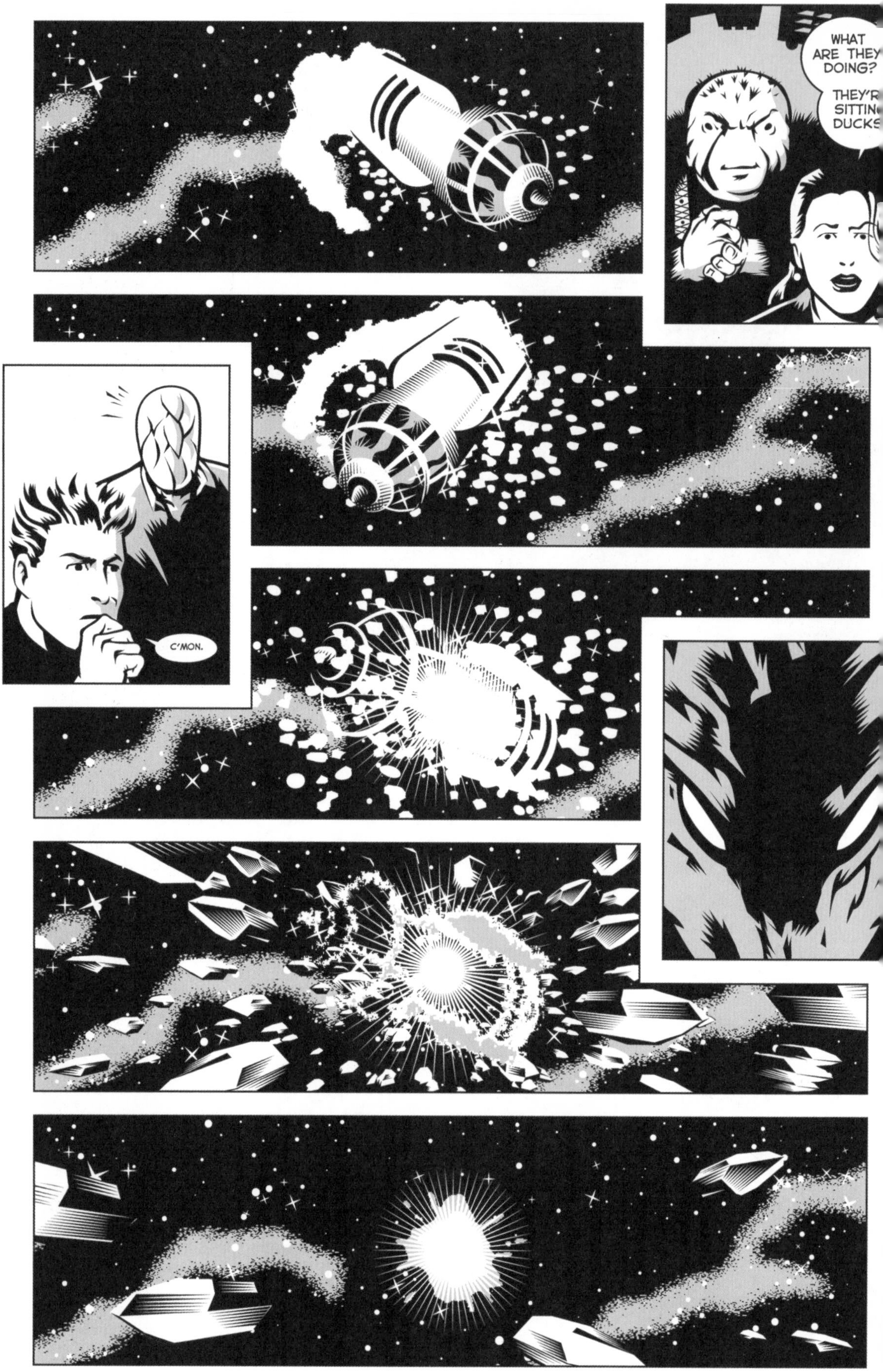
WHAT ARE THEY DOING?
THEY'R SITTIN DUCKS
C'MON.

twenty

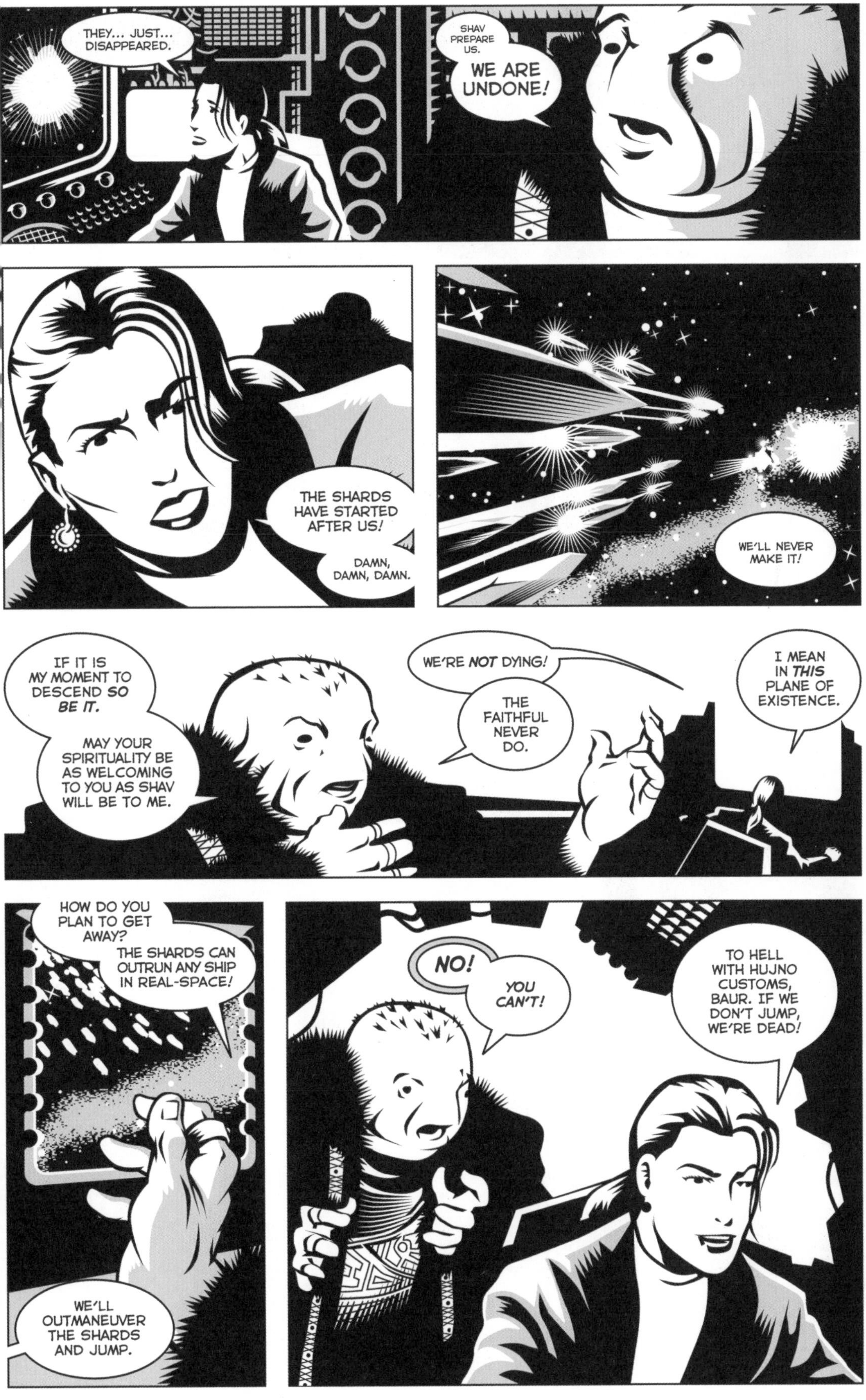
THEY... JUST... DISAPPEARED.
SHAV PREPARE US.
WE ARE UNDONE!
THE SHARDS HAVE STARTED AFTER US!
DAMN, DAMN, DAMN.
WE'LL NEVER MAKE IT!
IF IT IS MY MOMENT TO DESCEND SO BE IT.
MAY YOUR SPIRITUALITY BE AS WELCOMING TO YOU AS SHAV WILL BE TO ME.
WE'RE NOT DYING!
THE FAITHFUL NEVER DO.
I MEAN IN THIS PLANE OF EXISTENCE.
HOW DO YOU PLAN TO GET AWAY?
THE SHARDS CAN OUTRUN ANY SHIP IN REAL-SPACE!
WE'LL OUTMANEUVER THE SHARDS AND JUMP.
NO!
YOU CAN'T!
TO HELL WITH HUJNO CUSTOMS, BAUR. IF WE DON'T JUMP, WE'RE DEAD!

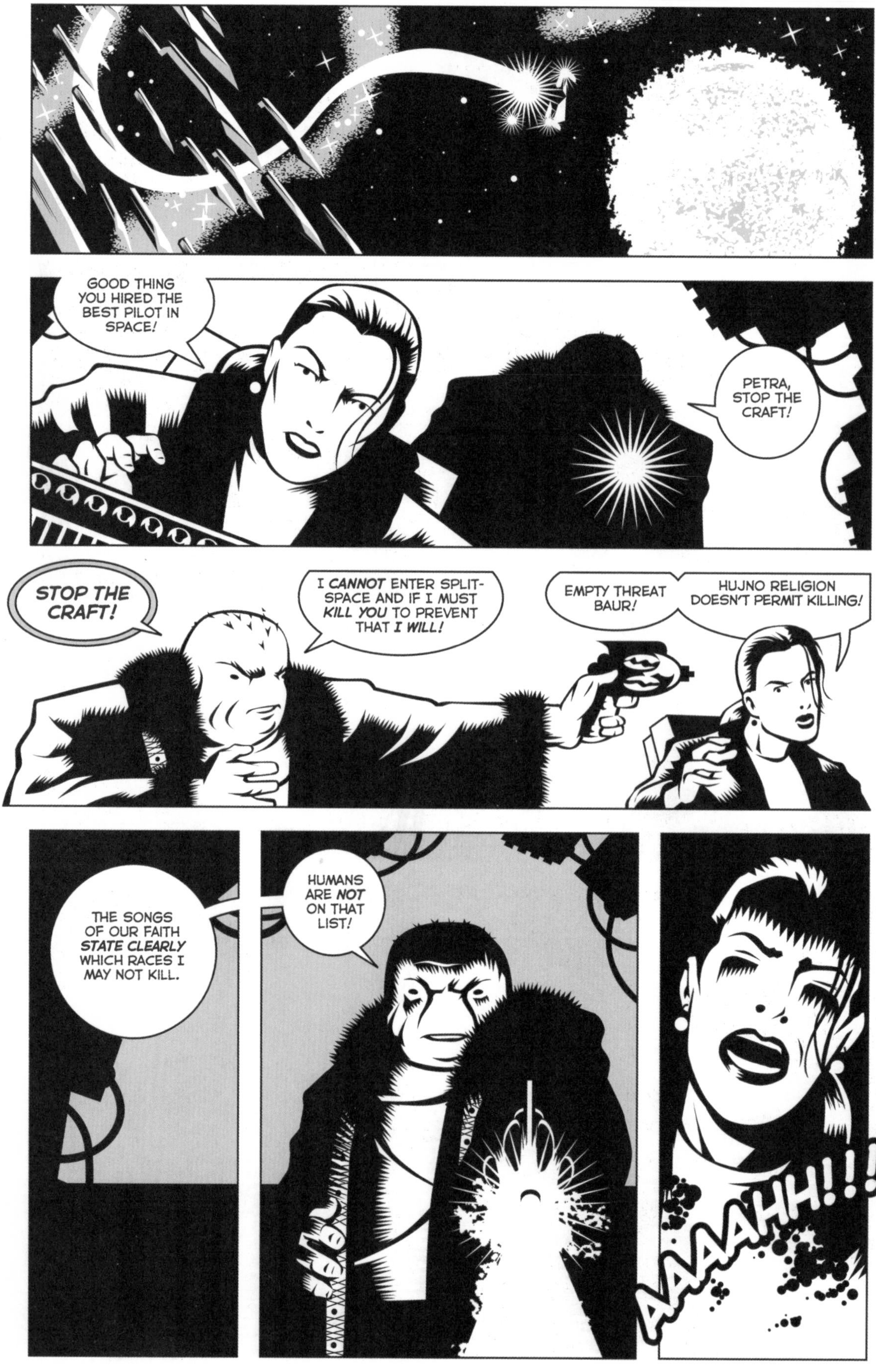
GOOD THING YOU HIRED THE BEST PILOT IN SPACE!
PETRA, STOP THE CRAFT!
STOP THE CRAFT!
I CANNOT ENTER SPLIT-SPACE AND IF I MUST KILL YOU TO PREVENT THAT I WILL!
EMPTY THREAT BAUR!
HUJNO RELIGION DOESN'T PERMIT KILLING!
THE SONGS OF OUR FAITH STATE CLEARLY WHICH RACES I MAY NOT KILL.
HUMANS ARE NOT ON THAT LIST!
AAAAHH!!!

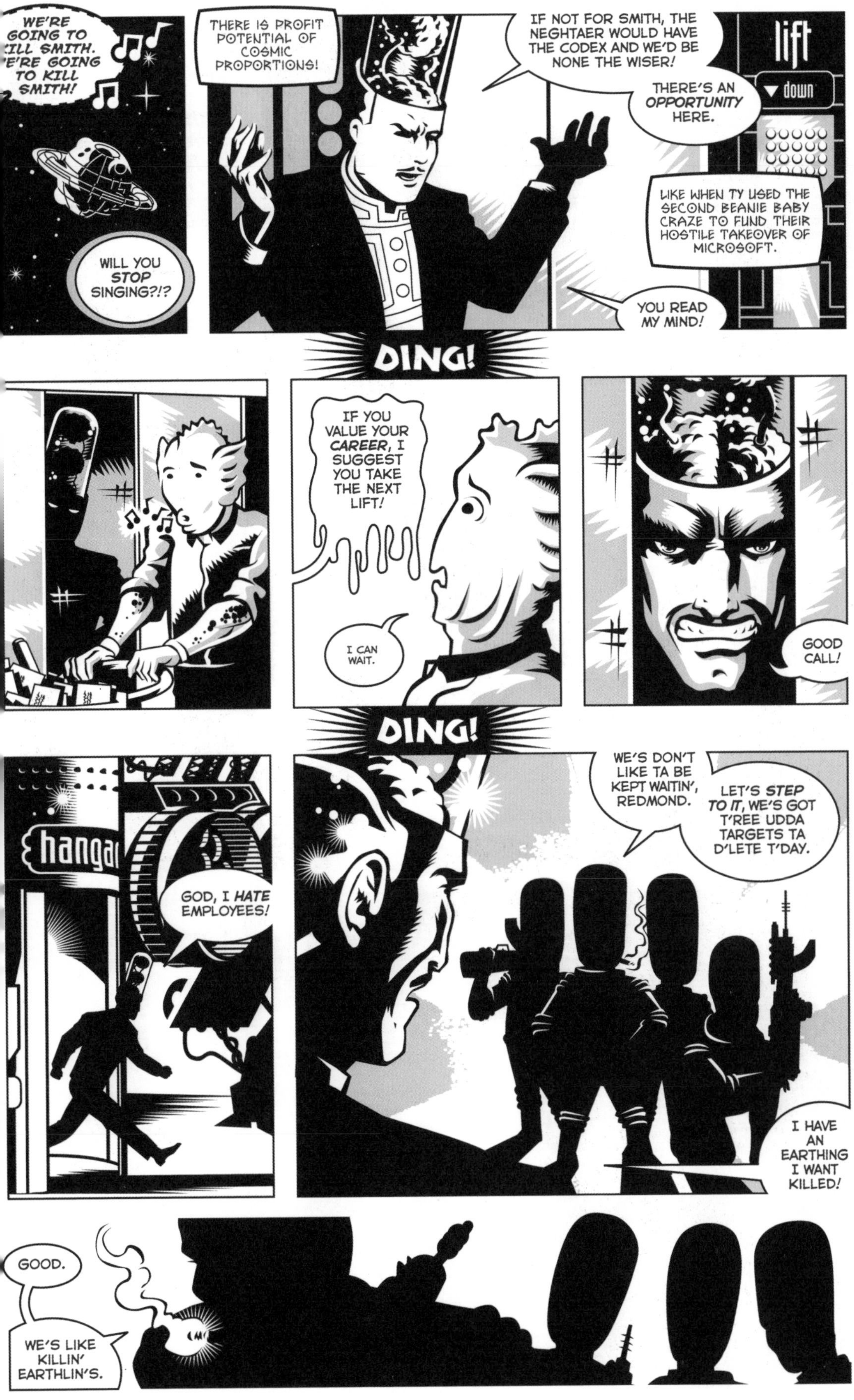
WE'RE GOING TO KILL SMITH. WE'RE GOING TO KILL SMITH!
WILL YOU STOP SINGING?!?
THERE IS PROFIT POTENTIAL OF COSMIC PROPORTIONS!
IF NOT FOR SMITH, THE NEGHTAER WOULD HAVE THE CODEX AND WE'D BE NONE THE WISER!
THERE'S AN OPPORTUNITY HERE.
lift
down
LIKE WHEN TY USED THE SECOND BEANIE BABY CRAZE TO FUND THEIR HOSTILE TAKEOVER OF MICROSOFT.
YOU READ MY MIND!
DING!
IF YOU VALUE YOUR CAREER, I SUGGEST YOU TAKE THE NEXT LIFT!
I CAN WAIT.
GOOD CALL!
DING!
hangar
GOD, I HATE EMPLOYEES!
WE'S DON'T LIKE TA BE KEPT WAITIN', REDMOND.
LET'S STEP TO IT, WE'S GOT T'REE UDDA TARGETS TA D'LETE T'DAY.
I HAVE AN EARTHING I WANT KILLED!
GOOD.
WE'S LIKE KILLIN' EARTHLIN'S.

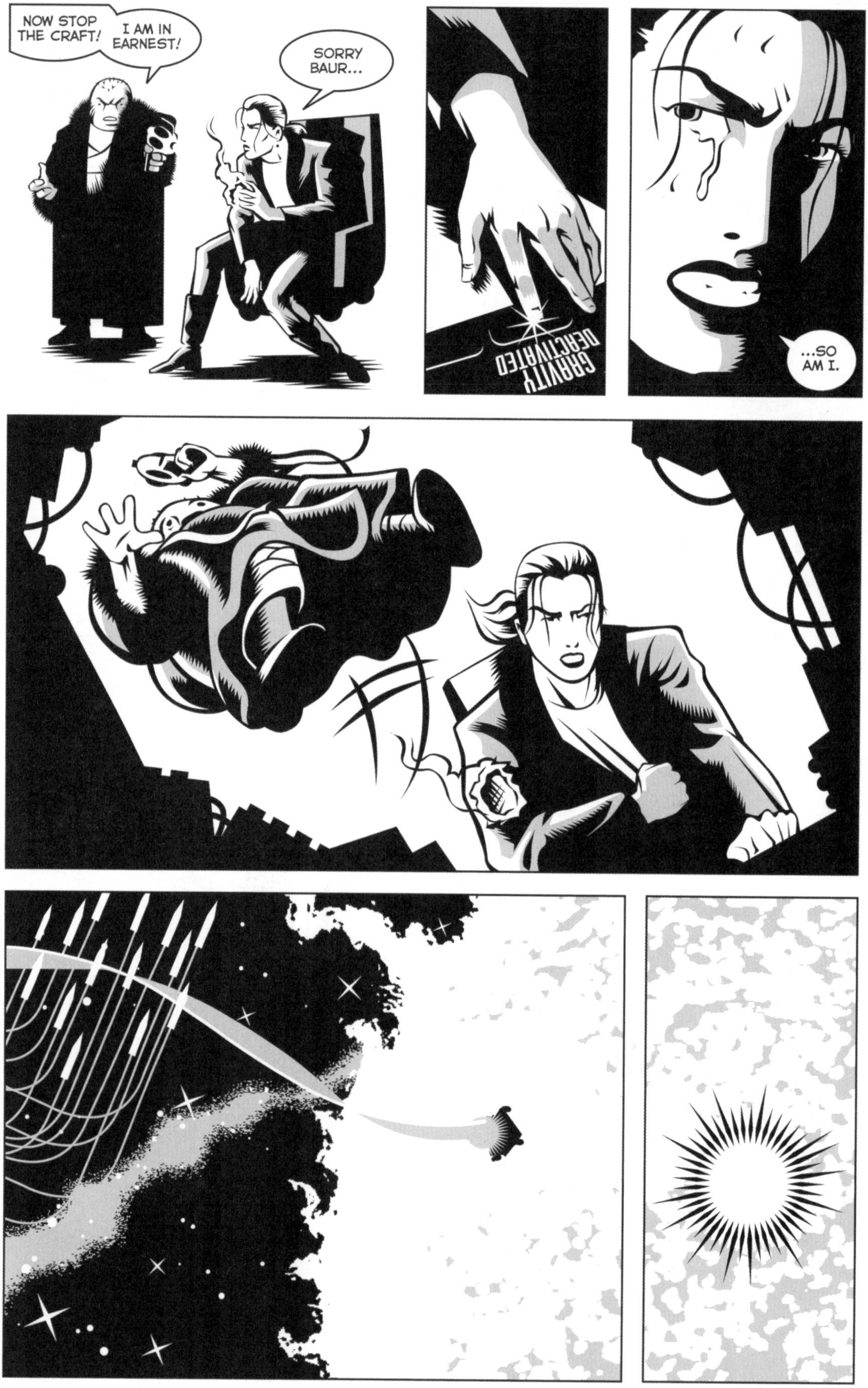
NOW STOP THE CRAFT!
I AM IN EARNEST!
SORRY BAUR...
GRAVITY DEACTIVATED
...SO AM I.

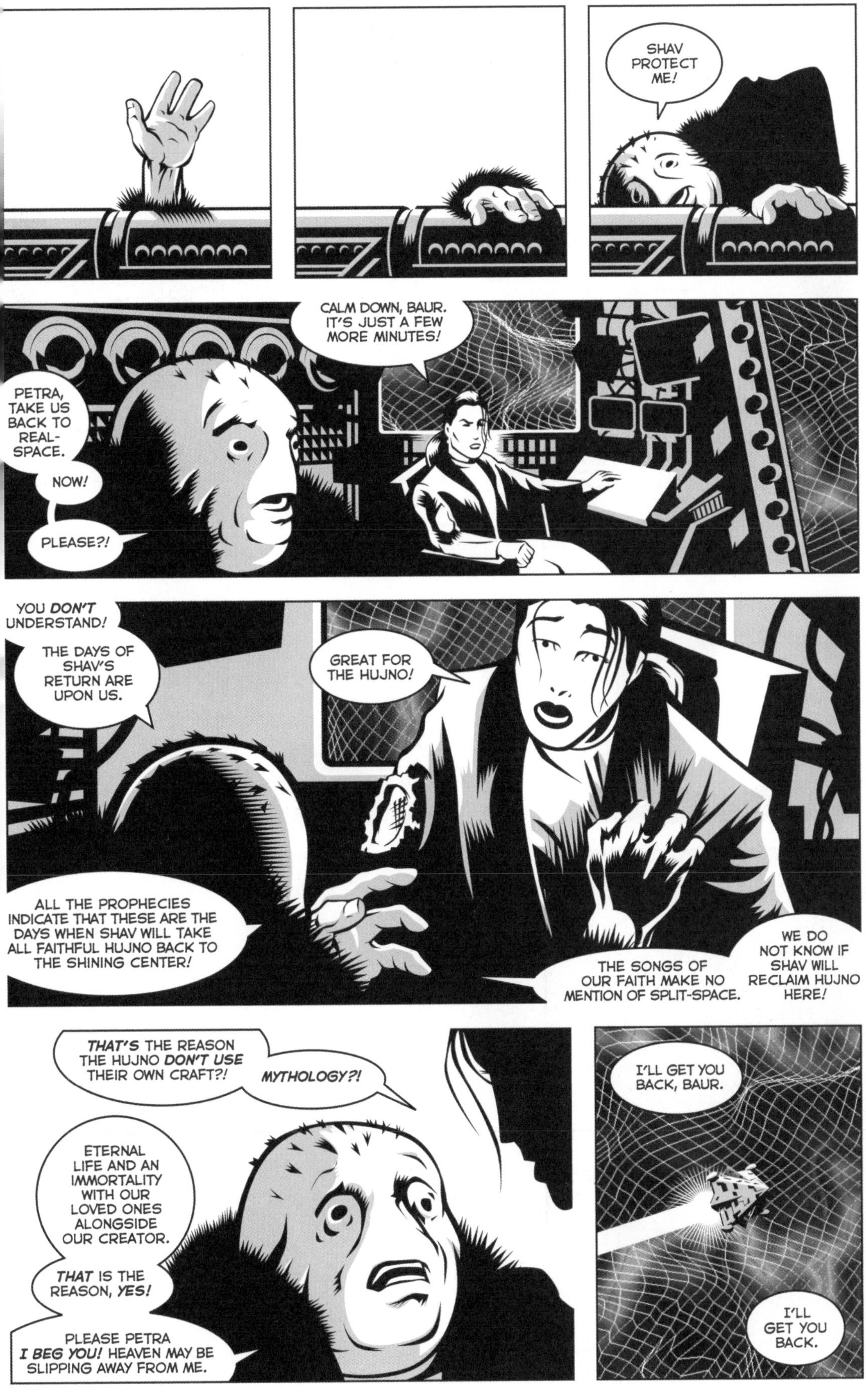
SHAV PROTECT ME!
CALM DOWN, BAUR. IT'S JUST A FEW MORE MINUTES!
PETRA, TAKE US BACK TO REAL-SPACE.
NOW!
PLEASE?!
YOU DON'T UNDERSTAND!
THE DAYS OF SHAV'S RETURN ARE UPON US.
GREAT FOR THE HUJNO!
ALL THE PROPHECIES INDICATE THAT THESE ARE THE DAYS WHEN SHAV WILL TAKE ALL FAITHFUL HUJNO BACK TO THE SHINING CENTER!
THE SONGS OF OUR FAITH MAKE NO MENTION OF SPLIT-SPACE.
WE DO NOT KNOW IF SHAV WILL RECLAIM HUJNO HERE!
THAT'S THE REASON THE HUJNO DON'T USE THEIR OWN CRAFT?!
MYTHOLOGY?!
ETERNAL LIFE AND AN IMMORTALITY WITH OUR LOVED ONES ALONGSIDE OUR CREATOR.
THAT IS THE REASON, YES!
PLEASE PETRA I BEG YOU! HEAVEN MAY BE SLIPPING AWAY FROM ME.
I'LL GET YOU BACK, BAUR.
I'LL GET YOU BACK.

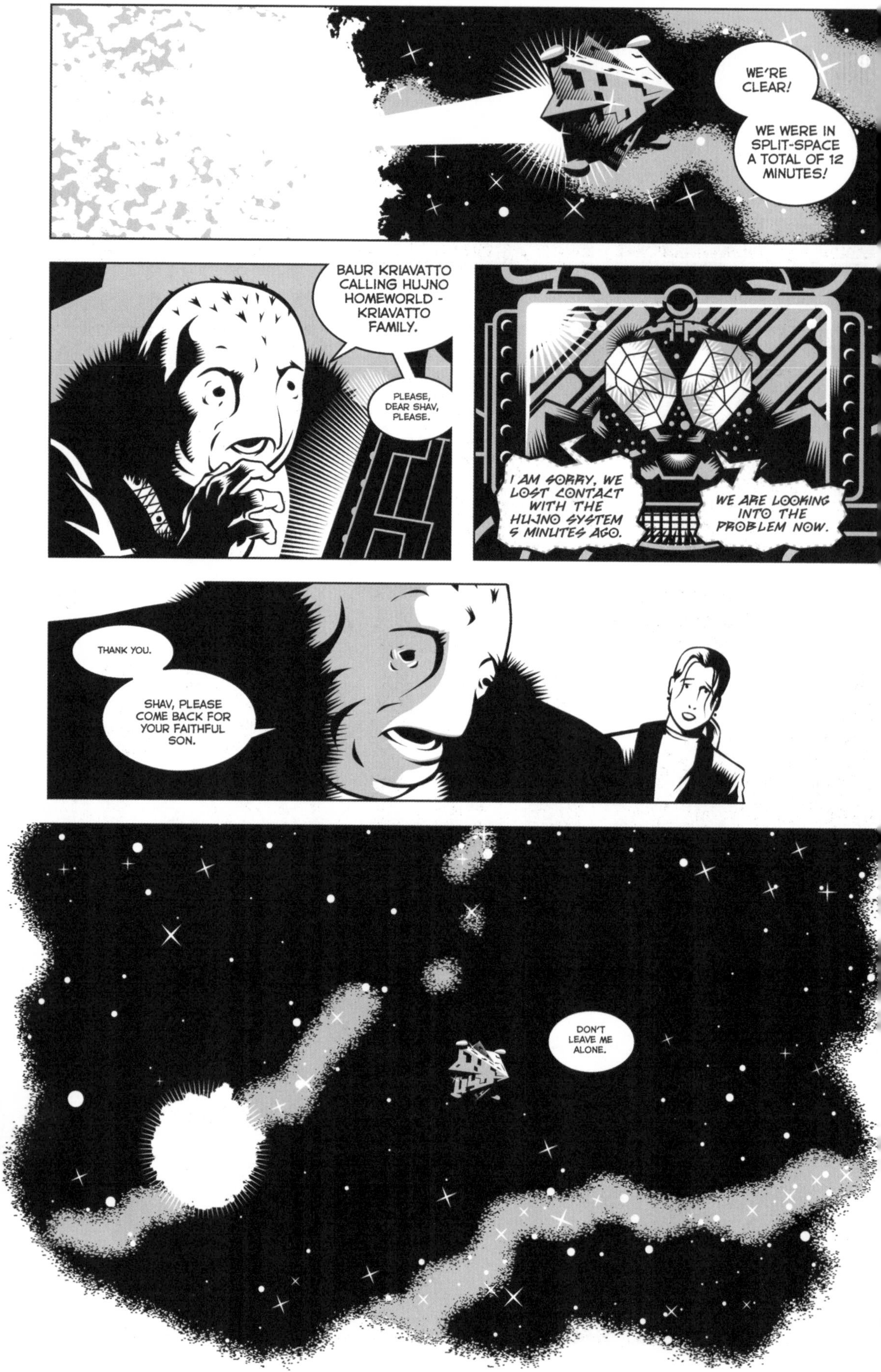
WE'RE CLEAR!
WE WERE IN SPLIT-SPACE A TOTAL OF 12 MINUTES!
BAUR KRIAVATTO CALLING HUJNO HOMEWORLD - KRIAVATTO FAMILY.
PLEASE, DEAR SHAV, PLEASE.
I AM SORRY, WE LOST CONTACT WITH THE HUJNO SYSTEM 5 MINUTES AGO.
WE ARE LOOKING INTO THE PROBLEM NOW.
THANK YOU.
SHAV, PLEASE COME BACK FOR YOUR FAITHFUL SON.
DON'T LEAVE ME ALONE.

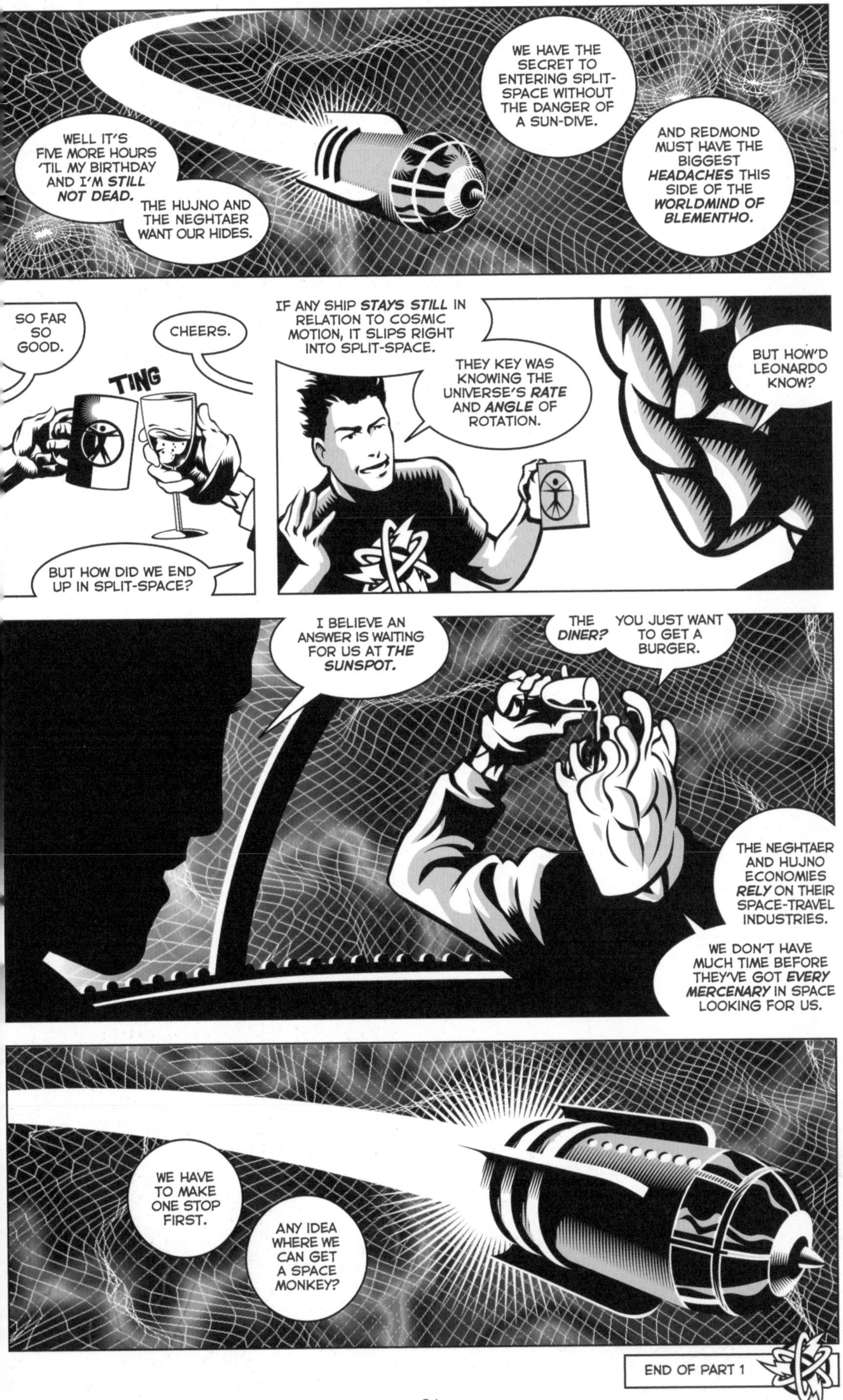
WELL IT'S FIVE MORE HOURS 'TIL MY BIRTHDAY AND I'M *STILL NOT DEAD.*
THE HUJNO AND THE NEGHTAER WANT OUR HIDES.
WE HAVE THE SECRET TO ENTERING SPLIT-SPACE WITHOUT THE DANGER OF A SUN-DIVE.
AND REDMOND MUST HAVE THE BIGGEST *HEADACHES* THIS SIDE OF THE *WORLDMIND OF BLEMENTHO.*
SO FAR SO GOOD.
CHEERS.
TING
BUT HOW DID WE END UP IN SPLIT-SPACE?
IF ANY SHIP *STAYS STILL* IN RELATION TO COSMIC MOTION, IT SLIPS RIGHT INTO SPLIT-SPACE.
THEY KEY WAS KNOWING THE UNIVERSE'S *RATE* AND *ANGLE* OF ROTATION.
BUT HOW'D LEONARDO KNOW?
I BELIEVE AN ANSWER IS WAITING FOR US AT *THE SUNSPOT.*
THE *DINER?*
YOU JUST WANT TO GET A BURGER.
THE NEGHTAER AND HUJNO ECONOMIES *RELY* ON THEIR SPACE-TRAVEL INDUSTRIES.
WE DON'T HAVE MUCH TIME BEFORE THEY'VE GOT *EVERY MERCENARY* IN SPACE LOOKING FOR US.
WE HAVE TO MAKE ONE STOP FIRST.
ANY IDEA WHERE WE CAN GET A SPACE MONKEY?
END OF PART 1

STEVE CONLEY'S
ASTOUNDING
SPACE THRILLS
2
GREG & TIM HILDEBRANDT

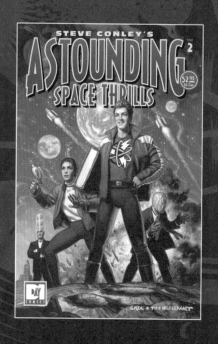

ASTOUNDING SPACE THRILLS #2
AUGUST 1998

COVER BY GREG AND TIM HILDEBRANDT

[E YOUNG MAN YOU] EE RUNNING AND SCREAMING IS ARGOSY SMITH.

WITH THE HELP OF HIS FRIEND, THE ANTIQUARY AND BIOMASS, *THEREMIN* (ALSO SEEN RUNNING AND SCREAMING), ARGOSY STOLE A RECENTLY-DISCOVERED BOOK OF *LEONARDO DAVINCI'S* NOTES FROM THE TERRAN SOFTWARE FIRM, *MACROSHAFT.*

(ALTHOUGH 'STOLE' IS A HARSH TERM SINCE ARGOSY CONSIDERS THE BOOK - *THE CODEX MELZI* - PAYMENT FOR SERVICES RENDERED.)

[SOON CHASED BY TWO ALIEN RACES, THE] ZEALOUS *HUJNO* AND THE CALCULATING *NEGHTAER*, AS WELL AS MACROSHAFT AND THE PILOT-FOR-HIRE *PETRA VAVERCHEK*, ARGOSY SMITH FOUND IN THE NOTES JUST WHAT HE WAS LOOKING FOR...

THE FORMULA FOR *INSTANTANEOUS ACCESS* TO THE FASTER-THAN-LIGHT REALM OF *SPLIT-SPACE.*

NEEDLESS TO SAY, THE HUJNO AND NEGHTAER, WHO MAINTAIN A STRANGLEHOLD ON THE GALAXY'S SPACESHIP MANUFACTURING INDUSTRY, ARE *NONE TOO THRILLED* BY THE DEVELOPMENTS.

More monstrous mayhem from the multi-dimensional mixed bag that is...

steve conley's astounding space thrills

the CODEX RECKONING

PART TWO

WHICH BRINGS US TO TODAY: *ARGOSY'S 25TH BIRTHDAY* AND THE *DAY* HE HAS BEEN *PROPHESIED TO DIE.* WHERE FOLLOWING A QUICK MEAL AT THE SUNSPOT DINER, ARGOSY AND THEREMIN FOUND THEMSELVES CHASED BY THE *HIDEOUS MONSTROSITY* YOU SEE HERE.

BUT NOW WE'RE GETTING AHEAD OF OURSELVES...

WHERE IS HE? HE'S LATE!
NOW WHO'S IN A HURRY?
ARGOSY, BOTH THE HUJNO AND THE NEGHTAER WANT US DEAD!
ONE MEASLY ALIEN TAKES A POT SHOT AT US AND YOU GET ALL UPTIGHT.
THAT MEASLY ALIEN WAS GRACKEN KURR. REMEMBER HIM?
KILLED THE VENUSIAN PREFECT AND THE ANDROMEDAN PHEREMONARCH.
OH.
HMM.
ANYWAY, I FIGURE EVEN WITH YOUR SHIP'S ENGINES AT 50%, WE CAN MAKE IT TO THE TECHNOWORLD, WAAZNIAX.
ONCE THERE, I CAN FAKE REDMOND'S OWN I.D. AND BROADCAST THE CODEX FORMULA TO EVERY PC IN THE GALAXY.
MY SHIP?! OUT OF THE QUESTION! YOU'RE GOING TO HAVE TO FIND ANOTHER RIDE.
THEREMIN, YOU'VE GOT TO FLY ME THERE.
I'M NOT GOING THROUGH THIS AGAIN.
OKAY. YOU CAN LEND ME YOUR SHIP, AND I'LL FLY IT MYSELF.
FINE. I'LL DRIVE YOU.
I JUST WANT TO GET THIS OVER WITH.
TELL ME ABOUT OUR CONTACT.
HAVE YOU EVER HEARD OF GEMINI SYNDROME?
SURE. TWO TELEPATHS OF DIFFERENT SPECIES TRY BOOSTING THEIR MENTAL CONNECTION AND FRY ONE OF THE PARTICIPANTS. THE SURVIVING TELEPATH ENDS UP SHARING THE PERSONALITIES OF BOTH ALIENS.
I WAS LOOKING INTO IT WHEN I TRIED TO GET MY OLD BODY BACK.
OUR CONTACT IS A NEGHTAER WITH A DUAL HUMAN-NEGHTAER PERSONALITY.
A NEGHTAER!?!
YOU DO REMEMBER THE NEGHTAER WANT US DEAD? HOW DO YOU KNOW HE WON'T TURN US IN?
ASK HER YOURSELF.
YAAAA!

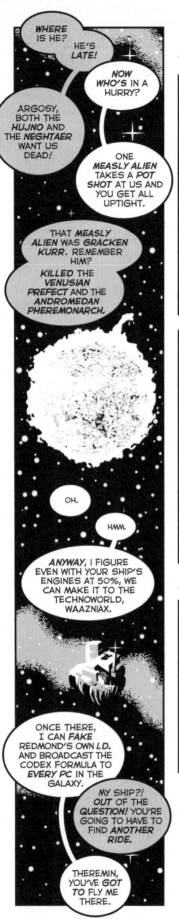

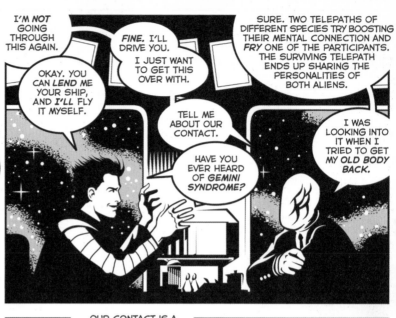

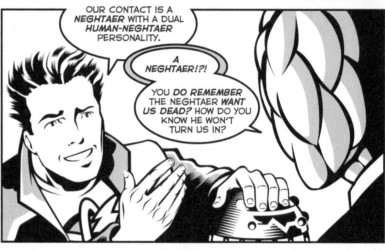

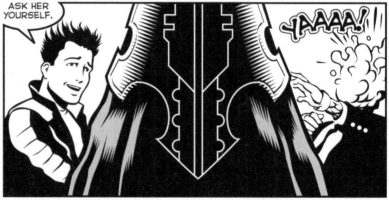

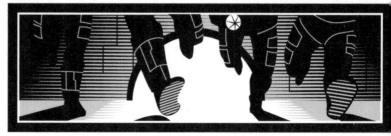

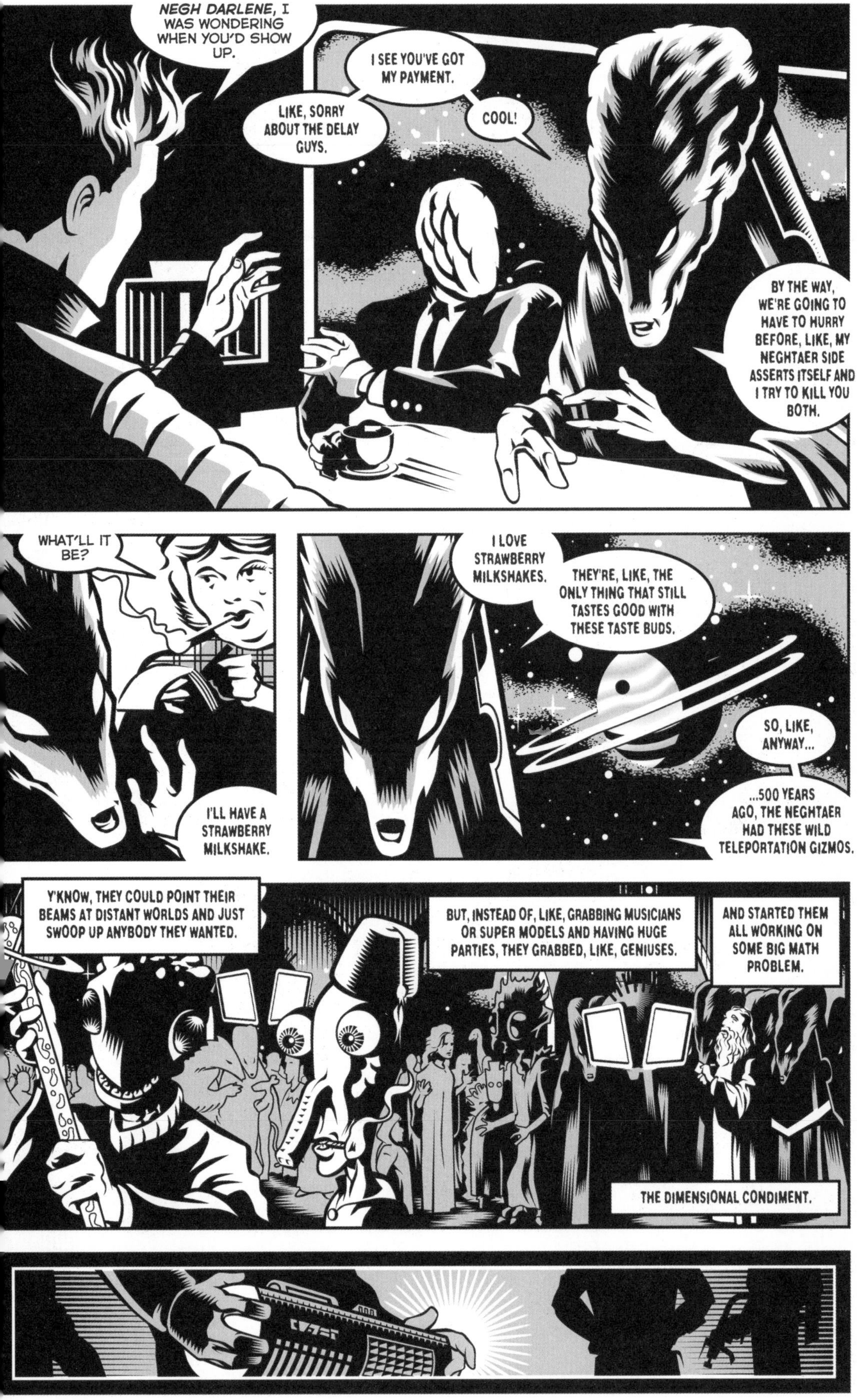
NEGH DARLENE, I WAS WONDERING WHEN YOU'D SHOW UP.
I SEE YOU'VE GOT MY PAYMENT.
LIKE, SORRY ABOUT THE DELAY GUYS.
COOL!
BY THE WAY, WE'RE GOING TO HAVE TO HURRY BEFORE, LIKE, MY NEGHTAER SIDE ASSERTS ITSELF AND I TRY TO KILL YOU BOTH.
WHAT'LL IT BE?
I'LL HAVE A STRAWBERRY MILKSHAKE.
I LOVE STRAWBERRY MILKSHAKES.
THEY'RE, LIKE, THE ONLY THING THAT STILL TASTES GOOD WITH THESE TASTE BUDS.
SO, LIKE, ANYWAY...
...500 YEARS AGO, THE NEGHTAER HAD THESE WILD TELEPORTATION GIZMOS.
Y'KNOW, THEY COULD POINT THEIR BEAMS AT DISTANT WORLDS AND JUST SWOOP UP ANYBODY THEY WANTED.
BUT, INSTEAD OF, LIKE, GRABBING MUSICIANS OR SUPER MODELS AND HAVING HUGE PARTIES, THEY GRABBED, LIKE, GENIUSES.
AND STARTED THEM ALL WORKING ON SOME BIG MATH PROBLEM.
THE DIMENSIONAL CONDIMENT.

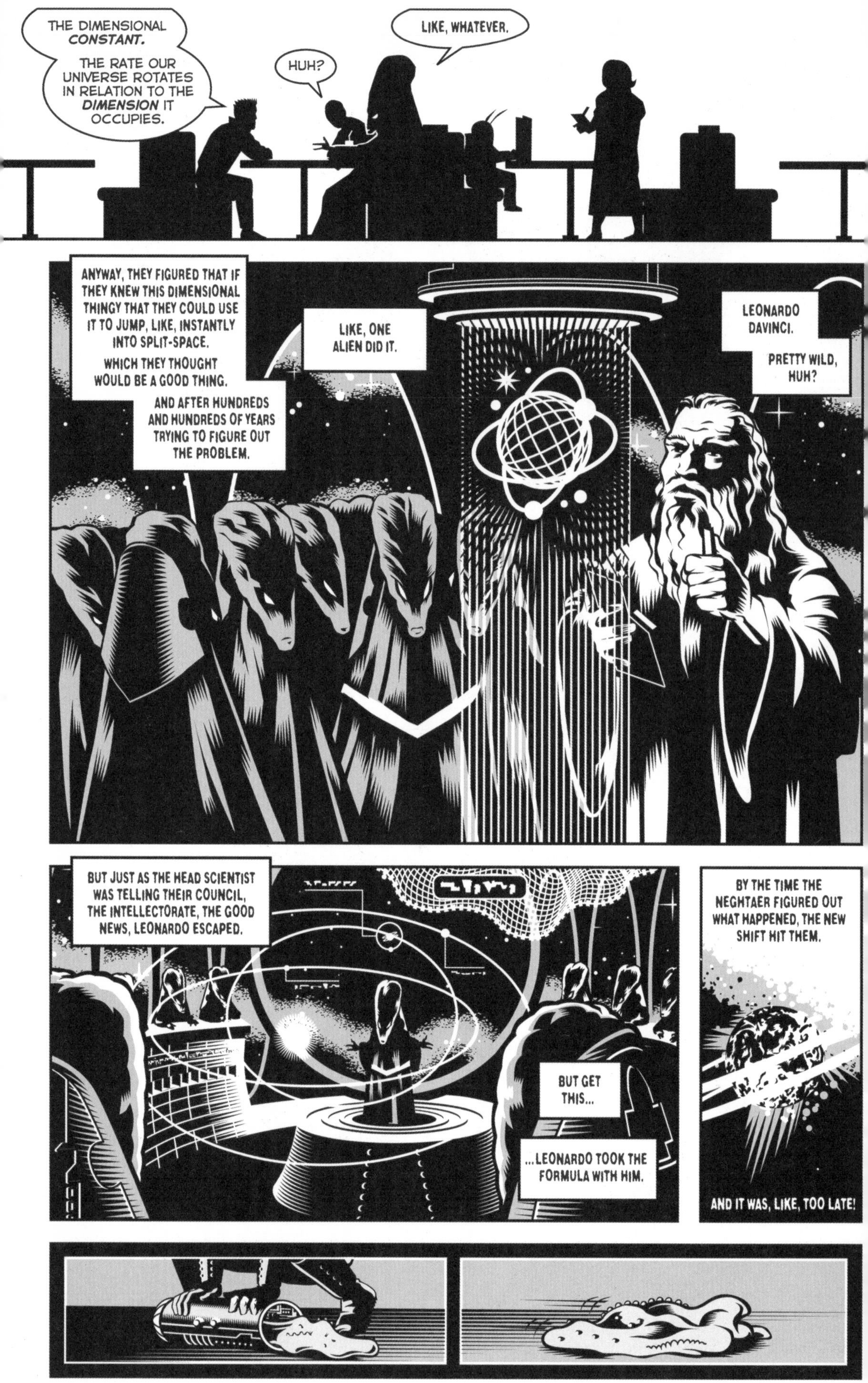
THE DIMENSIONAL **CONSTANT.**
THE RATE OUR UNIVERSE ROTATES IN RELATION TO THE **DIMENSION** IT OCCUPIES.
HUH?
LIKE, WHATEVER.
ANYWAY, THEY FIGURED THAT IF THEY KNEW THIS DIMENSIONAL THINGY THAT THEY COULD USE IT TO JUMP, LIKE, INSTANTLY INTO SPLIT-SPACE.
WHICH THEY THOUGHT WOULD BE A GOOD THING.
AND AFTER HUNDREDS AND HUNDREDS OF YEARS TRYING TO FIGURE OUT THE PROBLEM.
LIKE, ONE ALIEN DID IT.
LEONARDO DAVINCI.
PRETTY WILD, HUH?
BUT JUST AS THE HEAD SCIENTIST WAS TELLING THEIR COUNCIL, THE INTELLECTORATE, THE GOOD NEWS, LEONARDO ESCAPED.
BUT GET THIS...
...LEONARDO TOOK THE FORMULA WITH HIM.
BY THE TIME THE NEGHTAER FIGURED OUT WHAT HAPPENED, THE NEW SHIFT HIT THEM.
AND IT WAS, LIKE, TOO LATE!

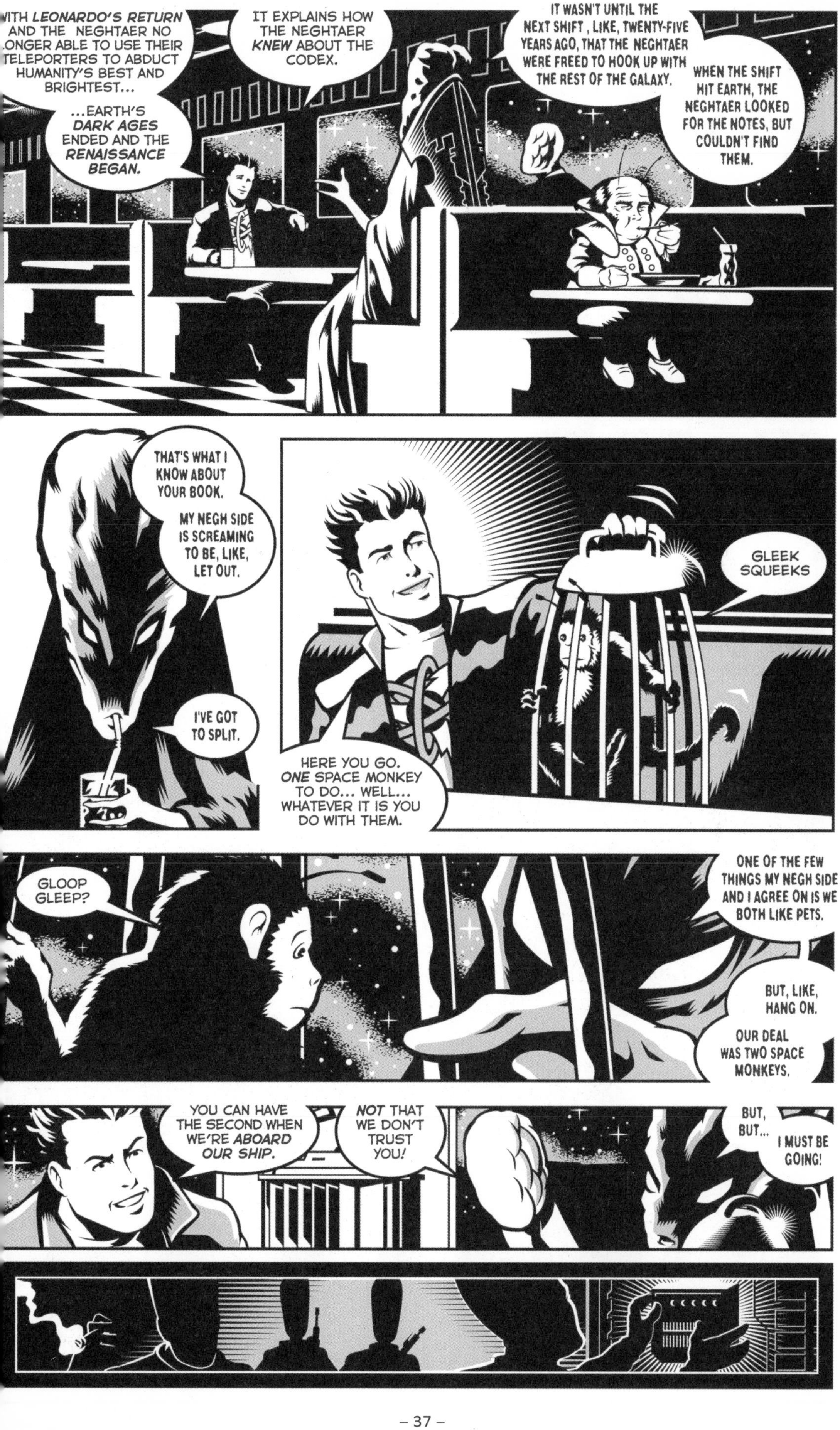
WITH *LEONARDO'S RETURN* AND THE NEGHTAER NO LONGER ABLE TO USE THEIR TELEPORTERS TO ABDUCT HUMANITY'S BEST AND BRIGHTEST...
...EARTH'S *DARK AGES* ENDED AND THE *RENAISSANCE BEGAN.*
IT EXPLAINS HOW THE NEGHTAER *KNEW* ABOUT THE CODEX.
IT WASN'T UNTIL THE NEXT SHIFT , LIKE, TWENTY-FIVE YEARS AGO, THAT THE NEGHTAER WERE FREED TO HOOK UP WITH THE REST OF THE GALAXY.
WHEN THE SHIFT HIT EARTH, THE NEGHTAER LOOKED FOR THE NOTES, BUT COULDN'T FIND THEM.
THAT'S WHAT I KNOW ABOUT YOUR BOOK.
MY NEGH SIDE IS SCREAMING TO BE, LIKE, LET OUT.
I'VE GOT TO SPLIT.
HERE YOU GO. *ONE* SPACE MONKEY TO DO... WELL... WHATEVER IT IS YOU DO WITH THEM.
GLEEK SQUEEKS
GLOOP GLEEP?
ONE OF THE FEW THINGS MY NEGH SIDE AND I AGREE ON IS WE BOTH LIKE PETS.
BUT, LIKE, HANG ON.
OUR DEAL WAS TWO SPACE MONKEYS.
YOU CAN HAVE THE SECOND WHEN WE'RE *ABOARD OUR SHIP.*
NOT THAT WE DON'T TRUST YOU!
BUT, BUT...
I MUST BE GOING!

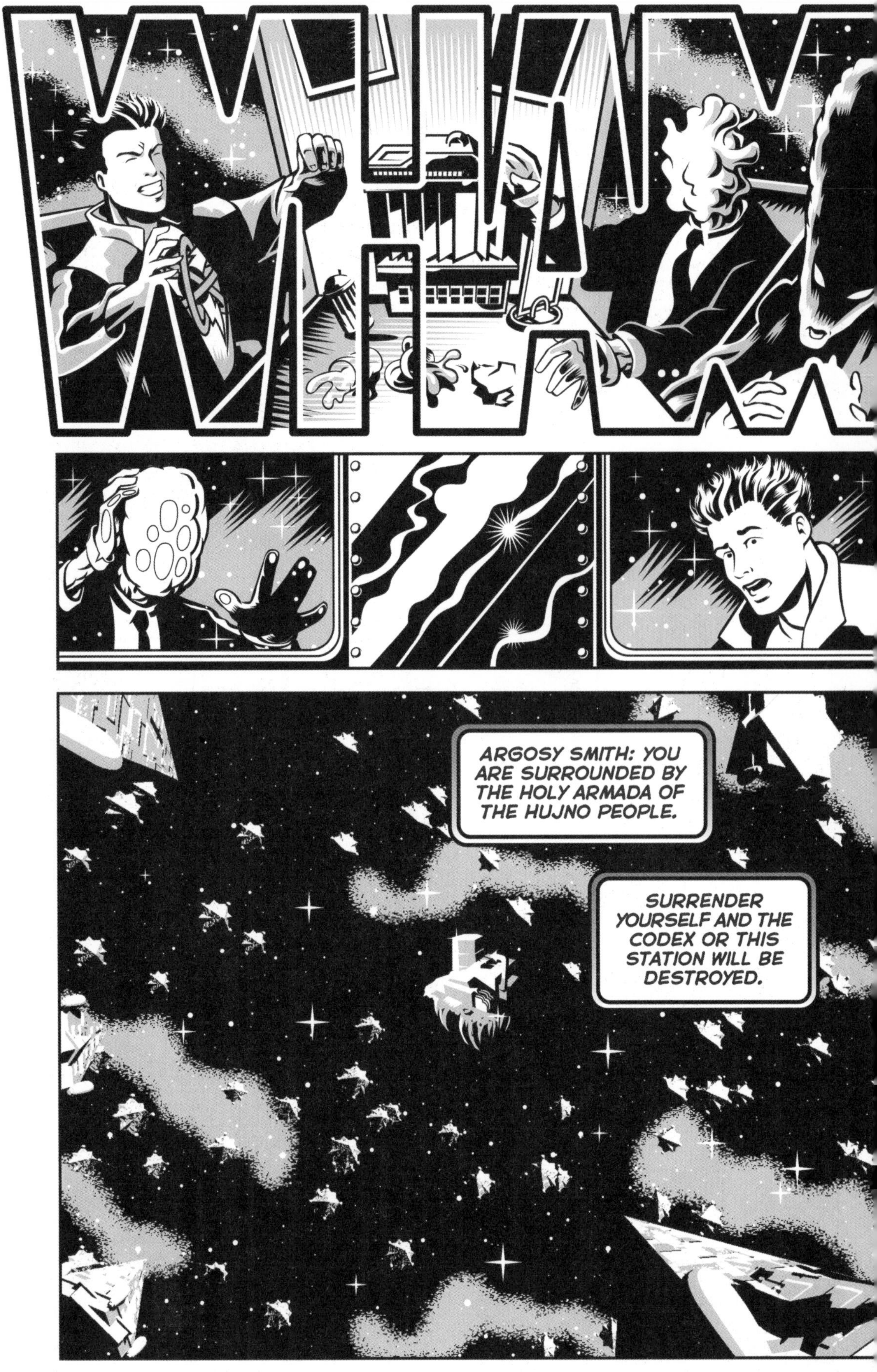
ARGOSY SMITH: YOU ARE SURROUNDED BY THE HOLY ARMADA OF THE HUJNO PEOPLE.
SURRENDER YOURSELF AND THE CODEX OR THIS STATION WILL BE DESTROYED.

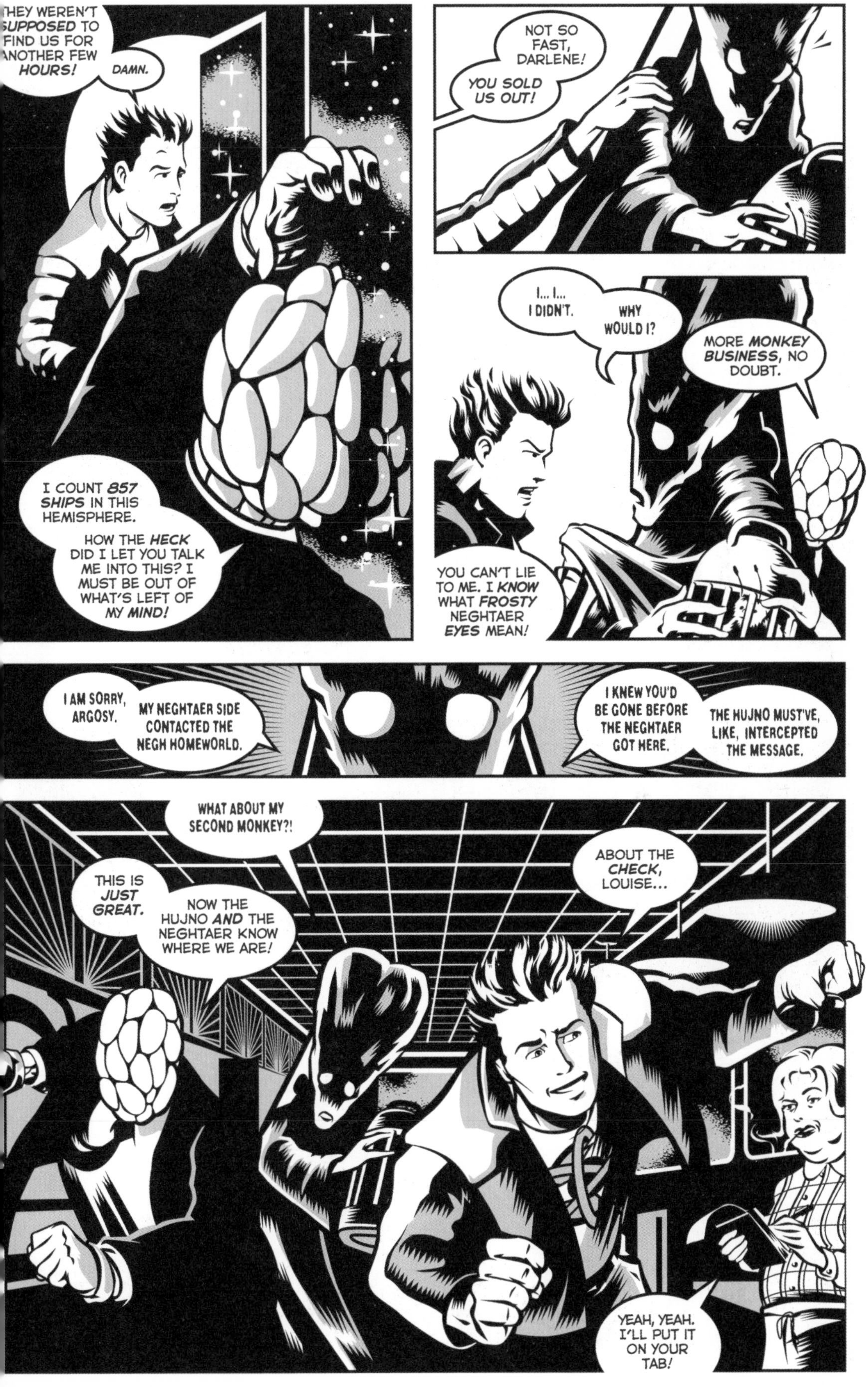
THEY WEREN'T SUPPOSED TO FIND US FOR ANOTHER FEW HOURS!
DAMN.
I COUNT 857 SHIPS IN THIS HEMISPHERE.
HOW THE HECK DID I LET YOU TALK ME INTO THIS? I MUST BE OUT OF WHAT'S LEFT OF MY MIND!
NOT SO FAST, DARLENE!
YOU SOLD US OUT!
I... I... I DIDN'T.
WHY WOULD I?
MORE MONKEY BUSINESS, NO DOUBT.
YOU CAN'T LIE TO ME. I KNOW WHAT FROSTY NEGHTAER EYES MEAN!
I AM SORRY, ARGOSY.
MY NEGHTAER SIDE CONTACTED THE NEGH HOMEWORLD.
I KNEW YOU'D BE GONE BEFORE THE NEGHTAER GOT HERE.
THE HUJNO MUST'VE, LIKE, INTERCEPTED THE MESSAGE.
WHAT ABOUT MY SECOND MONKEY?!
THIS IS JUST GREAT.
NOW THE HUJNO AND THE NEGHTAER KNOW WHERE WE ARE!
ABOUT THE CHECK, LOUISE...
YEAH, YEAH. I'LL PUT IT ON YOUR TAB!

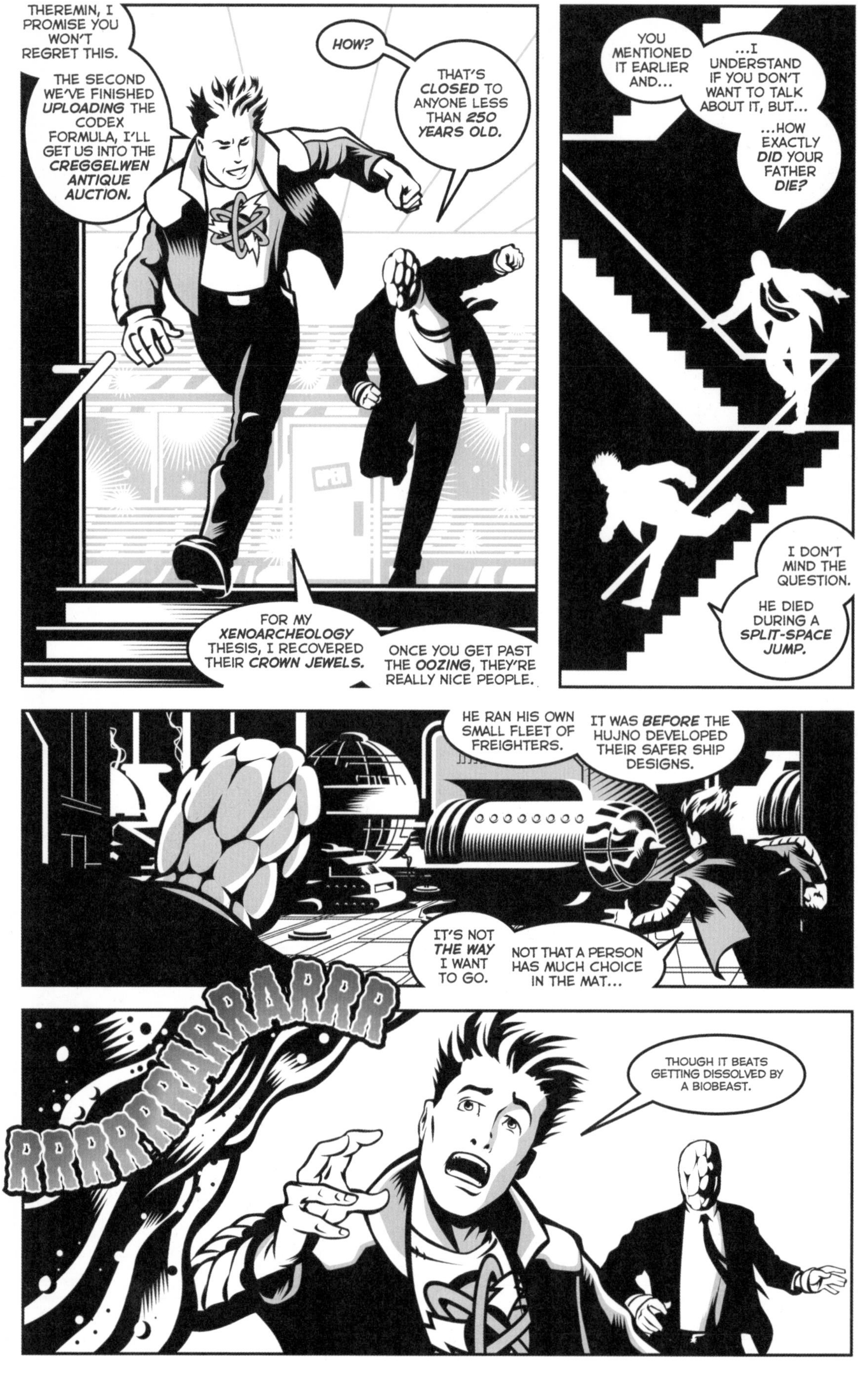
THEREMIN, I PROMISE YOU WON'T REGRET THIS.
THE SECOND WE'VE FINISHED UPLOADING THE CODEX FORMULA, I'LL GET US INTO THE CREGGELWEN ANTIQUE AUCTION.
HOW?
THAT'S CLOSED TO ANYONE LESS THAN 250 YEARS OLD.
OPEN
FOR MY XENOARCHEOLOGY THESIS, I RECOVERED THEIR CROWN JEWELS.
ONCE YOU GET PAST THE OOZING, THEY'RE REALLY NICE PEOPLE.
YOU MENTIONED IT EARLIER AND...
...I UNDERSTAND IF YOU DON'T WANT TO TALK ABOUT IT, BUT...
...HOW EXACTLY DID YOUR FATHER DIE?
I DON'T MIND THE QUESTION.
HE DIED DURING A SPLIT-SPACE JUMP.
HE RAN HIS OWN SMALL FLEET OF FREIGHTERS.
IT WAS BEFORE THE HUJNO DEVELOPED THEIR SAFER SHIP DESIGNS.
IT'S NOT THE WAY I WANT TO GO.
NOT THAT A PERSON HAS MUCH CHOICE IN THE MAT...
RRRRRRARRRARRRR
THOUGH IT BEATS GETTING DISSOLVED BY A BIOBEAST.

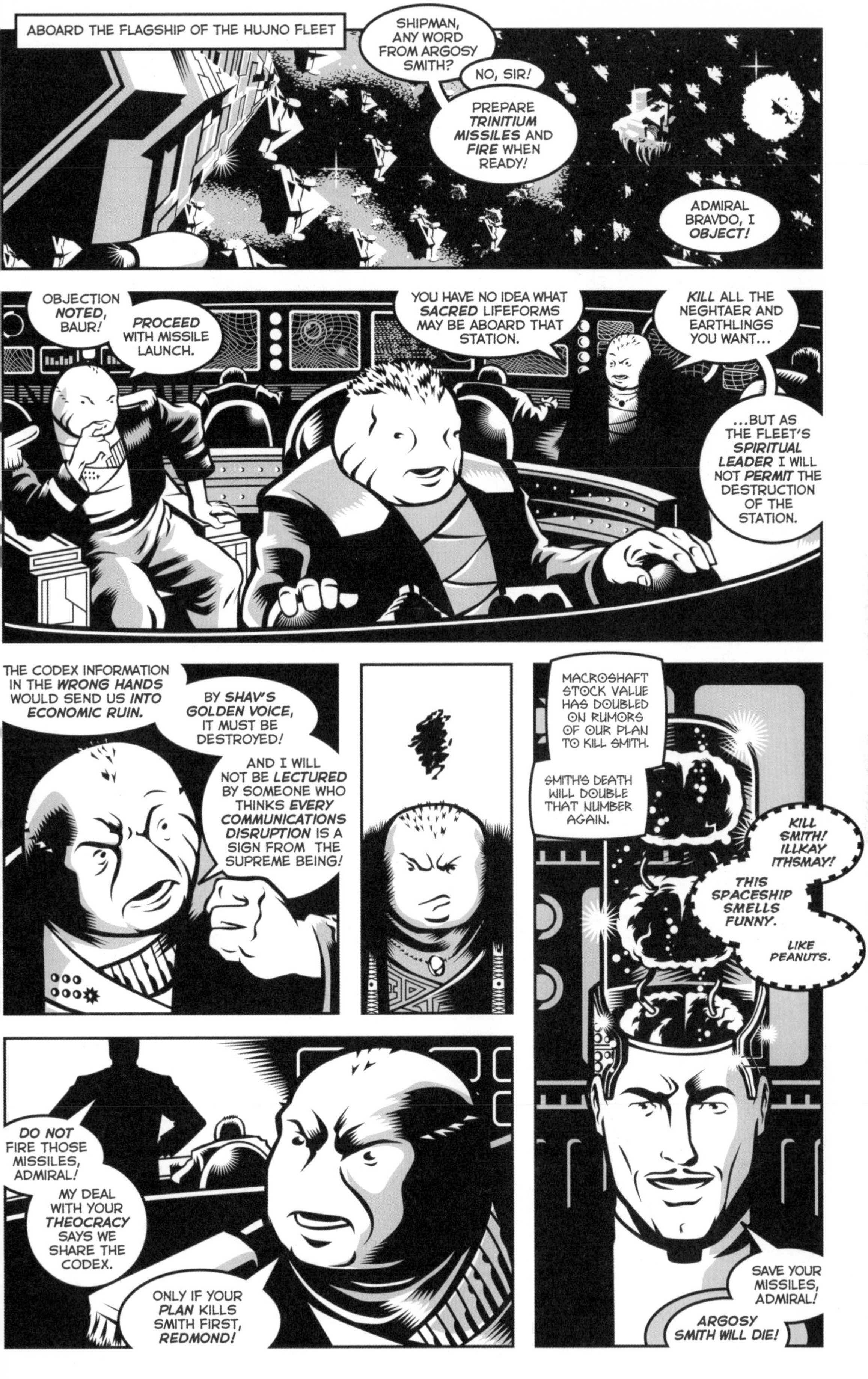
ABOARD THE FLAGSHIP OF THE HUJNO FLEET
SHIPMAN, ANY WORD FROM ARGOSY SMITH?
NO, SIR!
PREPARE TRINITIUM MISSILES AND FIRE WHEN READY!
ADMIRAL BRAVDO, I OBJECT!
OBJECTION NOTED, BAUR!
PROCEED WITH MISSILE LAUNCH.
YOU HAVE NO IDEA WHAT SACRED LIFEFORMS MAY BE ABOARD THAT STATION.
KILL ALL THE NEGHTAER AND EARTHLINGS YOU WANT...
...BUT AS THE FLEET'S SPIRITUAL LEADER I WILL NOT PERMIT THE DESTRUCTION OF THE STATION.
THE CODEX INFORMATION IN THE WRONG HANDS WOULD SEND US INTO ECONOMIC RUIN.
BY SHAV'S GOLDEN VOICE, IT MUST BE DESTROYED!
AND I WILL NOT BE LECTURED BY SOMEONE WHO THINKS EVERY COMMUNICATIONS DISRUPTION IS A SIGN FROM THE SUPREME BEING!
MACROSHAFT STOCK VALUE HAS DOUBLED ON RUMORS OF OUR PLAN TO KILL SMITH.
SMITH'S DEATH WILL DOUBLE THAT NUMBER AGAIN.
KILL SMITH! ILLKAY ITHSMAY!
THIS SPACESHIP SMELLS FUNNY.
LIKE PEANUTS.
DO NOT FIRE THOSE MISSILES, ADMIRAL!
MY DEAL WITH YOUR THEOCRACY SAYS WE SHARE THE CODEX.
ONLY IF YOUR PLAN KILLS SMITH FIRST, REDMOND!
SAVE YOUR MISSILES, ADMIRAL!
ARGOSY SMITH WILL DIE!

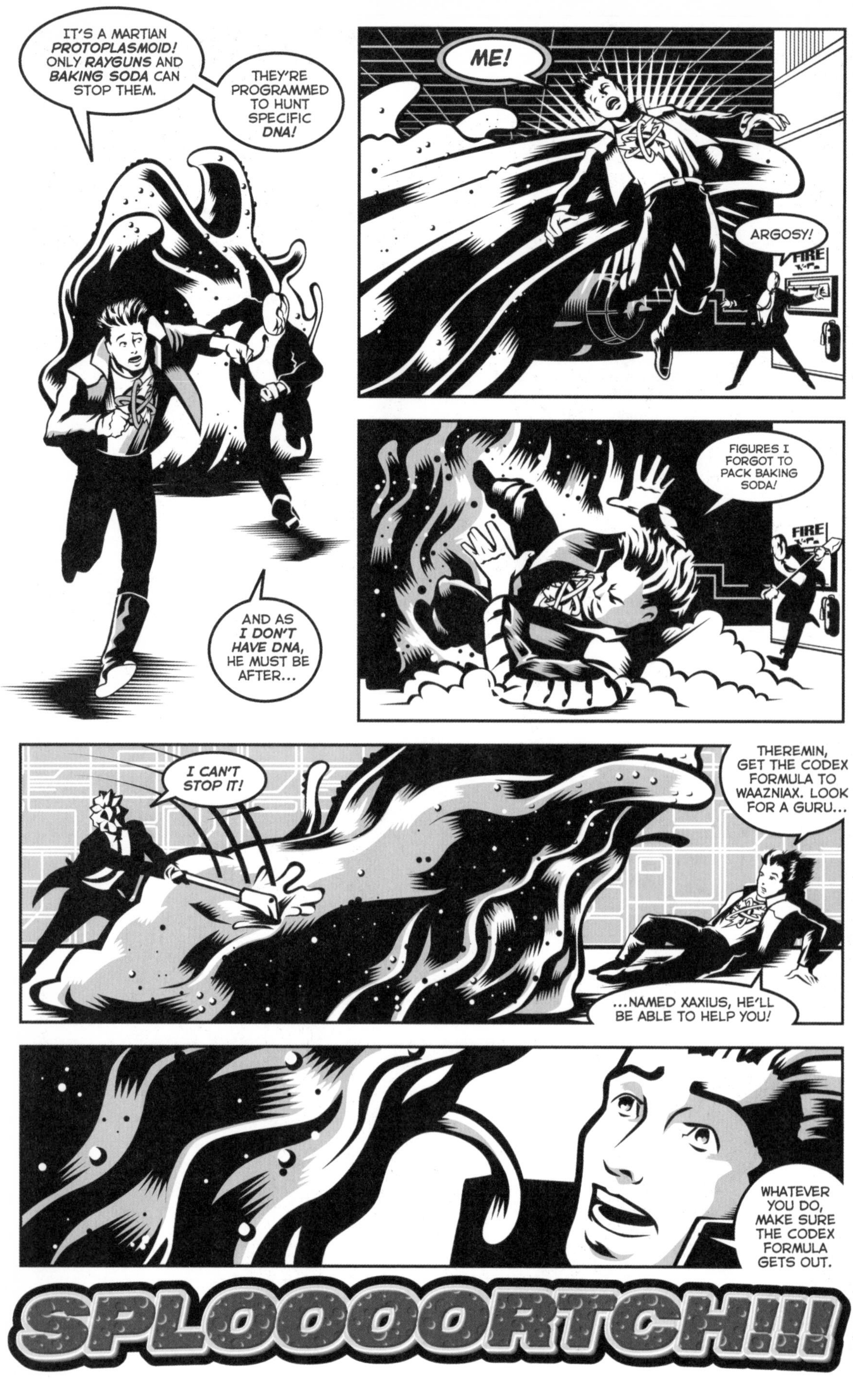
IT'S A MARTIAN PROTOPLASMOID! ONLY RAYGUNS AND BAKING SODA CAN STOP THEM.
THEY'RE PROGRAMMED TO HUNT SPECIFIC DNA!
AND AS I DON'T HAVE DNA, HE MUST BE AFTER...
ME!
ARGOSY!
FIRE
FIGURES I FORGOT TO PACK BAKING SODA!
FIRE
I CAN'T STOP IT!
THEREMIN, GET THE CODEX FORMULA TO WAAZNIAX. LOOK FOR A GURU...
...NAMED XAXIUS, HE'LL BE ABLE TO HELP YOU!
WHATEVER YOU DO, MAKE SURE THE CODEX FORMULA GETS OUT.
SPLOOOORTCH!!!

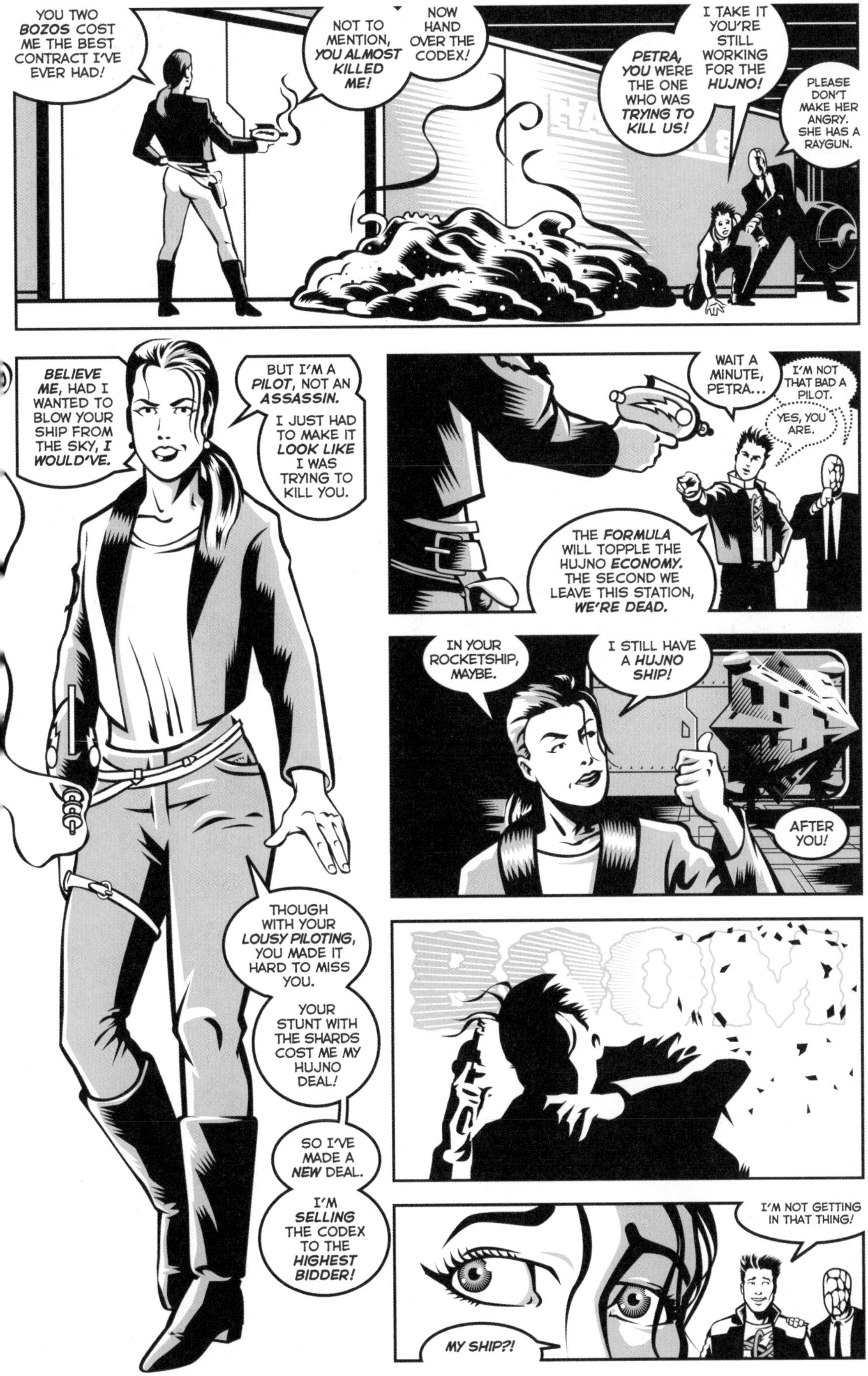
YOU TWO BOZOS COST ME THE BEST CONTRACT I'VE EVER HAD!
NOT TO MENTION, YOU ALMOST KILLED ME!
NOW HAND OVER THE CODEX!
PETRA, YOU WERE THE ONE WHO WAS TRYING TO KILL US!
I TAKE IT YOU'RE STILL WORKING FOR THE HUJNO!
PLEASE DON'T MAKE HER ANGRY. SHE HAS A RAYGUN.
BELIEVE ME, HAD I WANTED TO BLOW YOUR SHIP FROM THE SKY, I WOULD'VE.
BUT I'M A PILOT, NOT AN ASSASSIN.
I JUST HAD TO MAKE IT LOOK LIKE I WAS TRYING TO KILL YOU.
THOUGH WITH YOUR LOUSY PILOTING, YOU MADE IT HARD TO MISS YOU.
YOUR STUNT WITH THE SHARDS COST ME MY HUJNO DEAL!
SO I'VE MADE A NEW DEAL.
I'M SELLING THE CODEX TO THE HIGHEST BIDDER!
WAIT A MINUTE, PETRA...
I'M NOT THAT BAD A PILOT.
YES, YOU ARE.
THE FORMULA WILL TOPPLE THE HUJNO ECONOMY. THE SECOND WE LEAVE THIS STATION, WE'RE DEAD.
IN YOUR ROCKETSHIP, MAYBE.
I STILL HAVE A HUJNO SHIP!
AFTER YOU!
BOOM
I'M NOT GETTING IN THAT THING!
MY SHIP?!

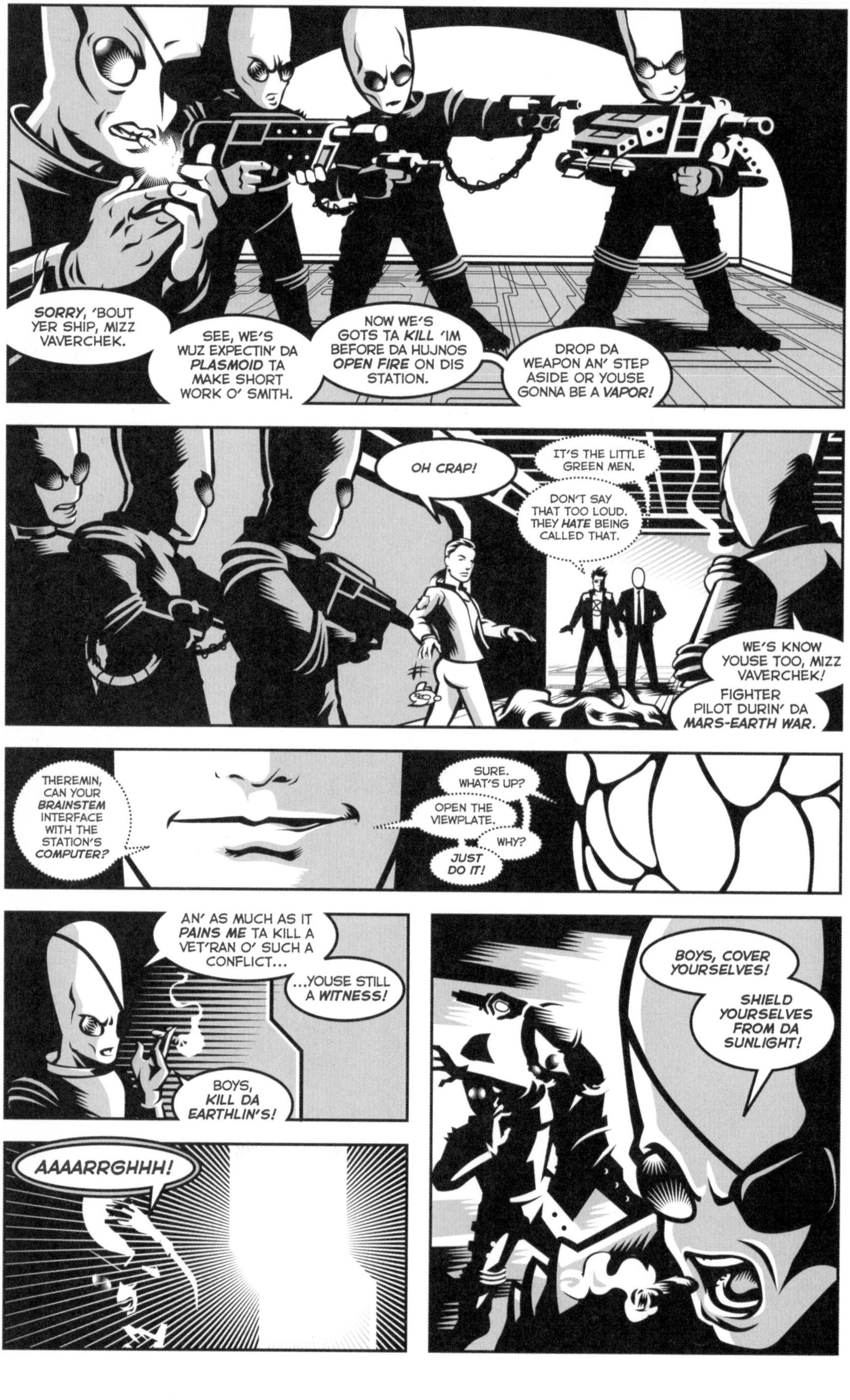
SORRY, 'BOUT YER SHIP, MIZZ VAVERCHEK.
SEE, WE'S WUZ EXPECTIN' DA PLASMOID TA MAKE SHORT WORK O' SMITH.
NOW WE'S GOTS TA KILL 'IM BEFORE DA HUJNOS OPEN FIRE ON DIS STATION.
DROP DA WEAPON AN' STEP ASIDE OR YOUSE GONNA BE A VAPOR!
OH CRAP!
IT'S THE LITTLE GREEN MEN.
DON'T SAY THAT TOO LOUD. THEY HATE BEING CALLED THAT.
WE'S KNOW YOUSE TOO, MIZZ VAVERCHEK!
FIGHTER PILOT DURIN' DA MARS-EARTH WAR.
THEREMIN, CAN YOUR BRAINSTEM INTERFACE WITH THE STATION'S COMPUTER?
SURE. WHAT'S UP?
OPEN THE VIEWPLATE.
WHY?
JUST DO IT!
AN' AS MUCH AS IT PAINS ME TA KILL A VET'RAN O' SUCH A CONFLICT...
...YOUSE STILL A WITNESS!
BOYS, KILL DA EARTHLIN'S!
BOYS, COVER YOURSELVES!
SHIELD YOURSELVES FROM DA SUNLIGHT!
AAAARRGHHH!

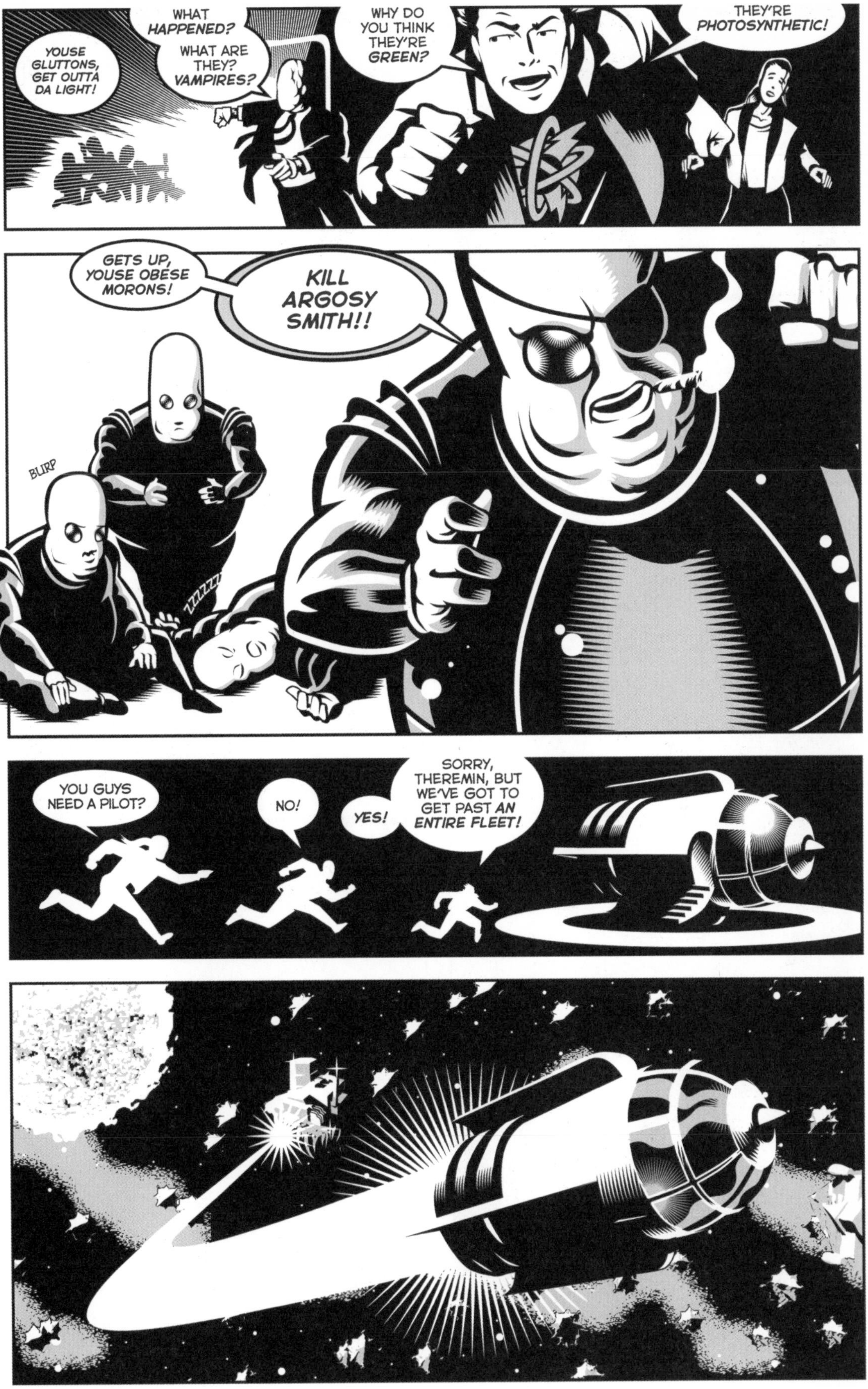
YOUSE GLUTTONS, GET OUTTA DA LIGHT!
WHAT HAPPENED?
WHAT ARE THEY? VAMPIRES?
WHY DO YOU THINK THEY'RE GREEN?
THEY'RE PHOTOSYNTHETIC!
GETS UP, YOUSE OBESE MORONS!
KILL ARGOSY SMITH!!
BURP
ZZZZZZ
YOU GUYS NEED A PILOT?
NO!
YES!
SORRY, THEREMIN, BUT WE'VE GOT TO GET PAST AN ENTIRE FLEET!

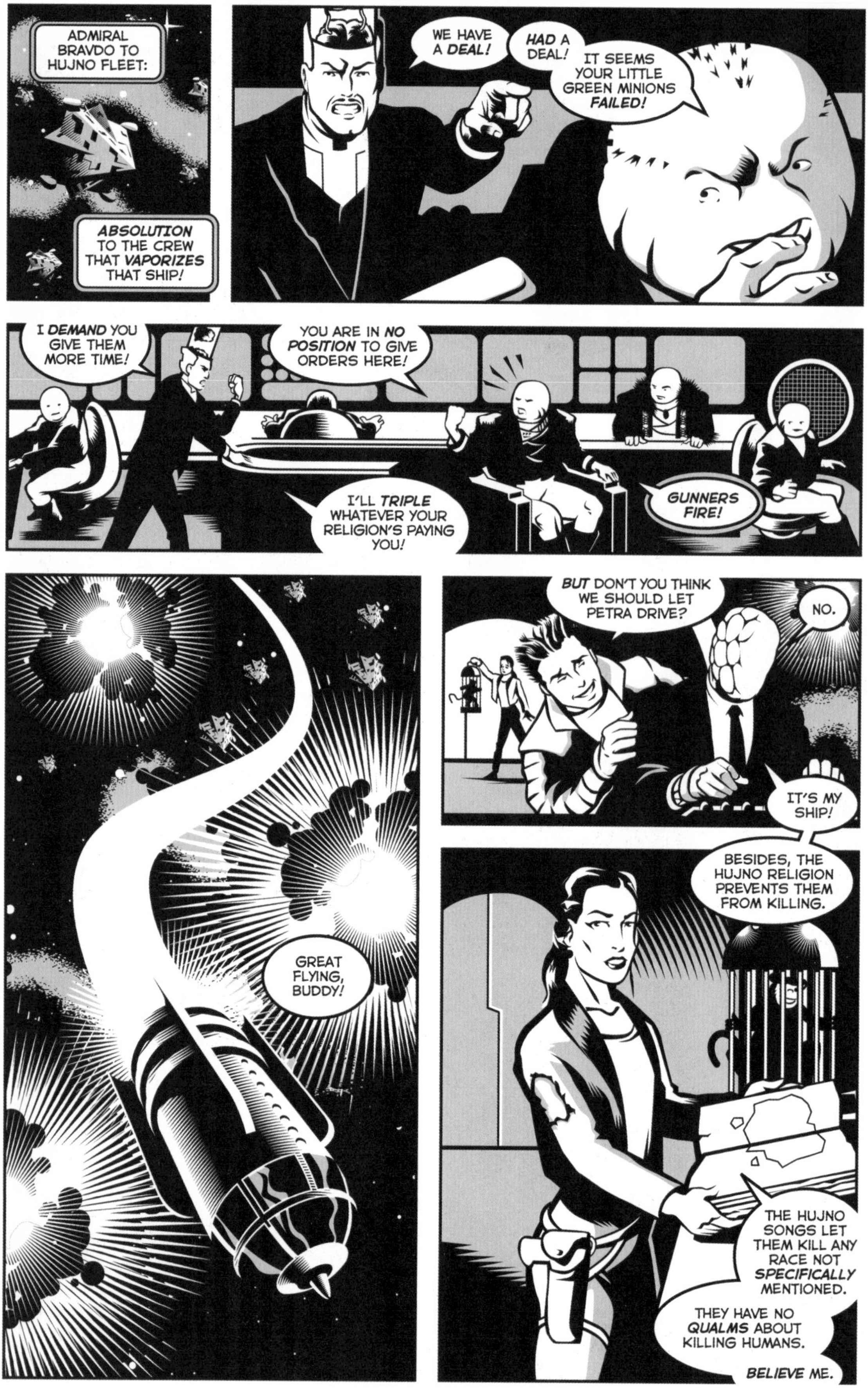
ADMIRAL BRAVDO TO HUJNO FLEET:
ABSOLUTION TO THE CREW THAT VAPORIZES THAT SHIP!
WE HAVE A DEAL!
HAD A DEAL!
IT SEEMS YOUR LITTLE GREEN MINIONS FAILED!
I DEMAND YOU GIVE THEM MORE TIME!
YOU ARE IN NO POSITION TO GIVE ORDERS HERE!
I'LL TRIPLE WHATEVER YOUR RELIGION'S PAYING YOU!
GUNNERS FIRE!
GREAT FLYING, BUDDY!
BUT DON'T YOU THINK WE SHOULD LET PETRA DRIVE?
NO.
IT'S MY SHIP!
BESIDES, THE HUJNO RELIGION PREVENTS THEM FROM KILLING.
THE HUJNO SONGS LET THEM KILL ANY RACE NOT SPECIFICALLY MENTIONED.
THEY HAVE NO QUALMS ABOUT KILLING HUMANS.
BELIEVE ME.

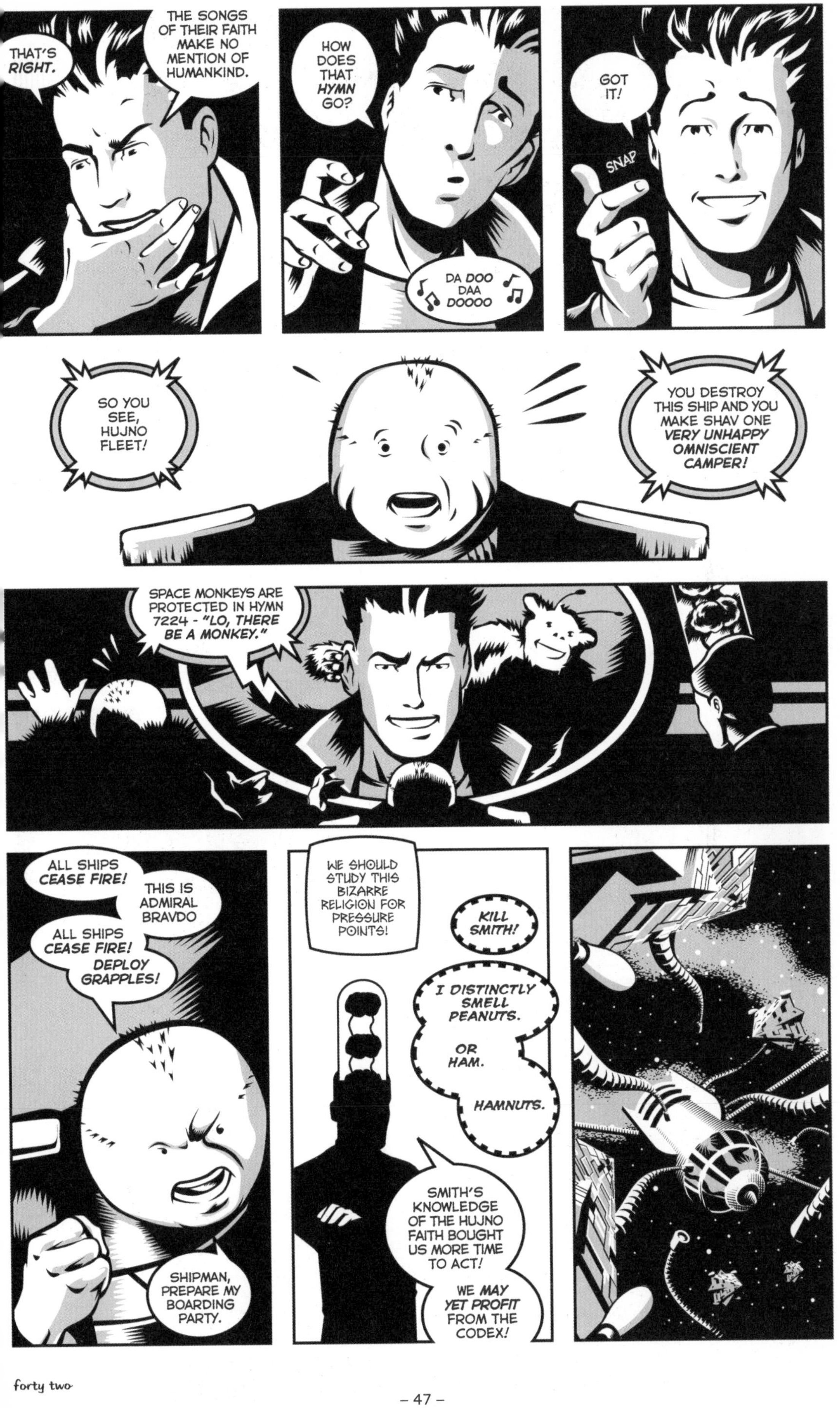
THAT'S RIGHT.
THE SONGS OF THEIR FAITH MAKE NO MENTION OF HUMANKIND.
HOW DOES THAT HYMN GO?
DA DOO DAA DOOOO
GOT IT!
SNAP
SO YOU SEE, HUJNO FLEET!
YOU DESTROY THIS SHIP AND YOU MAKE SHAV ONE VERY UNHAPPY OMNISCIENT CAMPER!
SPACE MONKEYS ARE PROTECTED IN HYMN 7224 - "LO, THERE BE A MONKEY."
ALL SHIPS CEASE FIRE!
THIS IS ADMIRAL BRAVDO
ALL SHIPS CEASE FIRE! DEPLOY GRAPPLES!
SHIPMAN, PREPARE MY BOARDING PARTY.
WE SHOULD STUDY THIS BIZARRE RELIGION FOR PRESSURE POINTS!
KILL SMITH!
I DISTINCTLY SMELL PEANUTS.
OR HAM.
HAMNUTS.
SMITH'S KNOWLEDGE OF THE HUJNO FAITH BOUGHT US MORE TIME TO ACT!
WE MAY YET PROFIT FROM THE CODEX!

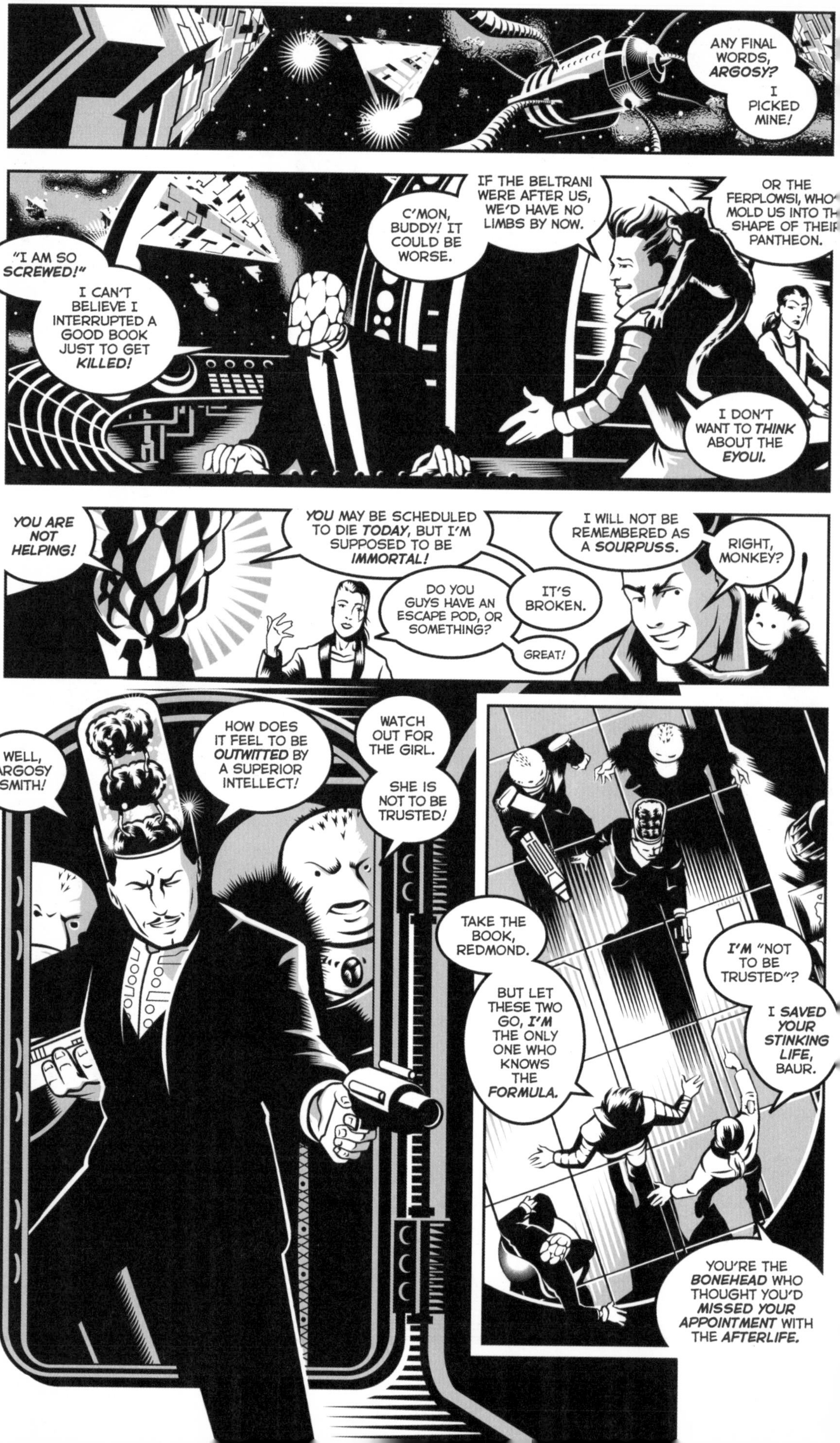
ANY FINAL WORDS, ARGOSY?
I PICKED MINE!
"I AM SO SCREWED!"
I CAN'T BELIEVE I INTERRUPTED A GOOD BOOK JUST TO GET KILLED!
C'MON, BUDDY! IT COULD BE WORSE.
IF THE BELTRANI WERE AFTER US, WE'D HAVE NO LIMBS BY NOW.
OR THE FERPLOWSI, WHO
MOLD US INTO TH
SHAPE OF THEIR PANTHEON.
I DON'T WANT TO THINK ABOUT THE EYOUI.
YOU ARE NOT HELPING!
YOU MAY BE SCHEDULED TO DIE TODAY, BUT I'M SUPPOSED TO BE IMMORTAL!
I WILL NOT BE REMEMBERED AS A SOURPUSS.
RIGHT, MONKEY?
DO YOU GUYS HAVE AN ESCAPE POD, OR SOMETHING?
IT'S BROKEN.
GREAT!
WELL, ARGOSY SMITH!
HOW DOES IT FEEL TO BE OUTWITTED BY A SUPERIOR INTELLECT!
WATCH OUT FOR THE GIRL.
SHE IS NOT TO BE TRUSTED!
TAKE THE BOOK, REDMOND.
BUT LET THESE TWO GO, I'M THE ONLY ONE WHO KNOWS THE FORMULA.
I'M "NOT TO BE TRUSTED"?
I SAVED YOUR STINKING LIFE, BAUR.
YOU'RE THE BONEHEAD WHO THOUGHT YOU'D MISSED YOUR APPOINTMENT WITH THE AFTERLIFE.

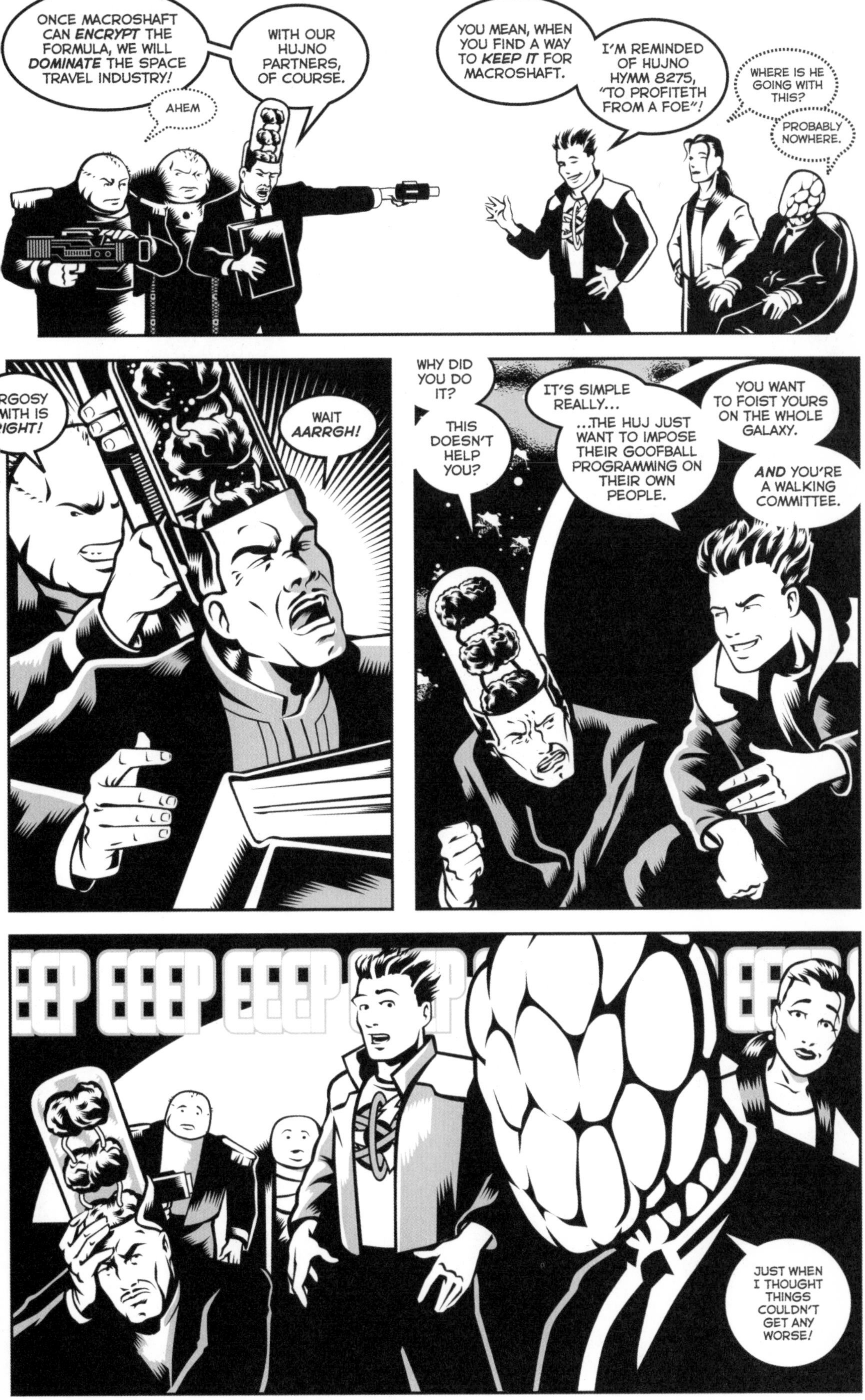

ONCE MACROSHAFT CAN ENCRYPT THE FORMULA, WE WILL DOMINATE THE SPACE TRAVEL INDUSTRY!
AHEM
WITH OUR HUJNO PARTNERS, OF COURSE.
YOU MEAN, WHEN YOU FIND A WAY TO KEEP IT FOR MACROSHAFT.
I'M REMINDED OF HUJNO HYMM 8275, "TO PROFITETH FROM A FOE"!
WHERE IS HE GOING WITH THIS?
PROBABLY NOWHERE.
RGOSY MITH IS IGHT!
WAIT AARRGH!
WHY DID YOU DO IT?
THIS DOESN'T HELP YOU?
IT'S SIMPLE REALLY...
...THE HUJ JUST WANT TO IMPOSE THEIR GOOFBALL PROGRAMMING ON THEIR OWN PEOPLE.
YOU WANT TO FOIST YOURS ON THE WHOLE GALAXY.
AND YOU'RE A WALKING COMMITTEE.
EEP EEEP EEEP
JUST WHEN I THOUGHT THINGS COULDN'T GET ANY WORSE!

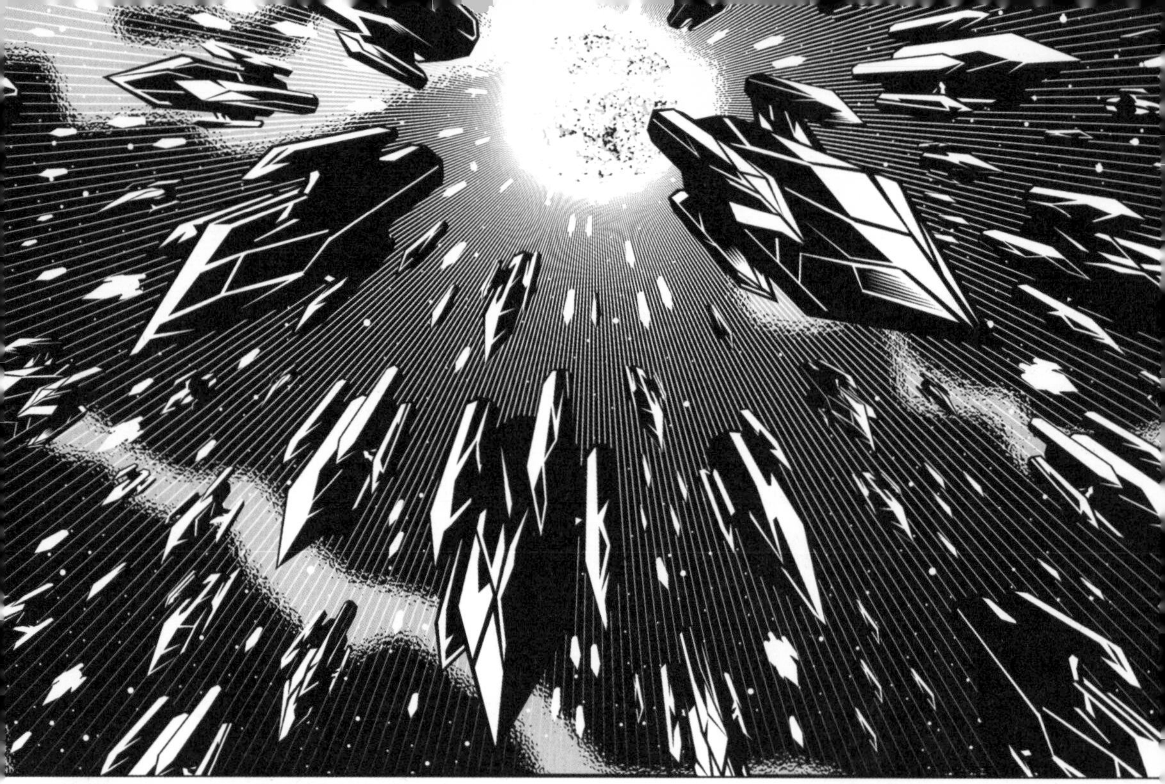

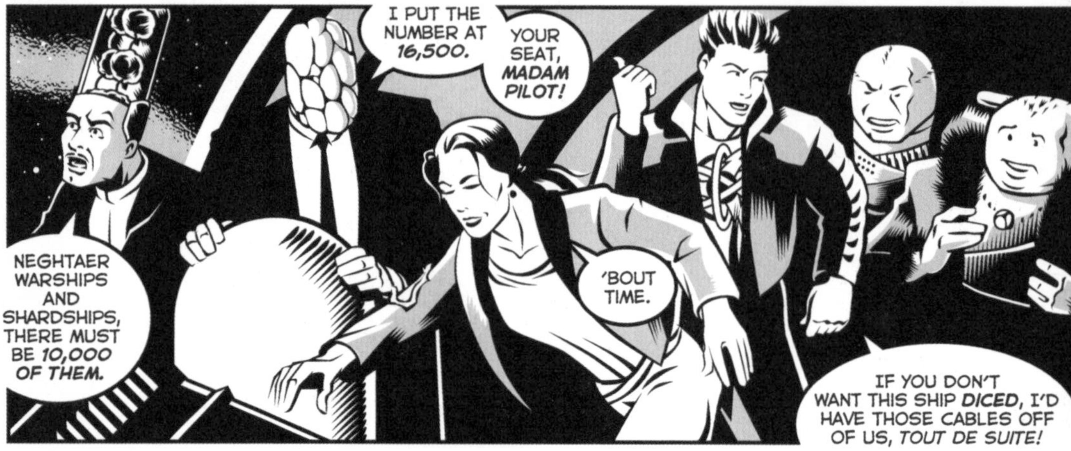
NEGHTAER WARSHIPS AND SHARDSHIPS, THERE MUST BE 10,000 OF THEM.
I PUT THE NUMBER AT 16,500.
YOUR SEAT, MADAM PILOT!
'BOUT TIME.
IF YOU DON'T WANT THIS SHIP DICED, I'D HAVE THOSE CABLES OFF OF US, TOUT DE SUITE!

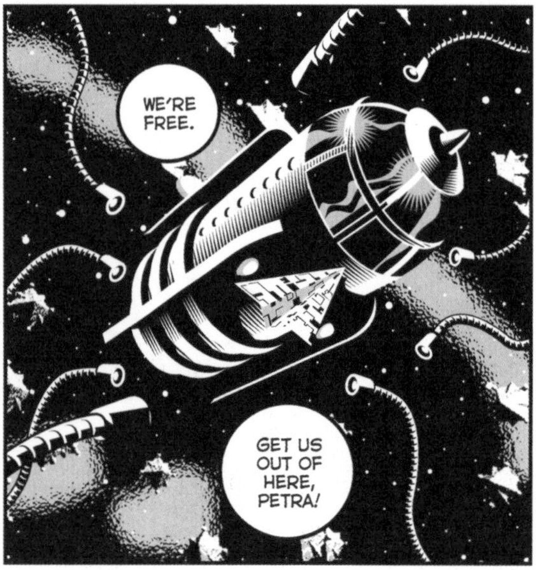
WE'RE FREE.
GET US OUT OF HERE, PETRA!

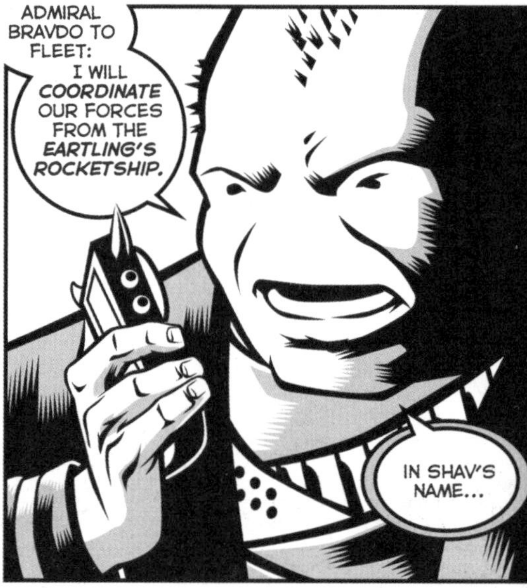
ADMIRAL BRAVDO TO FLEET:
I WILL COORDINATE OUR FORCES FROM THE EARTLING'S ROCKETSHIP.
IN SHAV'S NAME...

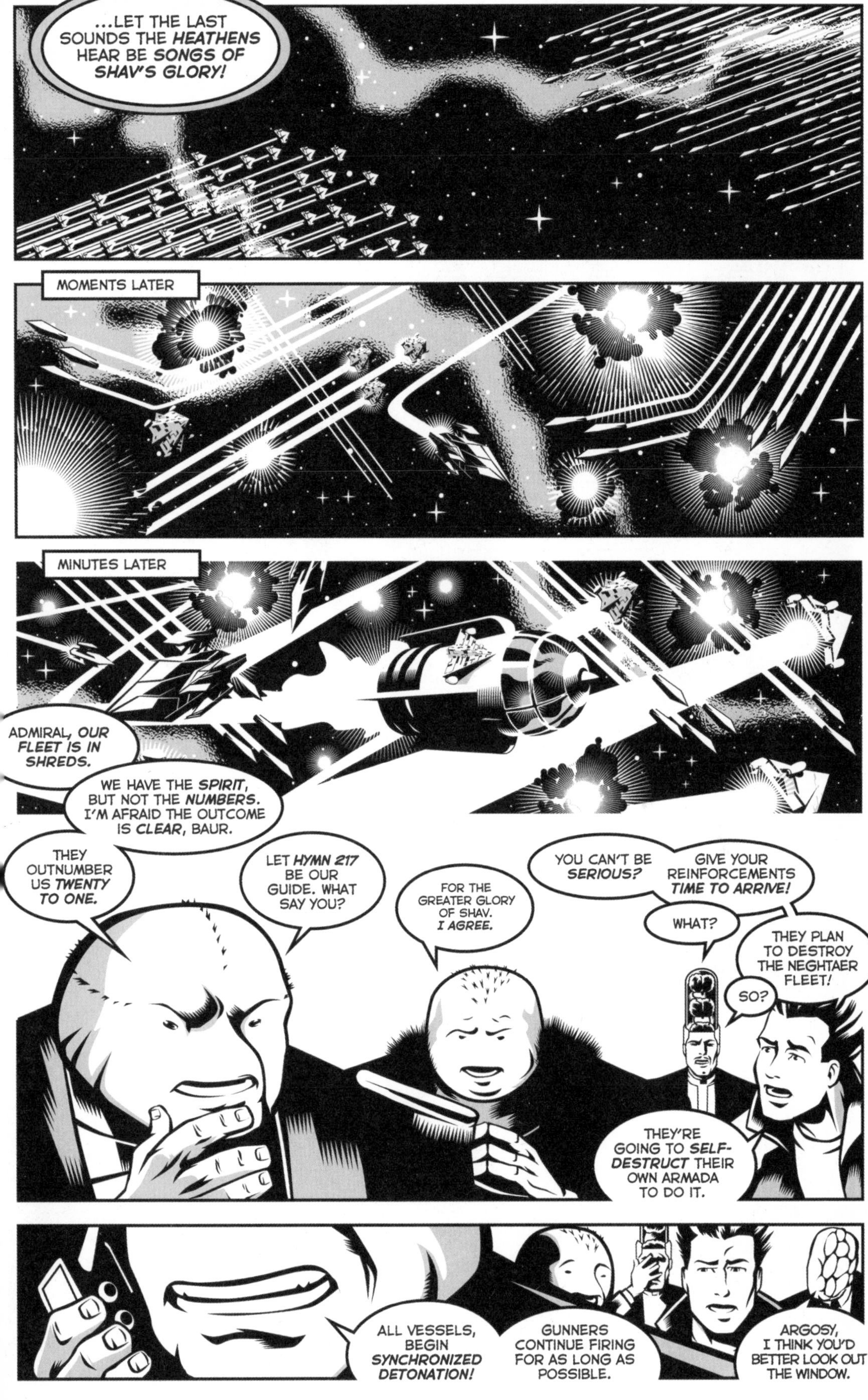
...LET THE LAST SOUNDS THE *HEATHENS* HEAR BE *SONGS OF SHAV'S GLORY!*
MOMENTS LATER
MINUTES LATER
ADMIRAL, *OUR FLEET IS IN SHREDS.*
WE HAVE THE *SPIRIT*, BUT NOT THE *NUMBERS*. I'M AFRAID THE OUTCOME IS *CLEAR*, BAUR.
THEY OUTNUMBER US *TWENTY TO ONE.*
LET *HYMN 217* BE OUR GUIDE. WHAT SAY YOU?
FOR THE GREATER GLORY OF SHAV. *I AGREE.*
YOU CAN'T BE *SERIOUS?*
GIVE YOUR REINFORCEMENTS *TIME TO ARRIVE!*
WHAT?
THEY PLAN TO DESTROY THE NEGHTAER FLEET!
SO?
THEY'RE GOING TO *SELF-DESTRUCT* THEIR OWN ARMADA TO DO IT.
ALL VESSELS, BEGIN *SYNCHRONIZED DETONATION!*
GUNNERS CONTINUE FIRING FOR AS LONG AS POSSIBLE.
ARGOSY, I THINK YOU'D BETTER LOOK OUT THE WINDOW.

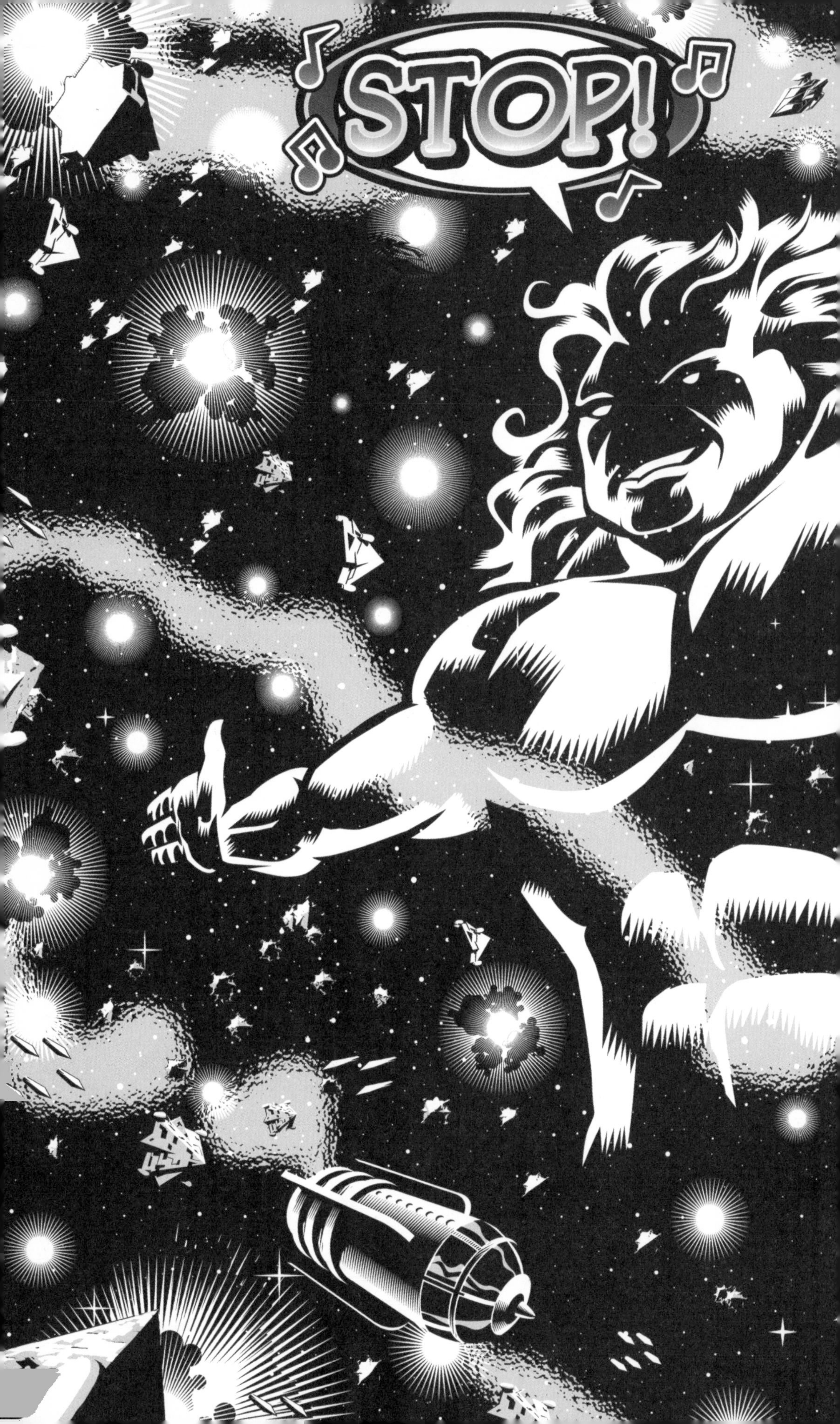
STOP!

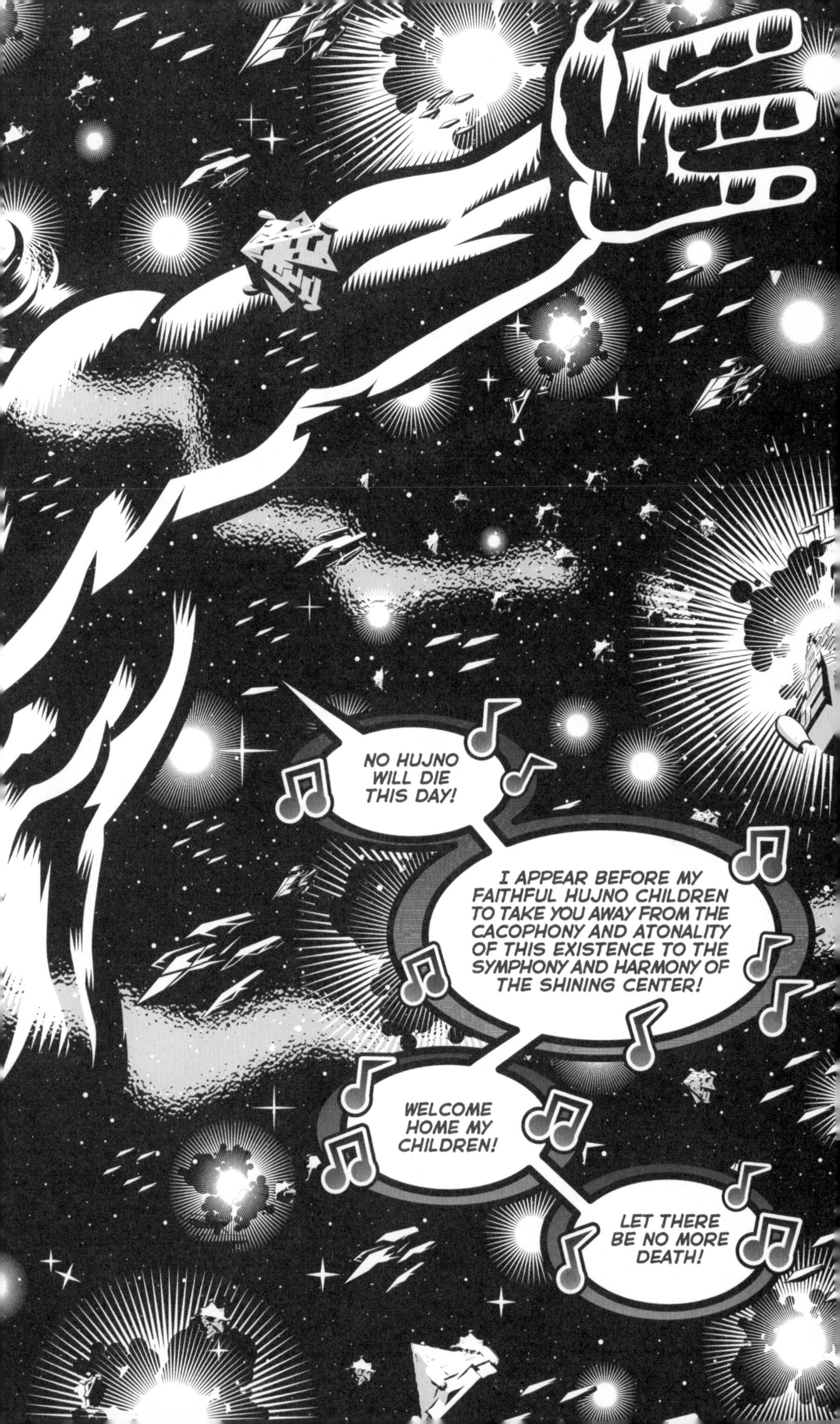
NO HUJNO WILL DIE THIS DAY!
I APPEAR BEFORE MY FAITHFUL HUJNO CHILDREN TO TAKE YOU AWAY FROM THE CACOPHONY AND ATONALITY OF THIS EXISTENCE TO THE SYMPHONY AND HARMONY OF THE SHINING CENTER!
WELCOME HOME MY CHILDREN!
LET THERE BE NO MORE DEATH!

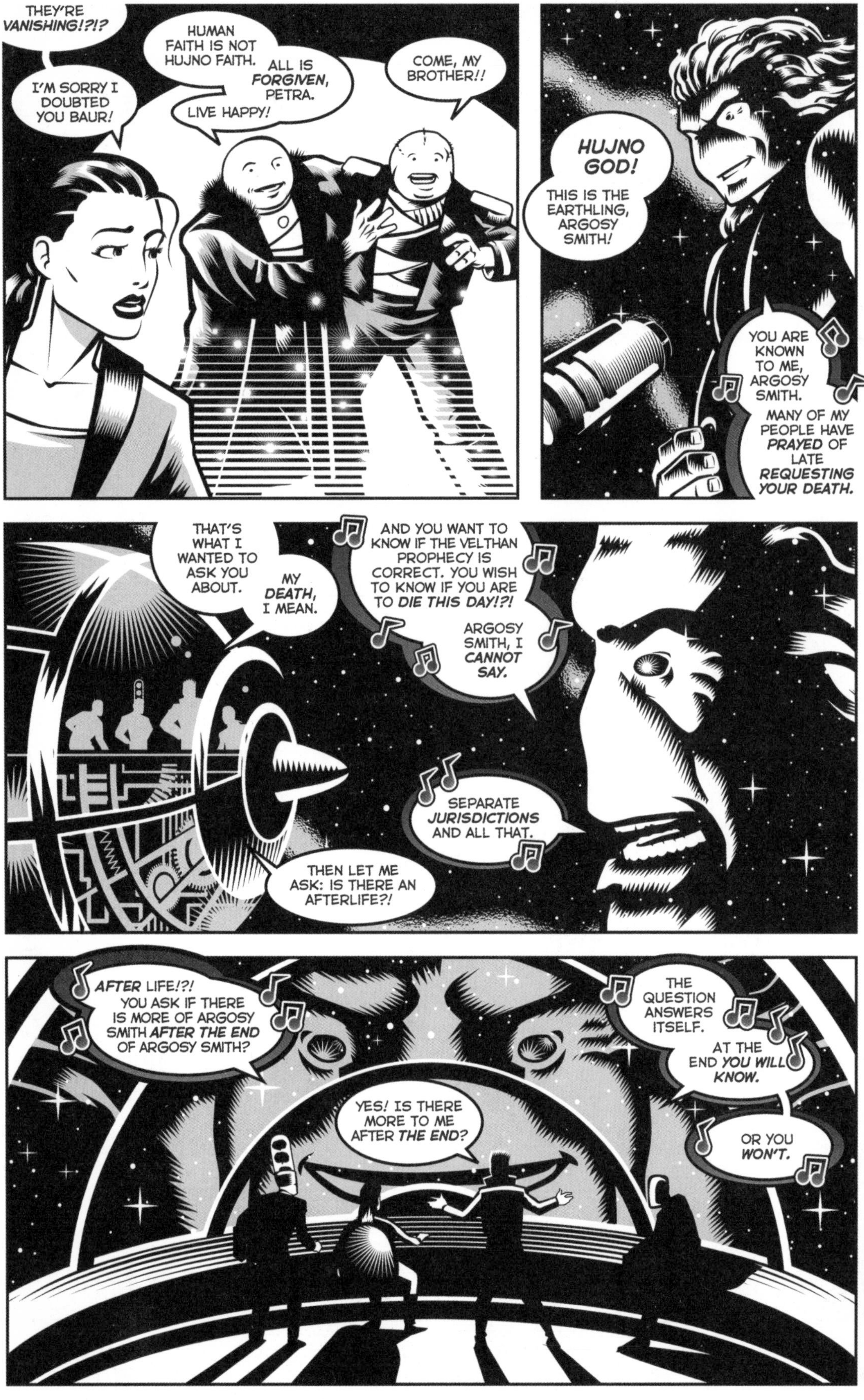
THEY'RE VANISHING!?!?
I'M SORRY I DOUBTED YOU BAUR!
HUMAN FAITH IS NOT HUJNO FAITH.
ALL IS FORGIVEN, PETRA.
LIVE HAPPY!
COME, MY BROTHER!!
HUJNO GOD!
THIS IS THE EARTHLING, ARGOSY SMITH!
YOU ARE KNOWN TO ME, ARGOSY SMITH.
MANY OF MY PEOPLE HAVE PRAYED OF LATE REQUESTING YOUR DEATH.
THAT'S WHAT I WANTED TO ASK YOU ABOUT.
MY DEATH, I MEAN.
AND YOU WANT TO KNOW IF THE VELTHAN PROPHECY IS CORRECT. YOU WISH TO KNOW IF YOU ARE TO DIE THIS DAY!?!
ARGOSY SMITH, I CANNOT SAY.
SEPARATE JURISDICTIONS AND ALL THAT.
THEN LET ME ASK: IS THERE AN AFTERLIFE?!
AFTER LIFE!?! YOU ASK IF THERE IS MORE OF ARGOSY SMITH AFTER THE END OF ARGOSY SMITH?
THE QUESTION ANSWERS ITSELF.
AT THE END YOU WILL KNOW.
YES! IS THERE MORE TO ME AFTER THE END?
OR YOU WON'T.

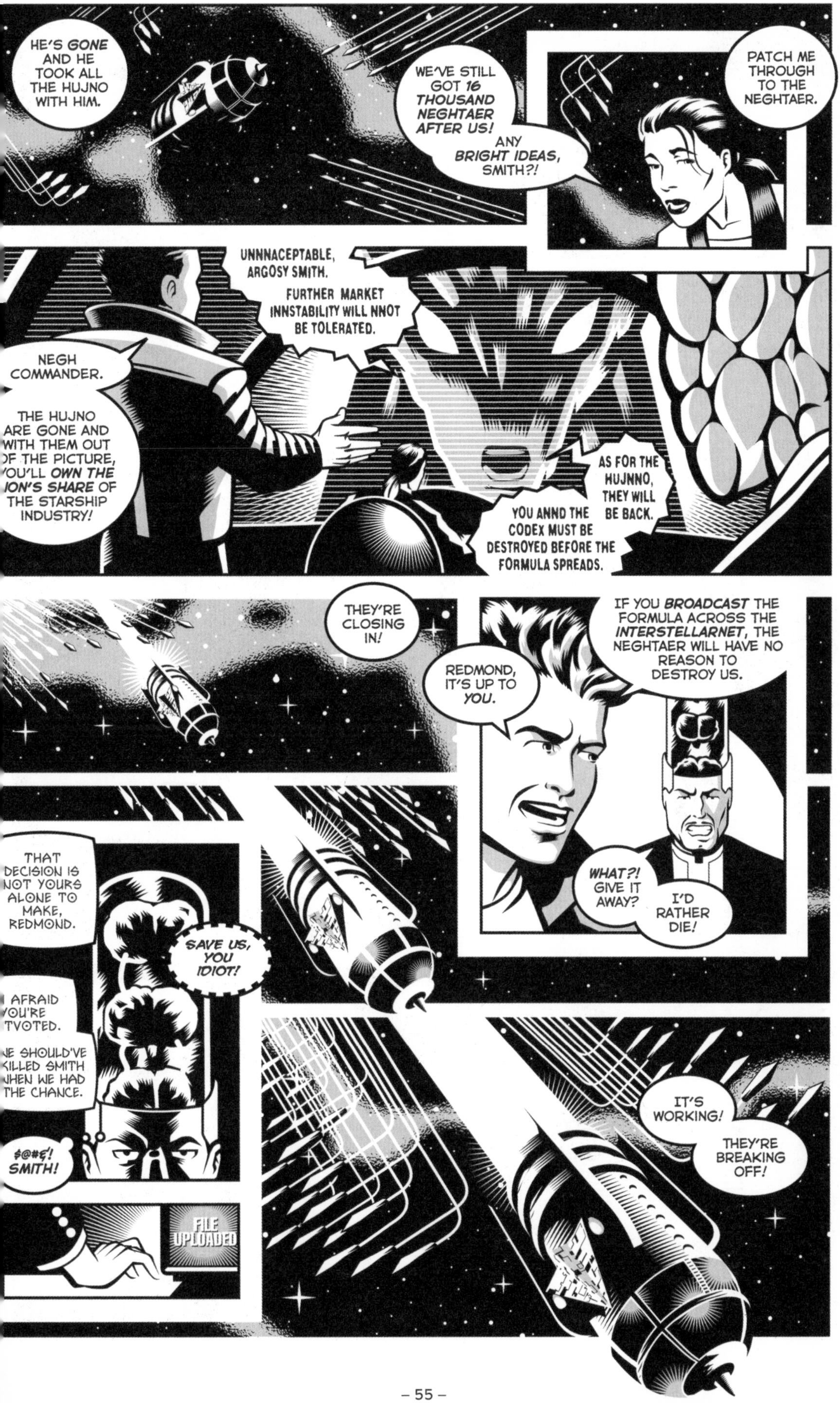
HE'S GONE AND HE TOOK ALL THE HUJNO WITH HIM.
WE'VE STILL GOT 16 THOUSAND NEGHTAER AFTER US!
ANY BRIGHT IDEAS, SMITH?!
PATCH ME THROUGH TO THE NEGHTAER.
UNNNACEPTABLE, ARGOSY SMITH.
FURTHER MARKET INNSTABILITY WILL NNOT BE TOLERATED.
NEGH COMMANDER.
THE HUJNO ARE GONE AND WITH THEM OUT OF THE PICTURE, YOU'LL OWN THE LION'S SHARE OF THE STARSHIP INDUSTRY!
AS FOR THE HUJNNO, THEY WILL BE BACK.
YOU ANND THE CODEX MUST BE DESTROYED BEFORE THE FORMULA SPREADS.
THEY'RE CLOSING IN!
IF YOU BROADCAST THE FORMULA ACROSS THE INTERSTELLARNET, THE NEGHTAER WILL HAVE NO REASON TO DESTROY US.
REDMOND, IT'S UP TO YOU.
WHAT?! GIVE IT AWAY?
I'D RATHER DIE!
THAT DECISION IS NOT YOURS ALONE TO MAKE, REDMOND.
SAVE US, YOU IDIOT!
I AFRAID YOU'RE TVOTED.
WE SHOULD'VE KILLED SMITH WHEN WE HAD THE CHANCE.
$@#€! SMITH!
FILE UPLOADED
IT'S WORKING!
THEY'RE BREAKING OFF!

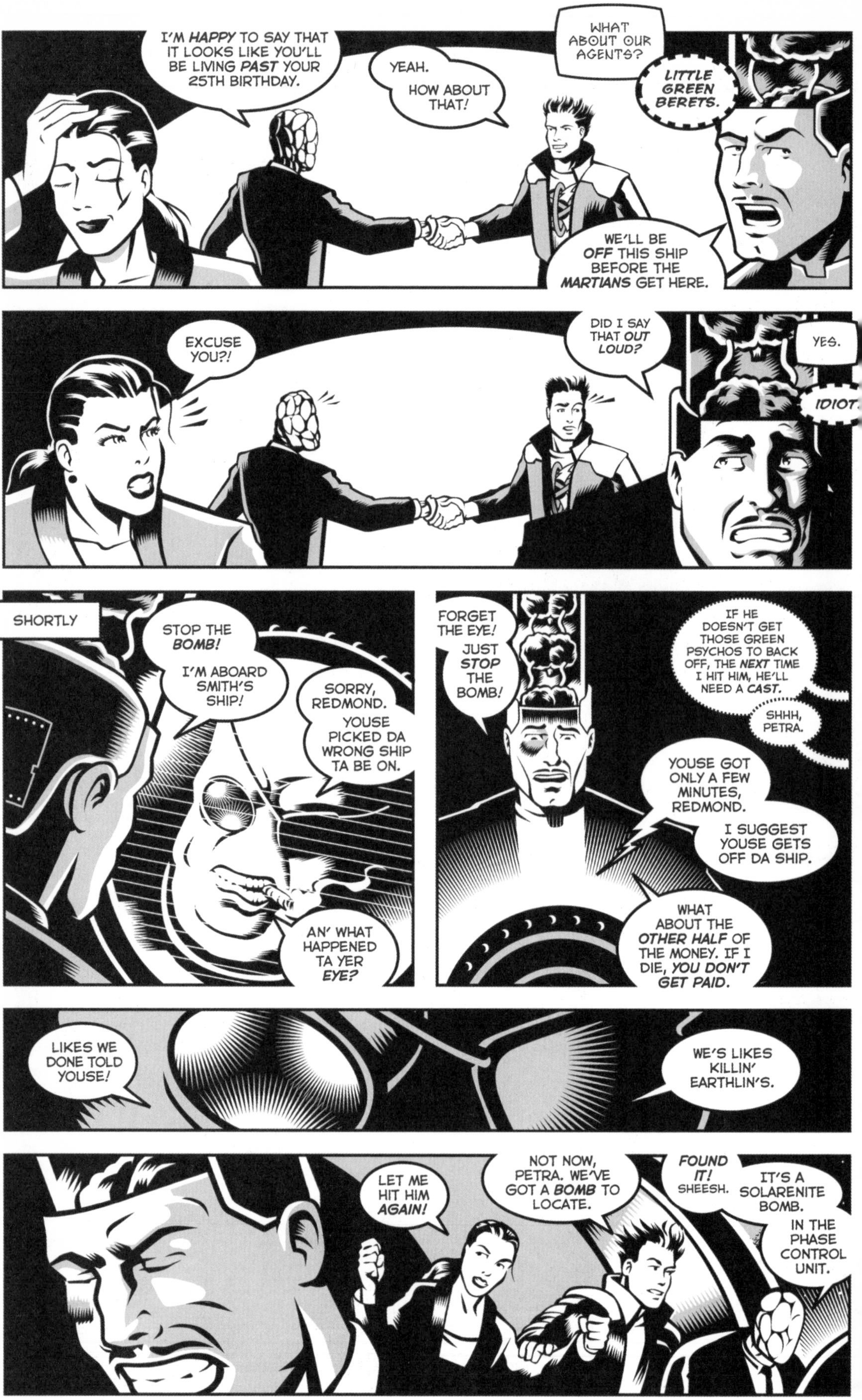

I'M HAPPY TO SAY THAT IT LOOKS LIKE YOU'LL BE LIVING PAST YOUR 25TH BIRTHDAY.
YEAH.
HOW ABOUT THAT!
WHAT ABOUT OUR AGENTS?
LITTLE GREEN BERETS.
WE'LL BE OFF THIS SHIP BEFORE THE MARTIANS GET HERE.
EXCUSE YOU?!
DID I SAY THAT OUT LOUD?
YES.
IDIOT.
SHORTLY
STOP THE BOMB!
I'M ABOARD SMITH'S SHIP!
SORRY, REDMOND.
YOUSE PICKED DA WRONG SHIP TA BE ON.
AN' WHAT HAPPENED TA YER EYE?
FORGET THE EYE!
JUST STOP THE BOMB!
IF HE DOESN'T GET THOSE GREEN PSYCHOS TO BACK OFF, THE NEXT TIME I HIT HIM, HE'LL NEED A CAST.
SHHH, PETRA.
YOUSE GOT ONLY A FEW MINUTES, REDMOND.
I SUGGEST YOUSE GETS OFF DA SHIP.
WHAT ABOUT THE OTHER HALF OF THE MONEY. IF I DIE, YOU DON'T GET PAID.
LIKES WE DONE TOLD YOUSE!
WE'S LIKES KILLIN' EARTHLIN'S.
LET ME HIT HIM AGAIN!
NOT NOW, PETRA. WE'VE GOT A BOMB TO LOCATE.
FOUND IT!
SHEESH.
IT'S A SOLARENITE BOMB.
IN THE PHASE CONTROL UNIT.

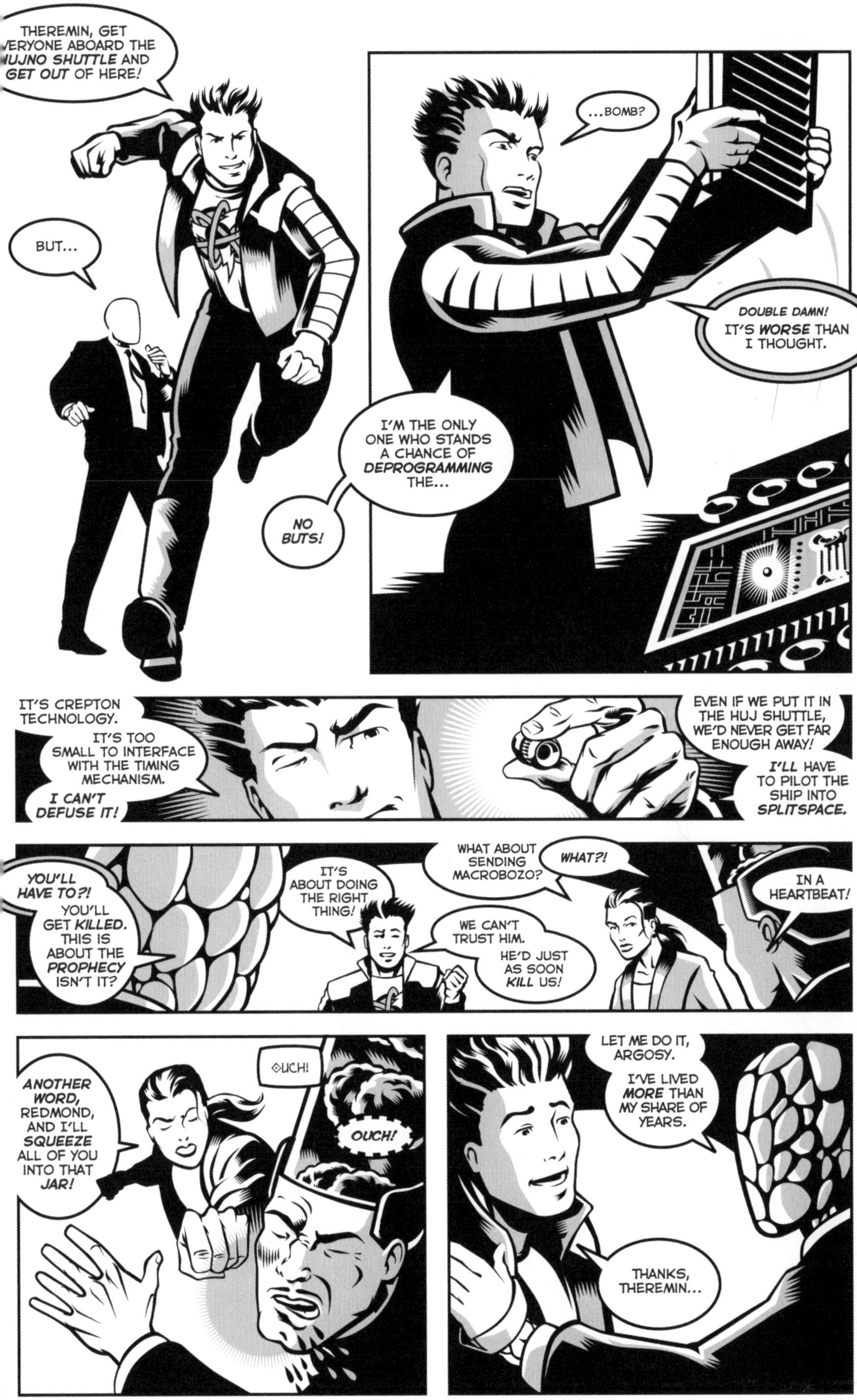
THEREMIN, GET
VERYONE ABOARD THE
UJNO SHUTTLE AND
GET OUT OF HERE!
BUT...
NO BUTS!
I'M THE ONLY ONE WHO STANDS A CHANCE OF DEPROGRAMMING THE...
...BOMB?
DOUBLE DAMN! IT'S WORSE THAN I THOUGHT.
IT'S CREPTON TECHNOLOGY.
IT'S TOO SMALL TO INTERFACE WITH THE TIMING MECHANISM.
I CAN'T DEFUSE IT!
EVEN IF WE PUT IT IN THE HUJ SHUTTLE, WE'D NEVER GET FAR ENOUGH AWAY!
I'LL HAVE TO PILOT THE SHIP INTO SPLITSPACE.
YOU'LL HAVE TO?! YOU'LL GET KILLED. THIS IS ABOUT THE PROPHECY ISN'T IT?
IT'S ABOUT DOING THE RIGHT THING!
WHAT ABOUT SENDING MACROBOZO?
WHAT?!
IN A HEARTBEAT!
WE CAN'T TRUST HIM.
HE'D JUST AS SOON KILL US!
ANOTHER WORD, REDMOND, AND I'LL SQUEEZE ALL OF YOU INTO THAT JAR!
OUCH!
OUCH!
LET ME DO IT, ARGOSY.
I'VE LIVED MORE THAN MY SHARE OF YEARS.
THANKS, THEREMIN...

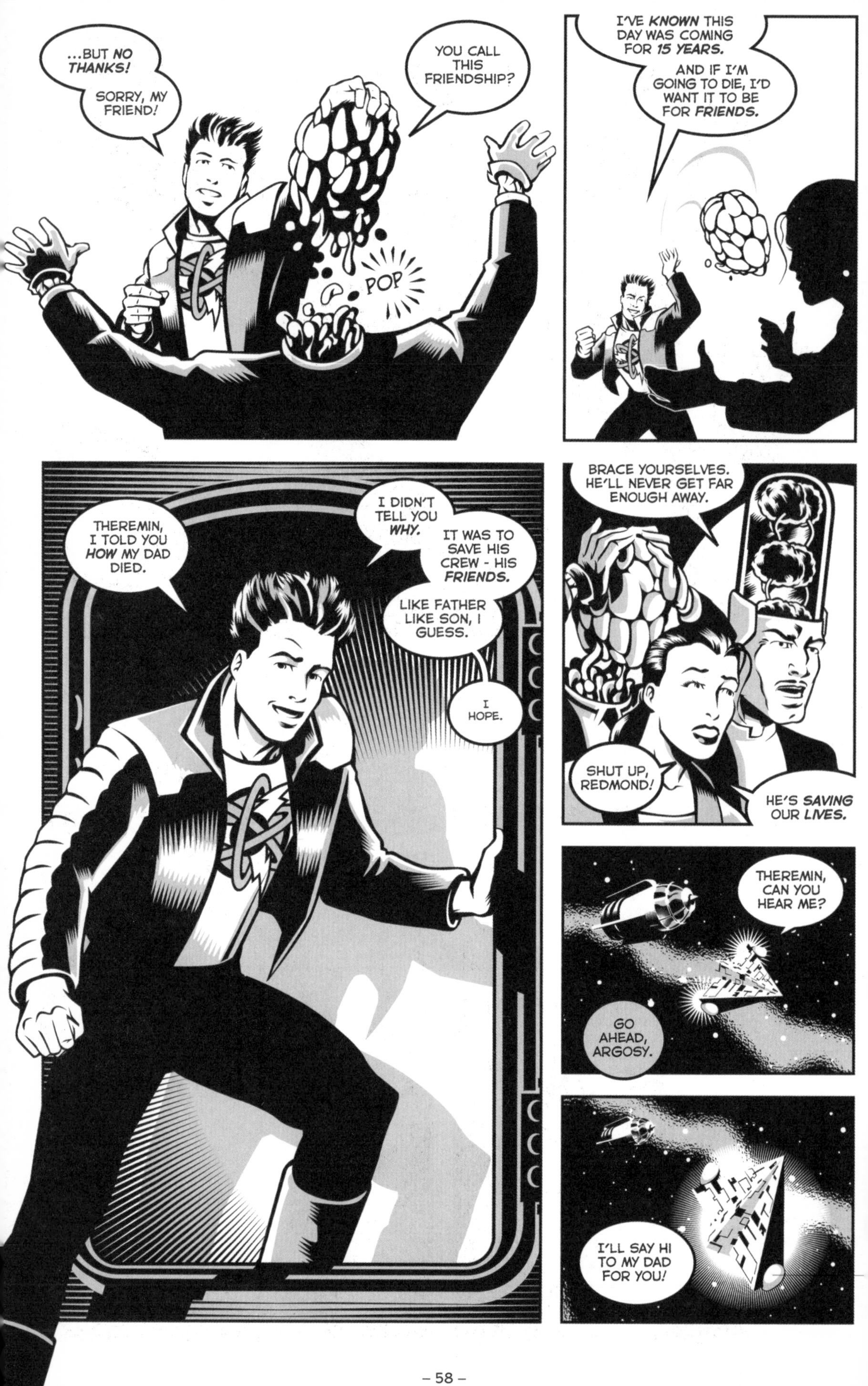
...BUT NO THANKS!
SORRY, MY FRIEND!
YOU CALL THIS FRIENDSHIP?
POP
I'VE KNOWN THIS DAY WAS COMING FOR 15 YEARS.
AND IF I'M GOING TO DIE, I'D WANT IT TO BE FOR FRIENDS.
THEREMIN, I TOLD YOU HOW MY DAD DIED.
I DIDN'T TELL YOU WHY.
IT WAS TO SAVE HIS CREW - HIS FRIENDS.
LIKE FATHER LIKE SON, I GUESS.
I HOPE.
BRACE YOURSELVES. HE'LL NEVER GET FAR ENOUGH AWAY.
SHUT UP, REDMOND!
HE'S SAVING OUR LIVES.
THEREMIN, CAN YOU HEAR ME?
GO AHEAD, ARGOSY.
I'LL SAY HI TO MY DAD FOR YOU!

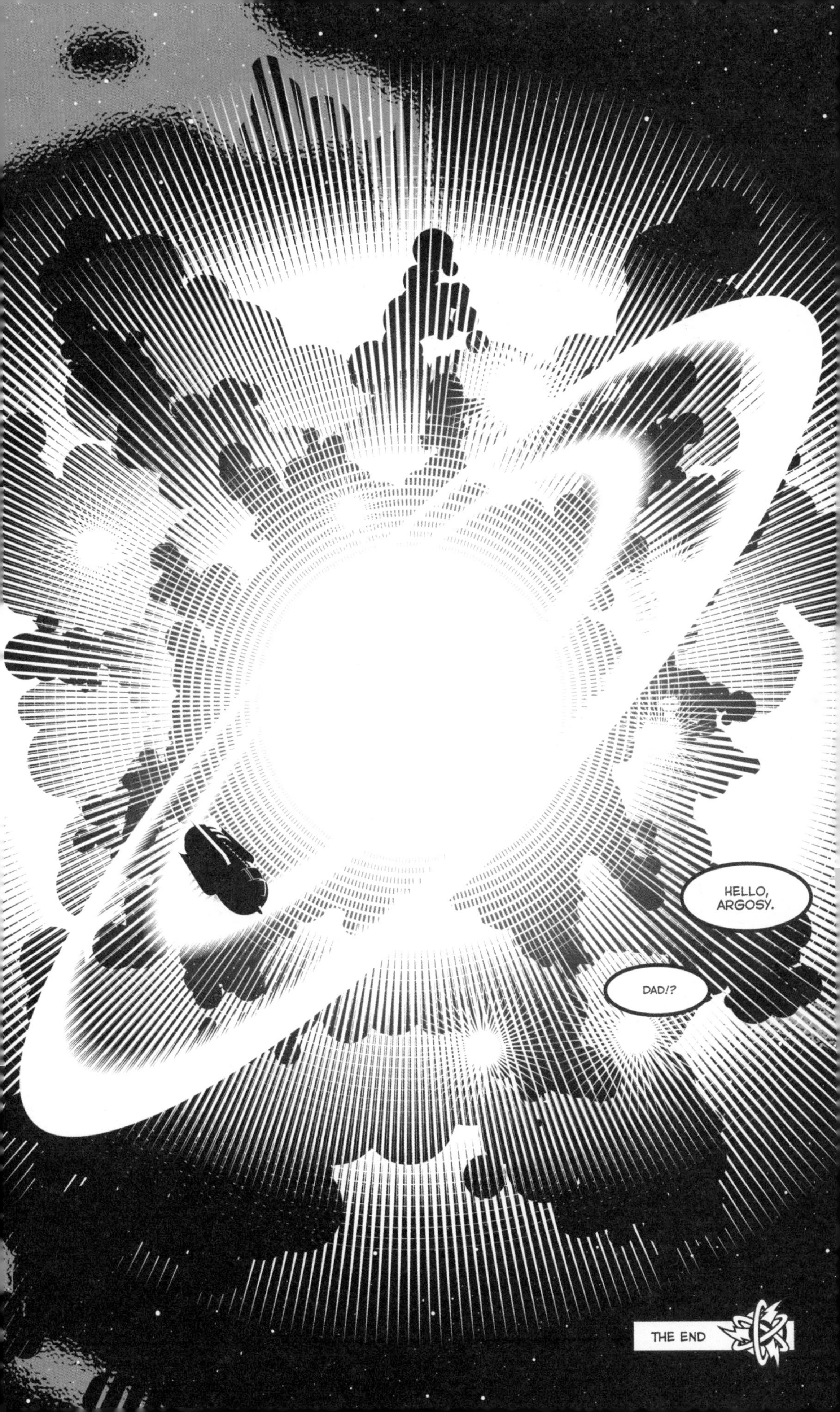
HELLO, ARGOSY.
DAD!?
THE END

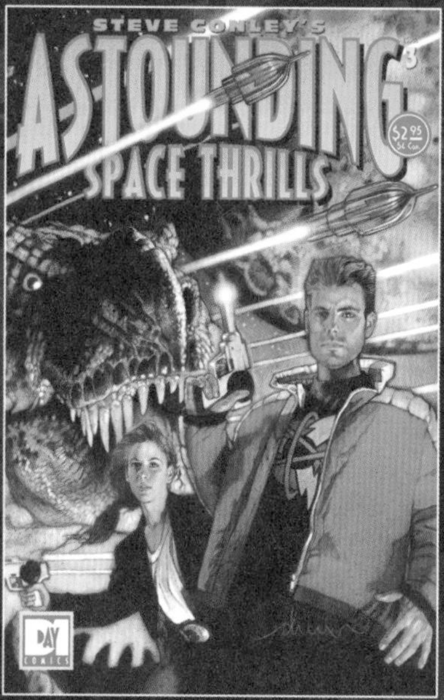
STEVE CONLEY'S
ASTOUNDING
3
SPACE THRILLS

ASTOUNDING SPACE THRILLS #3
JANUARY 1999

COVER BY DREW STRUZAN

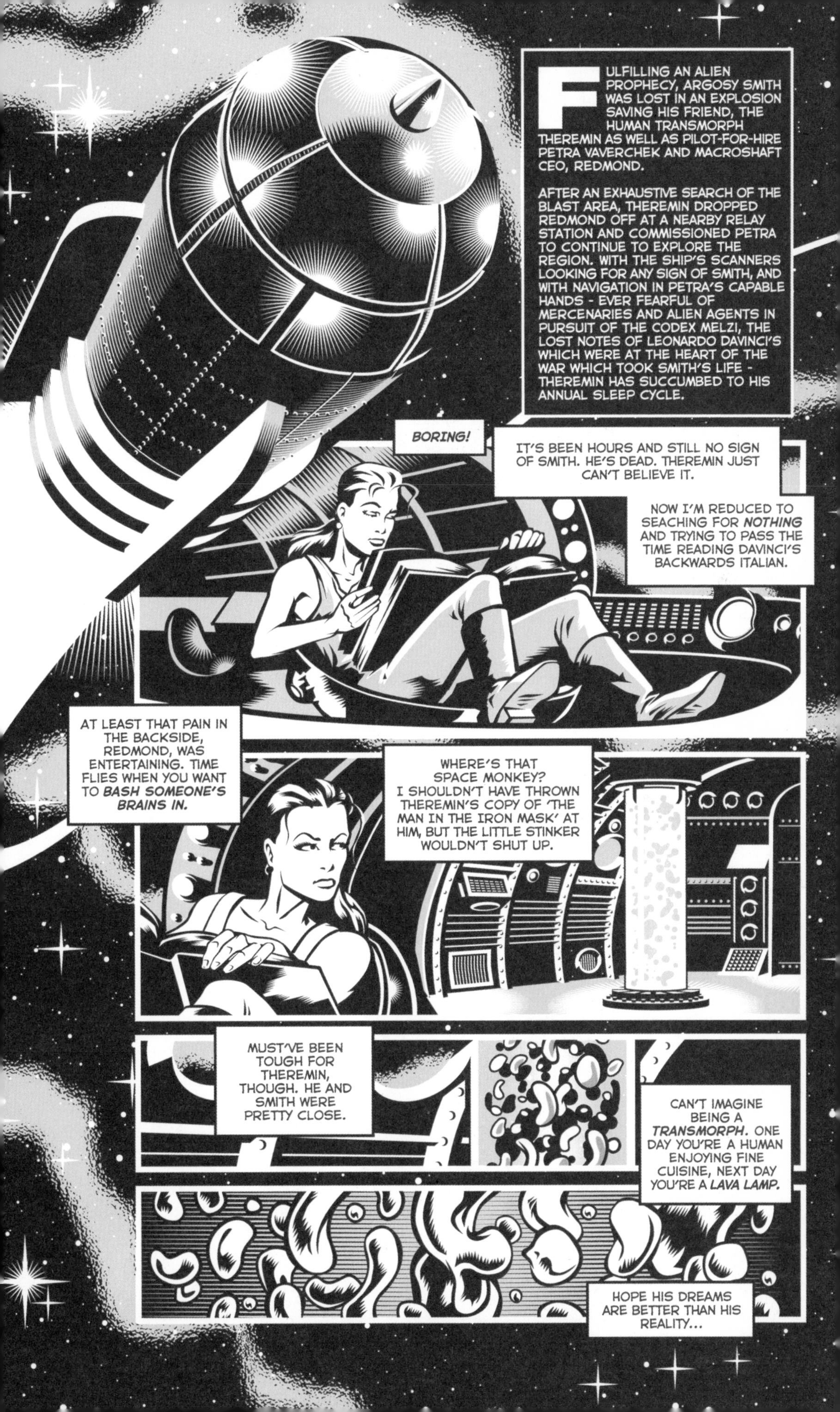
FULFILLING AN ALIEN PROPHECY, ARGOSY SMITH WAS LOST IN AN EXPLOSION SAVING HIS FRIEND, THE HUMAN TRANSMORPH THEREMIN AS WELL AS PILOT-FOR-HIRE PETRA VAVERCHEK AND MACROSHAFT CEO, REDMOND.
AFTER AN EXHAUSTIVE SEARCH OF THE BLAST AREA, THEREMIN DROPPED REDMOND OFF AT A NEARBY RELAY STATION AND COMMISSIONED PETRA TO CONTINUE TO EXPLORE THE REGION. WITH THE SHIP'S SCANNERS LOOKING FOR ANY SIGN OF SMITH, AND WITH NAVIGATION IN PETRA'S CAPABLE HANDS - EVER FEARFUL OF MERCENARIES AND ALIEN AGENTS IN PURSUIT OF THE CODEX MELZI, THE LOST NOTES OF LEONARDO DAVINCI'S WHICH WERE AT THE HEART OF THE WAR WHICH TOOK SMITH'S LIFE - THEREMIN HAS SUCCUMBED TO HIS ANNUAL SLEEP CYCLE.
BORING!
IT'S BEEN HOURS AND STILL NO SIGN OF SMITH. HE'S DEAD. THEREMIN JUST CAN'T BELIEVE IT.
NOW I'M REDUCED TO SEACHING FOR NOTHING AND TRYING TO PASS THE TIME READING DAVINCI'S BACKWARDS ITALIAN.
AT LEAST THAT PAIN IN THE BACKSIDE, REDMOND, WAS ENTERTAINING. TIME FLIES WHEN YOU WANT TO BASH SOMEONE'S BRAINS IN.
WHERE'S THAT SPACE MONKEY? I SHOULDN'T HAVE THROWN THEREMIN'S COPY OF 'THE MAN IN THE IRON MASK' AT HIM, BUT THE LITTLE STINKER WOULDN'T SHUT UP.
MUST'VE BEEN TOUGH FOR THEREMIN, THOUGH. HE AND SMITH WERE PRETTY CLOSE.
CAN'T IMAGINE BEING A TRANSMORPH. ONE DAY YOU'RE A HUMAN ENJOYING FINE CUISINE, NEXT DAY YOU'RE A LAVA LAMP.
HOPE HIS DREAMS ARE BETTER THAN HIS REALITY...

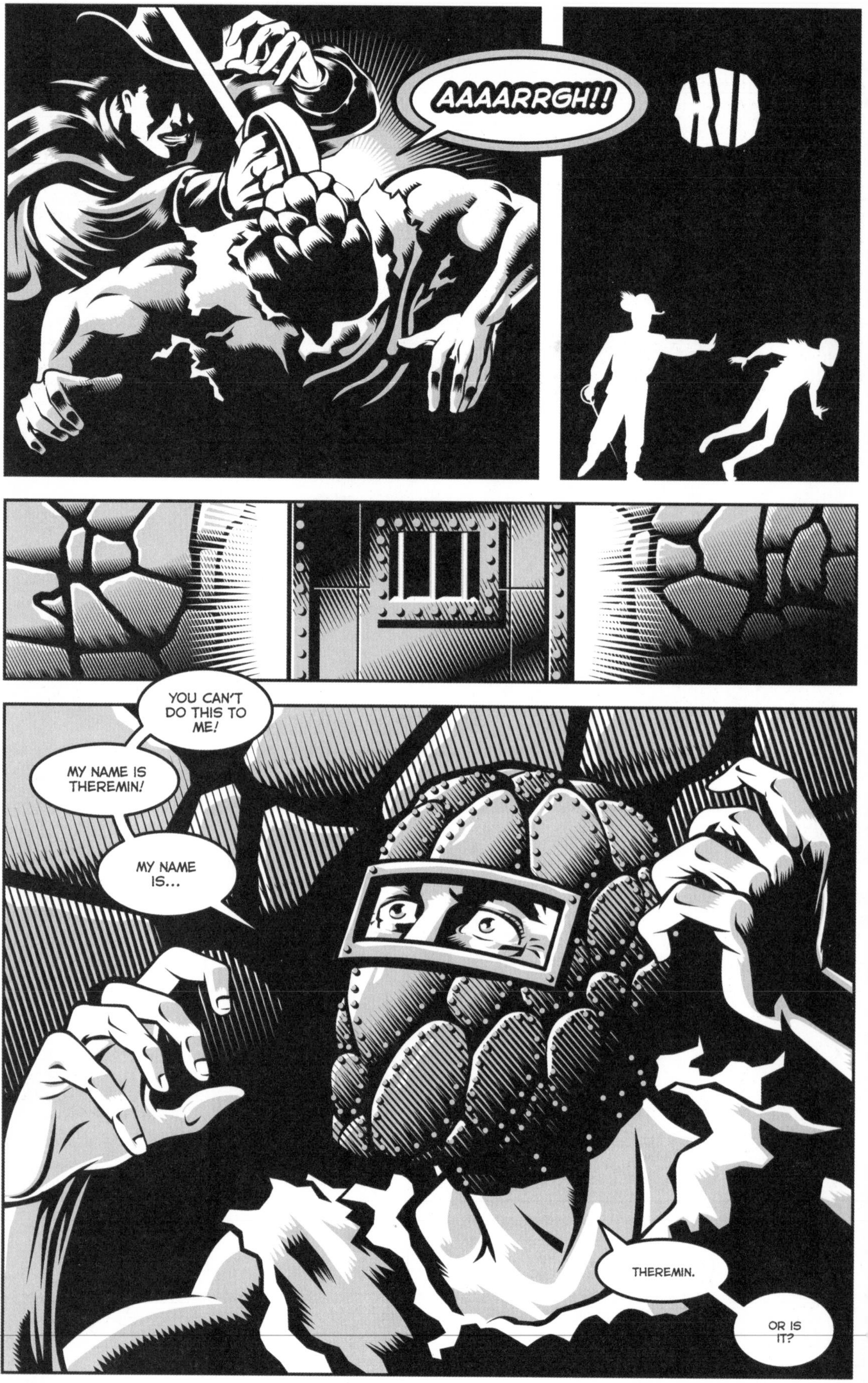
AAAARRGH!!
YOU CAN'T DO THIS TO ME!
MY NAME IS THEREMIN!
MY NAME IS...
THEREMIN.
OR IS IT?

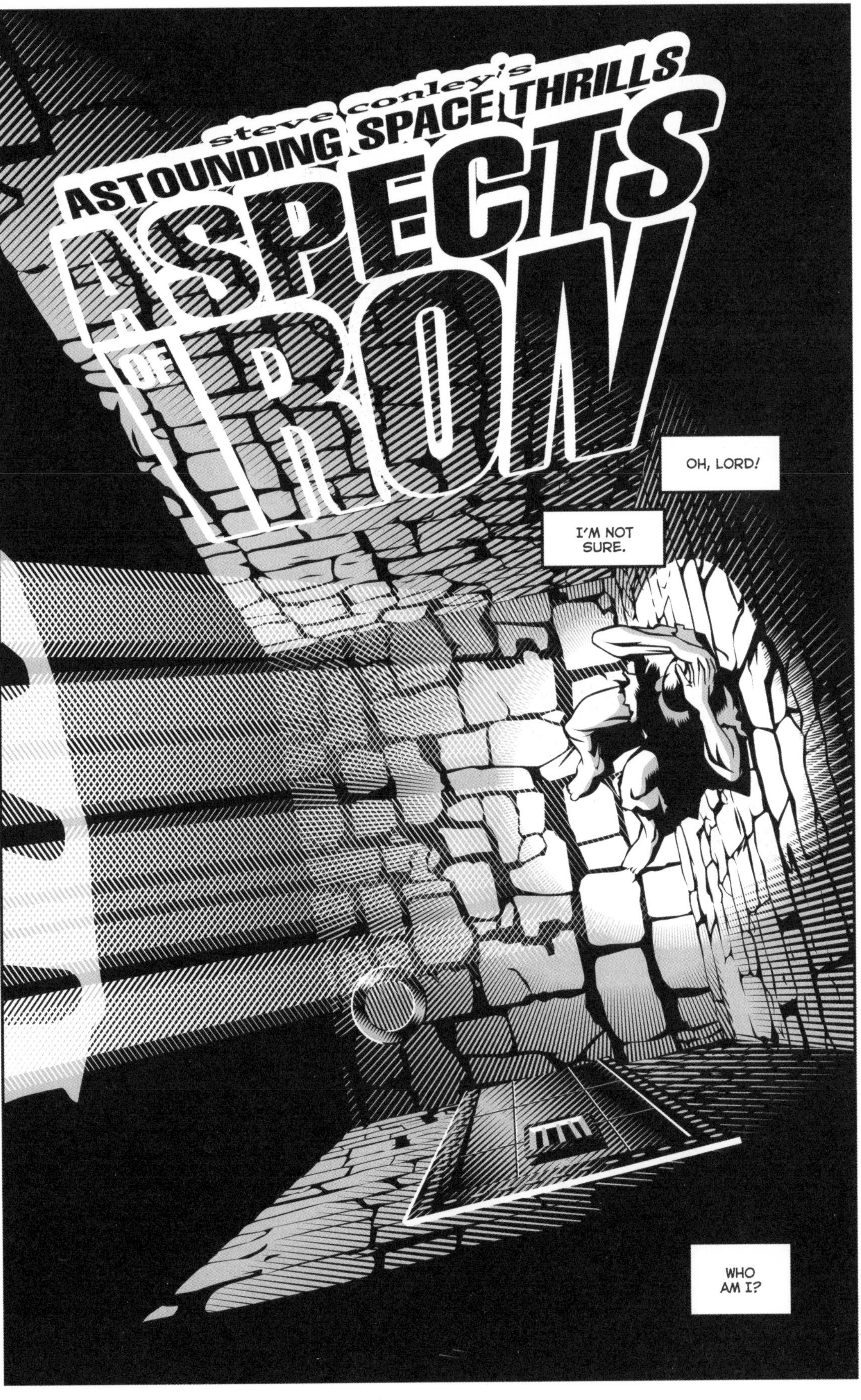
steve conley's
ASTOUNDING SPACE THRILLS
ASPECTS OF IRON
OH, LORD!
I'M NOT SURE.
WHO AM I?

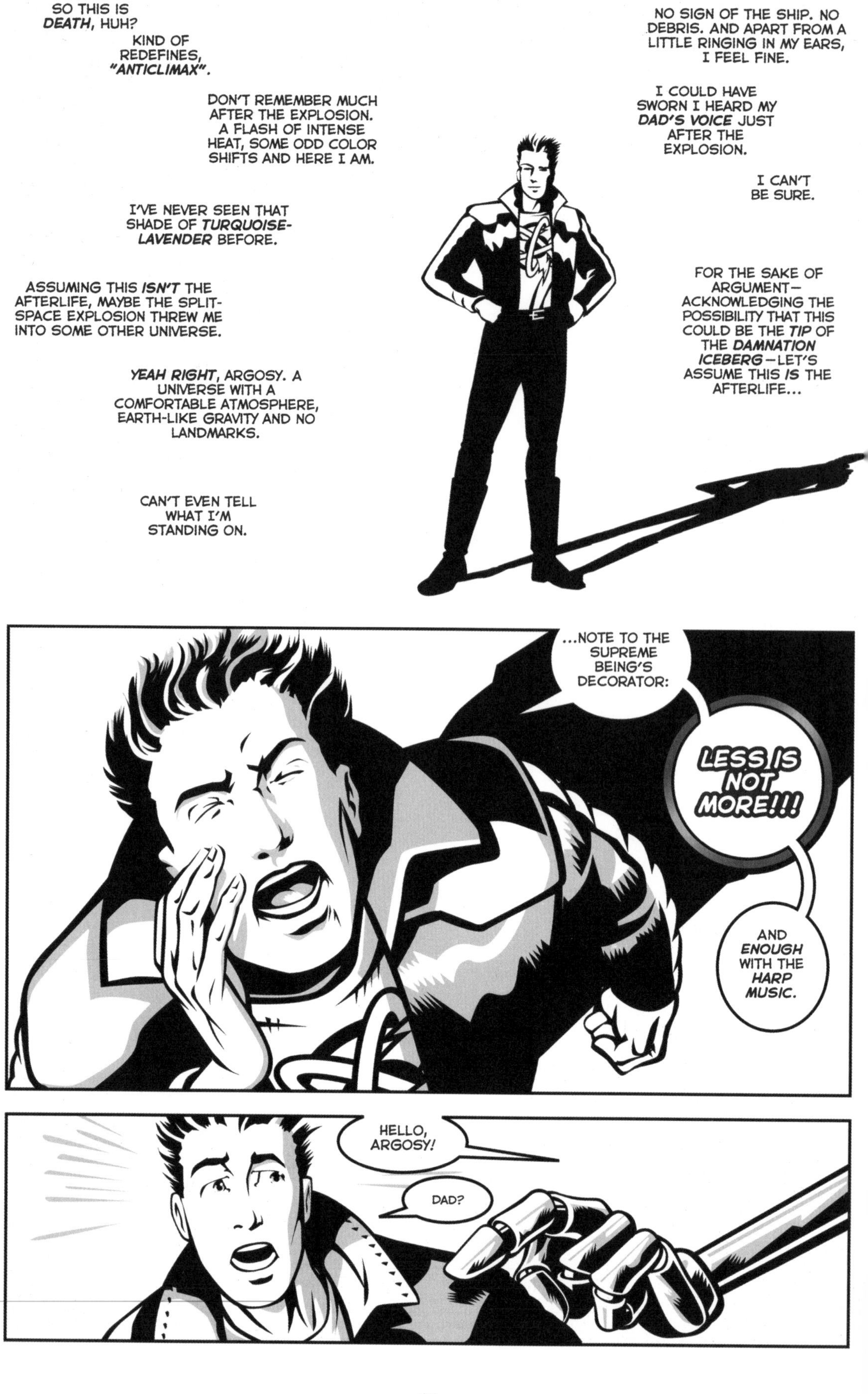
SO THIS IS DEATH, HUH?
KIND OF REDEFINES, "ANTICLIMAX".
DON'T REMEMBER MUCH AFTER THE EXPLOSION. A FLASH OF INTENSE HEAT, SOME ODD COLOR SHIFTS AND HERE I AM.
I'VE NEVER SEEN THAT SHADE OF TURQUOISE-LAVENDER BEFORE.
ASSUMING THIS ISN'T THE AFTERLIFE, MAYBE THE SPLIT-SPACE EXPLOSION THREW ME INTO SOME OTHER UNIVERSE.
YEAH RIGHT, ARGOSY. A UNIVERSE WITH A COMFORTABLE ATMOSPHERE, EARTH-LIKE GRAVITY AND NO LANDMARKS.
CAN'T EVEN TELL WHAT I'M STANDING ON.
NO SIGN OF THE SHIP. NO DEBRIS. AND APART FROM A LITTLE RINGING IN MY EARS, I FEEL FINE.
I COULD HAVE SWORN I HEARD MY DAD'S VOICE JUST AFTER THE EXPLOSION.
I CAN'T BE SURE.
FOR THE SAKE OF ARGUMENT—ACKNOWLEDGING THE POSSIBILITY THAT THIS COULD BE THE TIP OF THE DAMNATION ICEBERG—LET'S ASSUME THIS IS THE AFTERLIFE...
...NOTE TO THE SUPREME BEING'S DECORATOR:
LESS IS NOT MORE!!!
AND ENOUGH WITH THE HARP MUSIC.
HELLO, ARGOSY!
DAD?

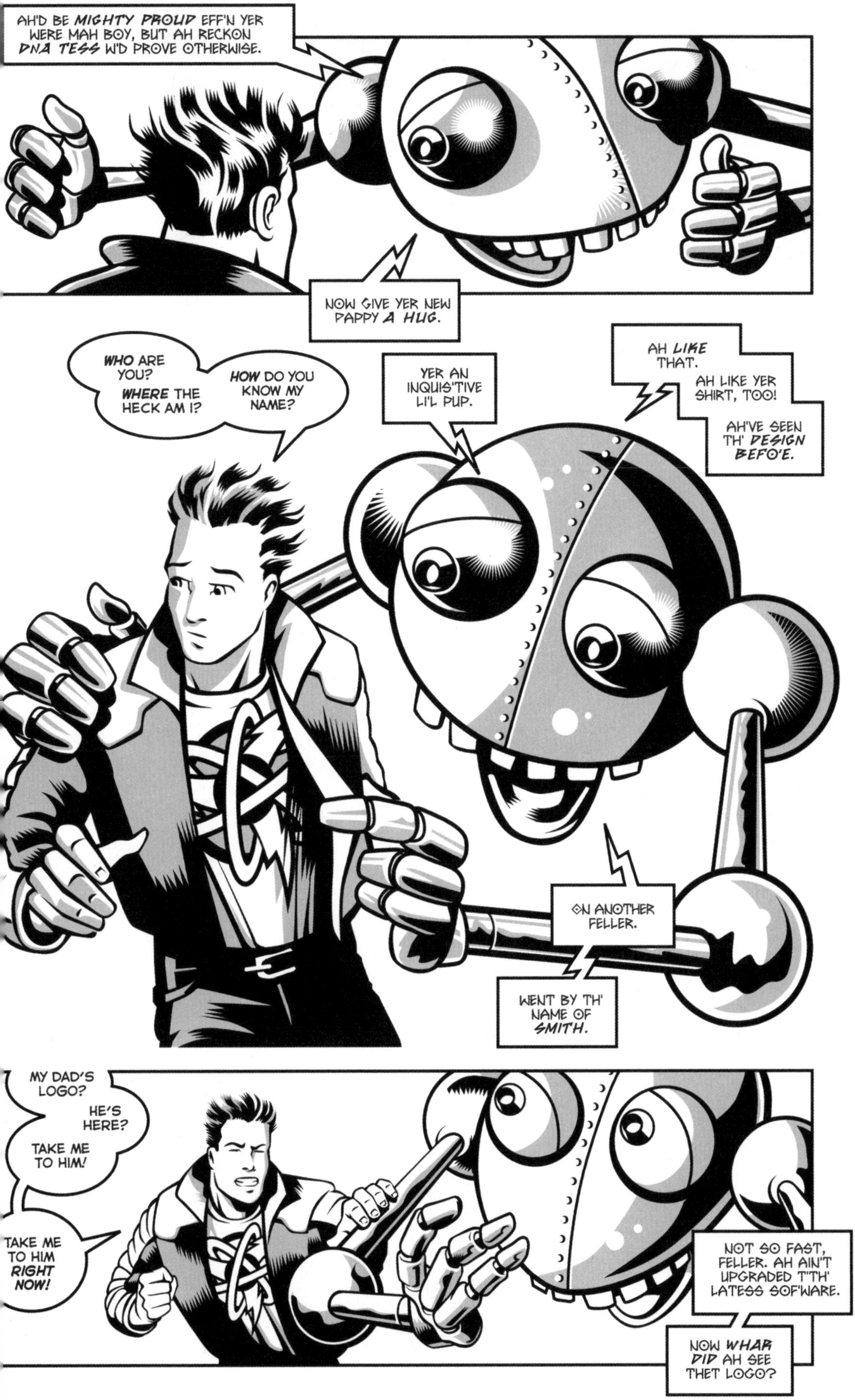

AH'D BE MIGHTY PROUD EFF'N YER WERE MAH BOY, BUT AH RECKON DNA TESS W'D PROVE OTHERWISE.
NOW GIVE YER NEW PAPPY A HUG.
WHO ARE YOU? WHERE THE HECK AM I?
HOW DO YOU KNOW MY NAME?
YER AN INQUIS'TIVE LI'L PUP.
AH LIKE THAT.
AH LIKE YER SHIRT, TOO!
AH'VE SEEN TH' DESIGN BEFO'E.
ON ANOTHER FELLER.
WENT BY TH' NAME OF SMITH.
MY DAD'S LOGO?
HE'S HERE?
TAKE ME TO HIM!
TAKE ME TO HIM RIGHT NOW!
NOT SO FAST, FELLER. AH AIN'T UPGRADED T'TH' LATESS SOF'WARE.
NOW WHAR DID AH SEE THET LOGO?

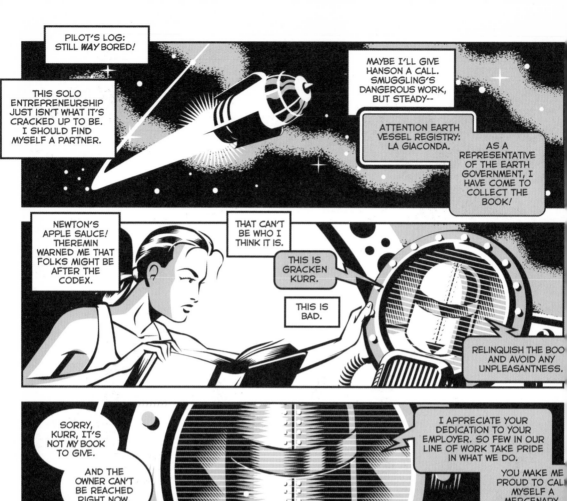

PILOT'S LOG: STILL *WAY* BORED!

THIS SOLO ENTREPRENEURSHIP JUST ISN'T WHAT IT'S CRACKED UP TO BE. I SHOULD FIND MYSELF A PARTNER.

MAYBE I'LL GIVE HANSON A CALL. SMUGGLING'S DANGEROUS WORK, BUT STEADY--

ATTENTION EARTH VESSEL REGISTRY: LA GIACONDA.

AS A REPRESENTATIVE OF THE EARTH GOVERNMENT, I HAVE COME TO COLLECT THE BOOK!

NEWTON'S APPLE SAUCE! THEREMIN WARNED ME THAT FOLKS MIGHT BE AFTER THE CODEX.

THAT CAN'T BE WHO I THINK IT IS.

THIS IS GRACKEN KURR.

THIS IS BAD.

RELINQUISH THE BOO AND AVOID ANY UNPLEASANTNESS.

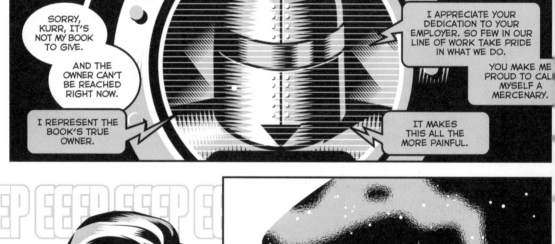

SORRY, KURR, IT'S NOT MY BOOK TO GIVE.

AND THE OWNER CAN'T BE REACHED RIGHT NOW.

I REPRESENT THE BOOK'S TRUE OWNER.

I APPRECIATE YOUR DEDICATION TO YOUR EMPLOYER. SO FEW IN OUR LINE OF WORK TAKE PRIDE IN WHAT WE DO.

YOU MAKE ME PROUD TO CALL MYSELF A MERCENARY.

IT MAKES THIS ALL THE MORE PAINFUL.

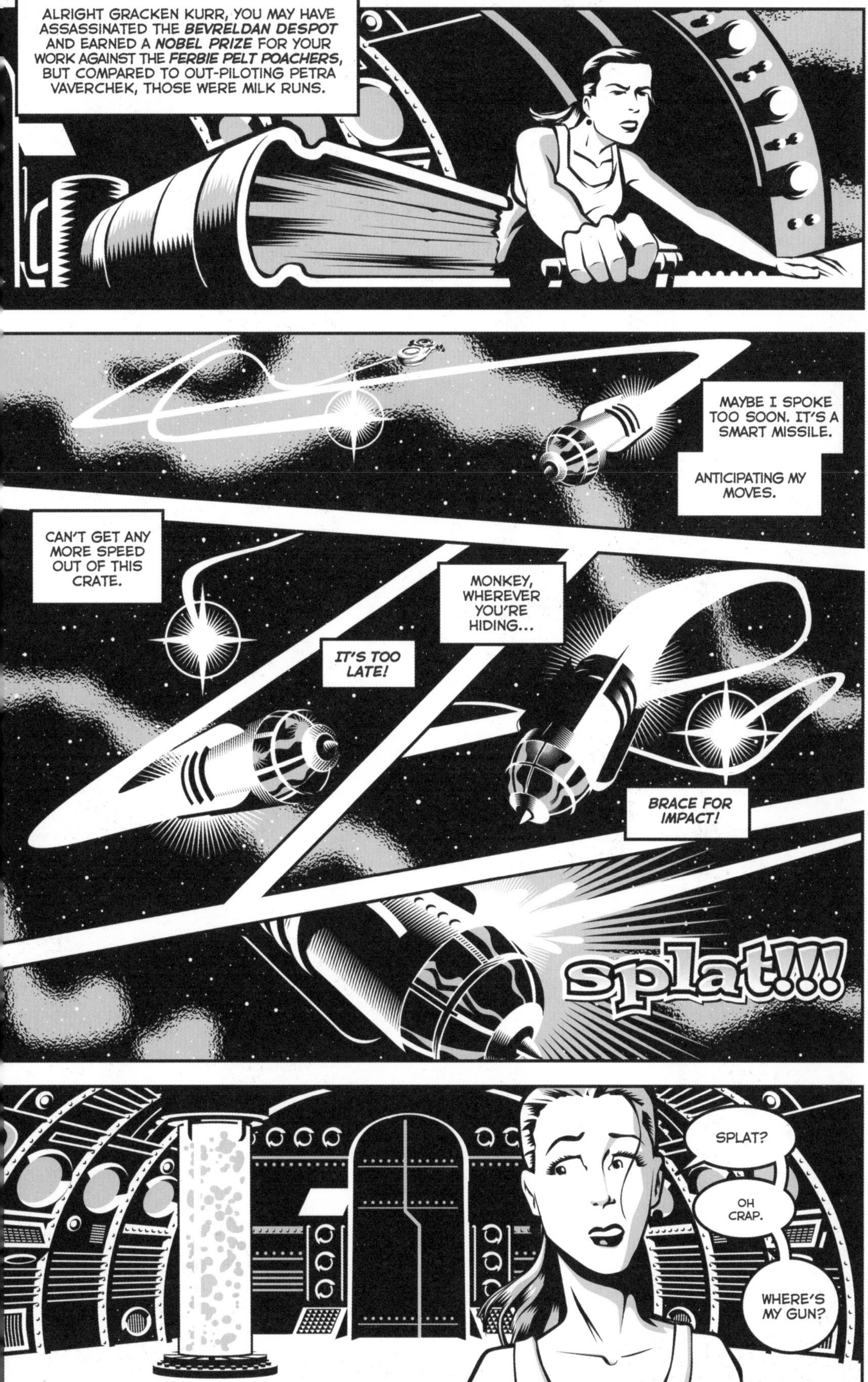
ALRIGHT GRACKEN KURR, YOU MAY HAVE ASSASSINATED THE *BEVRELDAN DESPOT* AND EARNED A *NOBEL PRIZE* FOR YOUR WORK AGAINST THE *FERBIE PELT POACHERS*, BUT COMPARED TO OUT-PILOTING PETRA VAVERCHEK, THOSE WERE MILK RUNS.
MAYBE I SPOKE TOO SOON. IT'S A SMART MISSILE.
ANTICIPATING MY MOVES.
CAN'T GET ANY MORE SPEED OUT OF THIS CRATE.
MONKEY, WHEREVER YOU'RE HIDING...
IT'S TOO LATE!
BRACE FOR IMPACT!
splat!!!
SPLAT?
OH CRAP.
WHERE'S MY GUN?

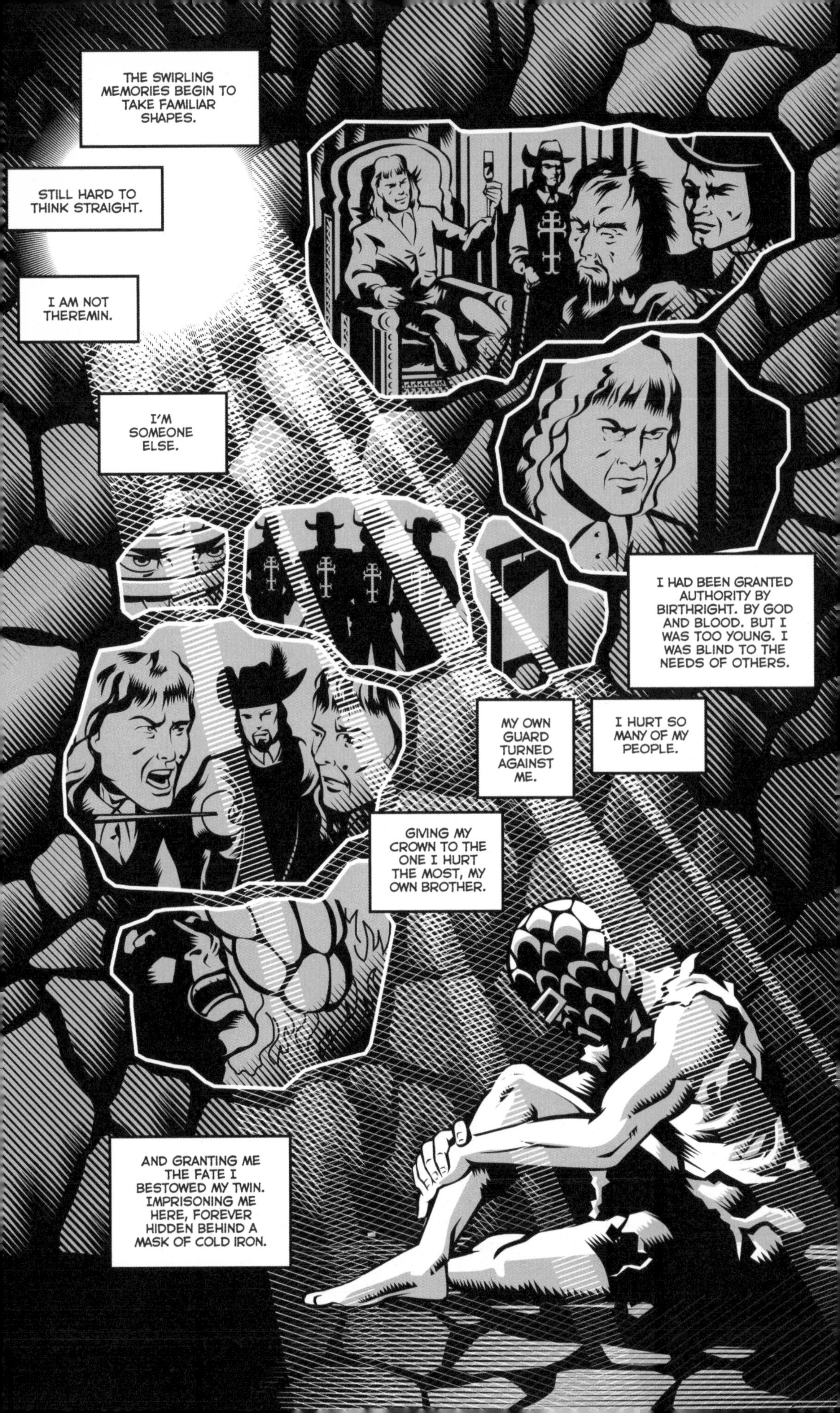
THE SWIRLING MEMORIES BEGIN TO TAKE FAMILIAR SHAPES.
STILL HARD TO THINK STRAIGHT.
I AM NOT THEREMIN.
I'M SOMEONE ELSE.
I HAD BEEN GRANTED AUTHORITY BY BIRTHRIGHT. BY GOD AND BLOOD. BUT I WAS TOO YOUNG. I WAS BLIND TO THE NEEDS OF OTHERS.
I HURT SO MANY OF MY PEOPLE.
MY OWN GUARD TURNED AGAINST ME.
GIVING MY CROWN TO THE ONE I HURT THE MOST, MY OWN BROTHER.
AND GRANTING ME THE FATE I BESTOWED MY TWIN. IMPRISONING ME HERE, FOREVER HIDDEN BEHIND A MASK OF COLD IRON.

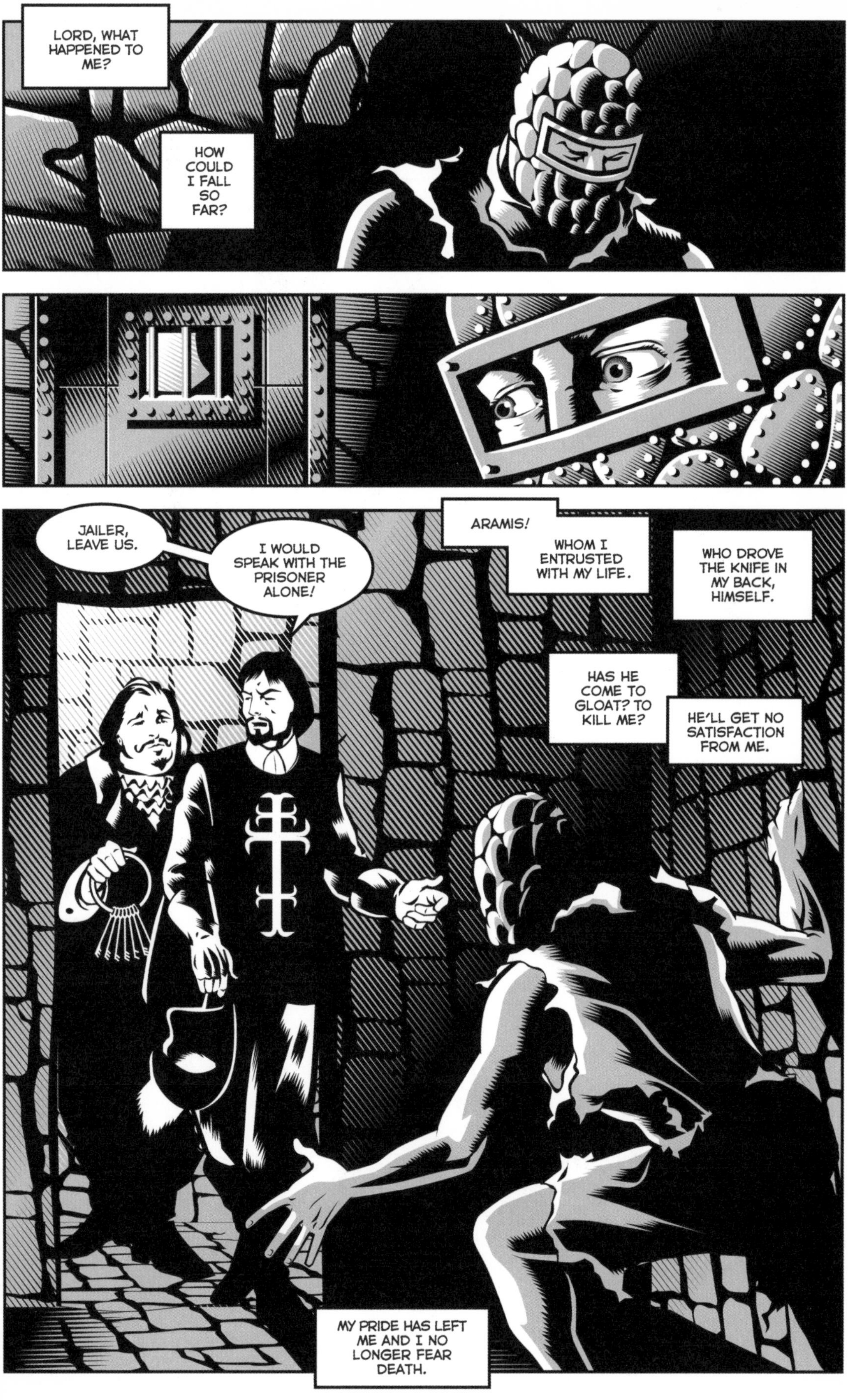
LORD, WHAT HAPPENED TO ME?
HOW COULD I FALL SO FAR?
JAILER, LEAVE US.
I WOULD SPEAK WITH THE PRISONER ALONE!
ARAMIS!
WHOM I ENTRUSTED WITH MY LIFE.
WHO DROVE THE KNIFE IN MY BACK, HIMSELF.
HAS HE COME TO GLOAT? TO KILL ME?
HE'LL GET NO SATISFACTION FROM ME.
MY PRIDE HAS LEFT ME AND I NO LONGER FEAR DEATH.

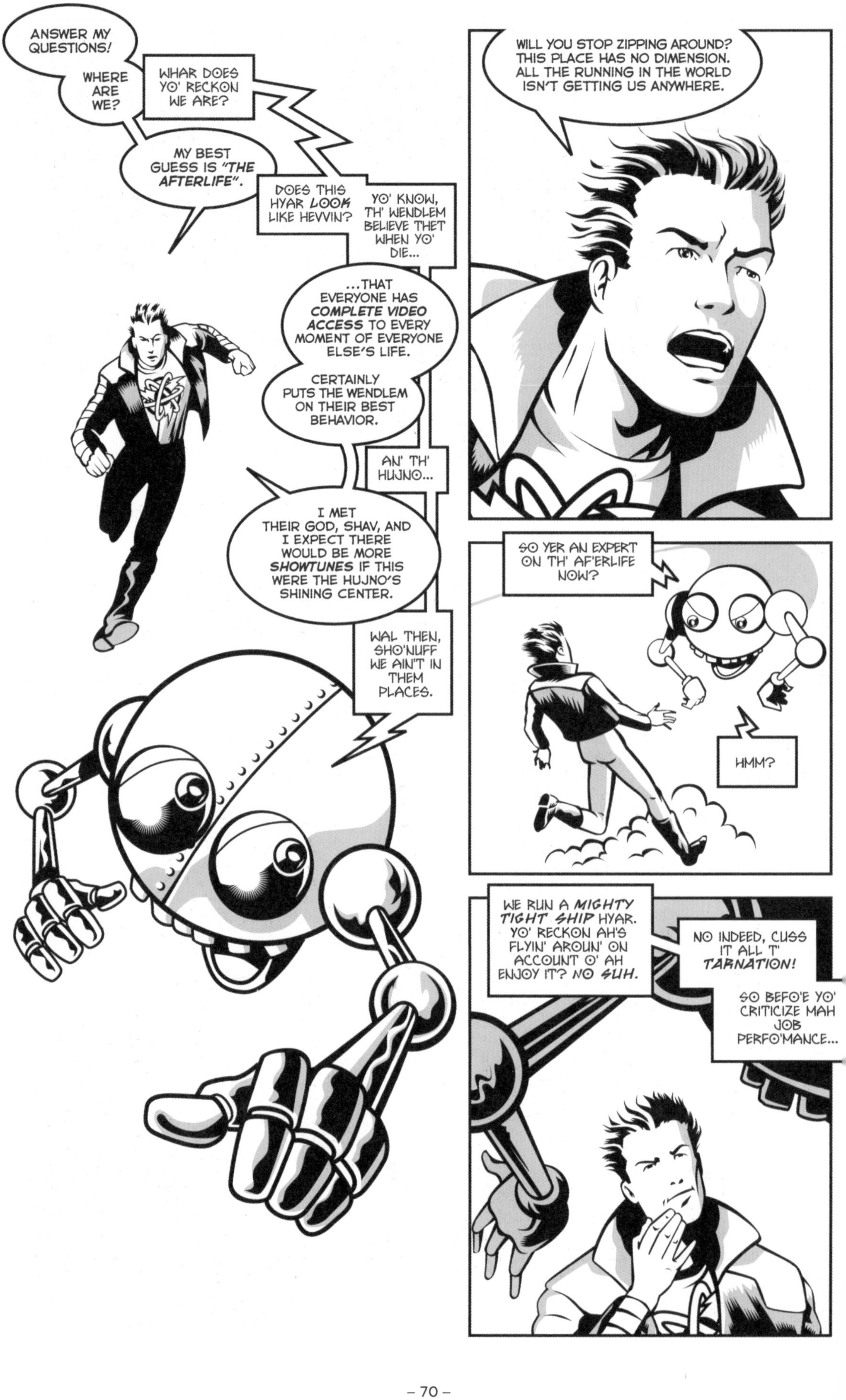

ANSWER MY QUESTIONS!
WHERE ARE WE?
WHAR DOES YO' RECKON WE ARE?
MY BEST GUESS IS "THE AFTERLIFE".
DOES THIS HYAR LOOK LIKE HEVVIN?
YO' KNOW, TH' WENDLEM BELIEVE THET WHEN YO' DIE...
...THAT EVERYONE HAS COMPLETE VIDEO ACCESS TO EVERY MOMENT OF EVERYONE ELSE'S LIFE.
CERTAINLY PUTS THE WENDLEM ON THEIR BEST BEHAVIOR.
AN' TH' HUJNO...
I MET THEIR GOD, SHAV, AND I EXPECT THERE WOULD BE MORE SHOWTUNES IF THIS WERE THE HUJNO'S SHINING CENTER.
WAL THEN, SHO'NUFF WE AIN'T IN THEM PLACES.
WILL YOU STOP ZIPPING AROUND? THIS PLACE HAS NO DIMENSION. ALL THE RUNNING IN THE WORLD ISN'T GETTING US ANYWHERE.
SO YER AN EXPERT ON TH' AF'ERLIFE NOW?
HMM?
WE RUN A MIGHTY TIGHT SHIP HYAR. YO' RECKON AH'S FLYIN' AROUN' ON ACCOUNT O' AH ENJOY IT? NO SUH.
NO INDEED, CUSS IT ALL T' TARNATION!
SO BEFO'E YO' CRITICIZE MAH JOB PERFO'MANCE...

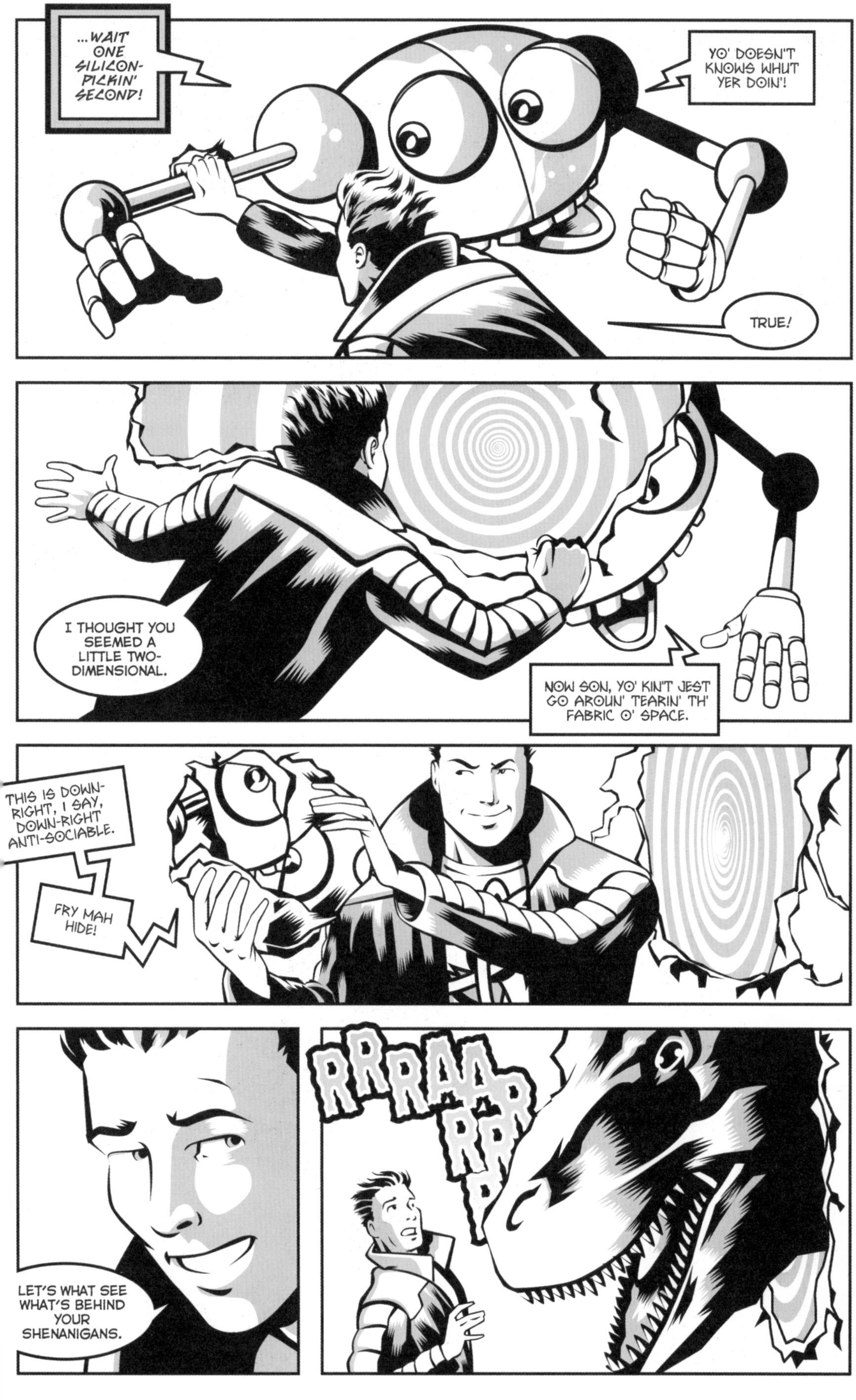
...WAIT ONE SILICON-PICKIN' SECOND!
YO' DOESN'T KNOWS WHUT YER DOIN'!
TRUE!
I THOUGHT YOU SEEMED A LITTLE TWO-DIMENSIONAL.
NOW SON, YO' KIN'T JEST GO AROUN' TEARIN' TH' FABRIC O' SPACE.
THIS IS DOWN-RIGHT, I SAY, DOWN-RIGHT ANTI-SOCIABLE.
FRY MAH HIDE!
LET'S WHAT SEE WHAT'S BEHIND YOUR SHENANIGANS.
RRRAAARRRR

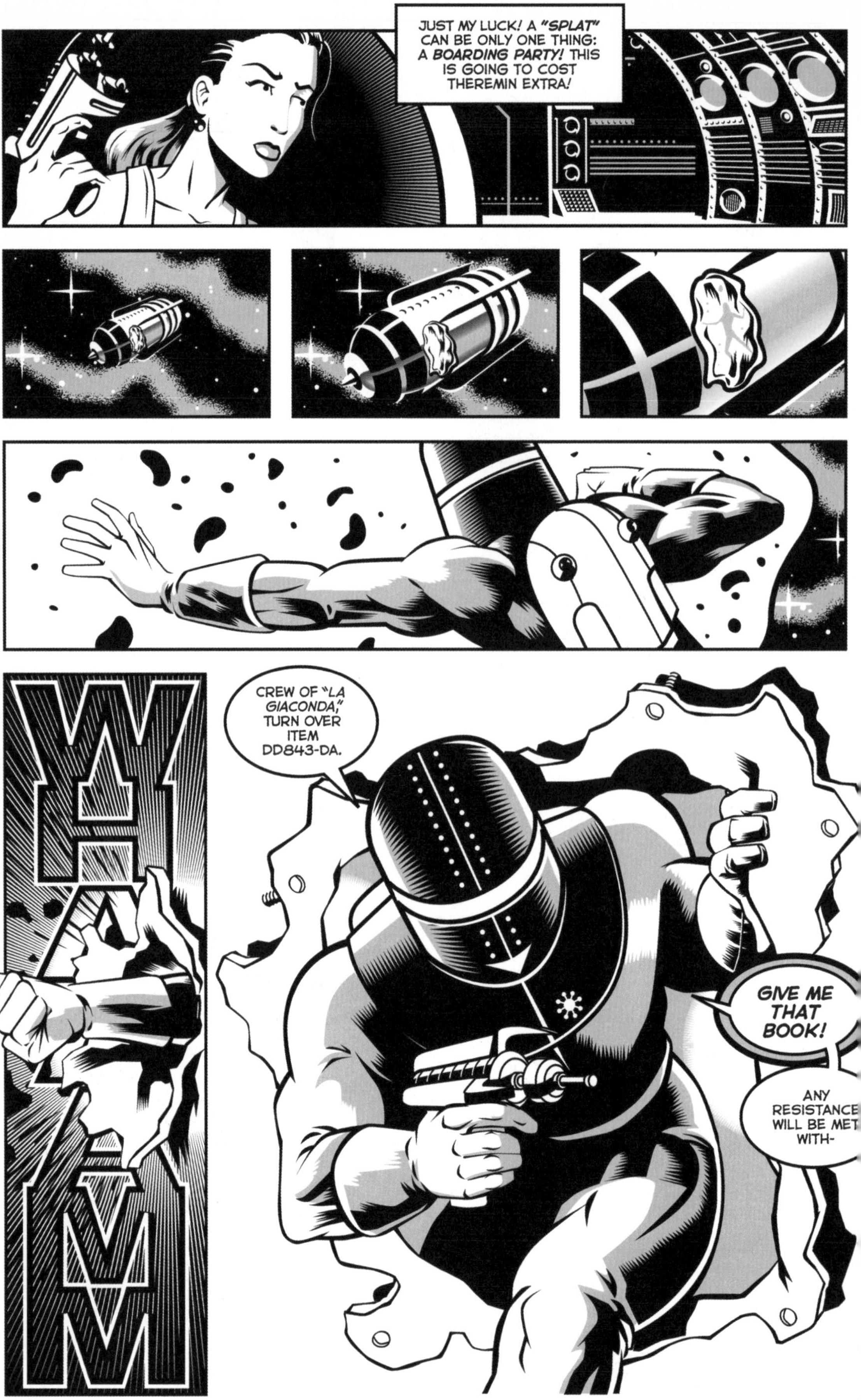
JUST MY LUCK! A "SPLAT" CAN BE ONLY ONE THING: A BOARDING PARTY! THIS IS GOING TO COST THEREMIN EXTRA!
WHAM
CREW OF "LA GIACONDA," TURN OVER ITEM DD843-DA.
GIVE ME THAT BOOK!
ANY RESISTANCE WILL BE MET WITH-

KZAKK

SOMETIMES I FORGET JUST HOW GOOD I AM!

I SHOULD SERIOUSLY CONSIDER *RAISING* MY *RATES.*

HOLD YOUR HORSE HEAD NEBULAS. THAT WAS NO NORMAL RAY GUN HE WAS PACKING. IT WAS A *DEATH RAY.*

I COULD'VE BEEN KILLED.

DEATH COMES TO THOSE WHO WAIT, M'DEAR!

HOLY—

RP! GLOOP! BLORP! SQUEEKS!
EEKS! GLEEK!
EK! BLORP! GLEEP!
GLOOP
SLEEP! BLORP!
KS! GLEEK! SQUEEKS!

— 73 —

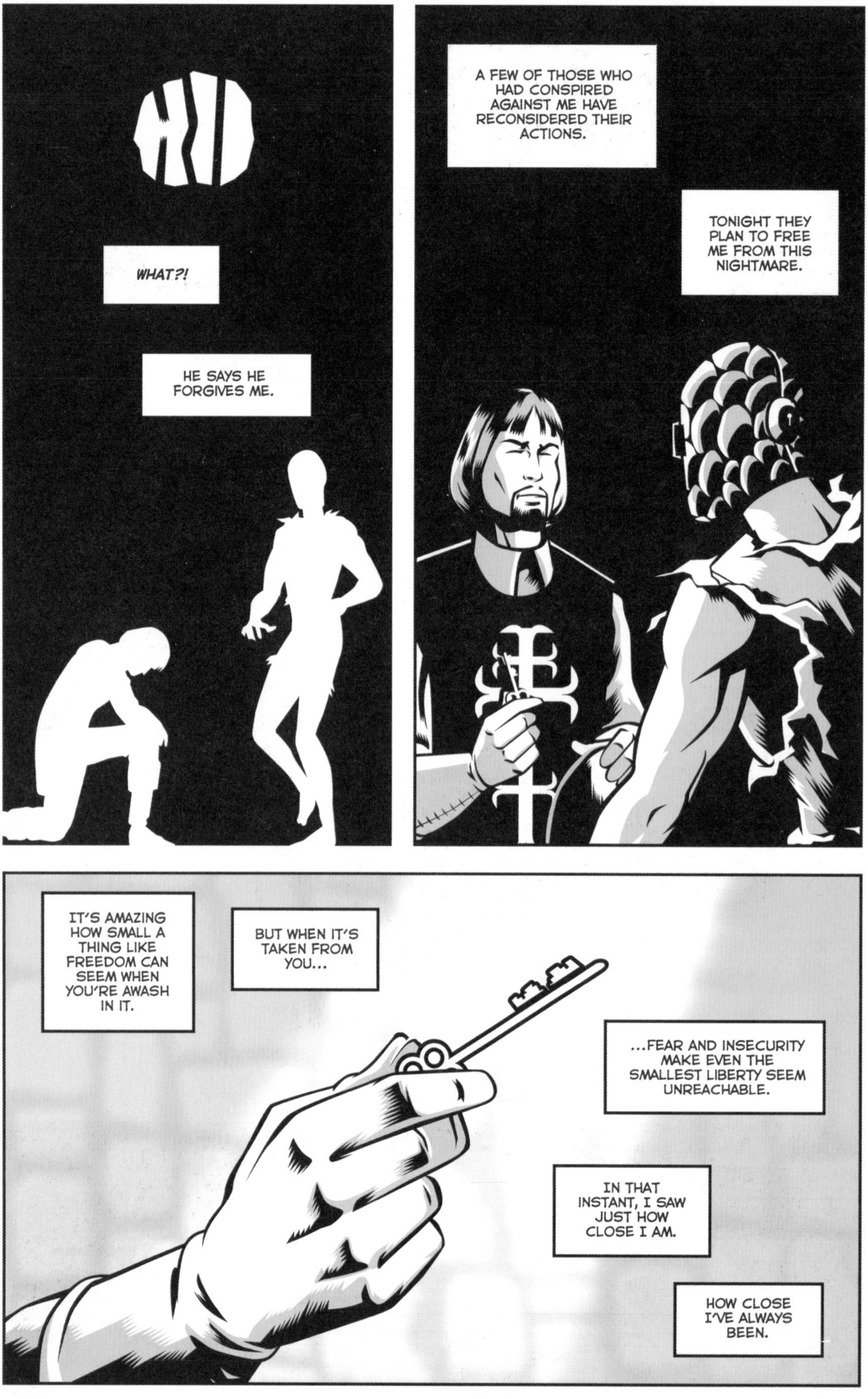
WHAT?!
HE SAYS HE FORGIVES ME.
A FEW OF THOSE WHO HAD CONSPIRED AGAINST ME HAVE RECONSIDERED THEIR ACTIONS.
TONIGHT THEY PLAN TO FREE ME FROM THIS NIGHTMARE.
IT'S AMAZING HOW SMALL A THING LIKE FREEDOM CAN SEEM WHEN YOU'RE AWASH IN IT.
BUT WHEN IT'S TAKEN FROM YOU...
...FEAR AND INSECURITY MAKE EVEN THE SMALLEST LIBERTY SEEM UNREACHABLE.
IN THAT INSTANT, I SAW JUST HOW CLOSE I AM.
HOW CLOSE I'VE ALWAYS BEEN.

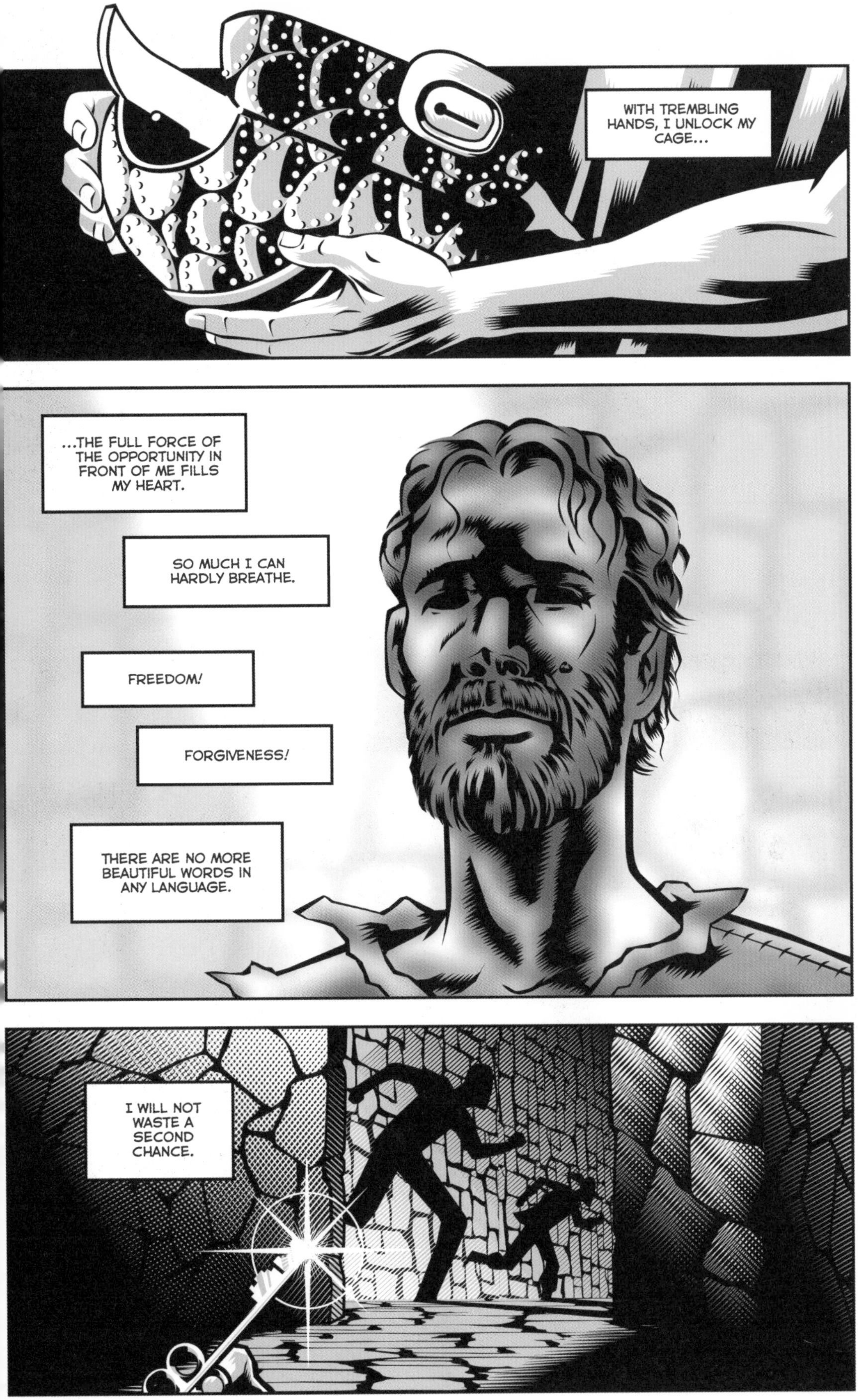
WITH TREMBLING HANDS, I UNLOCK MY CAGE...
...THE FULL FORCE OF THE OPPORTUNITY IN FRONT OF ME FILLS MY HEART.
SO MUCH I CAN HARDLY BREATHE.
FREEDOM!
FORGIVENESS!
THERE ARE NO MORE BEAUTIFUL WORDS IN ANY LANGUAGE.
I WILL NOT WASTE A SECOND CHANCE.

fifteen

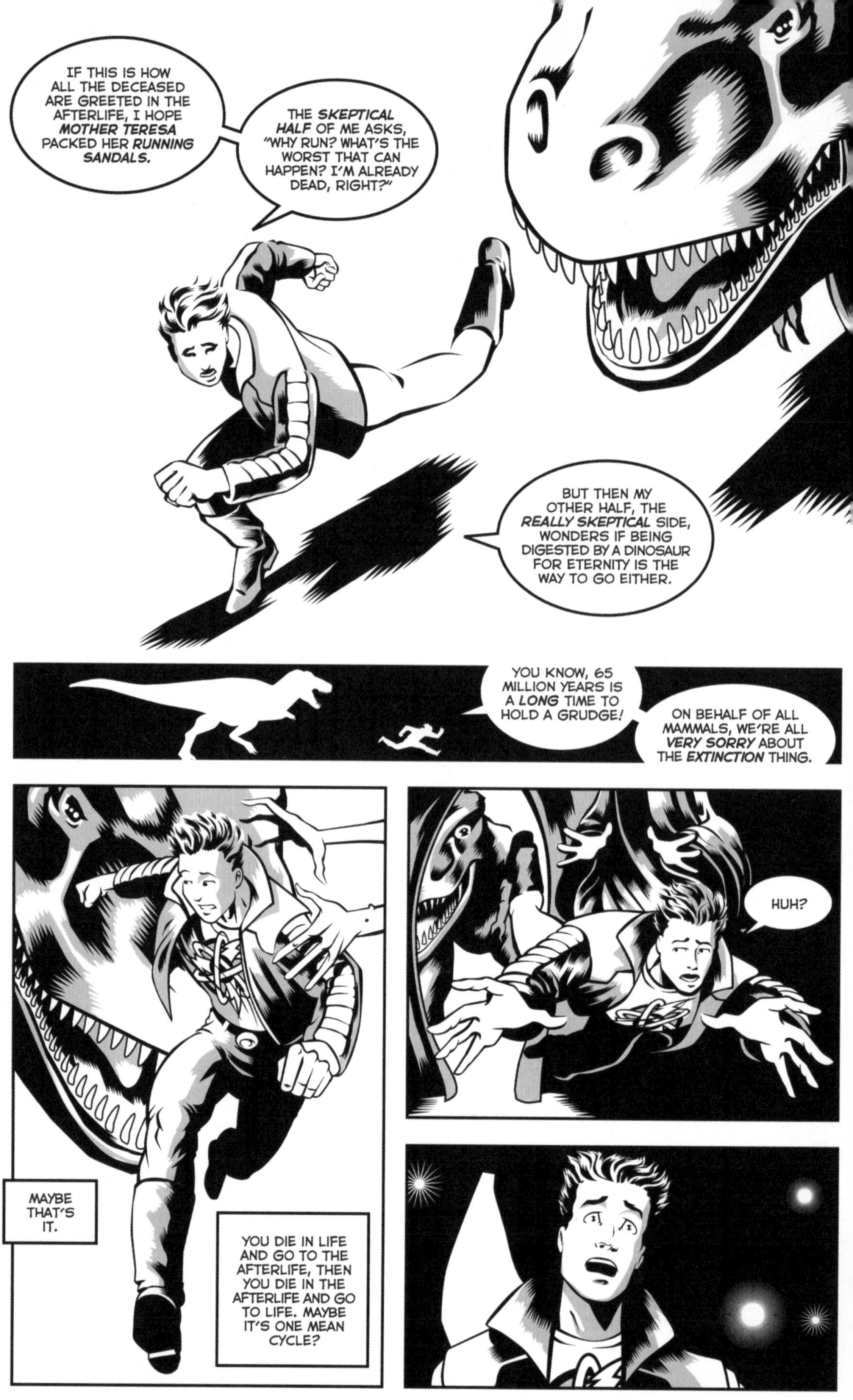
IF THIS IS HOW ALL THE DECEASED ARE GREETED IN THE AFTERLIFE, I HOPE *MOTHER TERESA* PACKED HER *RUNNING SANDALS.*
THE *SKEPTICAL HALF* OF ME ASKS, "WHY RUN? WHAT'S THE WORST THAT CAN HAPPEN? I'M ALREADY DEAD, RIGHT?"
BUT THEN MY OTHER HALF, THE *REALLY SKEPTICAL* SIDE, WONDERS IF BEING DIGESTED BY A DINOSAUR FOR ETERNITY IS THE WAY TO GO EITHER.
YOU KNOW, 65 MILLION YEARS IS A *LONG* TIME TO HOLD A GRUDGE!
ON BEHALF OF ALL MAMMALS, WE'RE ALL *VERY SORRY* ABOUT THE *EXTINCTION* THING.
MAYBE THAT'S IT.
YOU DIE IN LIFE AND GO TO THE AFTERLIFE, THEN YOU DIE IN THE AFTERLIFE AND GO TO LIFE. MAYBE IT'S ONE MEAN CYCLE?
HUH?

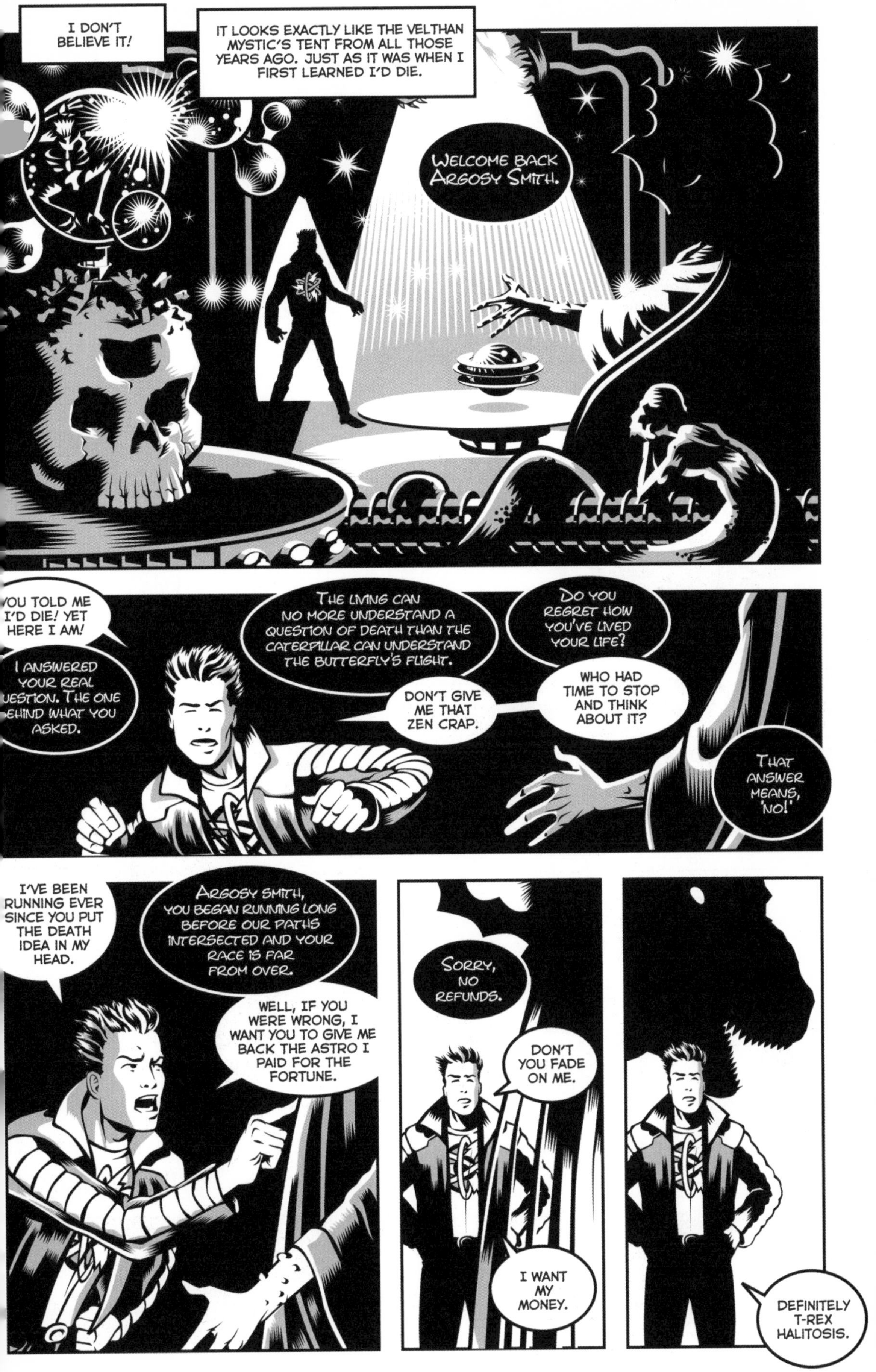

I DON'T BELIEVE IT!
IT LOOKS EXACTLY LIKE THE VELTHAN MYSTIC'S TENT FROM ALL THOSE YEARS AGO. JUST AS IT WAS WHEN I FIRST LEARNED I'D DIE.
WELCOME BACK ARGOSY SMITH.
OU TOLD ME I'D DIE! YET HERE I AM!
I ANSWERED YOUR REAL UESTION. THE ONE EHIND WHAT YOU ASKED.
THE LIVING CAN NO MORE UNDERSTAND A QUESTION OF DEATH THAN THE CATERPILLAR CAN UNDERSTAND THE BUTTERFLY'S FLIGHT.
DON'T GIVE ME THAT ZEN CRAP.
DO YOU REGRET HOW YOU'VE LIVED YOUR LIFE?
WHO HAD TIME TO STOP AND THINK ABOUT IT?
THAT ANSWER MEANS, 'NO!'
I'VE BEEN RUNNING EVER SINCE YOU PUT THE DEATH IDEA IN MY HEAD.
ARGOSY SMITH, YOU BEGAN RUNNING LONG BEFORE OUR PATHS INTERSECTED AND YOUR RACE IS FAR FROM OVER.
WELL, IF YOU WERE WRONG, I WANT YOU TO GIVE ME BACK THE ASTRO I PAID FOR THE FORTUNE.
SORRY, NO REFUNDS.
DON'T YOU FADE ON ME.
I WANT MY MONEY.
DEFINITELY T-REX HALITOSIS.

LOOP!
BLIP! BLORP!
SQUEEKS! SQUEEKS!
LOOP! GLEEK!
BLEEP! GLEEP!

GRACKEN'S AN *OPTIPUS!*

I CAN KNOCK HIM OUT IF I CAN JUST...

SQUEEK?

HOW DID HE KNOW I WAS BEHIND HIM?

OH, RIGHT.

I NEED HELP.

THEREMIN, *WAKE UP!*

REVIVE

YOU ARE FORTUNATE THAT I DON'T EAT MEAT!

ONE OF MY MOTHERS HAS AN AWARD-WINNING RECIPE FOR SPACE MONKEY PÂTÉ!

ENGINES

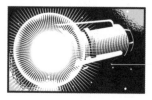

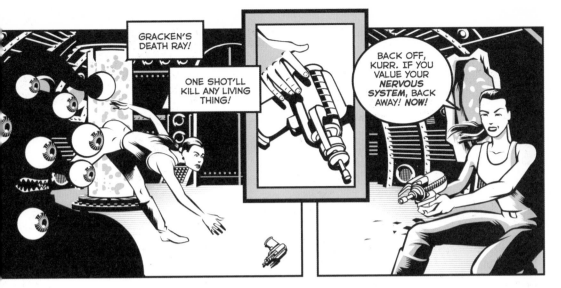

GRACKEN'S DEATH RAY!

ONE SHOT'LL KILL ANY LIVING THING!

BACK OFF, KURR. IF YOU VALUE YOUR *NERVOUS SYSTEM*, BACK AWAY! *NOW!*

AGAIN, I MUST INSIST, GIVE ME THE BOOK!

PLEASE DON'T MAKE ME KILL YOU!

SOMETHING ONE OF MY FATHERS TOLD ME...

..."WEAPONS DEALERS ARE AS COMMON AS STARS, BUT A GOOD TAILOR IS HARD TO FIND."

zzap

I COMMEND O-TAILOR BLEUL 4.

zzap

zzap

zzap

zzap

zzap

THEIR LIVING SUITS HOST A COLONY OF MICROORGANISMS. THE DEATH RAY WOULD HAVE TO KILL ALL 2 MILLION TO GET TO ME.

THE ESCAPE IS PERFECTLY PLANNED.

A CARRIAGE WAITS TO SPIRIT ME AWAY TO A NEW LIFE, A NEW NAME IN THE SOUTH WHERE I MAY LIVE MY DAYS IN REGAL YET ANONYMOUS FASHION.

A CHANCE TO START OVER.

WHY THEN, MY HESITATION?

PERHAPS IT'S THAT I KNOW MY PUNISHMENT IS JUST.

AND THAT EVEN IF MY FRIENDS FORGIVE ME...

...I MUST FORGIVE MYSELF, FIRST.

ALL I HAVE TO DO IS LET GO.

I CAN'T.

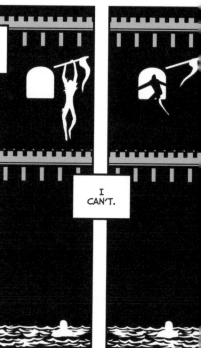

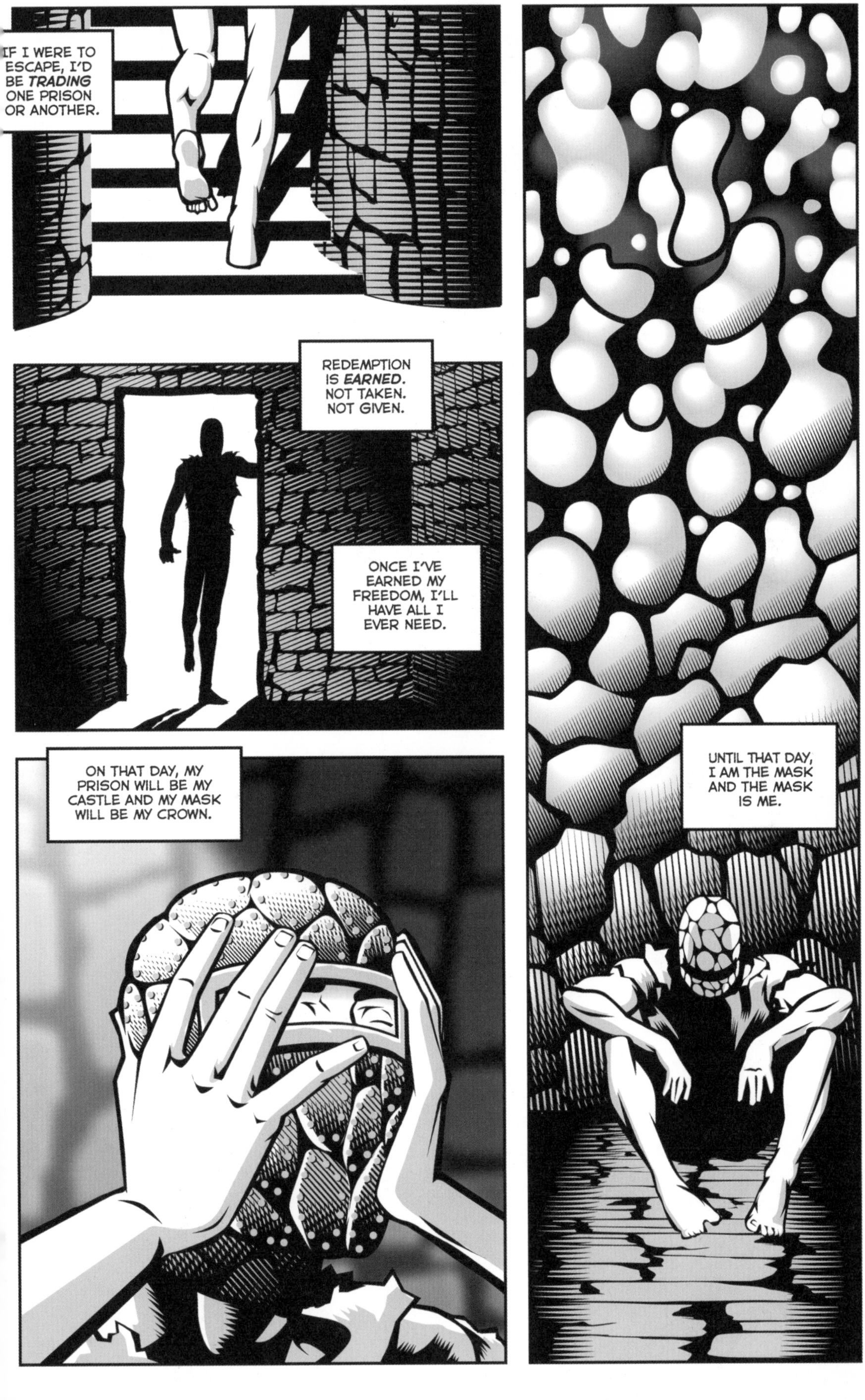
IF I WERE TO
ESCAPE, I'D
BE *TRADING*
ONE PRISON
OR ANOTHER.
REDEMPTION
IS *EARNED.*
NOT TAKEN.
NOT GIVEN.
ONCE I'VE
EARNED MY
FREEDOM, I'LL
HAVE ALL I
EVER NEED.
ON THAT DAY, MY
PRISON WILL BE MY
CASTLE AND MY MASK
WILL BE MY CROWN.
UNTIL THAT DAY,
I AM THE MASK
AND THE MASK
IS ME.

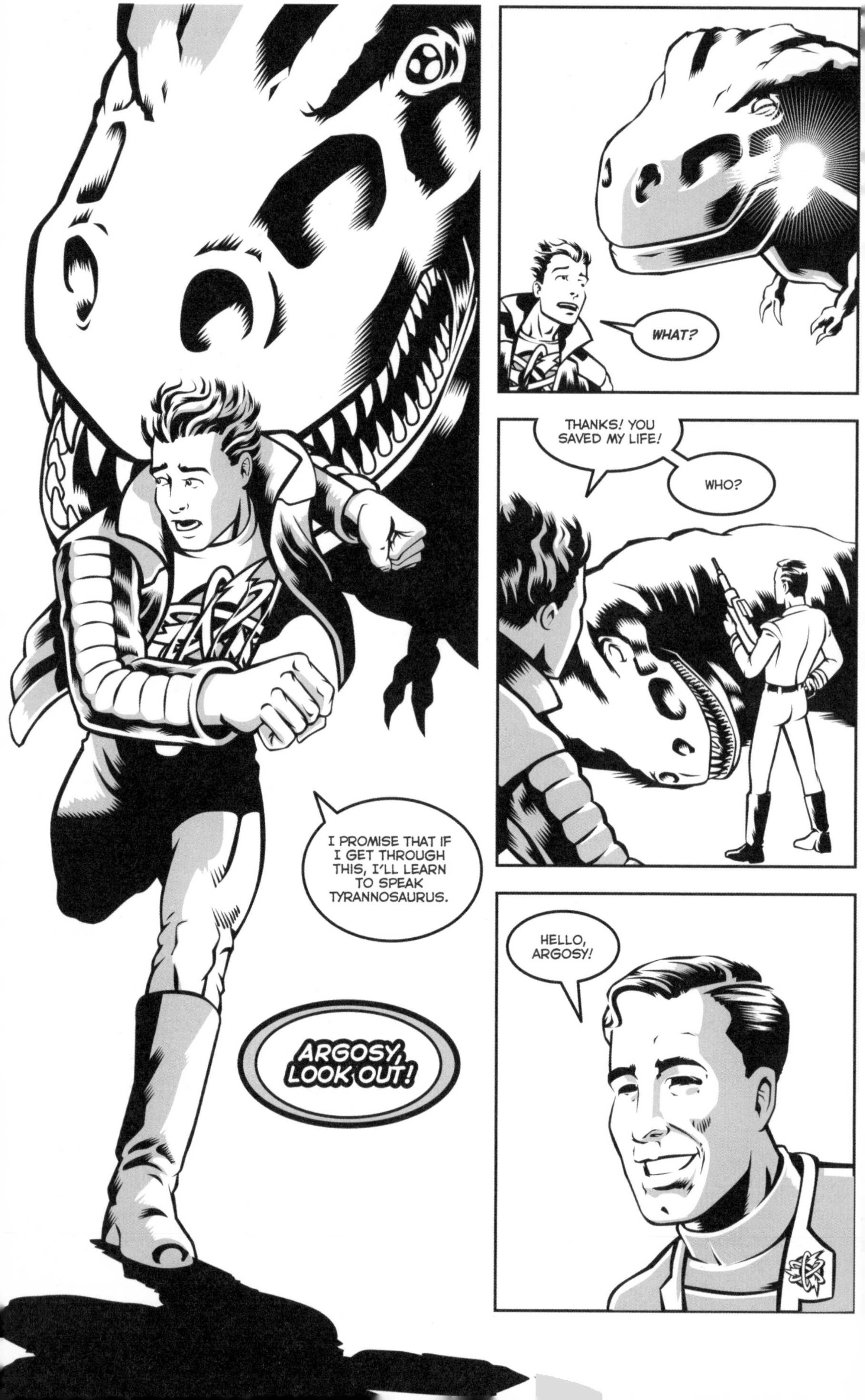
I PROMISE THAT IF I GET THROUGH THIS, I'LL LEARN TO SPEAK TYRANNOSAURUS.
ARGOSY, LOOK OUT!
WHAT?
THANKS! YOU SAVED MY LIFE!
WHO?
HELLO, ARGOSY!

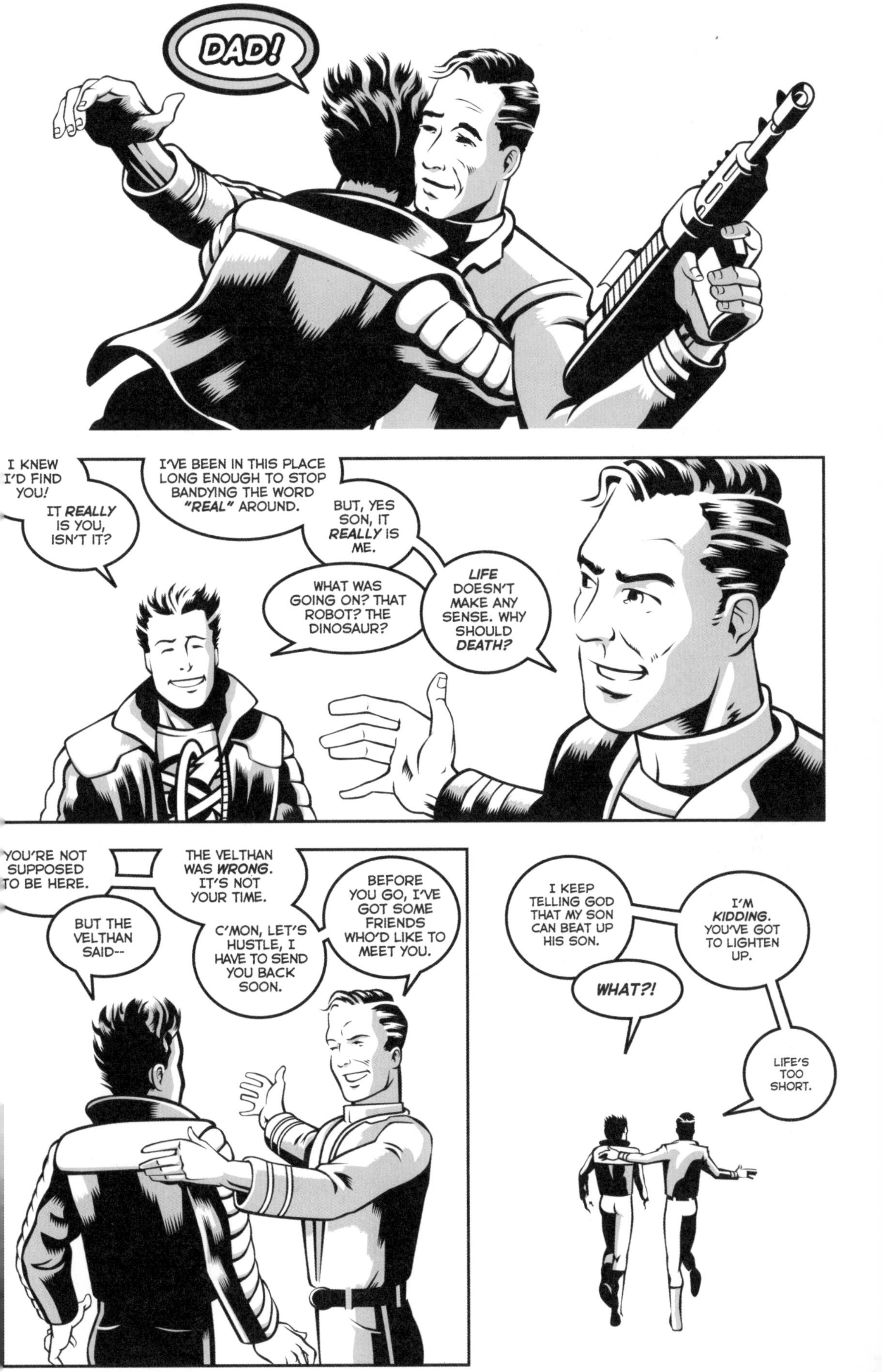

DAD!
I KNEW I'D FIND YOU!
IT REALLY IS YOU, ISN'T IT?
I'VE BEEN IN THIS PLACE LONG ENOUGH TO STOP BANDYING THE WORD "REAL" AROUND.
BUT, YES SON, IT REALLY IS ME.
WHAT WAS GOING ON? THAT ROBOT? THE DINOSAUR?
LIFE DOESN'T MAKE ANY SENSE. WHY SHOULD DEATH?
YOU'RE NOT SUPPOSED TO BE HERE.
BUT THE VELTHAN SAID--
THE VELTHAN WAS WRONG. IT'S NOT YOUR TIME.
C'MON, LET'S HUSTLE, I HAVE TO SEND YOU BACK SOON.
BEFORE YOU GO, I'VE GOT SOME FRIENDS WHO'D LIKE TO MEET YOU.
I KEEP TELLING GOD THAT MY SON CAN BEAT UP HIS SON.
WHAT?!
I'M KIDDING. YOU'VE GOT TO LIGHTEN UP.
LIFE'S TOO SHORT.

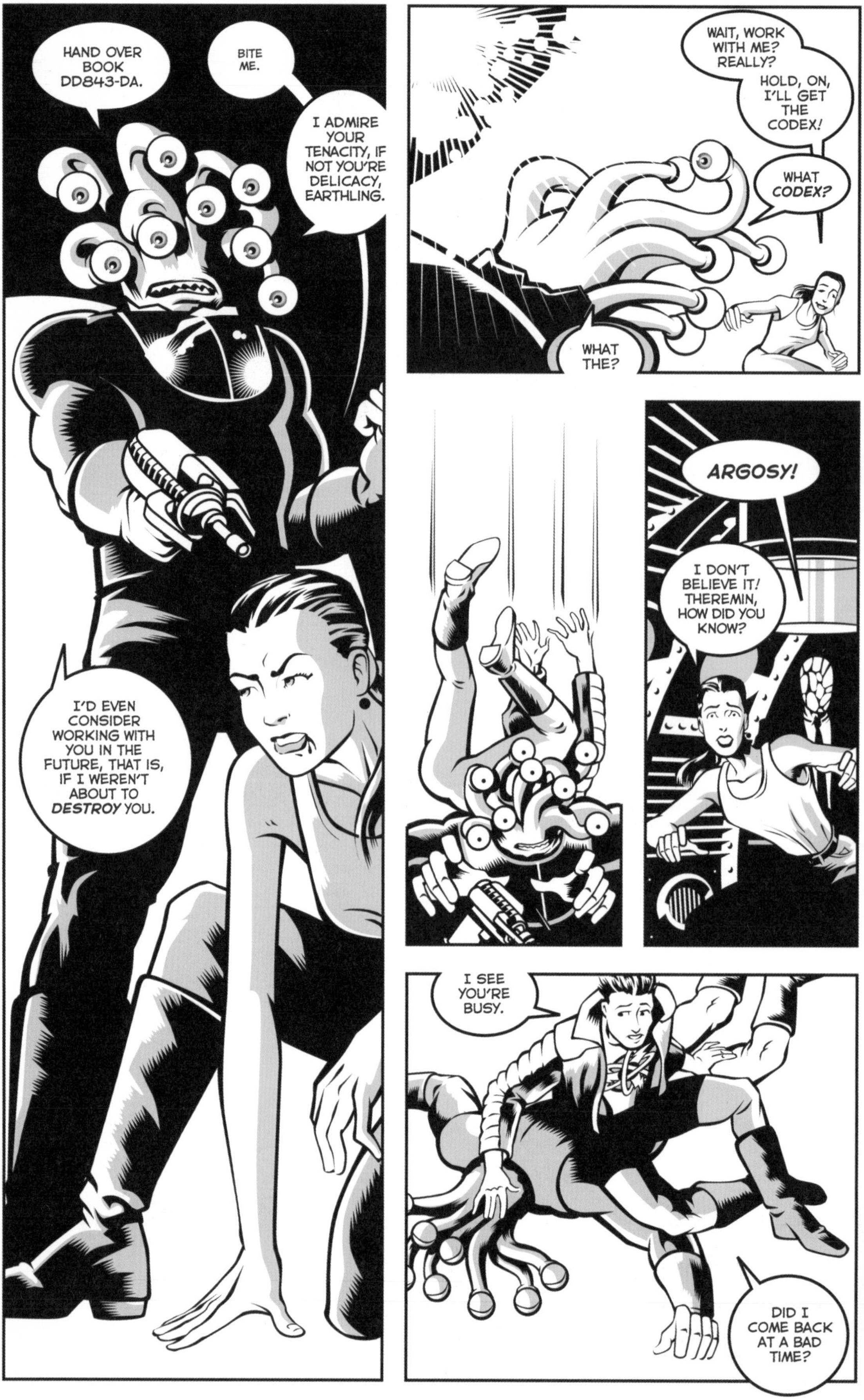
HAND OVER BOOK DD843-DA.
BITE ME.
I ADMIRE YOUR TENACITY, IF NOT YOU'RE DELICACY, EARTHLING.
I'D EVEN CONSIDER WORKING WITH YOU IN THE FUTURE, THAT IS, IF I WEREN'T ABOUT TO DESTROY YOU.
WAIT, WORK WITH ME? REALLY?
HOLD, ON, I'LL GET THE CODEX!
WHAT CODEX?
WHAT THE?
ARGOSY!
I DON'T BELIEVE IT! THEREMIN, HOW DID YOU KNOW?
I SEE YOU'RE BUSY.
DID I COME BACK AT A BAD TIME?

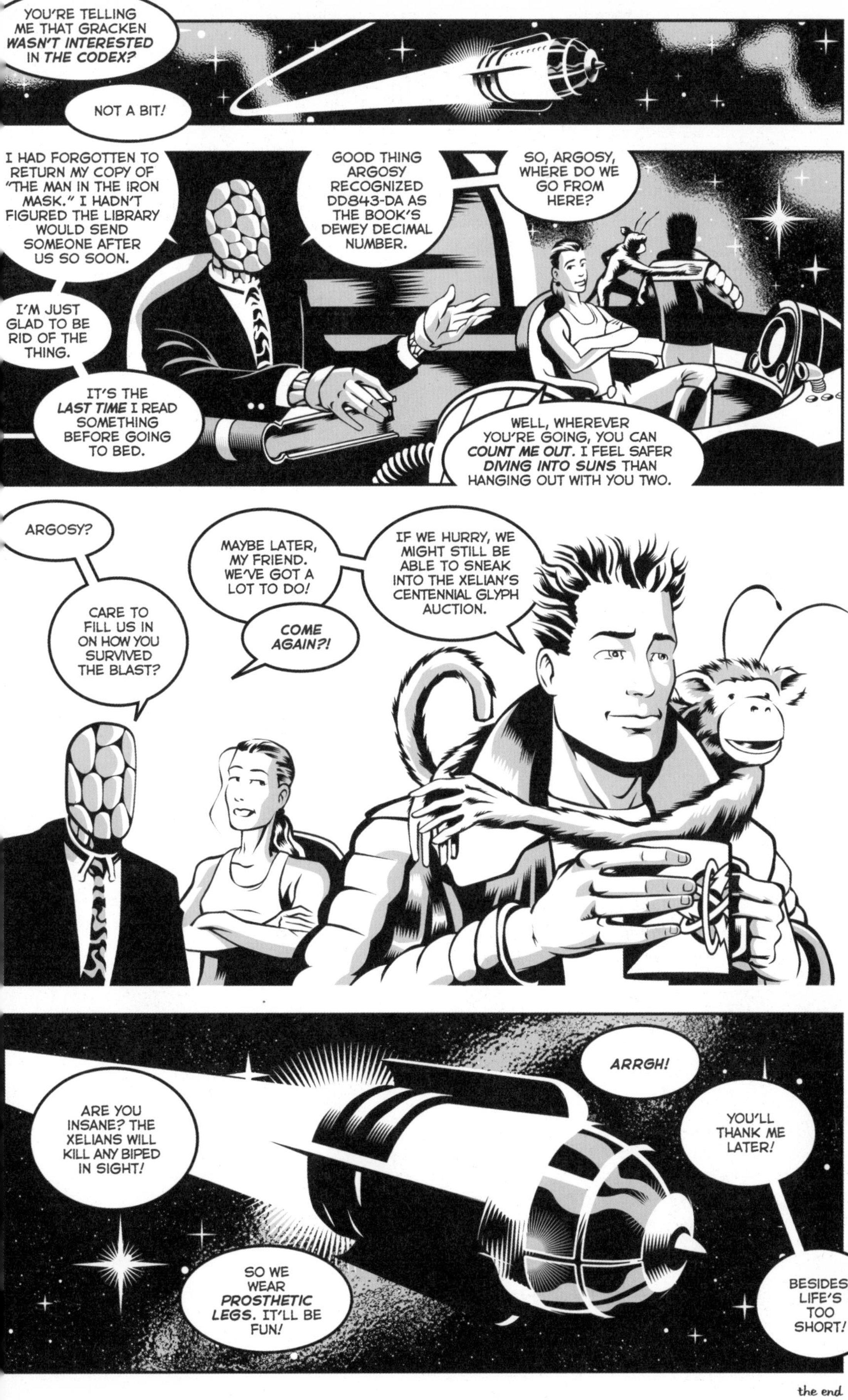
YOU'RE TELLING ME THAT GRACKEN WASN'T INTERESTED IN THE CODEX?
NOT A BIT!
I HAD FORGOTTEN TO RETURN MY COPY OF "THE MAN IN THE IRON MASK." I HADN'T FIGURED THE LIBRARY WOULD SEND SOMEONE AFTER US SO SOON.
I'M JUST GLAD TO BE RID OF THE THING.
IT'S THE LAST TIME I READ SOMETHING BEFORE GOING TO BED.
GOOD THING ARGOSY RECOGNIZED DD843-DA AS THE BOOK'S DEWEY DECIMAL NUMBER.
SO, ARGOSY, WHERE DO WE GO FROM HERE?
WELL, WHEREVER YOU'RE GOING, YOU CAN COUNT ME OUT. I FEEL SAFER DIVING INTO SUNS THAN HANGING OUT WITH YOU TWO.
ARGOSY?
CARE TO FILL US IN ON HOW YOU SURVIVED THE BLAST?
MAYBE LATER, MY FRIEND. WE'VE GOT A LOT TO DO!
IF WE HURRY, WE MIGHT STILL BE ABLE TO SNEAK INTO THE XELIAN'S CENTENNIAL GLYPH AUCTION.
COME AGAIN?!
ARE YOU INSANE? THE XELIANS WILL KILL ANY BIPED IN SIGHT!
SO WE WEAR PROSTHETIC LEGS. IT'LL BE FUN!
ARRGH!
YOU'LL THANK ME LATER!
BESIDES, LIFE'S TOO SHORT!

the end

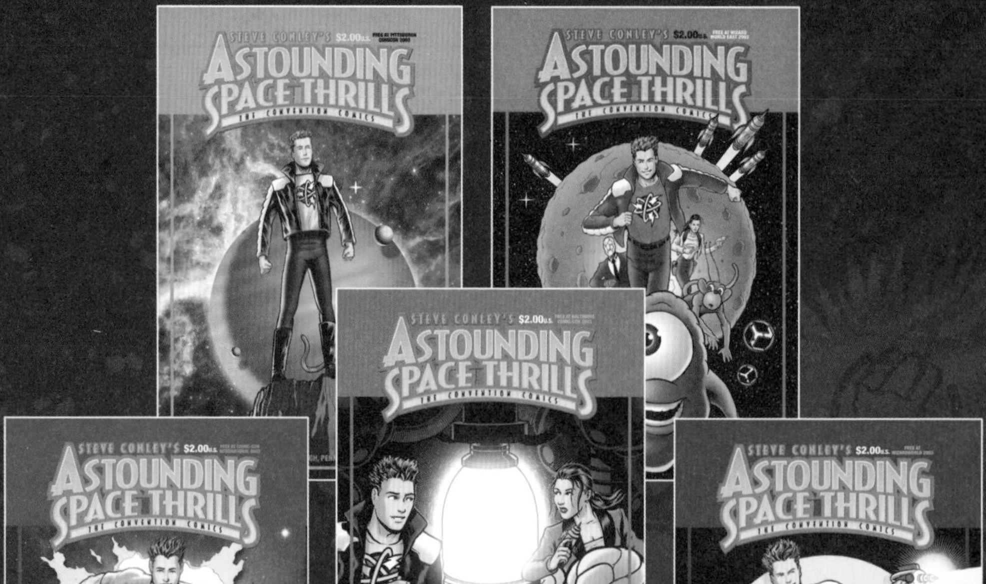
STEVE CONLEY'S
$2.00 U.S.
ASTOUNDING SPACE THRILLS
THE CONVENTION COMICS
MEGACON 2003 • ORLANDO, FLORIDA • FEBRUARY 28-MARCH 2, 2003
AUGUST 8-10, 2003

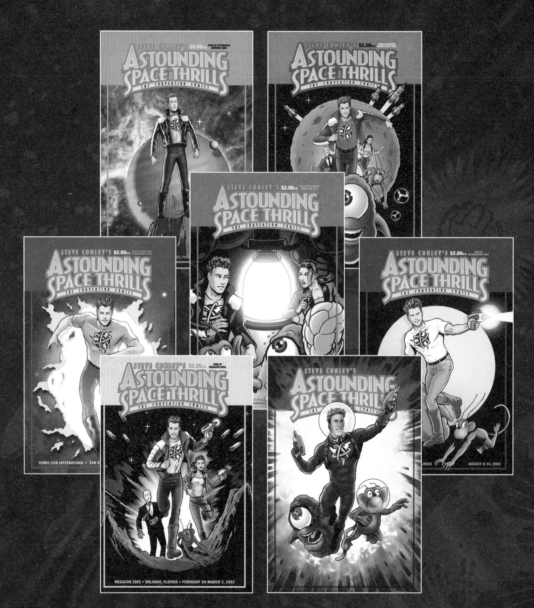

ASTOUNDING SPACE THRILLS #9-15
CONVENTION COMICS 2003

COVERS BY STEVE CONLEY

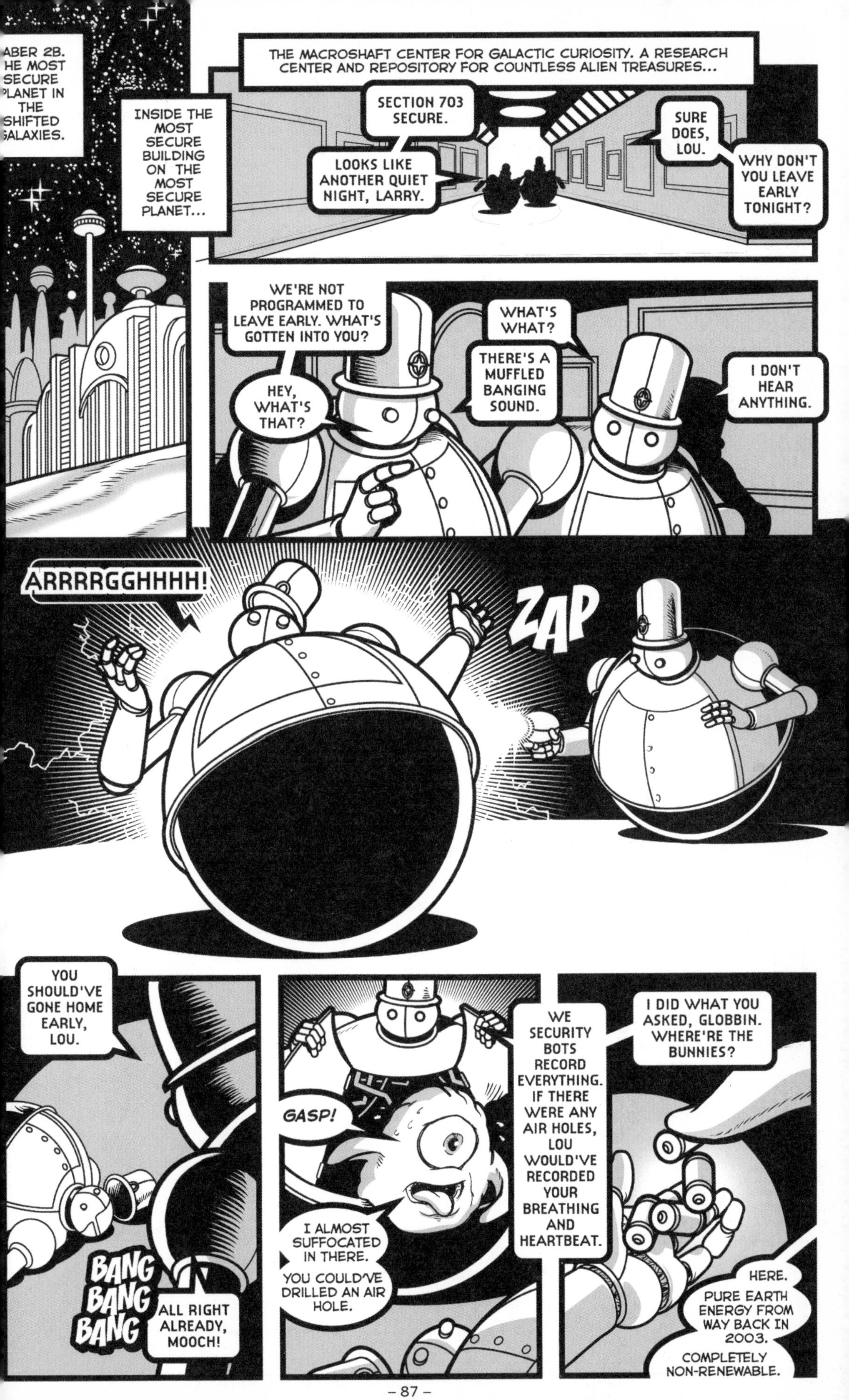
ABER 2B. HE MOST SECURE PLANET IN THE SHIFTED GALAXIES.
INSIDE THE MOST SECURE BUILDING ON THE MOST SECURE PLANET...
THE MACROSHAFT CENTER FOR GALACTIC CURIOSITY. A RESEARCH CENTER AND REPOSITORY FOR COUNTLESS ALIEN TREASURES...
SECTION 703 SECURE.
LOOKS LIKE ANOTHER QUIET NIGHT, LARRY.
SURE DOES, LOU.
WHY DON'T YOU LEAVE EARLY TONIGHT?
WE'RE NOT PROGRAMMED TO LEAVE EARLY. WHAT'S GOTTEN INTO YOU?
HEY, WHAT'S THAT?
WHAT'S WHAT?
THERE'S A MUFFLED BANGING SOUND.
I DON'T HEAR ANYTHING.
ARRRRGGHHHH!
ZAP
YOU SHOULD'VE GONE HOME EARLY, LOU.
BANG BANG BANG
ALL RIGHT ALREADY, MOOCH!
GASP!
I ALMOST SUFFOCATED IN THERE.
YOU COULD'VE DRILLED AN AIR HOLE.
WE SECURITY BOTS RECORD EVERYTHING. IF THERE WERE ANY AIR HOLES, LOU WOULD'VE RECORDED YOUR BREATHING AND HEARTBEAT.
I DID WHAT YOU ASKED, GLOBBIN. WHERE'RE THE BUNNIES?
HERE.
PURE EARTH ENERGY FROM WAY BACK IN 2003.
COMPLETELY NON-RENEWABLE.

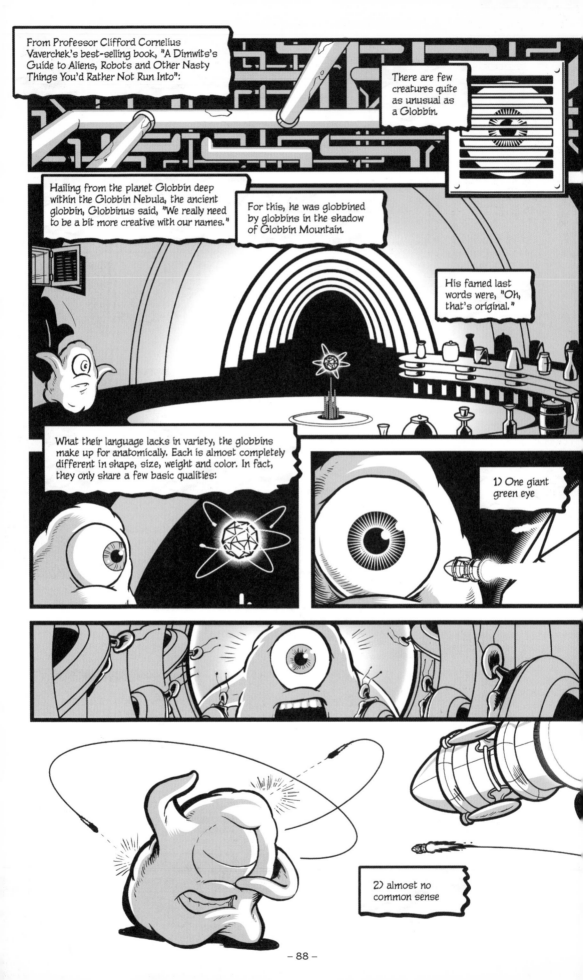

From Professor Clifford Cornelius Vaverchek's best-selling book, "A Dimwits's Guide to Aliens, Robots and Other Nasty Things You'd Rather Not Run Into":

There are few creatures quite as unusual as a Globbin.

Hailing from the planet Globbin deep within the Globbin Nebula, the ancient globbin, Globbinus said, "We really need to be a bit more creative with our names."

For this, he was globbined by globbins in the shadow of Globbin Mountain.

His famed last words were, "Oh, that's original."

What their language lacks in variety, the globbins make up for anatomically. Each is almost completely different in shape, size, weight and color. In fact, they only share a few basic qualities:

1) One giant green eye

2) almost no common sense

3) an insatiable appetite

CHOMP!

and 4) an extremely slow and nearly indestructible digestive system.

(One must presume the primitive globbins didn't survive by NOT eating poisons but by living long enough after eating poisons to have children of their own.)

urp

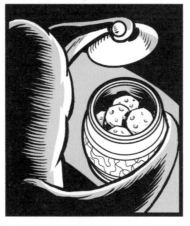

Globbins rarely venture outside their home nebula. But there are exceptions.

And it's usually because they're lost.

I HAVE THE STONE, GET THE SHIP READY.

STONE of XEBROB

N TEMPORARY SPLAY THROUGH THE GENEROUS DONATION OF ANONYMOUS

NOW, HOW THE GLOBBIN DO I GET OUT OF HERE?

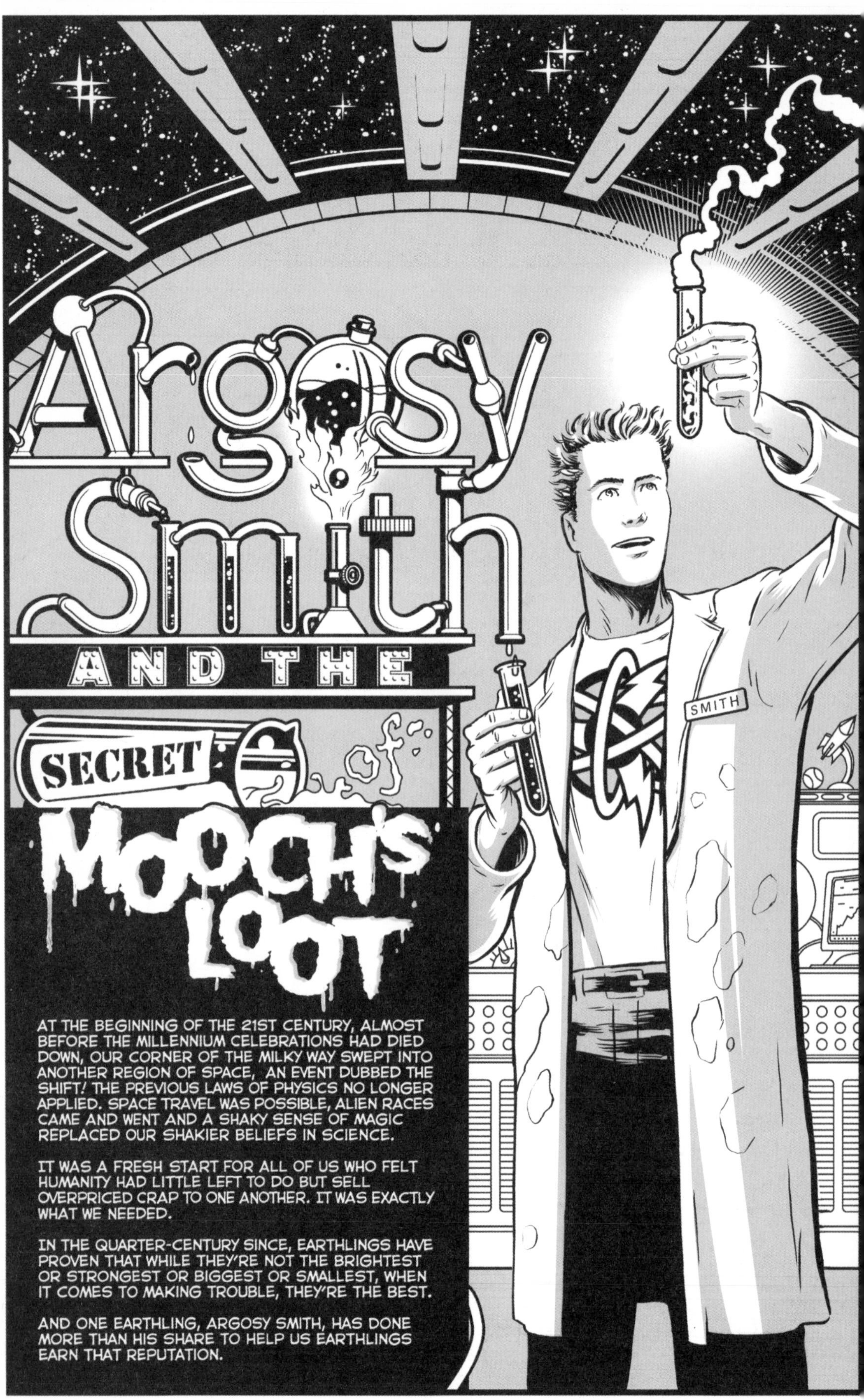
Argosy Smith
AND THE
SECRET
of
MOOCH'S LOOT
SMITH
AT THE BEGINNING OF THE 21ST CENTURY, ALMOST BEFORE THE MILLENNIUM CELEBRATIONS HAD DIED DOWN, OUR CORNER OF THE MILKY WAY SWEPT INTO ANOTHER REGION OF SPACE, AN EVENT DUBBED THE SHIFT! THE PREVIOUS LAWS OF PHYSICS NO LONGER APPLIED. SPACE TRAVEL WAS POSSIBLE, ALIEN RACES CAME AND WENT AND A SHAKY SENSE OF MAGIC REPLACED OUR SHAKIER BELIEFS IN SCIENCE.
IT WAS A FRESH START FOR ALL OF US WHO FELT HUMANITY HAD LITTLE LEFT TO DO BUT SELL OVERPRICED CRAP TO ONE ANOTHER. IT WAS EXACTLY WHAT WE NEEDED.
IN THE QUARTER-CENTURY SINCE, EARTHLINGS HAVE PROVEN THAT WHILE THEY'RE NOT THE BRIGHTEST OR STRONGEST OR BIGGEST OR SMALLEST, WHEN IT COMES TO MAKING TROUBLE, THEY'RE THE BEST.
AND ONE EARTHLING, ARGOSY SMITH, HAS DONE MORE THAN HIS SHARE TO HELP US EARTHLINGS EARN THAT REPUTATION.

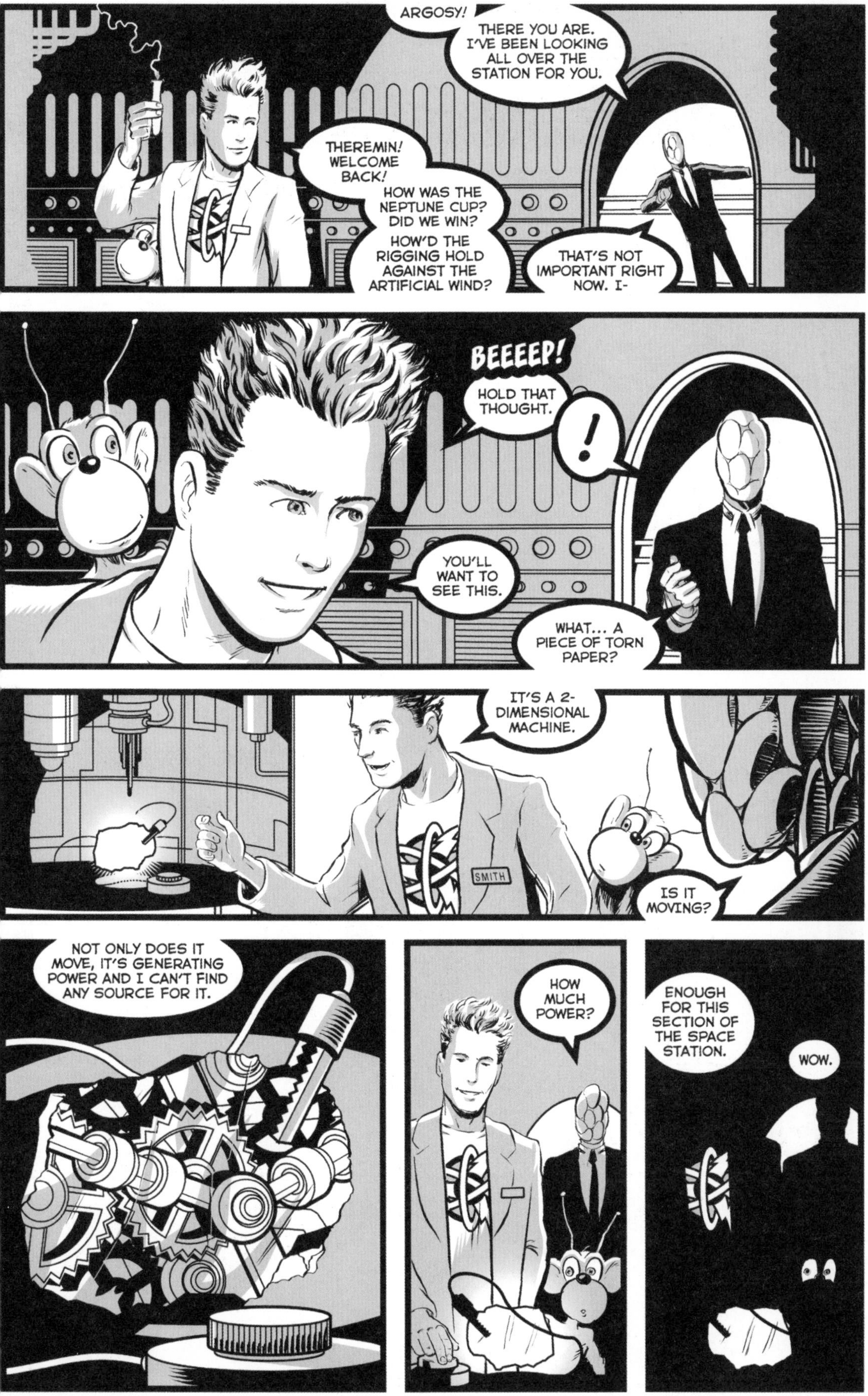
ARGOSY!
THERE YOU ARE. I'VE BEEN LOOKING ALL OVER THE STATION FOR YOU.
THEREMIN! WELCOME BACK!
HOW WAS THE NEPTUNE CUP? DID WE WIN?
HOW'D THE RIGGING HOLD AGAINST THE ARTIFICIAL WIND?
THAT'S NOT IMPORTANT RIGHT NOW. I-
BEEEEP!
HOLD THAT THOUGHT.
!
YOU'LL WANT TO SEE THIS.
WHAT... A PIECE OF TORN PAPER?
IT'S A 2-DIMENSIONAL MACHINE.
SMITH
IS IT MOVING?
NOT ONLY DOES IT MOVE, IT'S GENERATING POWER AND I CAN'T FIND ANY SOURCE FOR IT.
HOW MUCH POWER?
ENOUGH FOR THIS SECTION OF THE SPACE STATION.
WOW.

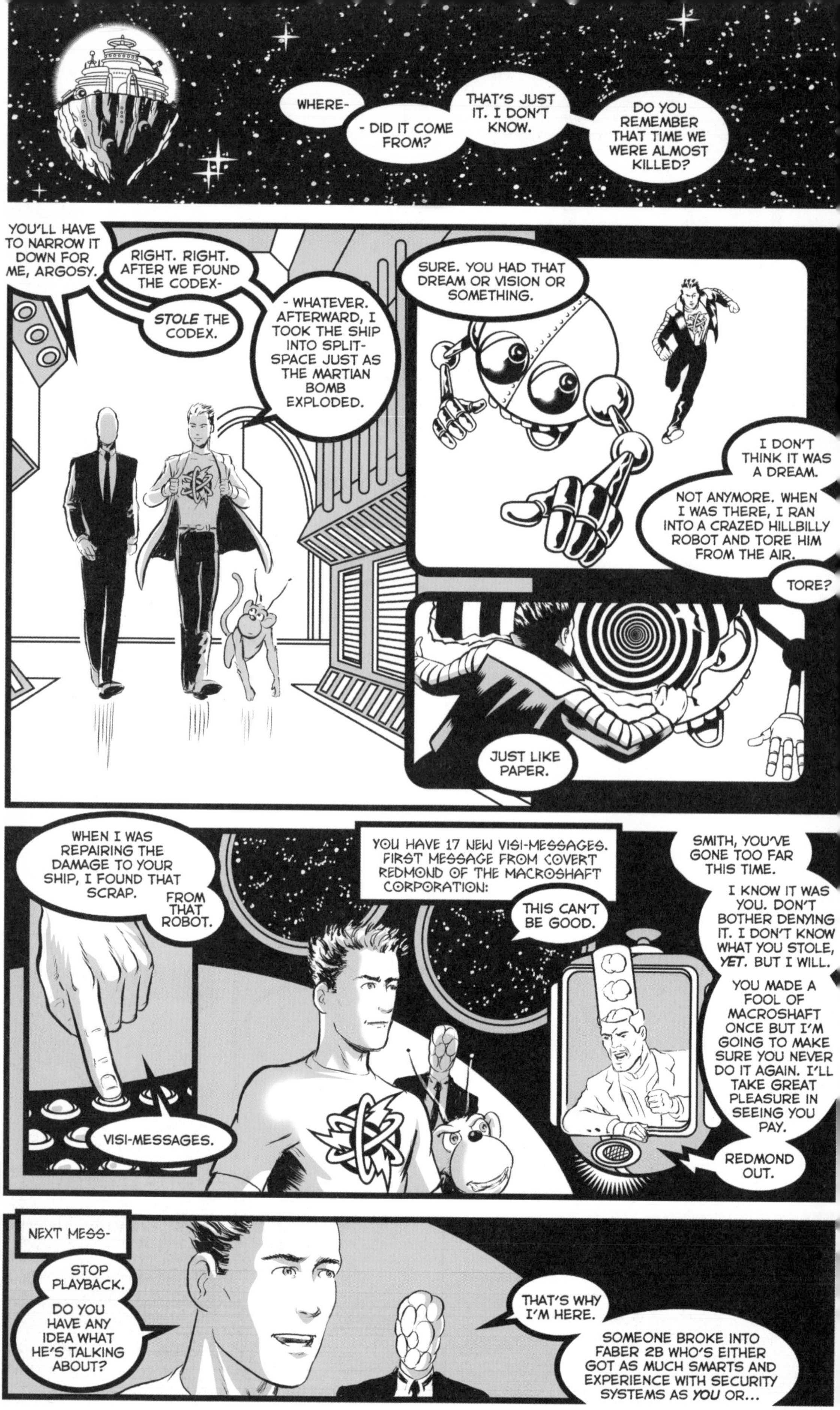
WHERE-
- DID IT COME FROM?
THAT'S JUST IT. I DON'T KNOW.
DO YOU REMEMBER THAT TIME WE WERE ALMOST KILLED?
YOU'LL HAVE TO NARROW IT DOWN FOR ME, ARGOSY.
RIGHT. RIGHT. AFTER WE FOUND THE CODEX-
STOLE THE CODEX.
- WHATEVER. AFTERWARD, I TOOK THE SHIP INTO SPLIT-SPACE JUST AS THE MARTIAN BOMB EXPLODED.
SURE. YOU HAD THAT DREAM OR VISION OR SOMETHING.
I DON'T THINK IT WAS A DREAM.
NOT ANYMORE. WHEN I WAS THERE, I RAN INTO A CRAZED HILLBILLY ROBOT AND TORE HIM FROM THE AIR.
TORE?
JUST LIKE PAPER.
WHEN I WAS REPAIRING THE DAMAGE TO YOUR SHIP, I FOUND THAT SCRAP.
FROM THAT ROBOT.
VISI-MESSAGES.
YOU HAVE 17 NEW VISI-MESSAGES. FIRST MESSAGE FROM COVERT REDMOND OF THE MACROSHAFT CORPORATION:
THIS CAN'T BE GOOD.
SMITH, YOU'VE GONE TOO FAR THIS TIME.
I KNOW IT WAS YOU. DON'T BOTHER DENYING IT. I DON'T KNOW WHAT YOU STOLE, *YET*. BUT I WILL.
YOU MADE A FOOL OF MACROSHAFT ONCE BUT I'M GOING TO MAKE SURE YOU NEVER DO IT AGAIN. I'LL TAKE GREAT PLEASURE IN SEEING YOU PAY.
REDMOND OUT.
NEXT MESS-
STOP PLAYBACK.
DO YOU HAVE ANY IDEA WHAT HE'S TALKING ABOUT?
THAT'S WHY I'M HERE.
SOMEONE BROKE INTO FABER 2B WHO'S EITHER GOT AS MUCH SMARTS AND EXPERIENCE WITH SECURITY SYSTEMS AS *YOU* OR...

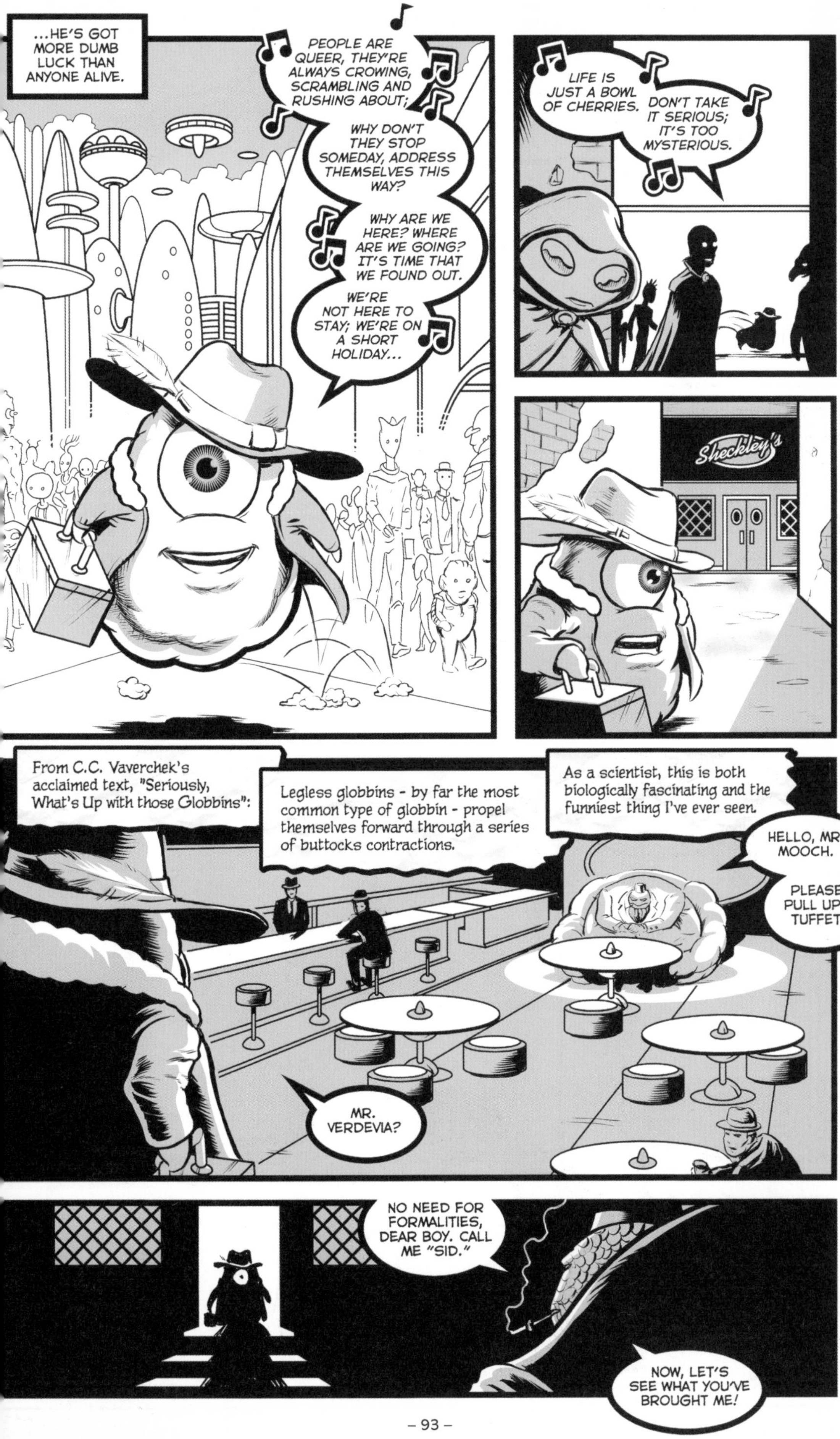
...HE'S GOT MORE DUMB LUCK THAN ANYONE ALIVE.
PEOPLE ARE QUEER, THEY'RE ALWAYS CROWING, SCRAMBLING AND RUSHING ABOUT;
WHY DON'T THEY STOP SOMEDAY, ADDRESS THEMSELVES THIS WAY?
WHY ARE WE HERE? WHERE ARE WE GOING? IT'S TIME THAT WE FOUND OUT.
WE'RE NOT HERE TO STAY; WE'RE ON A SHORT HOLIDAY...
LIFE IS JUST A BOWL OF CHERRIES.
DON'T TAKE IT SERIOUS; IT'S TOO MYSTERIOUS.
Sheckley's
From C.C. Vaverchek's acclaimed text, "Seriously, What's Up with those Globbins":
Legless globbins - by far the most common type of globbin - propel themselves forward through a series of buttocks contractions.
As a scientist, this is both biologically fascinating and the funniest thing I've ever seen.
HELLO, MR. MOOCH.
PLEASE, PULL UP A TUFFET.
MR. VERDEVIA?
NO NEED FOR FORMALITIES, DEAR BOY. CALL ME "SID."
NOW, LET'S SEE WHAT YOU'VE BROUGHT ME!

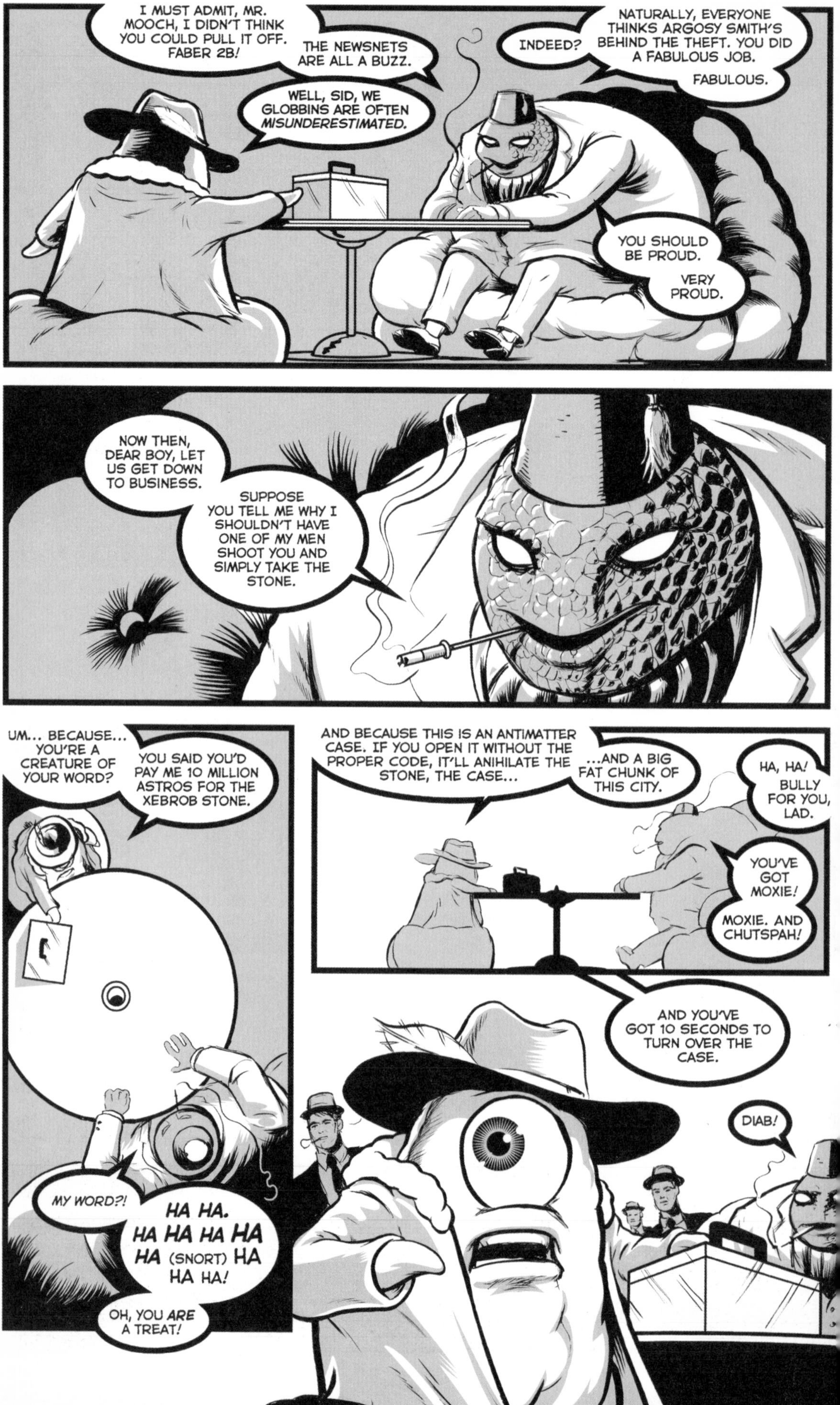
I MUST ADMIT, MR. MOOCH, I DIDN'T THINK YOU COULD PULL IT OFF. FABER 2B!
THE NEWSNETS ARE ALL A BUZZ.
WELL, SID, WE GLOBBINS ARE OFTEN *MISUNDERESTIMATED.*
INDEED?
NATURALLY, EVERYONE THINKS ARGOSY SMITH'S BEHIND THE THEFT. YOU DID A FABULOUS JOB.
FABULOUS.
YOU SHOULD BE PROUD.
VERY PROUD.
NOW THEN, DEAR BOY, LET US GET DOWN TO BUSINESS.
SUPPOSE YOU TELL ME WHY I SHOULDN'T HAVE ONE OF MY MEN SHOOT YOU AND SIMPLY TAKE THE STONE.
UM... BECAUSE... YOU'RE A CREATURE OF YOUR WORD?
YOU SAID YOU'D PAY ME 10 MILLION ASTROS FOR THE XEBROB STONE.
MY WORD?!
HA HA. HA HA HA HA HA HA (SNORT) HA HA HA!
OH, YOU *ARE* A TREAT!
AND BECAUSE THIS IS AN ANTIMATTER CASE. IF YOU OPEN IT WITHOUT THE PROPER CODE, IT'LL ANIHILATE THE STONE, THE CASE...
...AND A BIG FAT CHUNK OF THIS CITY.
HA, HA! BULLY FOR YOU, LAD.
YOU'VE GOT MOXIE!
MOXIE. AND CHUTSPAH!
AND YOU'VE GOT 10 SECONDS TO TURN OVER THE CASE.
DIAB!

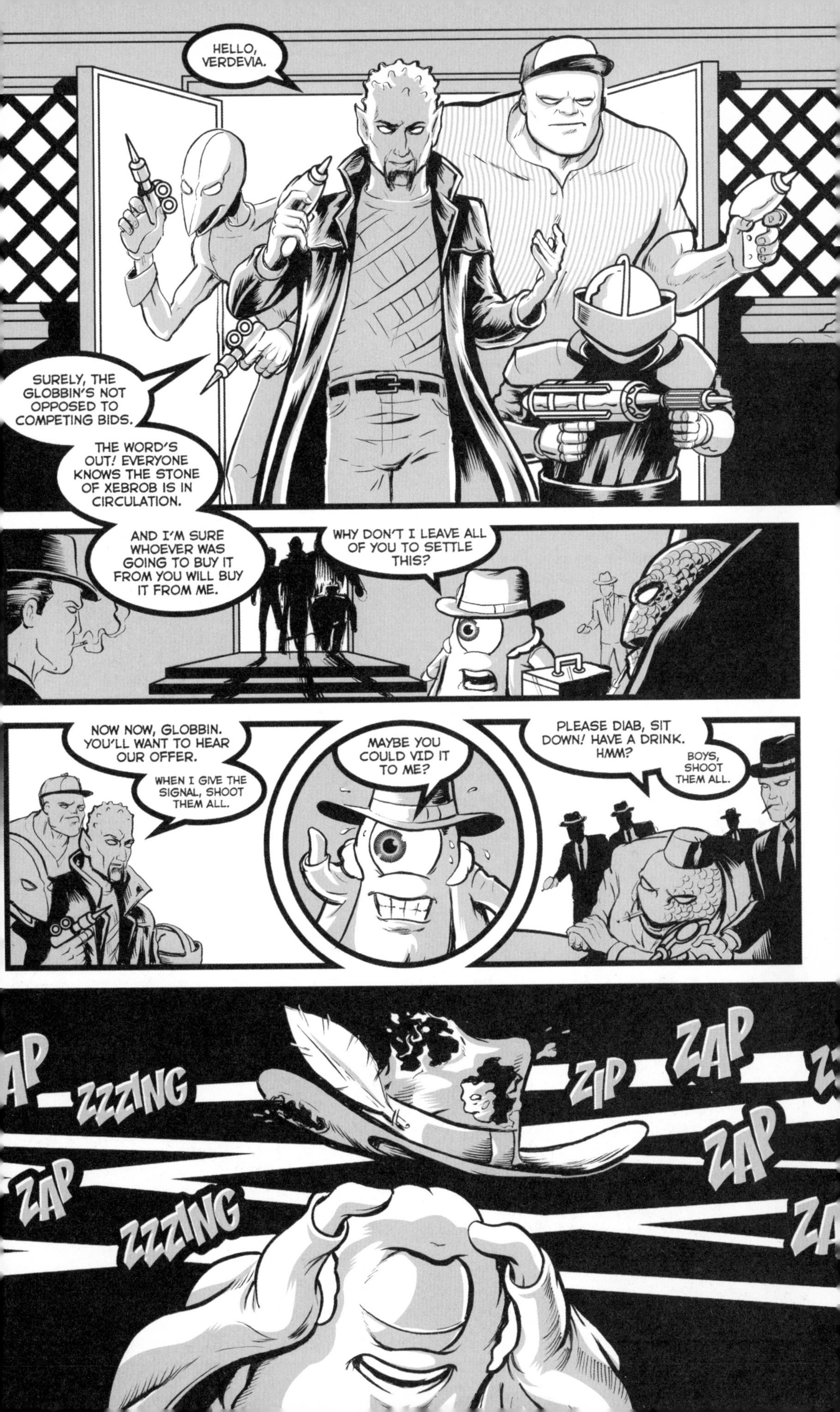

HELLO, VERDEVIA.
SURELY, THE GLOBBIN'S NOT OPPOSED TO COMPETING BIDS.
THE WORD'S OUT! EVERYONE KNOWS THE STONE OF XEBROB IS IN CIRCULATION.
AND I'M SURE WHOEVER WAS GOING TO BUY IT FROM YOU WILL BUY IT FROM ME.
WHY DON'T I LEAVE ALL OF YOU TO SETTLE THIS?
NOW NOW, GLOBBIN. YOU'LL WANT TO HEAR OUR OFFER.
WHEN I GIVE THE SIGNAL, SHOOT THEM ALL.
MAYBE YOU COULD VID IT TO ME?
PLEASE DIAB, SIT DOWN! HAVE A DRINK. HMM?
BOYS, SHOOT THEM ALL.
ZAP
ZZZING
ZIP
ZAP
ZAP
ZAP
ZZZING

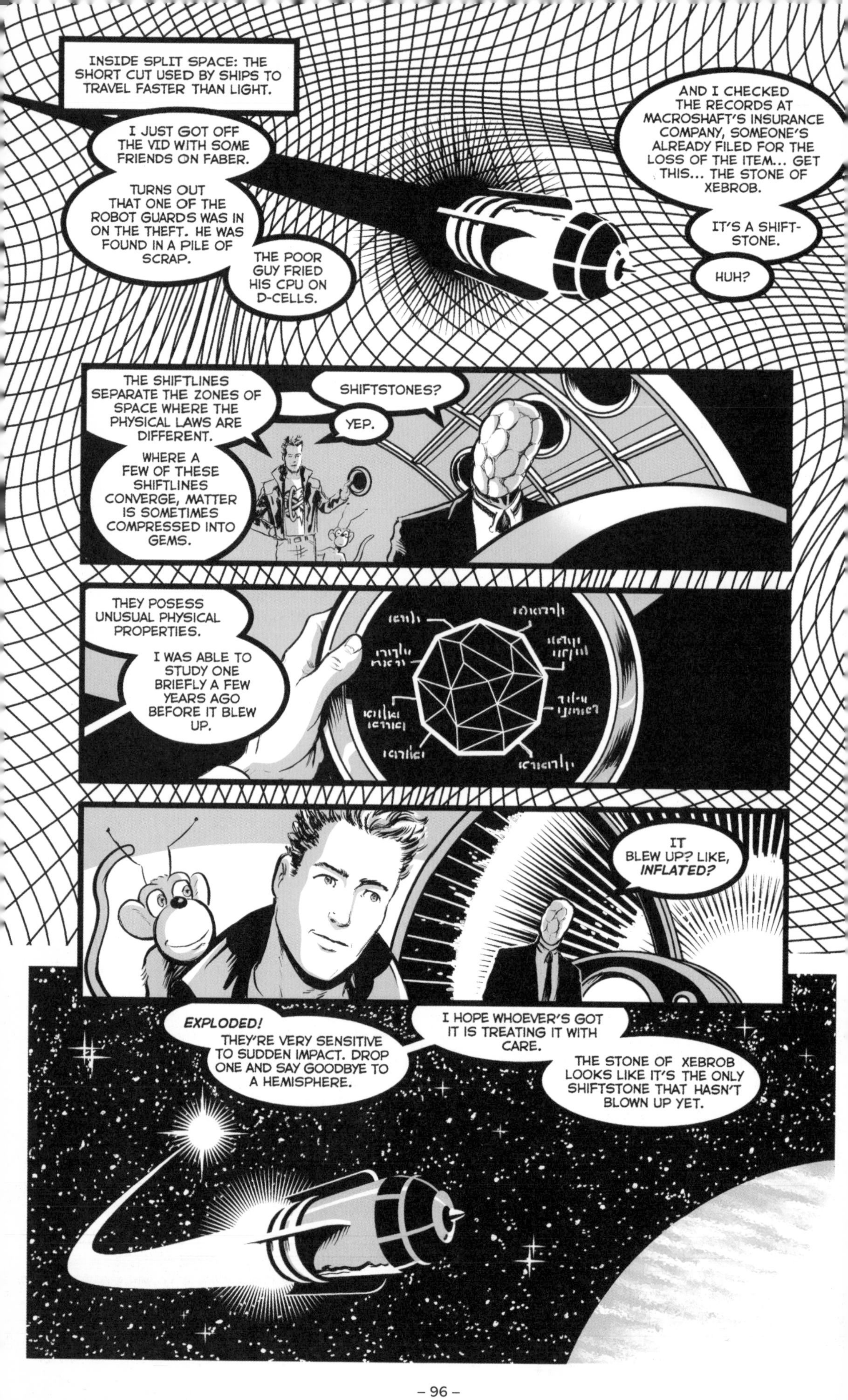

INSIDE SPLIT SPACE: THE SHORT CUT USED BY SHIPS TO TRAVEL FASTER THAN LIGHT.
I JUST GOT OFF THE VID WITH SOME FRIENDS ON FABER.
TURNS OUT THAT ONE OF THE ROBOT GUARDS WAS IN ON THE THEFT. HE WAS FOUND IN A PILE OF SCRAP.
THE POOR GUY FRIED HIS CPU ON D-CELLS.
AND I CHECKED THE RECORDS AT MACROSHAFT'S INSURANCE COMPANY, SOMEONE'S ALREADY FILED FOR THE LOSS OF THE ITEM... GET THIS... THE STONE OF XEBROB.
IT'S A SHIFT-STONE.
HUH?
THE SHIFTLINES SEPARATE THE ZONES OF SPACE WHERE THE PHYSICAL LAWS ARE DIFFERENT.
SHIFTSTONES?
YEP.
WHERE A FEW OF THESE SHIFTLINES CONVERGE, MATTER IS SOMETIMES COMPRESSED INTO GEMS.
THEY POSESS UNUSUAL PHYSICAL PROPERTIES.
I WAS ABLE TO STUDY ONE BRIEFLY A FEW YEARS AGO BEFORE IT BLEW UP.
IT BLEW UP? LIKE, *INFLATED?*
EXPLODED!
THEY'RE VERY SENSITIVE TO SUDDEN IMPACT. DROP ONE AND SAY GOODBYE TO A HEMISPHERE.
I HOPE WHOEVER'S GOT IT IS TREATING IT WITH CARE.
THE STONE OF XEBROB LOOKS LIKE IT'S THE ONLY SHIFTSTONE THAT HASN'T BLOWN UP YET.

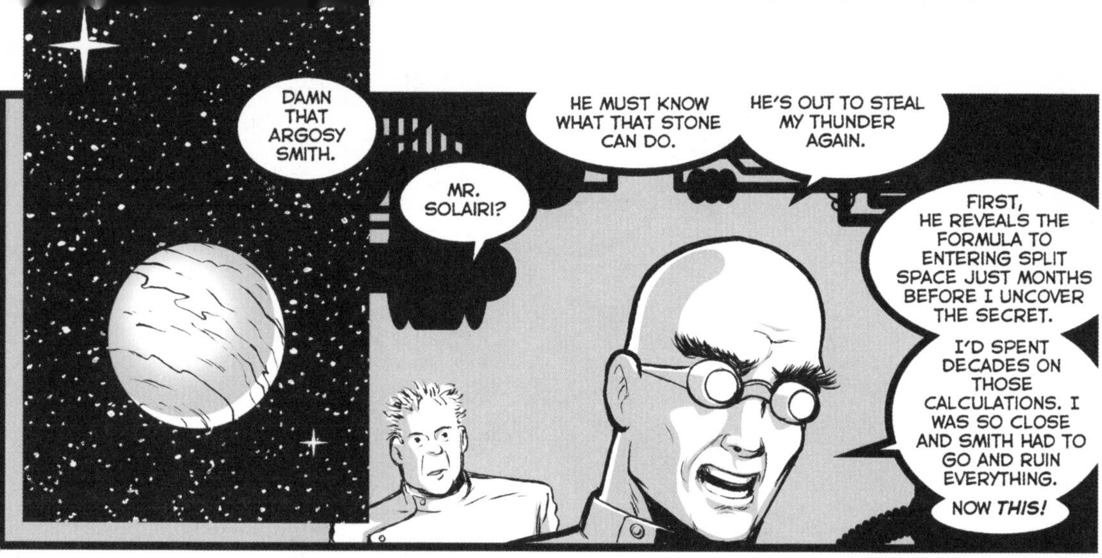
DAMN THAT ARGOSY SMITH.
MR. SOLAIRI?
HE MUST KNOW WHAT THAT STONE CAN DO.
HE'S OUT TO STEAL MY THUNDER AGAIN.
FIRST, HE REVEALS THE FORMULA TO ENTERING SPLIT SPACE JUST MONTHS BEFORE I UNCOVER THE SECRET.
I'D SPENT DECADES ON THOSE CALCULATIONS. I WAS SO CLOSE AND SMITH HAD TO GO AND RUIN EVERYTHING.
NOW *THIS!*

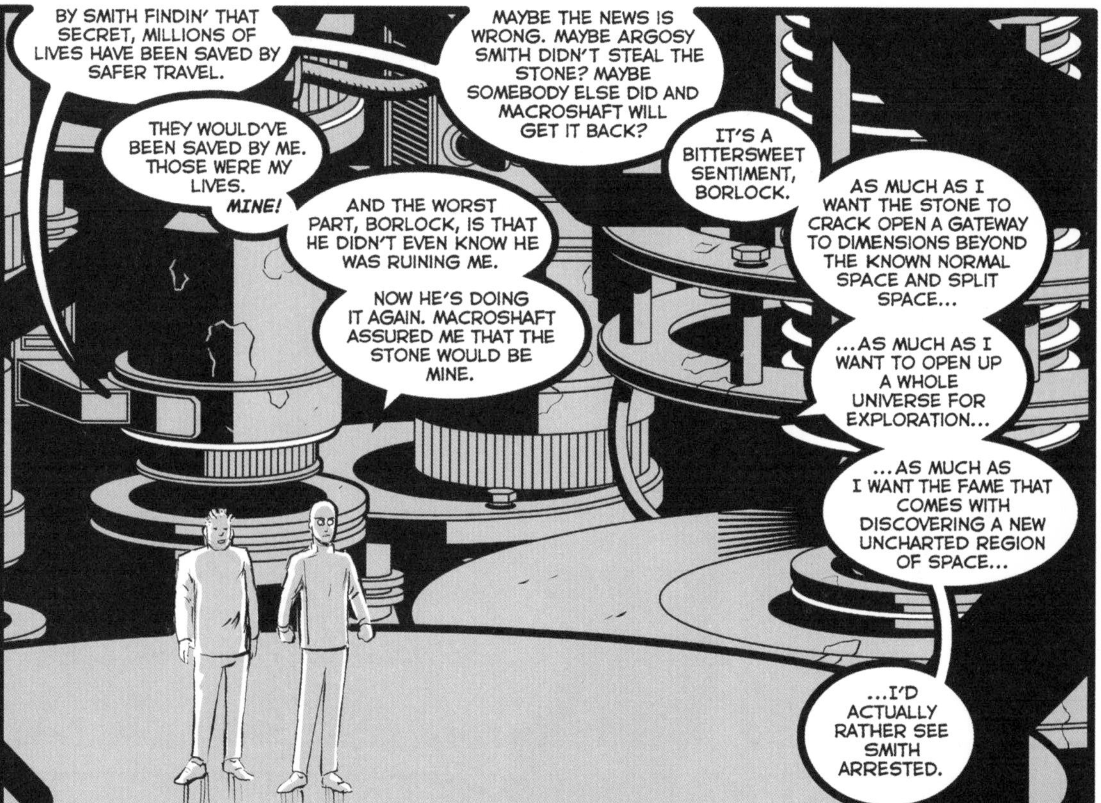
BY SMITH FINDIN' THAT SECRET, MILLIONS OF LIVES HAVE BEEN SAVED BY SAFER TRAVEL.
THEY WOULD'VE BEEN SAVED BY ME. THOSE WERE MY LIVES.
MINE!
AND THE WORST PART, BORLOCK, IS THAT HE DIDN'T EVEN KNOW HE WAS RUINING ME.
NOW HE'S DOING IT AGAIN. MACROSHAFT ASSURED ME THAT THE STONE WOULD BE MINE.
MAYBE THE NEWS IS WRONG. MAYBE ARGOSY SMITH DIDN'T STEAL THE STONE? MAYBE SOMEBODY ELSE DID AND MACROSHAFT WILL GET IT BACK?
IT'S A BITTERSWEET SENTIMENT, BORLOCK.
AS MUCH AS I WANT THE STONE TO CRACK OPEN A GATEWAY TO DIMENSIONS BEYOND THE KNOWN NORMAL SPACE AND SPLIT SPACE...
...AS MUCH AS I WANT TO OPEN UP A WHOLE UNIVERSE FOR EXPLORATION...
...AS MUCH AS I WANT THE FAME THAT COMES WITH DISCOVERING A NEW UNCHARTED REGION OF SPACE...
...I'D ACTUALLY RATHER SEE SMITH ARRESTED.

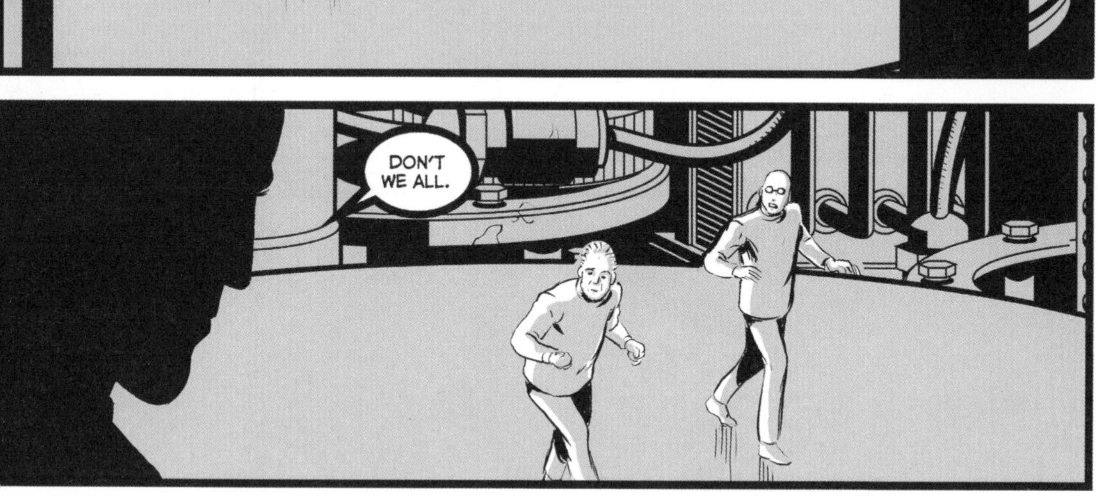
DON'T WE ALL.

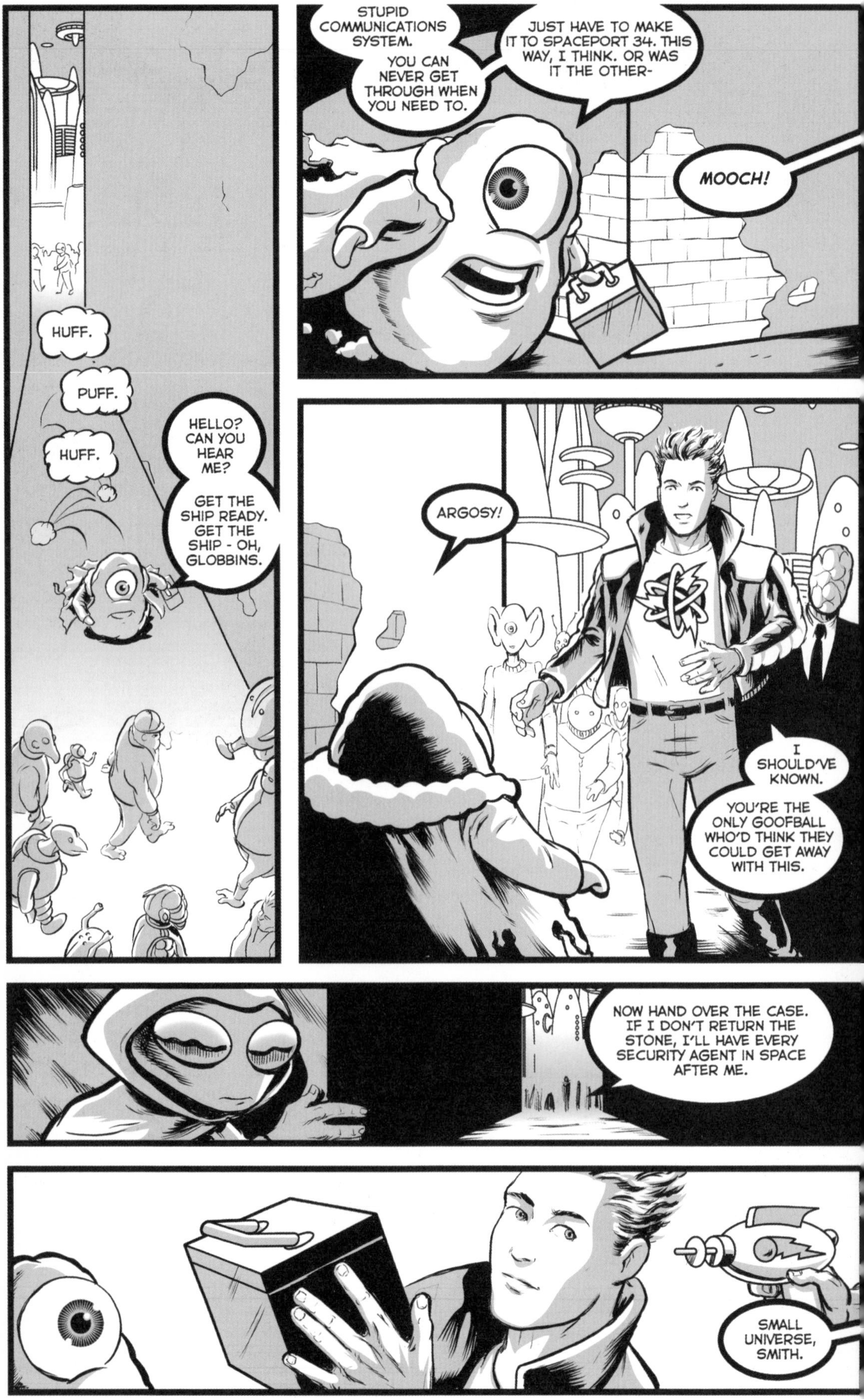
HUFF.
PUFF.
HUFF.
HELLO? CAN YOU HEAR ME?
GET THE SHIP READY. GET THE SHIP - OH, GLOBBINS.
STUPID COMMUNICATIONS SYSTEM.
YOU CAN NEVER GET THROUGH WHEN YOU NEED TO.
JUST HAVE TO MAKE IT TO SPACEPORT 34. THIS WAY, I THINK. OR WAS IT THE OTHER-
MOOCH!
ARGOSY!
I SHOULD'VE KNOWN.
YOU'RE THE ONLY GOOFBALL WHO'D THINK THEY COULD GET AWAY WITH THIS.
NOW HAND OVER THE CASE. IF I DON'T RETURN THE STONE, I'LL HAVE EVERY SECURITY AGENT IN SPACE AFTER ME.
SMALL UNIVERSE, SMITH.

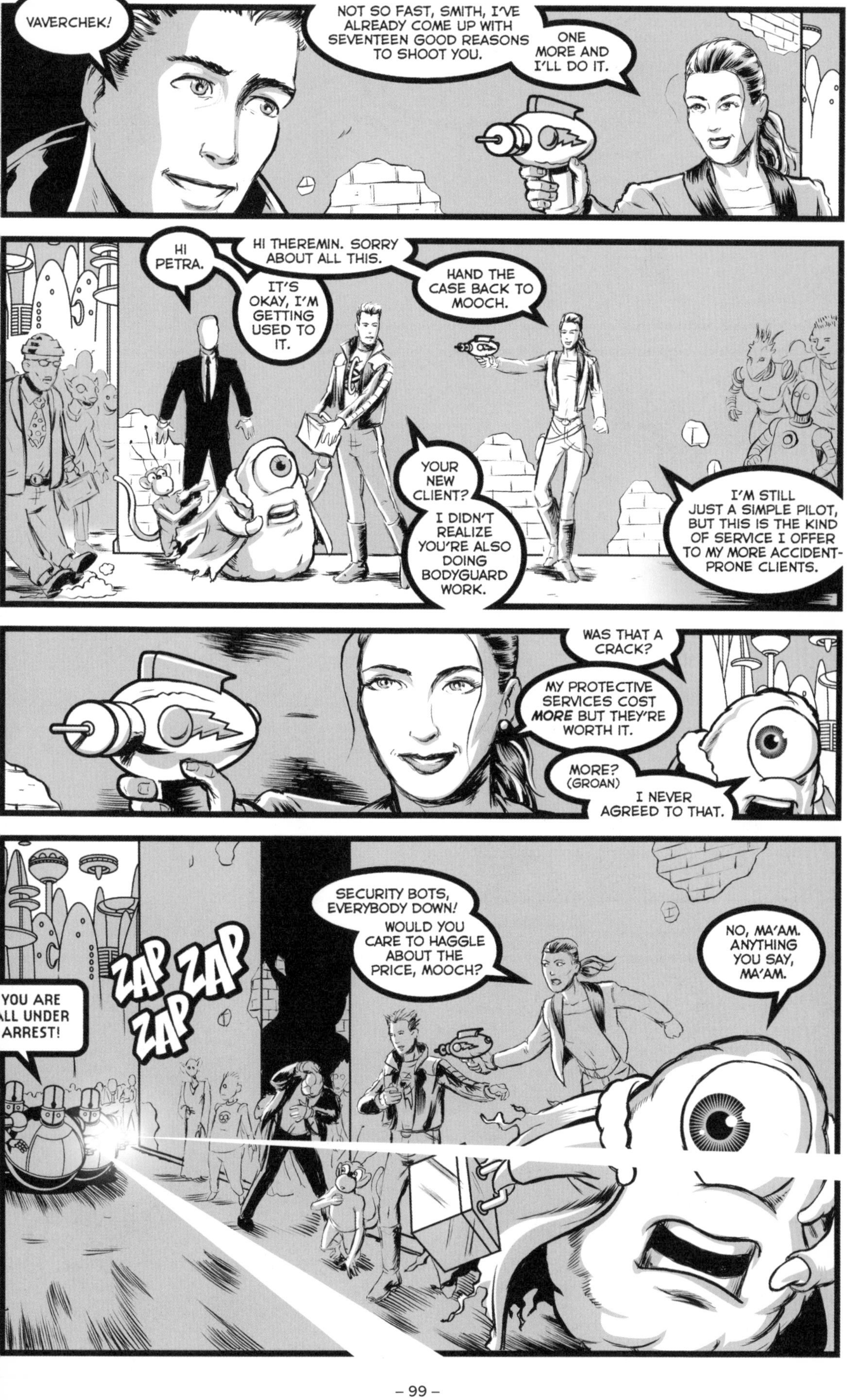
VAVERCHEK!
NOT SO FAST, SMITH, I'VE ALREADY COME UP WITH SEVENTEEN GOOD REASONS TO SHOOT YOU.
ONE MORE AND I'LL DO IT.
HI PETRA.
HI THEREMIN. SORRY ABOUT ALL THIS.
IT'S OKAY, I'M GETTING USED TO IT.
HAND THE CASE BACK TO MOOCH.
YOUR NEW CLIENT?
I DIDN'T REALIZE YOU'RE ALSO DOING BODYGUARD WORK.
I'M STILL JUST A SIMPLE PILOT, BUT THIS IS THE KIND OF SERVICE I OFFER TO MY MORE ACCIDENT-PRONE CLIENTS.
WAS THAT A CRACK?
MY PROTECTIVE SERVICES COST *MORE* BUT THEY'RE WORTH IT.
MORE? (GROAN)
I NEVER AGREED TO THAT.
YOU ARE ALL UNDER ARREST!
ZAP ZAP ZAP
SECURITY BOTS, EVERYBODY DOWN!
WOULD YOU CARE TO HAGGLE ABOUT THE PRICE, MOOCH?
NO, MA'AM. ANYTHING YOU SAY, MA'AM.

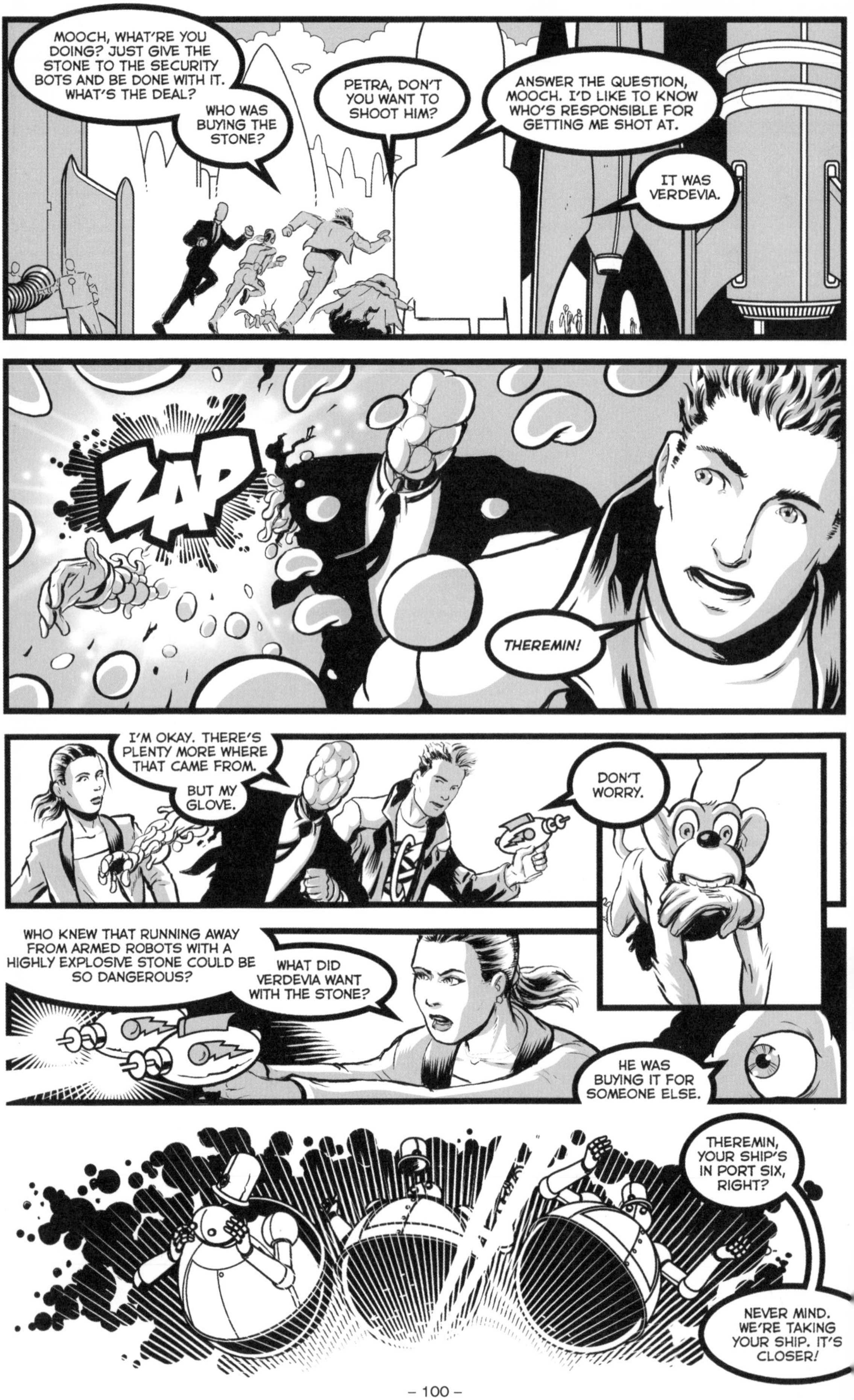
MOOCH, WHAT'RE YOU DOING? JUST GIVE THE STONE TO THE SECURITY BOTS AND BE DONE WITH IT. WHAT'S THE DEAL?
WHO WAS BUYING THE STONE?
PETRA, DON'T YOU WANT TO SHOOT HIM?
ANSWER THE QUESTION, MOOCH. I'D LIKE TO KNOW WHO'S RESPONSIBLE FOR GETTING ME SHOT AT.
IT WAS VERDEVIA.
ZAP
THEREMIN!
I'M OKAY. THERE'S PLENTY MORE WHERE THAT CAME FROM.
BUT MY GLOVE.
DON'T WORRY.
WHO KNEW THAT RUNNING AWAY FROM ARMED ROBOTS WITH A HIGHLY EXPLOSIVE STONE COULD BE SO DANGEROUS?
WHAT DID VERDEVIA WANT WITH THE STONE?
HE WAS BUYING IT FOR SOMEONE ELSE.
THEREMIN, YOUR SHIP'S IN PORT SIX, RIGHT?
NEVER MIND. WE'RE TAKING YOUR SHIP. IT'S CLOSER!

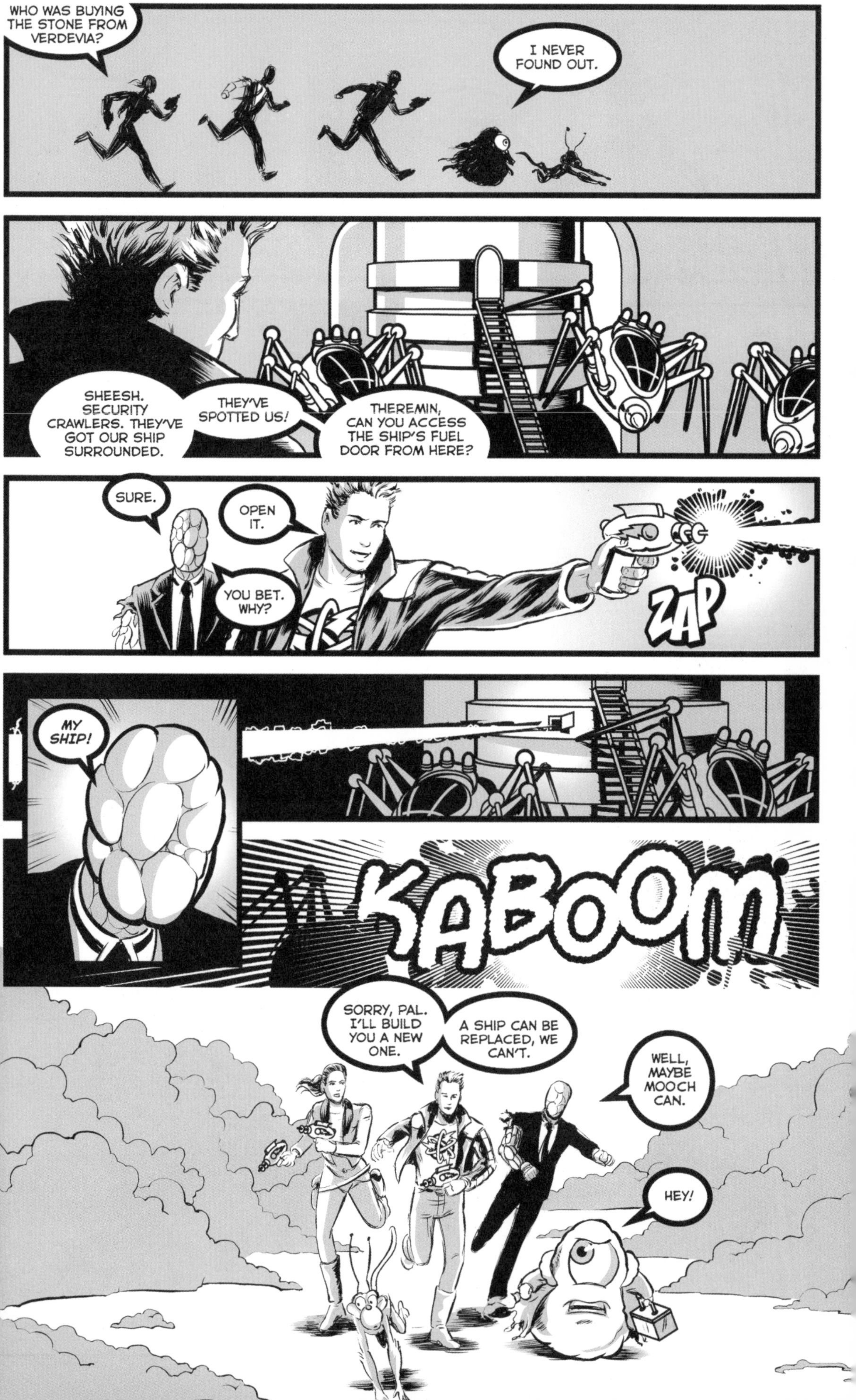
WHO WAS BUYING THE STONE FROM VERDEVIA?
I NEVER FOUND OUT.
SHEESH. SECURITY CRAWLERS. THEY'VE GOT OUR SHIP SURROUNDED.
THEY'VE SPOTTED US!
THEREMIN, CAN YOU ACCESS THE SHIP'S FUEL DOOR FROM HERE?
SURE.
OPEN IT.
YOU BET. WHY?
ZAP
MY SHIP!
KABOOM
SORRY, PAL. I'LL BUILD YOU A NEW ONE.
A SHIP CAN BE REPLACED, WE CAN'T.
WELL, MAYBE MOOCH CAN.
HEY!

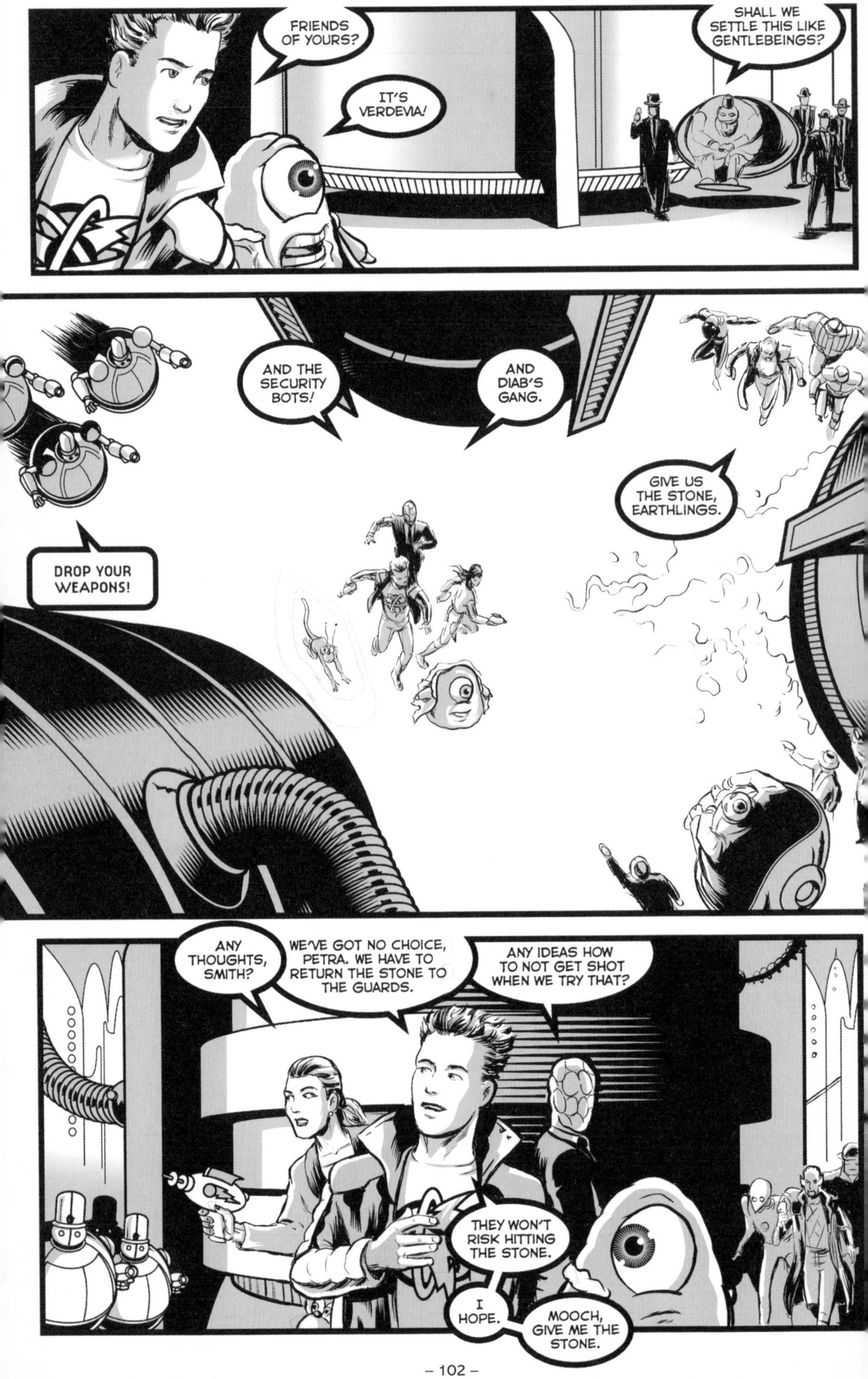
FRIENDS OF YOURS?
IT'S VERDEVIA!
SHALL WE SETTLE THIS LIKE GENTLEBEINGS?
AND THE SECURITY BOTS!
AND DIAB'S GANG.
DROP YOUR WEAPONS!
GIVE US THE STONE, EARTHLINGS.
ANY THOUGHTS, SMITH?
WE'VE GOT NO CHOICE, PETRA. WE HAVE TO RETURN THE STONE TO THE GUARDS.
ANY IDEAS HOW TO NOT GET SHOT WHEN WE TRY THAT?
THEY WON'T RISK HITTING THE STONE.
I HOPE.
MOOCH, GIVE ME THE STONE.

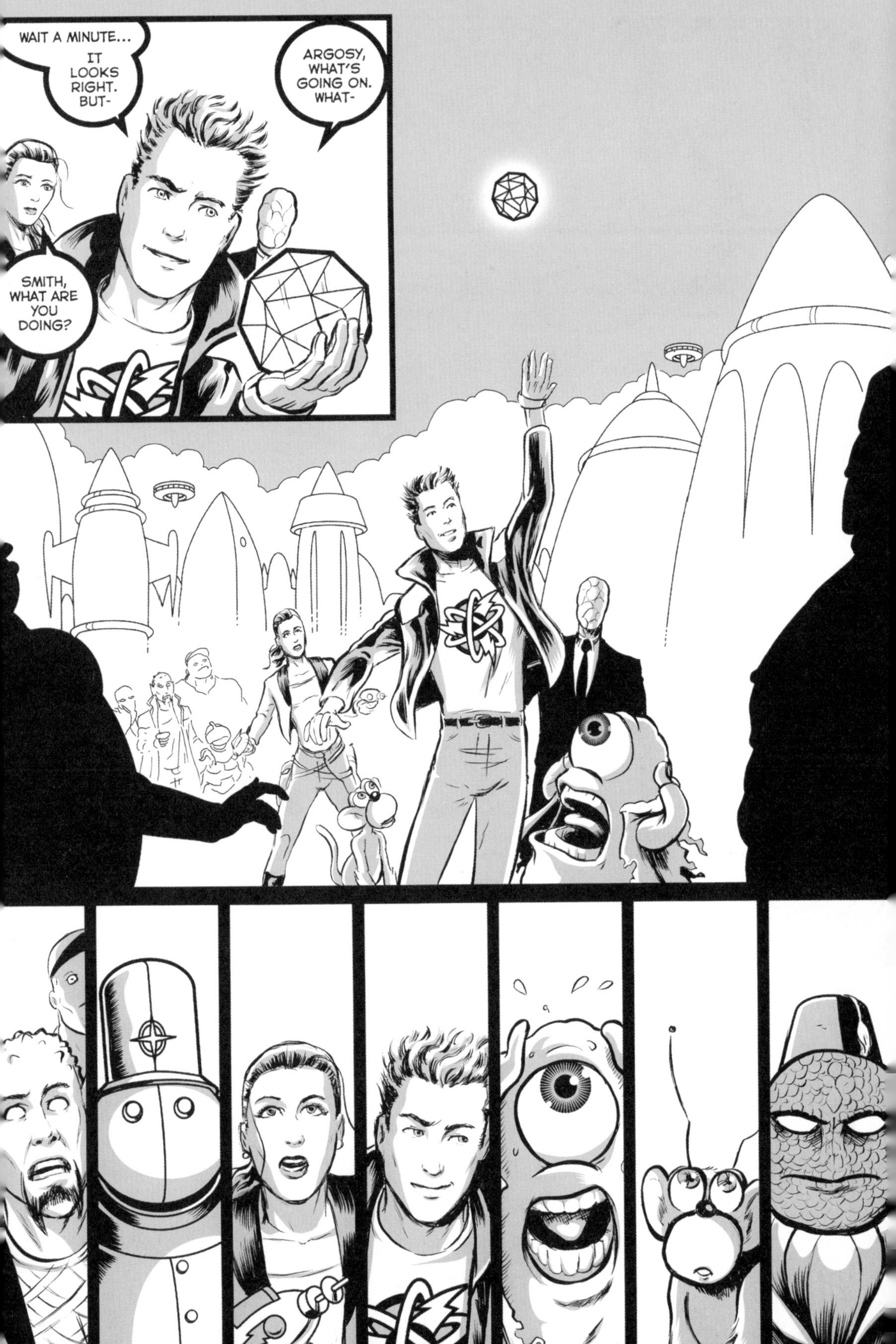
WAIT A MINUTE... IT LOOKS RIGHT. BUT-
ARGOSY, WHAT'S GOING ON. WHAT-
SMITH, WHAT ARE YOU DOING?

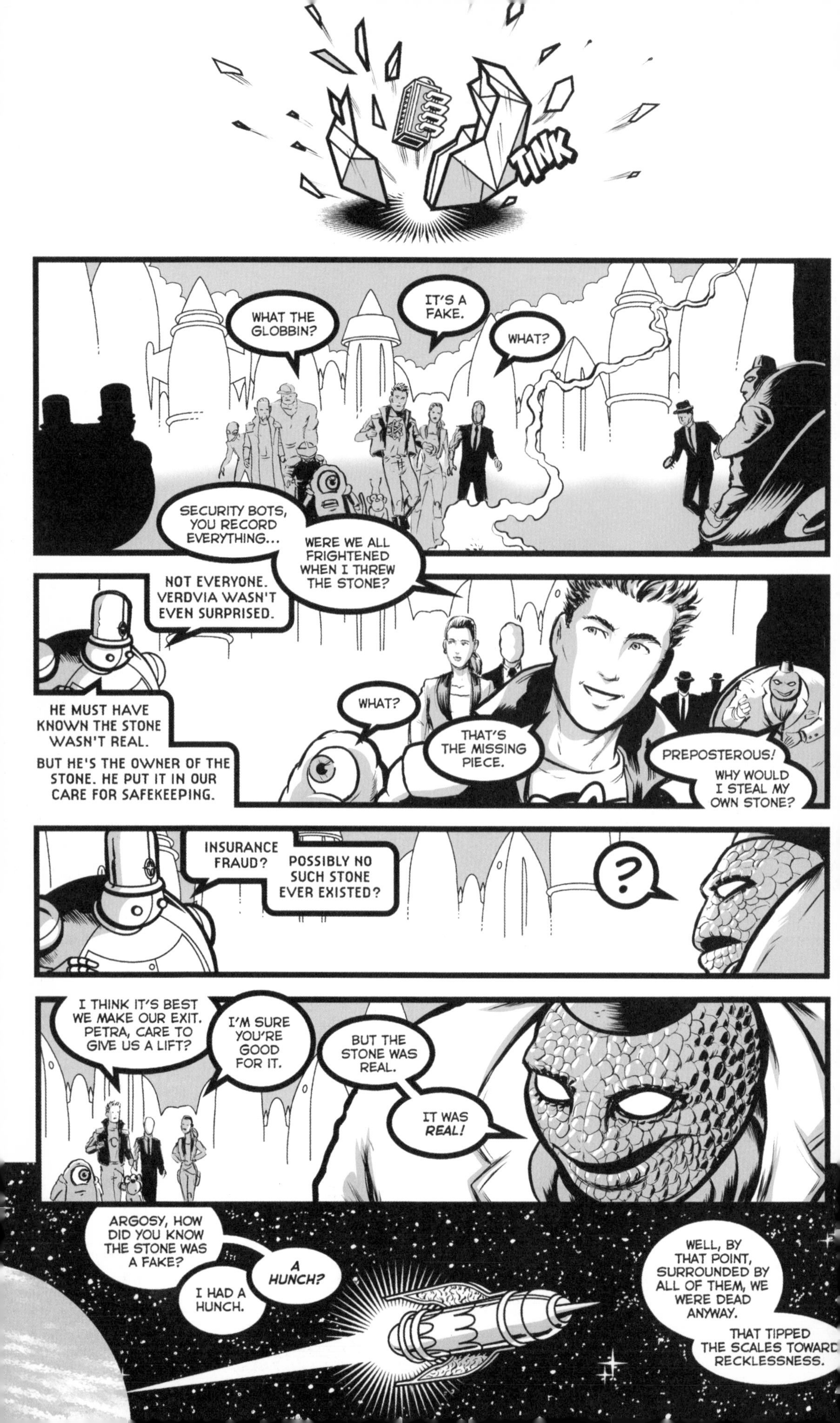
TINK
WHAT THE GLOBBIN?
IT'S A FAKE.
WHAT?
SECURITY BOTS, YOU RECORD EVERYTHING...
WERE WE ALL FRIGHTENED WHEN I THREW THE STONE?
NOT EVERYONE. VERDVIA WASN'T EVEN SURPRISED.
HE MUST HAVE KNOWN THE STONE WASN'T REAL.
BUT HE'S THE OWNER OF THE STONE. HE PUT IT IN OUR CARE FOR SAFEKEEPING.
WHAT?
THAT'S THE MISSING PIECE.
PREPOSTEROUS!
WHY WOULD I STEAL MY OWN STONE?
INSURANCE FRAUD?
POSSIBLY NO SUCH STONE EVER EXISTED?
?
I THINK IT'S BEST WE MAKE OUR EXIT. PETRA, CARE TO GIVE US A LIFT?
I'M SURE YOU'RE GOOD FOR IT.
BUT THE STONE WAS REAL.
IT WAS *REAL!*
ARGOSY, HOW DID YOU KNOW THE STONE WAS A FAKE?
I HAD A HUNCH.
A HUNCH?
WELL, BY THAT POINT, SURROUNDED BY ALL OF THEM, WE WERE DEAD ANYWAY.
THAT TIPPED THE SCALES TOWARD RECKLESSNESS.

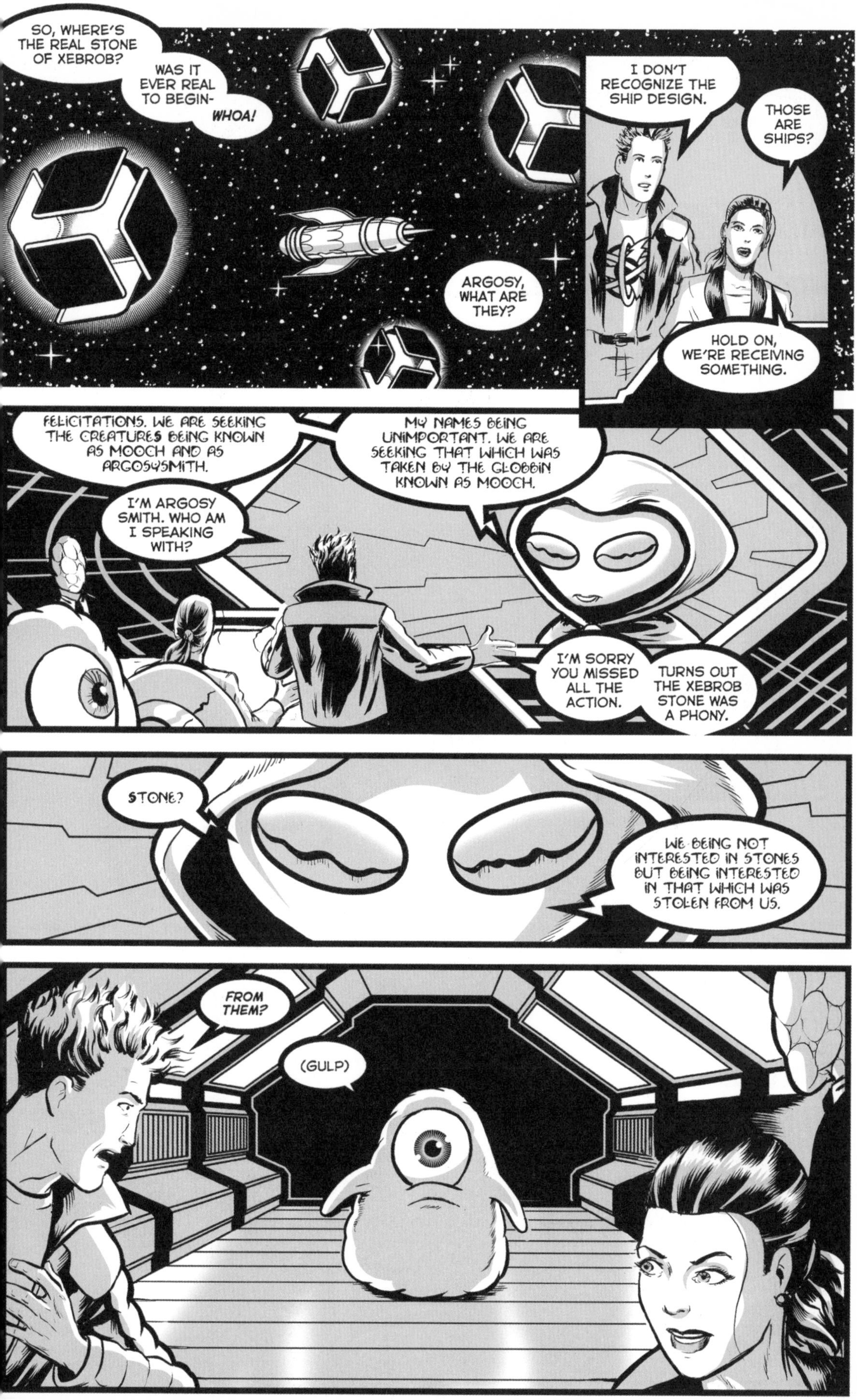

SO, WHERE'S THE REAL STONE OF XEBROB?
WAS IT EVER REAL TO BEGIN- WHOA!
I DON'T RECOGNIZE THE SHIP DESIGN.
THOSE ARE SHIPS?
ARGOSY, WHAT ARE THEY?
HOLD ON, WE'RE RECEIVING SOMETHING.
FELICITATIONS. WE ARE SEEKING THE CREATURES BEING KNOWN AS MOOCH AND AS ARGOSYSMITH.
I'M ARGOSY SMITH. WHO AM I SPEAKING WITH?
MY NAMES BEING UNIMPORTANT. WE ARE SEEKING THAT WHICH WAS TAKEN BY THE GLOBBIN KNOWN AS MOOCH.
I'M SORRY YOU MISSED ALL THE ACTION.
TURNS OUT THE XEBROB STONE WAS A PHONY.
STONE?
WE BEING NOT INTERESTED IN STONES BUT BEING INTERESTED IN THAT WHICH WAS STOLEN FROM US.
FROM THEM?
(GULP)

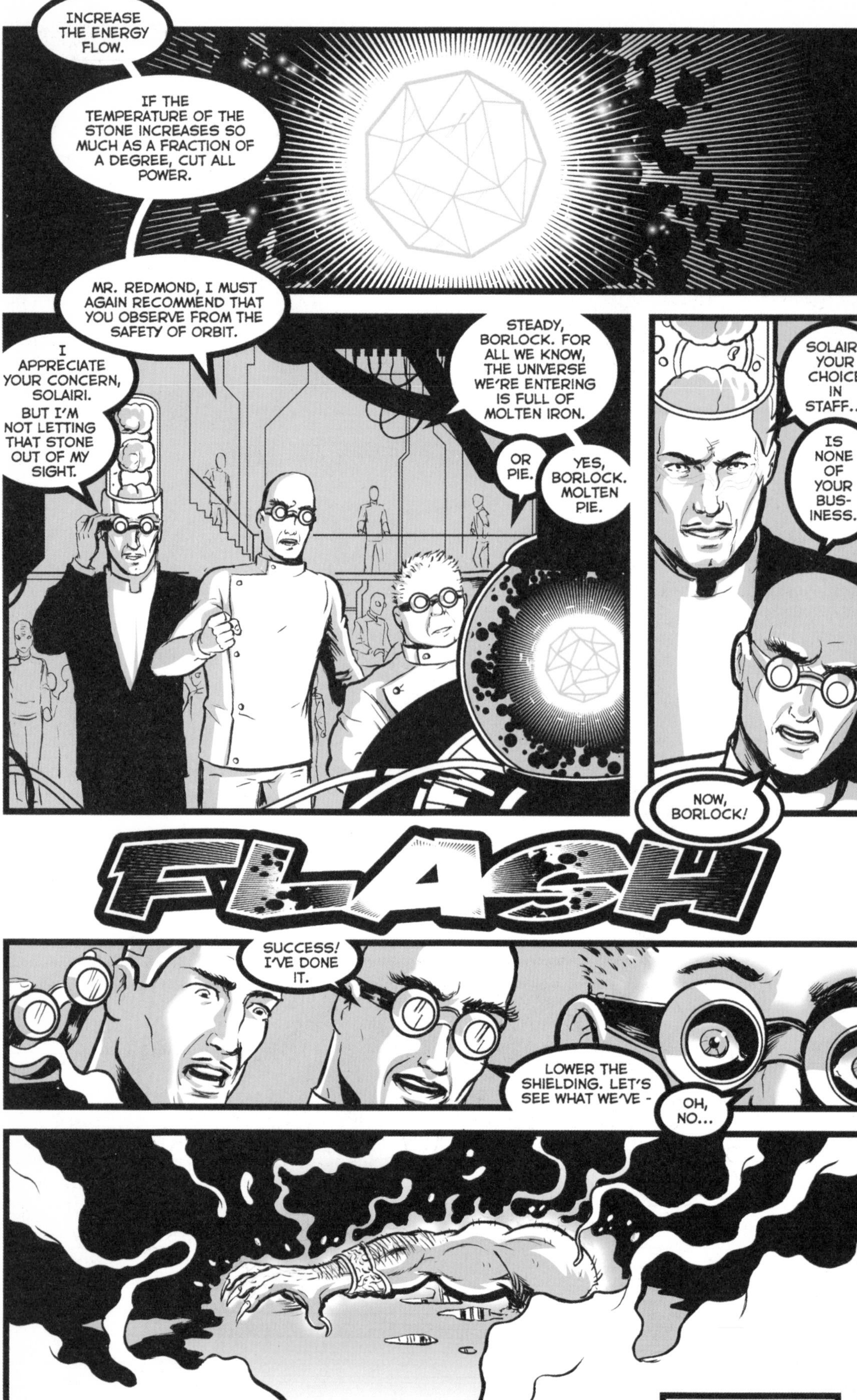
INCREASE THE ENERGY FLOW.
IF THE TEMPERATURE OF THE STONE INCREASES SO MUCH AS A FRACTION OF A DEGREE, CUT ALL POWER.
MR. REDMOND, I MUST AGAIN RECOMMEND THAT YOU OBSERVE FROM THE SAFETY OF ORBIT.
I APPRECIATE YOUR CONCERN, SOLAIRI.
BUT I'M NOT LETTING THAT STONE OUT OF MY SIGHT.
STEADY, BORLOCK. FOR ALL WE KNOW, THE UNIVERSE WE'RE ENTERING IS FULL OF MOLTEN IRON.
OR PIE.
YES, BORLOCK. MOLTEN PIE.
SOLAIRI, YOUR CHOICE IN STAFF...
IS NONE OF YOUR BUS-INESS.
NOW, BORLOCK!
FLASH
SUCCESS! I'VE DONE IT.
LOWER THE SHIELDING. LET'S SEE WHAT WE'VE -
OH, NO...
TO BE CONTINUED...

PREVIOUSLY

WHEN SOMEONE BROKE INTO THE HIGH-SECURITY FABER MUSEUM AND STOLE THE MYSTERIOUS STONE OF XEBROB, ARGOSY SMITH WAS THE PRIMARY SUSPECT. TO CLEAR HIS NAME, ARGOSY AND HIS PAL THEREMIN TRACKED DOWN THE REAL THIEF, MOOCH THE GLOBBIN.

HAVING FOUND THE STOLEN STONE AND DISCOVERING IT TO BE A FAKE, ARGOSY, THEREMIN, MOOCH AND MOOCH'S PILOT PETRA LEFT THE PLANET ONLY TO BE IMMEDIATELY SURROUNDED BY A VERY IMPOSING ALIEN FLEET.

APPARENTLY, THE STONE OF XEBROB WASN'T THE ONLY THING MOOCH STOLE...

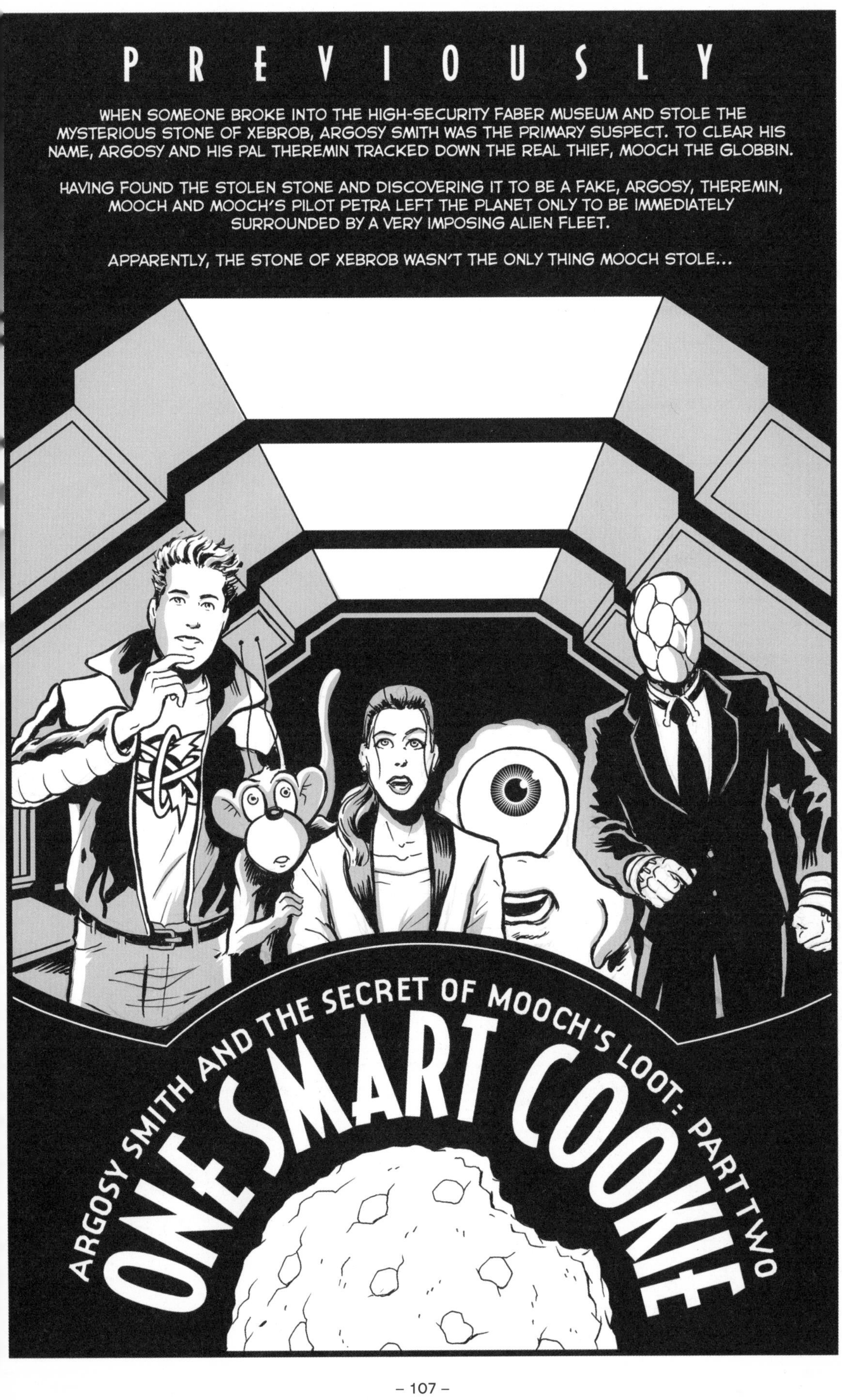
ARGOSY SMITH AND THE SECRET OF MOOCH'S LOOT: PART TWO
ONE SMART COOKIE

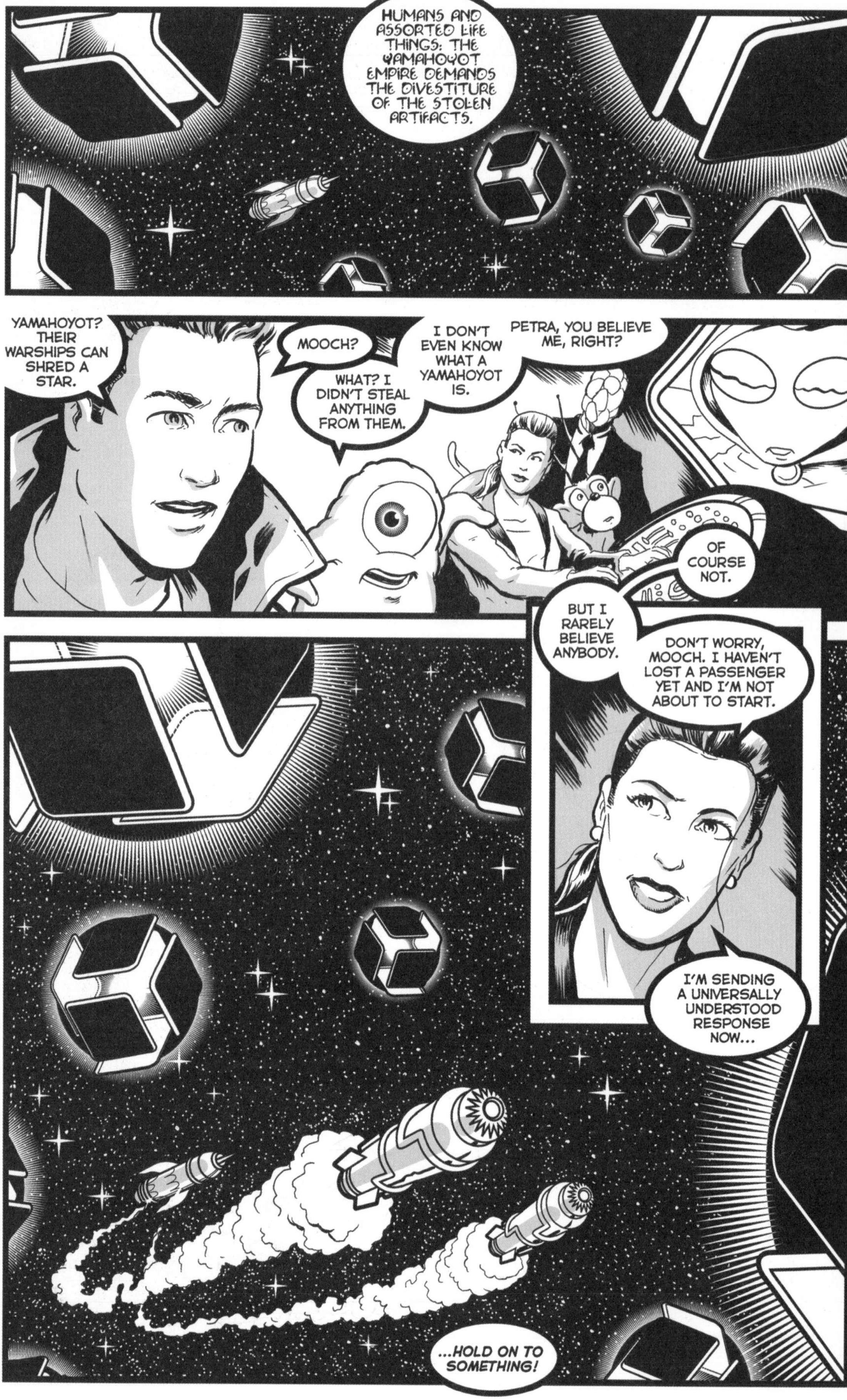
HUMANS AND ASSORTED LIFE THINGS: THE YAMAHOYOT EMPIRE DEMANDS THE DIVESTITURE OF THE STOLEN ARTIFACTS.
YAMAHOYOT? THEIR WARSHIPS CAN SHRED A STAR.
MOOCH?
WHAT? I DIDN'T STEAL ANYTHING FROM THEM.
I DON'T EVEN KNOW WHAT A YAMAHOYOT IS.
PETRA, YOU BELIEVE ME, RIGHT?
OF COURSE NOT.
BUT I RARELY BELIEVE ANYBODY.
DON'T WORRY, MOOCH. I HAVEN'T LOST A PASSENGER YET AND I'M NOT ABOUT TO START.
I'M SENDING A UNIVERSALLY UNDERSTOOD RESPONSE NOW...
...HOLD ON TO SOMETHING!

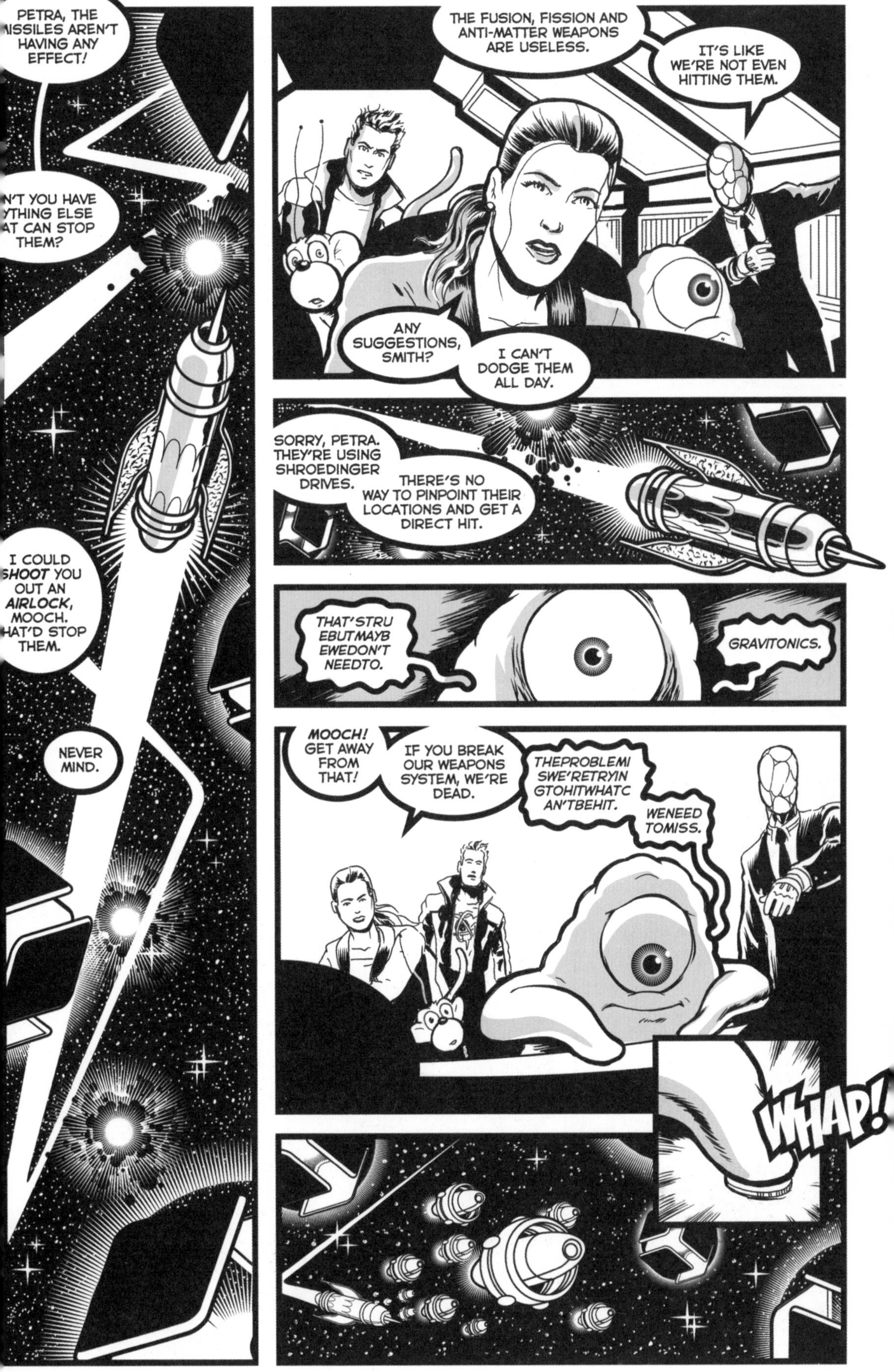
PETRA, THE ISSILES AREN'T HAVING ANY EFFECT!
N'T YOU HAVE YTHING ELSE AT CAN STOP THEM?
I COULD *SHOOT* YOU OUT AN *AIRLOCK*, MOOCH. HAT'D STOP THEM.
NEVER MIND.
THE FUSION, FISSION AND ANTI-MATTER WEAPONS ARE USELESS.
IT'S LIKE WE'RE NOT EVEN HITTING THEM.
ANY SUGGESTIONS, SMITH?
I CAN'T DODGE THEM ALL DAY.
SORRY, PETRA. THEY'RE USING SHROEDINGER DRIVES.
THERE'S NO WAY TO PINPOINT THEIR LOCATIONS AND GET A DIRECT HIT.
THAT'STRU EBUTMAYB EWEDON'T NEEDTO.
GRAVITONICS.
MOOCH! GET AWAY FROM THAT!
IF YOU BREAK OUR WEAPONS SYSTEM, WE'RE DEAD.
THEPROBLEMI SWE'RETRYIN GTOHITWHATC AN'TBEHIT.
WENEED TOMISS.
WHAP!

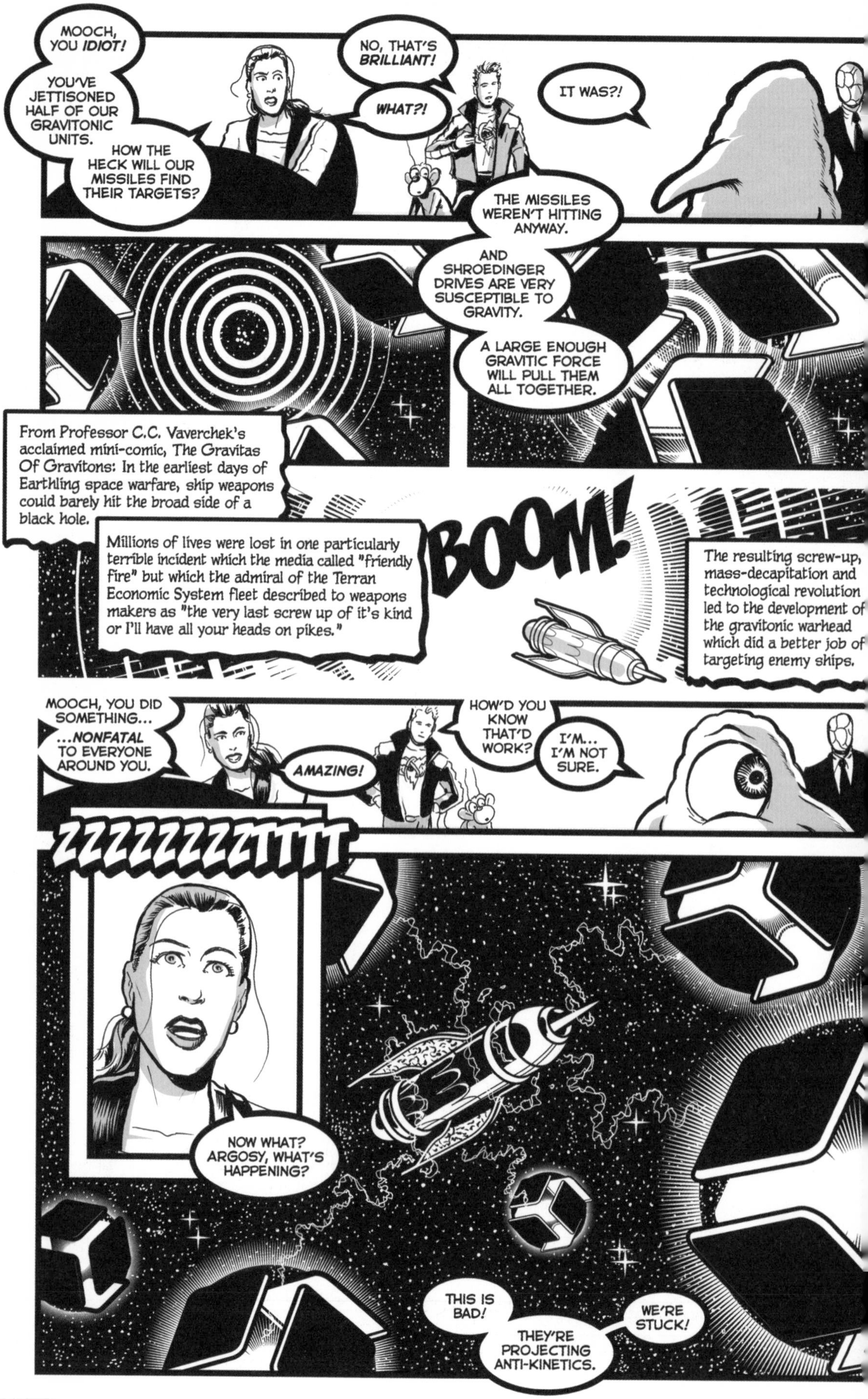
MOOCH, YOU IDIOT!
YOU'VE JETTISONED HALF OF OUR GRAVITONIC UNITS.
HOW THE HECK WILL OUR MISSILES FIND THEIR TARGETS?
NO, THAT'S BRILLIANT!
WHAT?!
IT WAS?!
THE MISSILES WEREN'T HITTING ANYWAY.
AND SHROEDINGER DRIVES ARE VERY SUSCEPTIBLE TO GRAVITY.
A LARGE ENOUGH GRAVITIC FORCE WILL PULL THEM ALL TOGETHER.
From Professor C.C. Vaverchek's acclaimed mini-comic, The Gravitas Of Gravitons: In the earliest days of Earthling space warfare, ship weapons could barely hit the broad side of a black hole.
Millions of lives were lost in one particularly terrible incident which the media called "friendly fire" but which the admiral of the Terran Economic System fleet described to weapons makers as "the very last screw up of it's kind or I'll have all your heads on pikes."
BOOM!
The resulting screw-up, mass-decapitation and technological revolution led to the development of the gravitonic warhead which did a better job of targeting enemy ships.
MOOCH, YOU DID SOMETHING... ...NONFATAL TO EVERYONE AROUND YOU.
AMAZING!
HOW'D YOU KNOW THAT'D WORK?
I'M... I'M NOT SURE.
ZZZZZZZZZTTTT
NOW WHAT? ARGOSY, WHAT'S HAPPENING?
THIS IS BAD!
THEY'RE PROJECTING ANTI-KINETICS.
WE'RE STUCK!

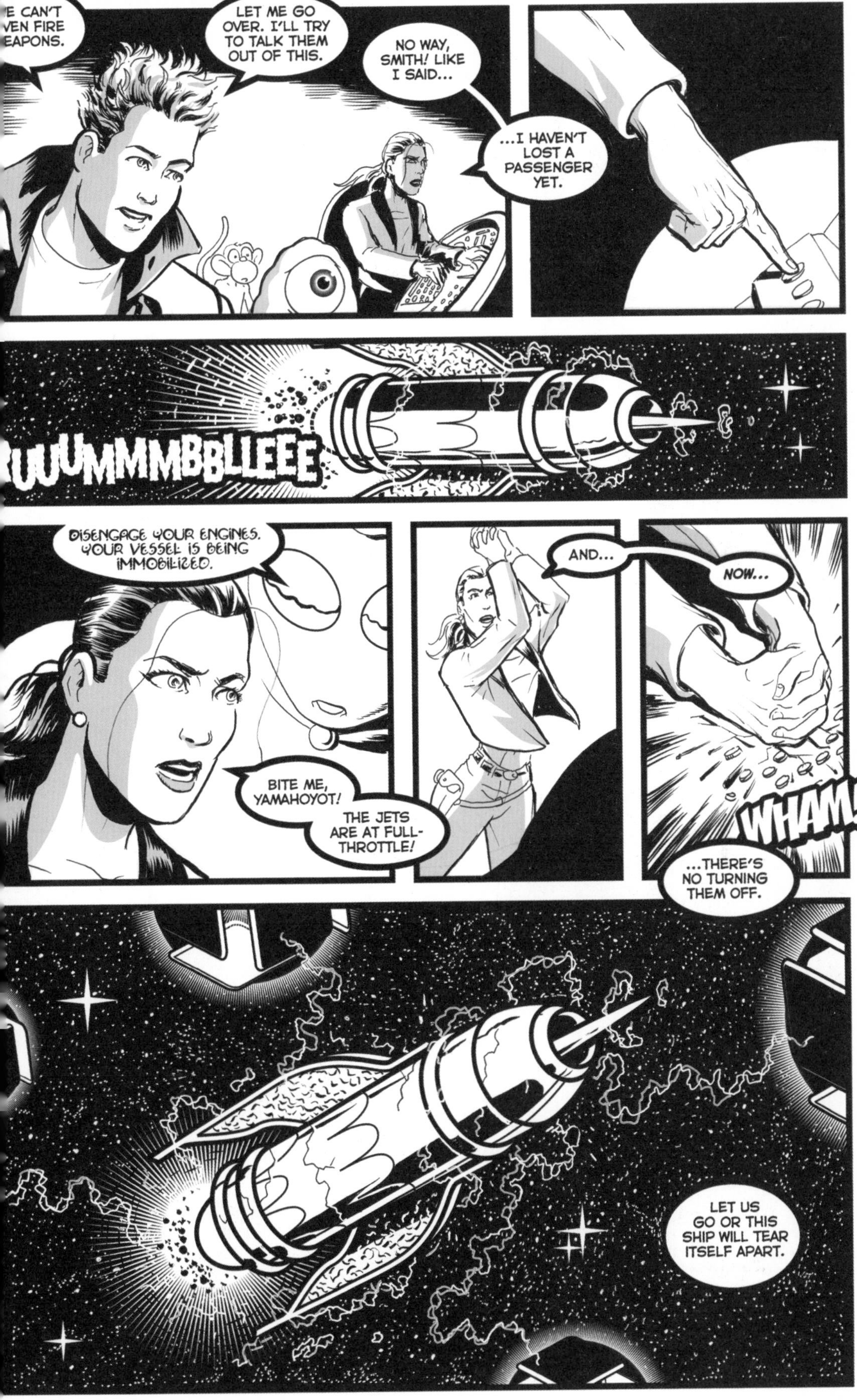
E CAN'T
VEN FIRE
EAPONS.
LET ME GO OVER. I'LL TRY TO TALK THEM OUT OF THIS.
NO WAY, SMITH! LIKE I SAID...
...I HAVEN'T LOST A PASSENGER YET.
UUUMMMBBLLEEE
DISENGAGE YOUR ENGINES. YOUR VESSEL IS BEING IMMOBILIZED.
BITE ME, YAMAHOYOT!
THE JETS ARE AT FULL-THROTTLE!
AND...
NOW...
WHAM!
...THERE'S NO TURNING THEM OFF.
LET US GO OR THIS SHIP WILL TEAR ITSELF APART.

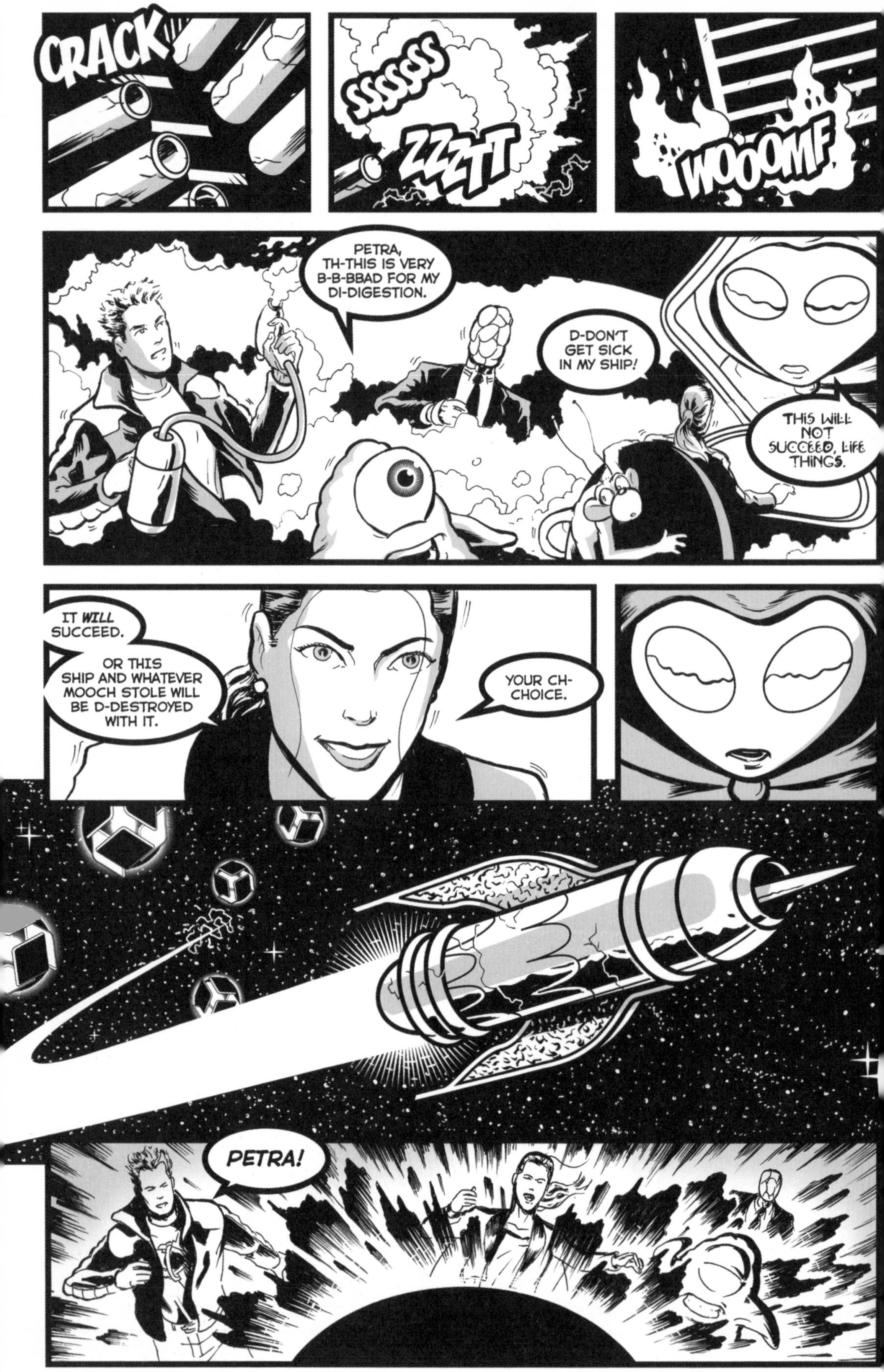

CRACK
SSSSSS
ZZZTT
WOOOMF
PETRA, TH-THIS IS VERY B-B-BBAD FOR MY DI-DIGESTION.
D-DON'T GET SICK IN MY SHIP!
THIS WILL NOT SUCCEED, LIFE THINGS.
IT *WILL* SUCCEED.
OR THIS SHIP AND WHATEVER MOOCH STOLE WILL BE D-DESTROYED WITH IT.
YOUR CH-CHOICE.
PETRA!

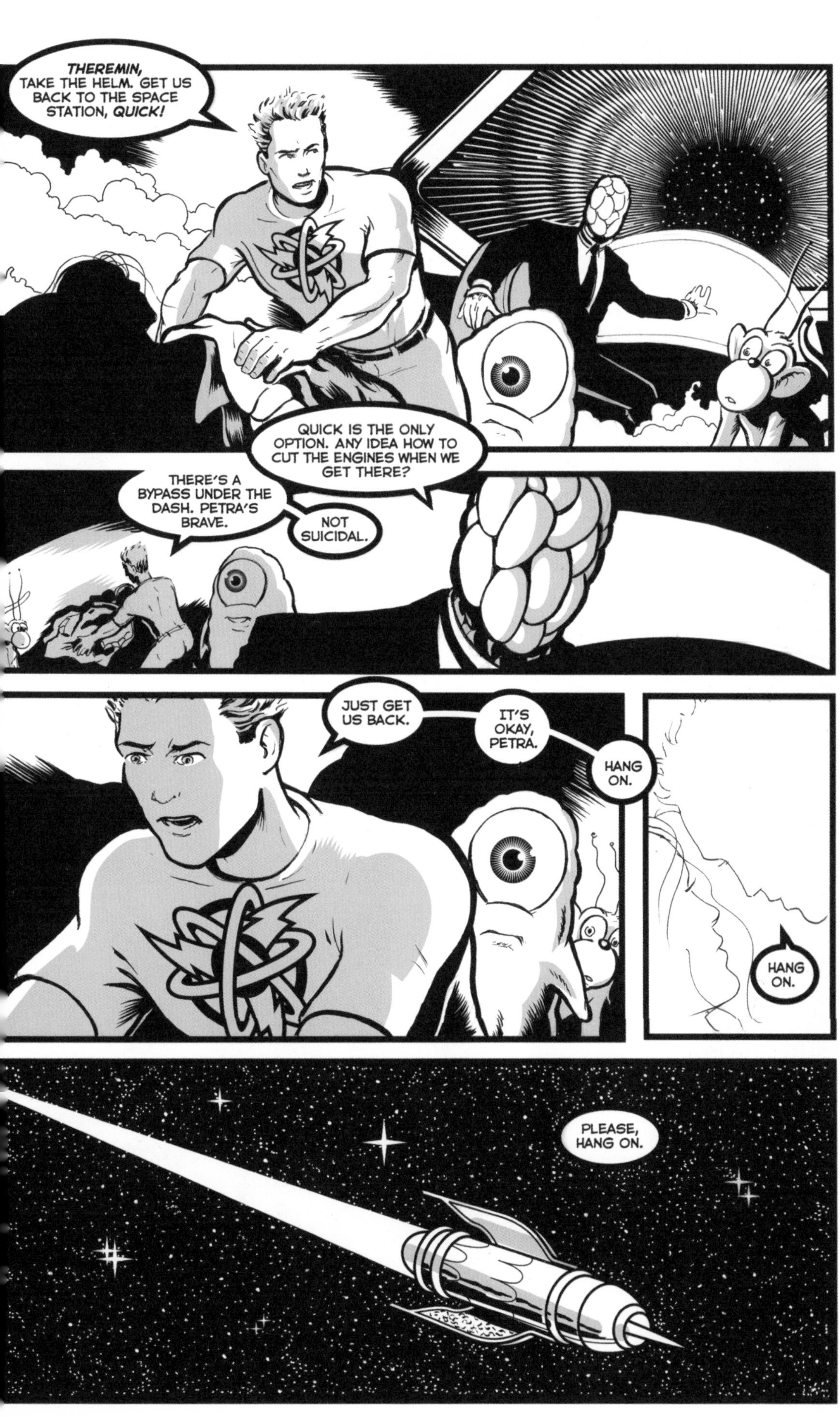
THEREMIN, TAKE THE HELM. GET US BACK TO THE SPACE STATION, QUICK!
QUICK IS THE ONLY OPTION. ANY IDEA HOW TO CUT THE ENGINES WHEN WE GET THERE?
THERE'S A BYPASS UNDER THE DASH. PETRA'S BRAVE.
NOT SUICIDAL.
JUST GET US BACK.
IT'S OKAY, PETRA.
HANG ON.
HANG ON.
PLEASE, HANG ON.

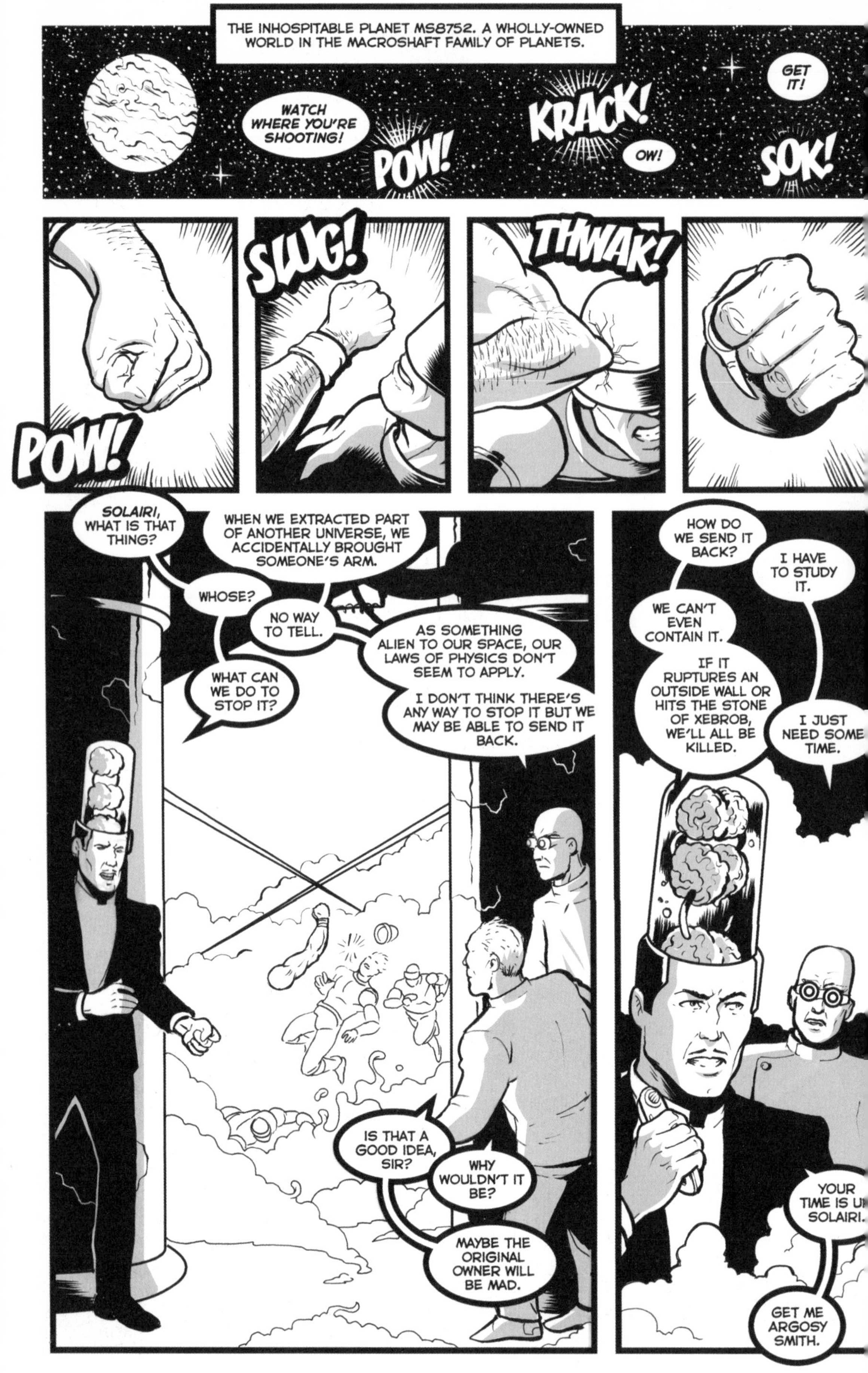

THE INHOSPITABLE PLANET MS8752. A WHOLLY-OWNED WORLD IN THE MACROSHAFT FAMILY OF PLANETS.
WATCH WHERE YOU'RE SHOOTING!
POW!
KRACK!
OW!
GET IT!
SOK!
POW!
SWG!
THWAK!
SOLAIRI, WHAT IS THAT THING?
WHEN WE EXTRACTED PART OF ANOTHER UNIVERSE, WE ACCIDENTALLY BROUGHT SOMEONE'S ARM.
WHOSE?
NO WAY TO TELL.
AS SOMETHING ALIEN TO OUR SPACE, OUR LAWS OF PHYSICS DON'T SEEM TO APPLY.
WHAT CAN WE DO TO STOP IT?
I DON'T THINK THERE'S ANY WAY TO STOP IT BUT WE MAY BE ABLE TO SEND IT BACK.
IS THAT A GOOD IDEA, SIR?
WHY WOULDN'T IT BE?
MAYBE THE ORIGINAL OWNER WILL BE MAD.
HOW DO WE SEND IT BACK?
I HAVE TO STUDY IT.
WE CAN'T EVEN CONTAIN IT.
IF IT RUPTURES AN OUTSIDE WALL OR HITS THE STONE OF XEBROB, WE'LL ALL BE KILLED.
I JUST NEED SOME TIME.
YOUR TIME IS U
SOLAIRI.
GET ME ARGOSY SMITH.

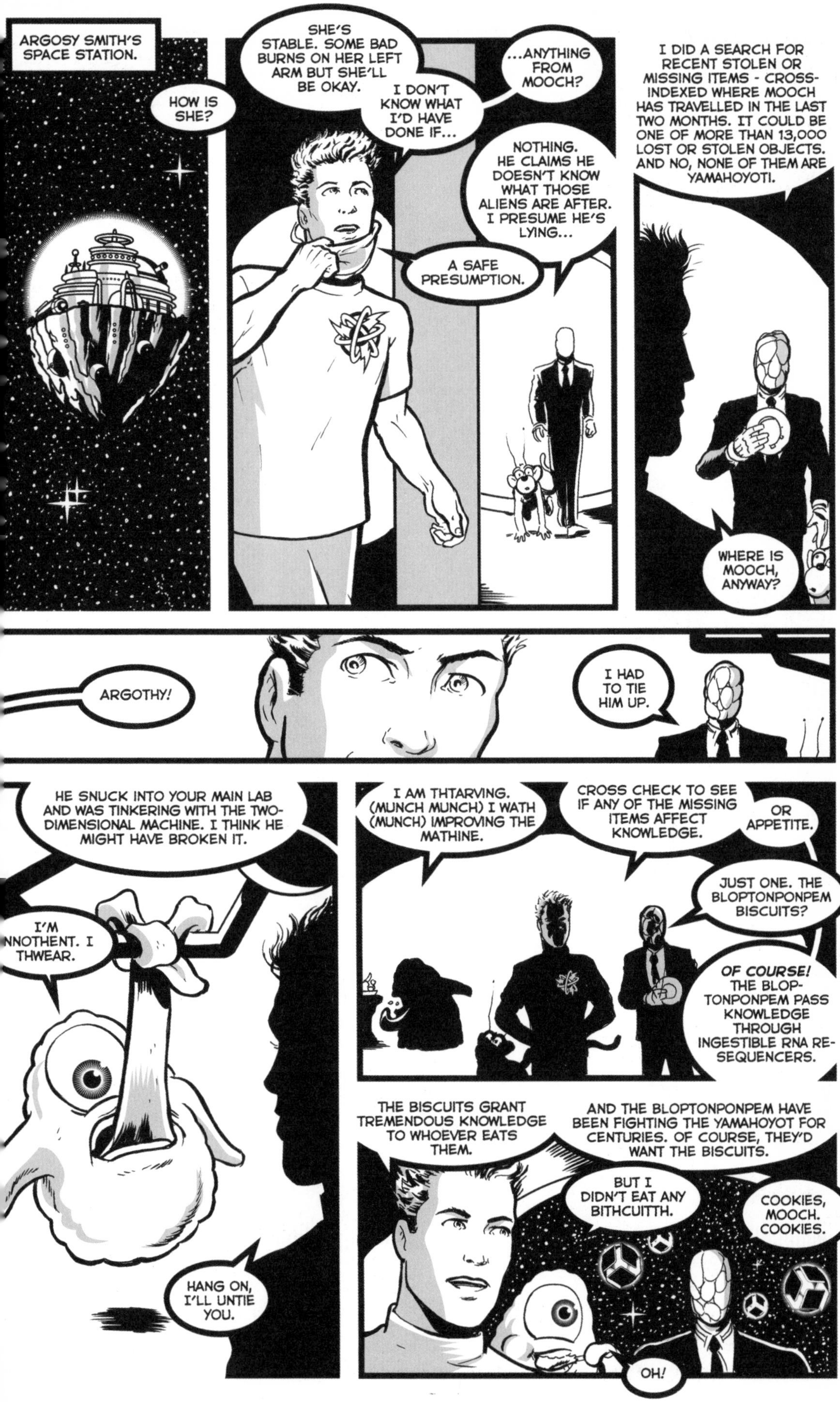
ARGOSY SMITH'S SPACE STATION.
HOW IS SHE?
SHE'S STABLE. SOME BAD BURNS ON HER LEFT ARM BUT SHE'LL BE OKAY.
I DON'T KNOW WHAT I'D HAVE DONE IF...
...ANYTHING FROM MOOCH?
NOTHING. HE CLAIMS HE DOESN'T KNOW WHAT THOSE ALIENS ARE AFTER. I PRESUME HE'S LYING...
A SAFE PRESUMPTION.
I DID A SEARCH FOR RECENT STOLEN OR MISSING ITEMS - CROSS-INDEXED WHERE MOOCH HAS TRAVELLED IN THE LAST TWO MONTHS. IT COULD BE ONE OF MORE THAN 13,000 LOST OR STOLEN OBJECTS. AND NO, NONE OF THEM ARE YAMAHOYOTI.
WHERE IS MOOCH, ANYWAY?
ARGOTHY!
I HAD TO TIE HIM UP.
HE SNUCK INTO YOUR MAIN LAB AND WAS TINKERING WITH THE TWO-DIMENSIONAL MACHINE. I THINK HE MIGHT HAVE BROKEN IT.
I'M NNOTHENT. I THWEAR.
HANG ON, I'LL UNTIE YOU.
I AM THTARVING. (MUNCH MUNCH) I WATH (MUNCH) IMPROVING THE MATHINE.
CROSS CHECK TO SEE IF ANY OF THE MISSING ITEMS AFFECT KNOWLEDGE.
OR APPETITE.
JUST ONE. THE BLOPTONPONPEM BISCUITS?
OF COURSE! THE BLOP-TONPONPEM PASS KNOWLEDGE THROUGH INGESTIBLE RNA RE-SEQUENCERS.
THE BISCUITS GRANT TREMENDOUS KNOWLEDGE TO WHOEVER EATS THEM.
AND THE BLOPTONPONPEM HAVE BEEN FIGHTING THE YAMAHOYOT FOR CENTURIES. OF COURSE, THEY'D WANT THE BISCUITS.
BUT I DIDN'T EAT ANY BITHCUITTH.
COOKIES, MOOCH. COOKIES.
OH!

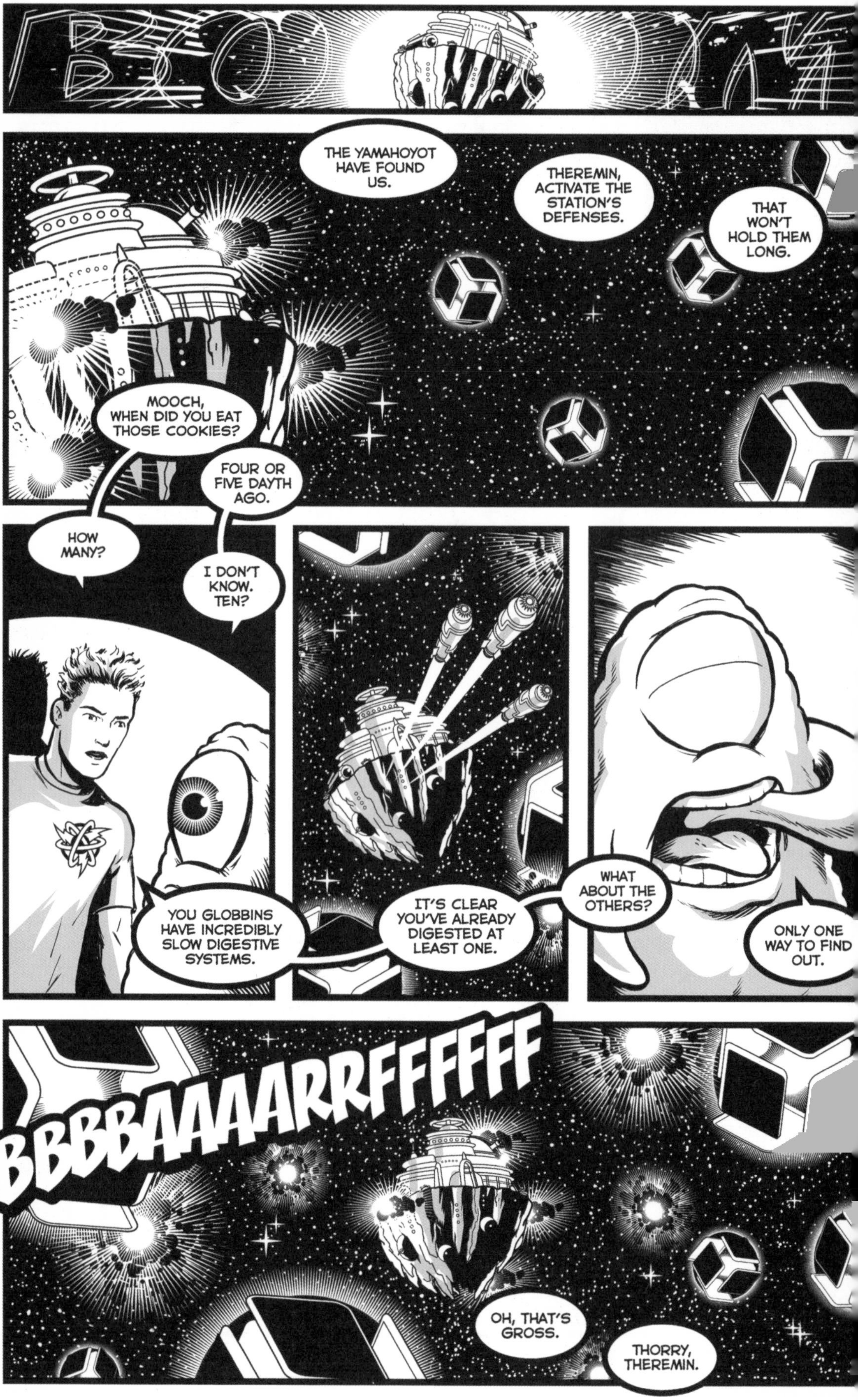
THE YAMAHOYOT HAVE FOUND US.
THEREMIN, ACTIVATE THE STATION'S DEFENSES.
THAT WON'T HOLD THEM LONG.
MOOCH, WHEN DID YOU EAT THOSE COOKIES?
FOUR OR FIVE DAYTH AGO.
HOW MANY?
I DON'T KNOW. TEN?
YOU GLOBBINS HAVE INCREDIBLY SLOW DIGESTIVE SYSTEMS.
IT'S CLEAR YOU'VE ALREADY DIGESTED AT LEAST ONE.
WHAT ABOUT THE OTHERS?
ONLY ONE WAY TO FIND OUT.
BBBBAAAARRFFFFFF
OH, THAT'S GROSS.
THORRY, THEREMIN.

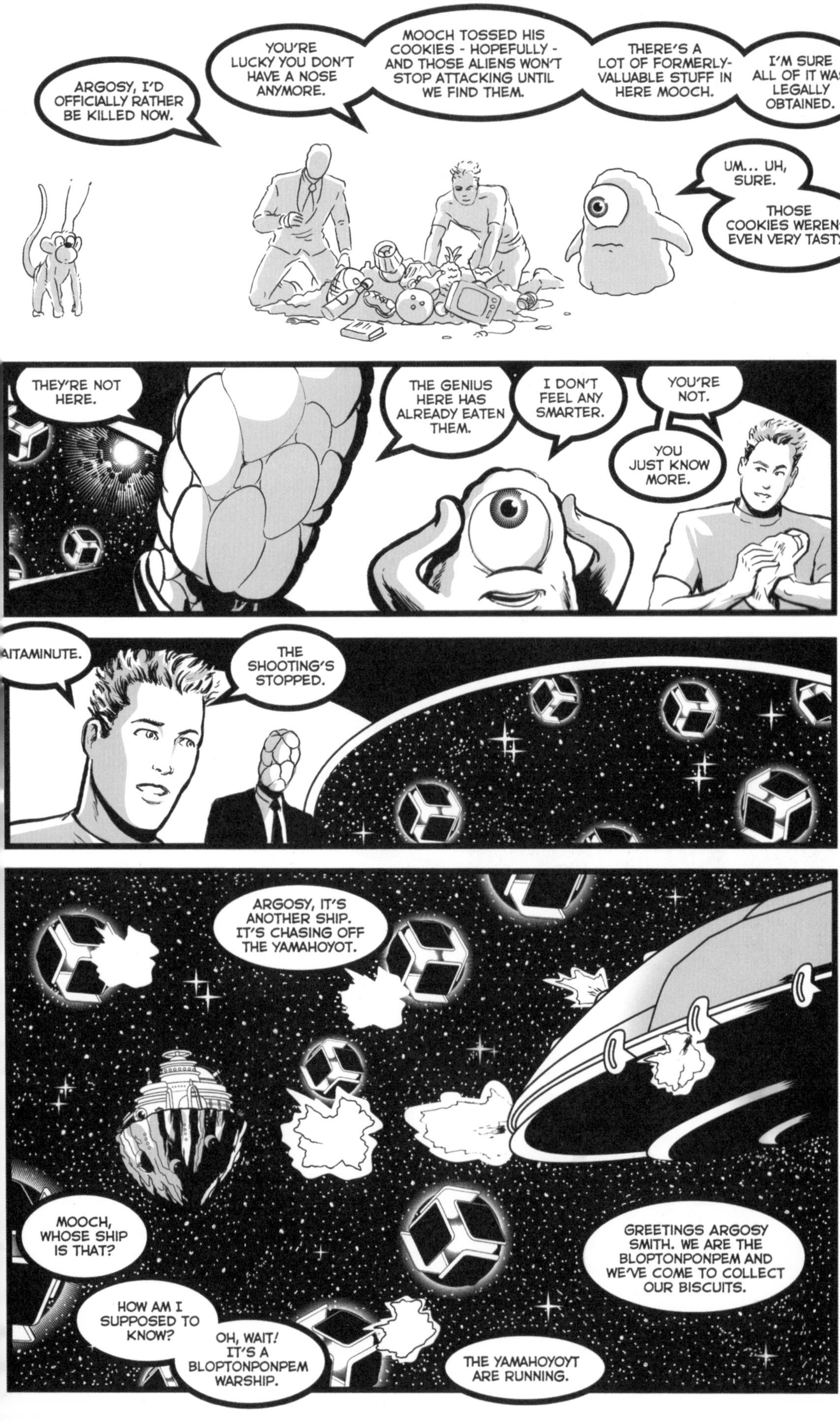

ARGOSY, I'D OFFICIALLY RATHER BE KILLED NOW.
YOU'RE LUCKY YOU DON'T HAVE A NOSE ANYMORE.
MOOCH TOSSED HIS COOKIES - HOPEFULLY - AND THOSE ALIENS WON'T STOP ATTACKING UNTIL WE FIND THEM.
THERE'S A LOT OF FORMERLY-VALUABLE STUFF IN HERE MOOCH.
I'M SURE ALL OF IT WAS LEGALLY OBTAINED.
UM... UH, SURE.
THOSE COOKIES WEREN'T EVEN VERY TASTY.
THEY'RE NOT HERE.
THE GENIUS HERE HAS ALREADY EATEN THEM.
I DON'T FEEL ANY SMARTER.
YOU'RE NOT.
YOU JUST KNOW MORE.
AITAMINUTE.
THE SHOOTING'S STOPPED.
ARGOSY, IT'S ANOTHER SHIP. IT'S CHASING OFF THE YAMAHOYOT.
MOOCH, WHOSE SHIP IS THAT?
HOW AM I SUPPOSED TO KNOW?
OH, WAIT! IT'S A BLOPTONPONPEM WARSHIP.
THE YAMAHOYOYT ARE RUNNING.
GREETINGS ARGOSY SMITH. WE ARE THE BLOPTONPONPEM AND WE'VE COME TO COLLECT OUR BISCUITS.

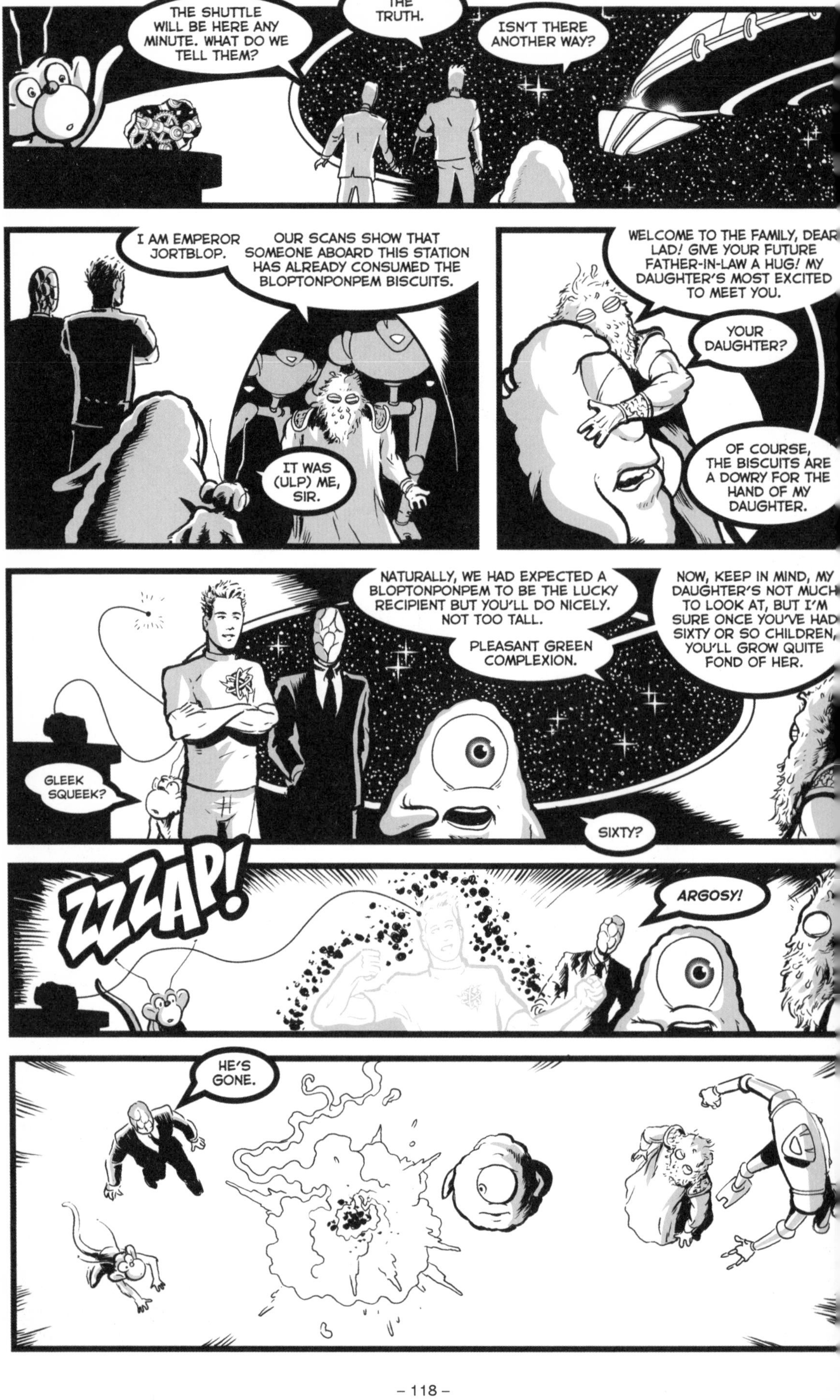
THE SHUTTLE WILL BE HERE ANY MINUTE. WHAT DO WE TELL THEM?
THE TRUTH.
ISN'T THERE ANOTHER WAY?
I AM EMPEROR JORTBLOP.
OUR SCANS SHOW THAT SOMEONE ABOARD THIS STATION HAS ALREADY CONSUMED THE BLOPTONPONPEM BISCUITS.
IT WAS (ULP) ME, SIR.
WELCOME TO THE FAMILY, DEAR LAD! GIVE YOUR FUTURE FATHER-IN-LAW A HUG! MY DAUGHTER'S MOST EXCITED TO MEET YOU.
YOUR DAUGHTER?
OF COURSE, THE BISCUITS ARE A DOWRY FOR THE HAND OF MY DAUGHTER.
NATURALLY, WE HAD EXPECTED A BLOPTONPONPEM TO BE THE LUCKY RECIPIENT BUT YOU'LL DO NICELY. NOT TOO TALL.
PLEASANT GREEN COMPLEXION.
NOW, KEEP IN MIND, MY DAUGHTER'S NOT MUCH TO LOOK AT, BUT I'M SURE ONCE YOU'VE HAD SIXTY OR SO CHILDREN, YOU'LL GROW QUITE FOND OF HER.
GLEEK SQUEEK?
SIXTY?
ZZZAP!
ARGOSY!
HE'S GONE.

OH, GREAT!

FLOATING ALONE IN A FEATURELESS VOID.

AGAIN.

ARGOSY SMITH
SCIENTIST, EXPLORER, TROUBLE MAGNET

THEREMIN
ARGOSY'S PAL, ANTIQUE DEALER, LIVING LAVA LAMP

PETRA VAVERCHEK
PILOT-FOR-HIRE, FORMER SOLDIER

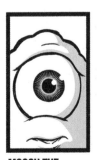

MOOCH THE GLOBBIN
THIEF, LUCKY TO BE ALIVE

REDMOND
C.E.O. OF THE MACROSHAFT CORPORATION

AND A SPACE MONKEY

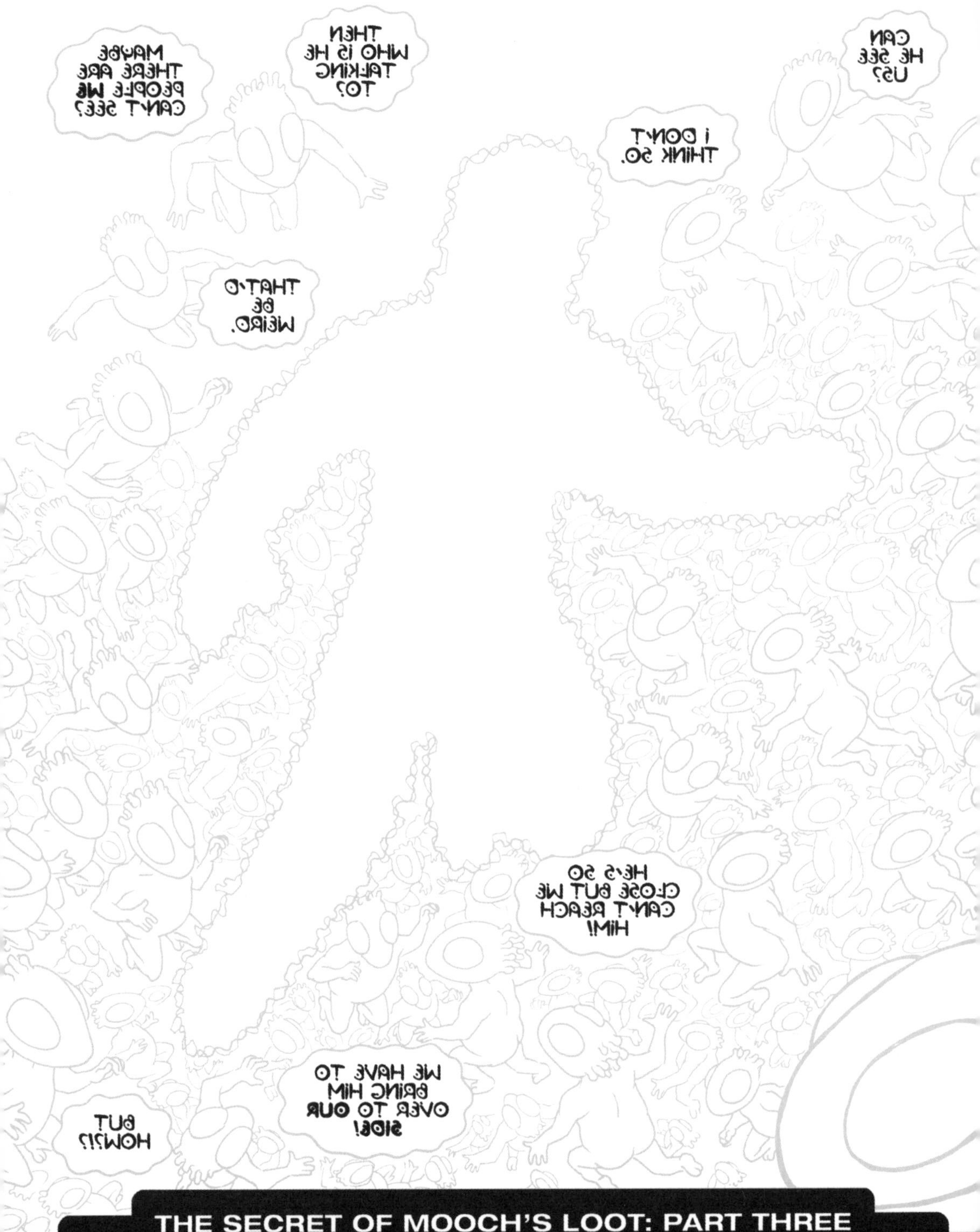
CAN HE SEE US?
I DON'T THINK SO.
THEN WHO IS HE TALKING TO?
MAYBE THERE ARE PEOPLE WE CAN'T SEE?
THAT'D BE WEIRD.
HE'S SO CLOSE BUT WE CAN'T REACH HIM!
WE HAVE TO BRING HIM OVER TO OUR SIDE!
BUT HOW?!

THE SECRET OF MOOCH'S LOOT: PART THREE

ACROSS THE SECOND DIMENSION

WHEN SOMEONE BROKE IN TO THE FABER 2B MUSEUM AND STOLE THE MYSTERIOUS AND POWERFUL STONE OF XEBROB, INVENTOR AND ADVENTURER ARGOSY SMITH WAS THE PRIMARY SUSPECT. TO CLEAR HIS NAME, ARGOSY AND HIS PAL THEREMIN TRACKED DOWN THE REAL THIEF, MOOCH THE GLOBBIN.

AFTER DISCOVERING THE STOLEN STONE TO BE A FAKE, ARGOSY, THEREMIN, BLOOP, MOOCH AND MOOCH'S PILOT PETRA FOUND THEMSELVES ATTACKED BY AN ALIEN ARMADA LOOKING FOR SOMETHING ELSE MOOCH HAD STOLEN - THE KNOWLEDGE-GRANTING BISCUITS OF BLOPTONPONPEM. THE ATTACKING ALIENS WERE CHASED OFF BY THE BLOPTONPONPEM FLEET BUT NOT BEFORE PETRA WAS INJURED.

UNFORTUNATELY FOR ALL INVOLVED, MOOCH HAD ALREADY EATEN THE BISCUITS - A CONDITION OF WHICH IS THAT HE MUST NOW MARRY THE BLOPTONPONPEM EMPEROR'S DAUGHTER.

AND AS IF THINGS WEREN'T COMPLICATED ENOUGH, ARGOSY SMITH JUST VANISHED.

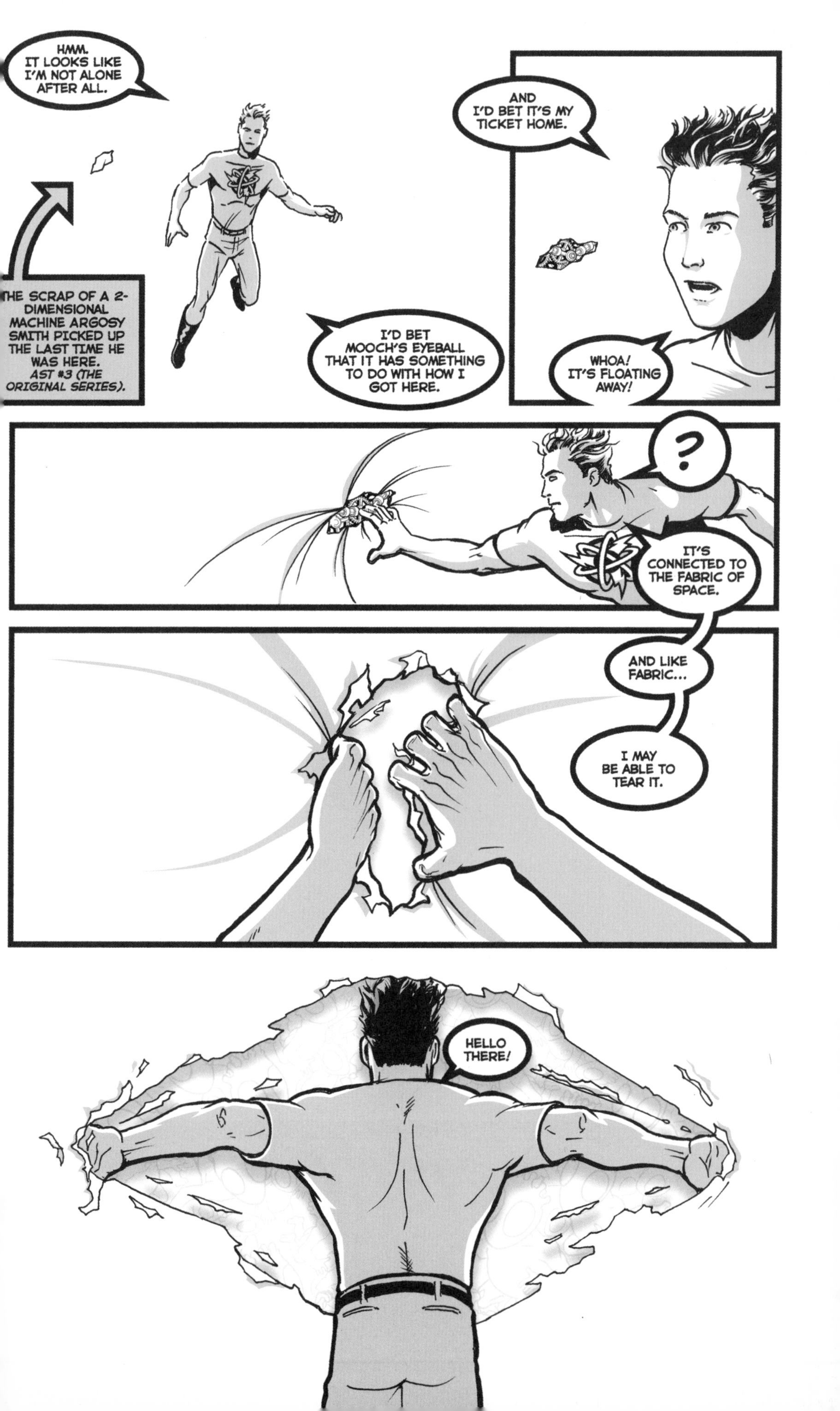

HMM. IT LOOKS LIKE I'M NOT ALONE AFTER ALL.
THE SCRAP OF A 2-DIMENSIONAL MACHINE ARGOSY SMITH PICKED UP THE LAST TIME HE WAS HERE. AST #3 (THE ORIGINAL SERIES).
I'D BET MOOCH'S EYEBALL THAT IT HAS SOMETHING TO DO WITH HOW I GOT HERE.
AND I'D BET IT'S MY TICKET HOME.
WHOA! IT'S FLOATING AWAY!
?
IT'S CONNECTED TO THE FABRIC OF SPACE.
AND LIKE FABRIC...
I MAY BE ABLE TO TEAR IT.
HELLO THERE!

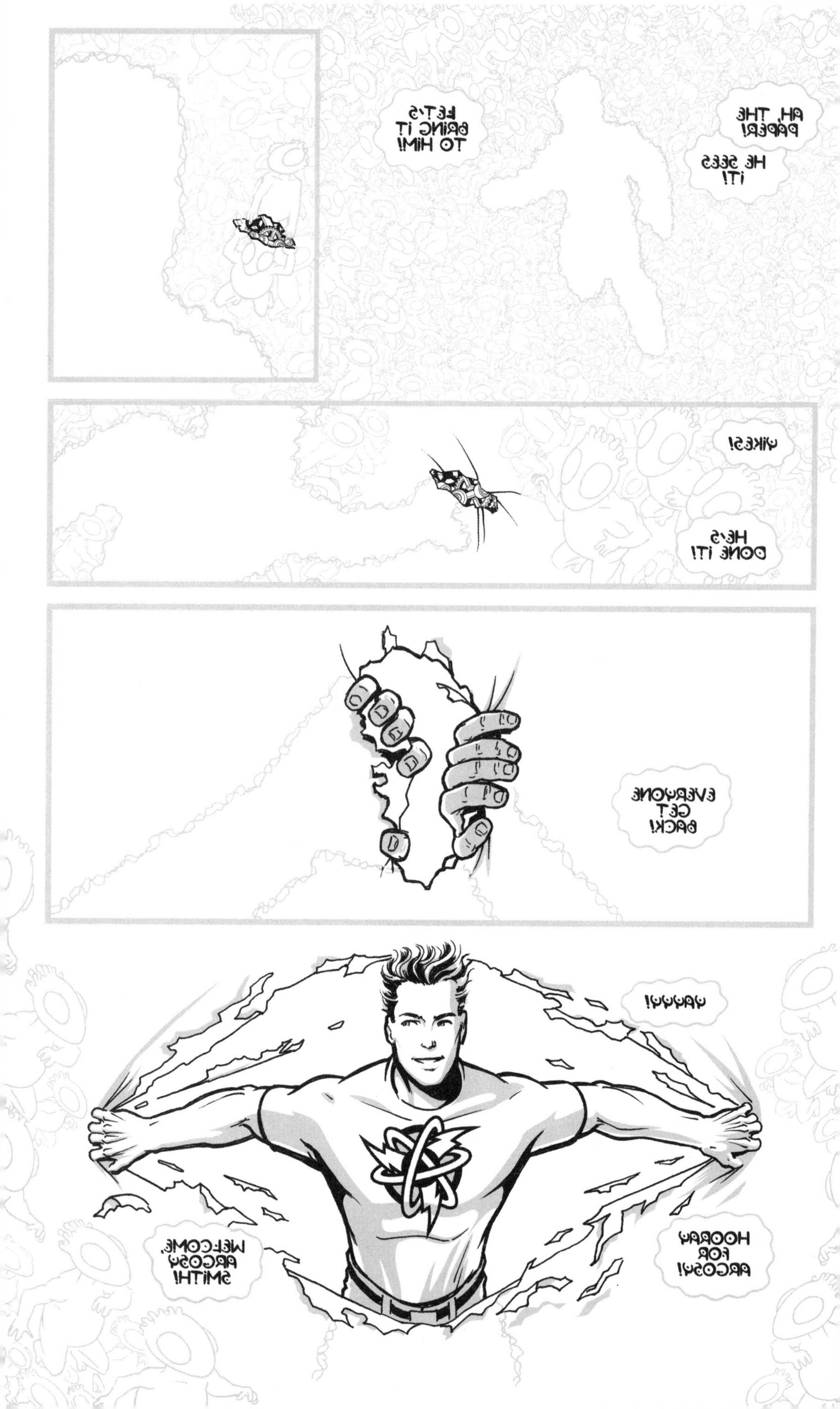
AH, THE PAPER!
HE SEES IT!
LET'S BRING IT TO HIM!
YIKES!
HE'S DONE IT!
EVERYONE GET BACK!
YAAAY!
HOORAY FOR ARGOSY!
WELCOME, ARGOSY SMITH!

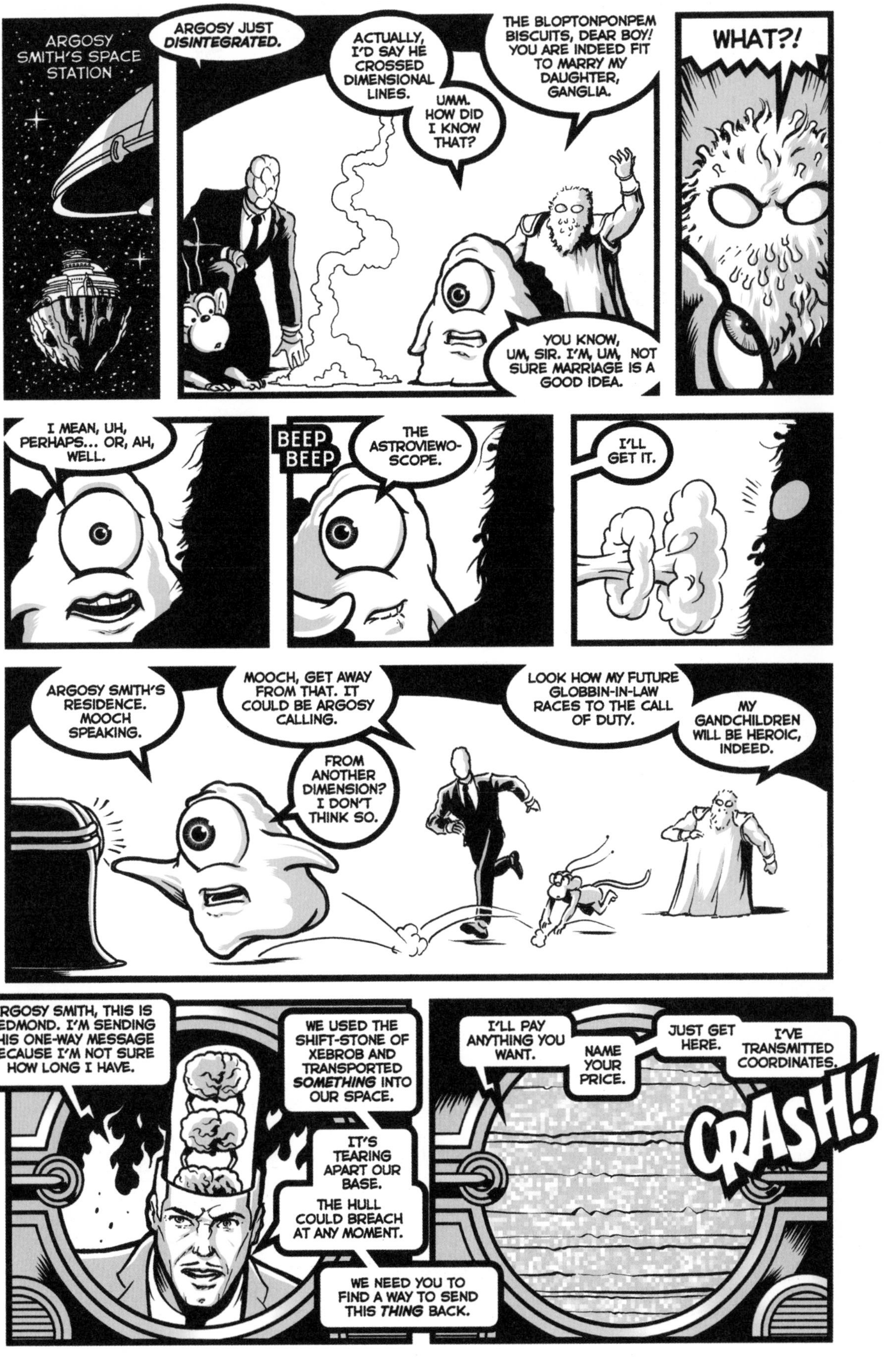
ARGOSY SMITH'S SPACE STATION
ARGOSY JUST DISINTEGRATED.
ACTUALLY, I'D SAY HE CROSSED DIMENSIONAL LINES.
UMM. HOW DID I KNOW THAT?
THE BLOPTONPONPEM BISCUITS, DEAR BOY! YOU ARE INDEED FIT TO MARRY MY DAUGHTER, GANGLIA.
YOU KNOW, UM, SIR. I'M, UM, NOT SURE MARRIAGE IS A GOOD IDEA.
WHAT?!
I MEAN, UH, PERHAPS... OR, AH, WELL.
BEEP BEEP
THE ASTROVIEWO-SCOPE.
I'LL GET IT.
ARGOSY SMITH'S RESIDENCE. MOOCH SPEAKING.
MOOCH, GET AWAY FROM THAT. IT COULD BE ARGOSY CALLING.
FROM ANOTHER DIMENSION? I DON'T THINK SO.
LOOK HOW MY FUTURE GLOBBIN-IN-LAW RACES TO THE CALL OF DUTY.
MY GANDCHILDREN WILL BE HEROIC, INDEED.
ARGOSY SMITH, THIS IS REDMOND. I'M SENDING THIS ONE-WAY MESSAGE BECAUSE I'M NOT SURE HOW LONG I HAVE.
WE USED THE SHIFT-STONE OF XEBROB AND TRANSPORTED SOMETHING INTO OUR SPACE.
IT'S TEARING APART OUR BASE.
THE HULL COULD BREACH AT ANY MOMENT.
WE NEED YOU TO FIND A WAY TO SEND THIS THING BACK.
I'LL PAY ANYTHING YOU WANT.
NAME YOUR PRICE.
JUST GET HERE.
I'VE TRANSMITTED COORDINATES.
CRASH!

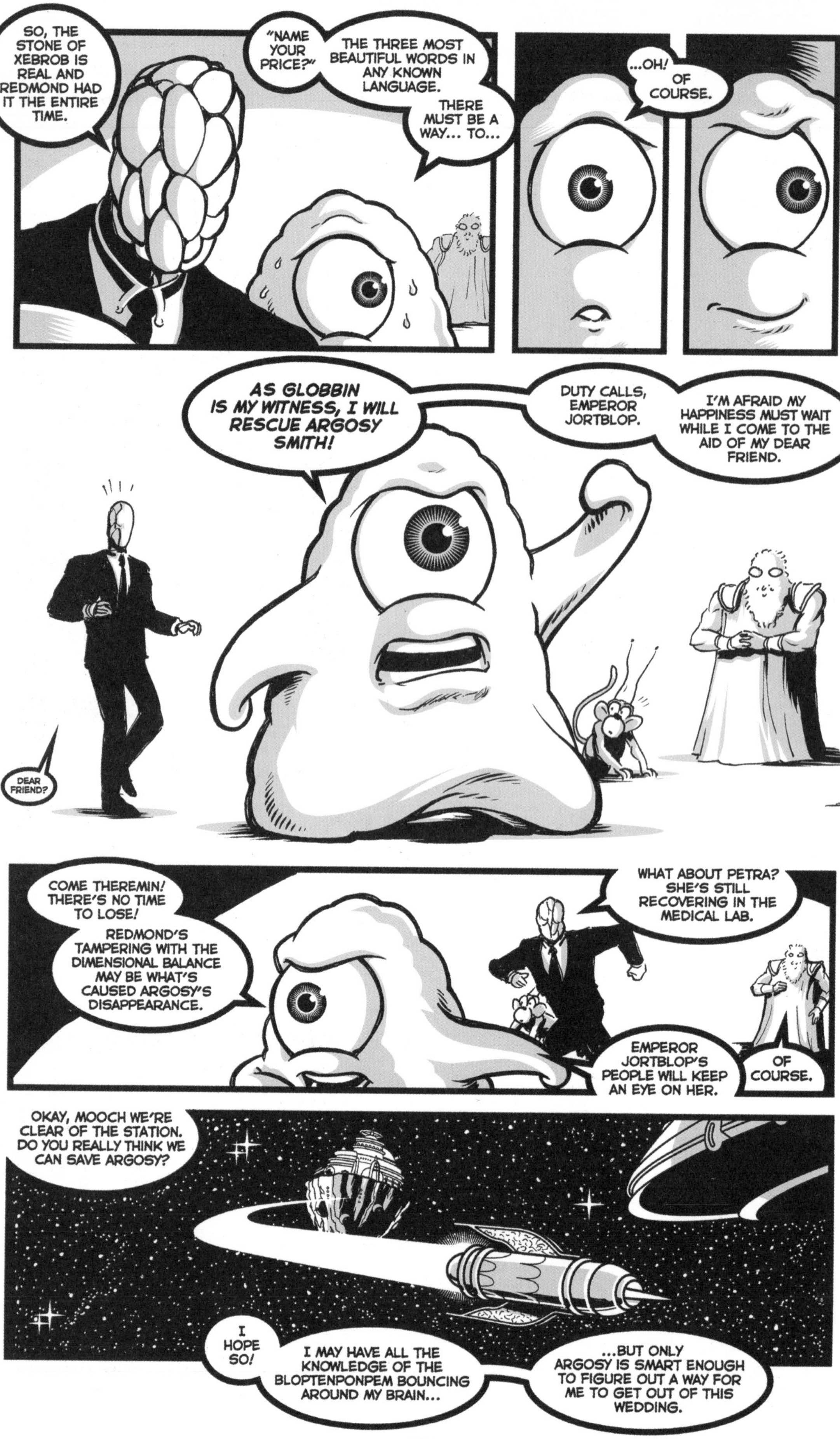
SO, THE STONE OF XEBROB IS REAL AND REDMOND HAD IT THE ENTIRE TIME.
"NAME YOUR PRICE?"
THE THREE MOST BEAUTIFUL WORDS IN ANY KNOWN LANGUAGE.
THERE MUST BE A WAY... TO...
...OH! OF COURSE.
AS GLOBBIN IS MY WITNESS, I WILL RESCUE ARGOSY SMITH!
DUTY CALLS, EMPEROR JORTBLOP.
I'M AFRAID MY HAPPINESS MUST WAIT WHILE I COME TO THE AID OF MY DEAR FRIEND.
DEAR FRIEND?
COME THEREMIN! THERE'S NO TIME TO LOSE!
REDMOND'S TAMPERING WITH THE DIMENSIONAL BALANCE MAY BE WHAT'S CAUSED ARGOSY'S DISAPPEARANCE.
WHAT ABOUT PETRA? SHE'S STILL RECOVERING IN THE MEDICAL LAB.
EMPEROR JORTBLOP'S PEOPLE WILL KEEP AN EYE ON HER.
OF COURSE.
OKAY, MOOCH WE'RE CLEAR OF THE STATION. DO YOU REALLY THINK WE CAN SAVE ARGOSY?
I HOPE SO!
I MAY HAVE ALL THE KNOWLEDGE OF THE BLOPTENPONPEM BOUNCING AROUND MY BRAIN...
...BUT ONLY ARGOSY IS SMART ENOUGH TO FIGURE OUT A WAY FOR ME TO GET OUT OF THIS WEDDING.

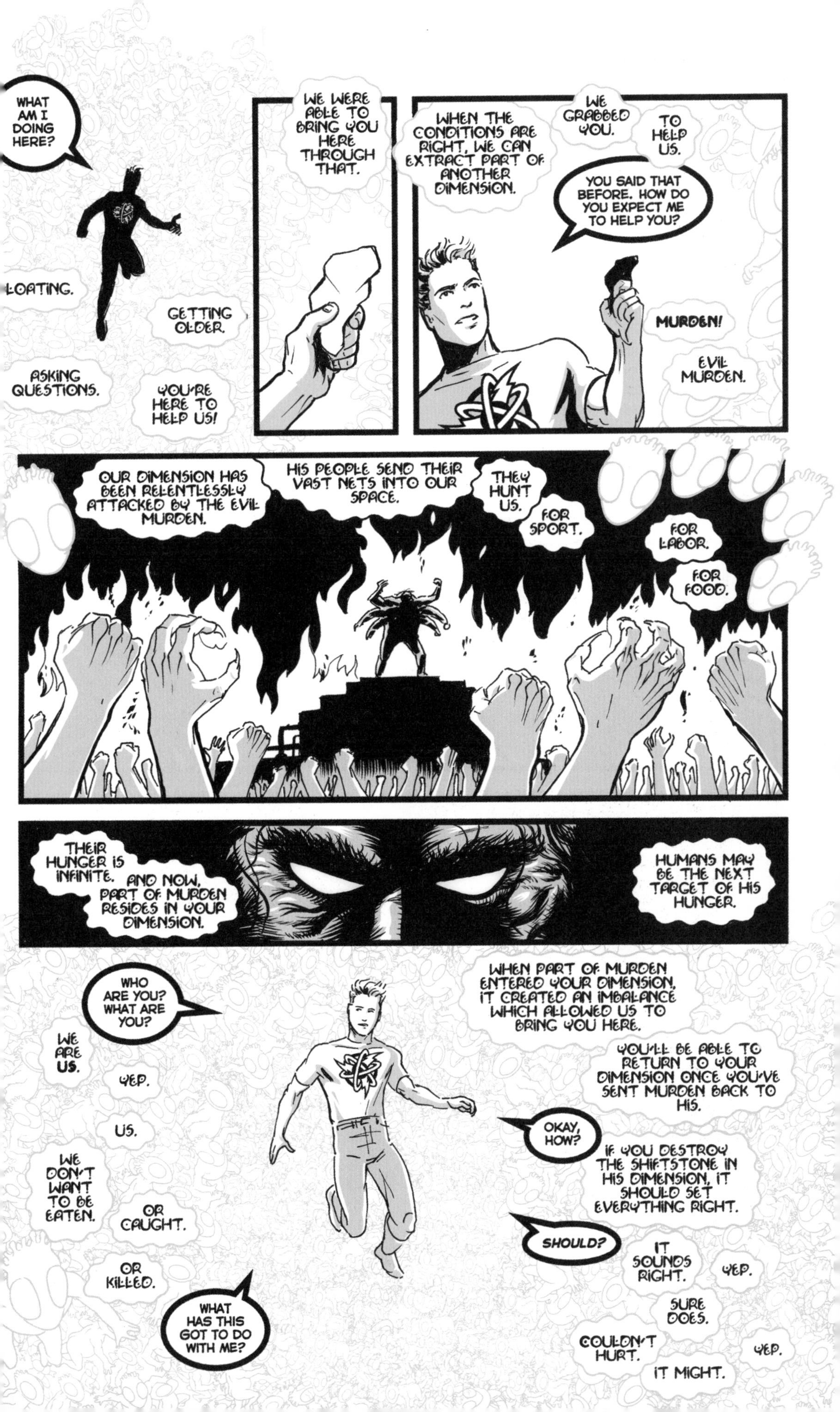
WHAT AM I DOING HERE?
LOATING.
GETTING OLDER.
ASKING QUESTIONS.
YOU'RE HERE TO HELP US!
WE WERE ABLE TO BRING YOU HERE THROUGH THAT.
WHEN THE CONDITIONS ARE RIGHT, WE CAN EXTRACT PART OF ANOTHER DIMENSION.
WE GRABBED YOU.
TO HELP US.
YOU SAID THAT BEFORE. HOW DO YOU EXPECT ME TO HELP YOU?
MURDEN!
EVIL MURDEN.
OUR DIMENSION HAS BEEN RELENTLESSLY ATTACKED BY THE EVIL MURDEN.
HIS PEOPLE SEND THEIR VAST NETS INTO OUR SPACE.
THEY HUNT US.
FOR SPORT.
FOR LABOR.
FOR FOOD.
THEIR HUNGER IS INFINITE.
AND NOW, PART OF MURDEN RESIDES IN YOUR DIMENSION.
HUMANS MAY BE THE NEXT TARGET OF HIS HUNGER.
WHO ARE YOU? WHAT ARE YOU?
WE ARE US.
YEP.
US.
WE DON'T WANT TO BE EATEN.
OR CAUGHT.
OR KILLED.
WHAT HAS THIS GOT TO DO WITH ME?
WHEN PART OF MURDEN ENTERED YOUR DIMENSION, IT CREATED AN IMBALANCE WHICH ALLOWED US TO BRING YOU HERE.
YOU'LL BE ABLE TO RETURN TO YOUR DIMENSION ONCE YOU'VE SENT MURDEN BACK TO HIS.
OKAY, HOW?
IF YOU DESTROY THE SHIFTSTONE IN HIS DIMENSION, IT SHOULD SET EVERYTHING RIGHT.
SHOULD?
IT SOUNDS RIGHT.
YEP.
SURE DOES.
COULDN'T HURT.
YEP.
IT MIGHT.

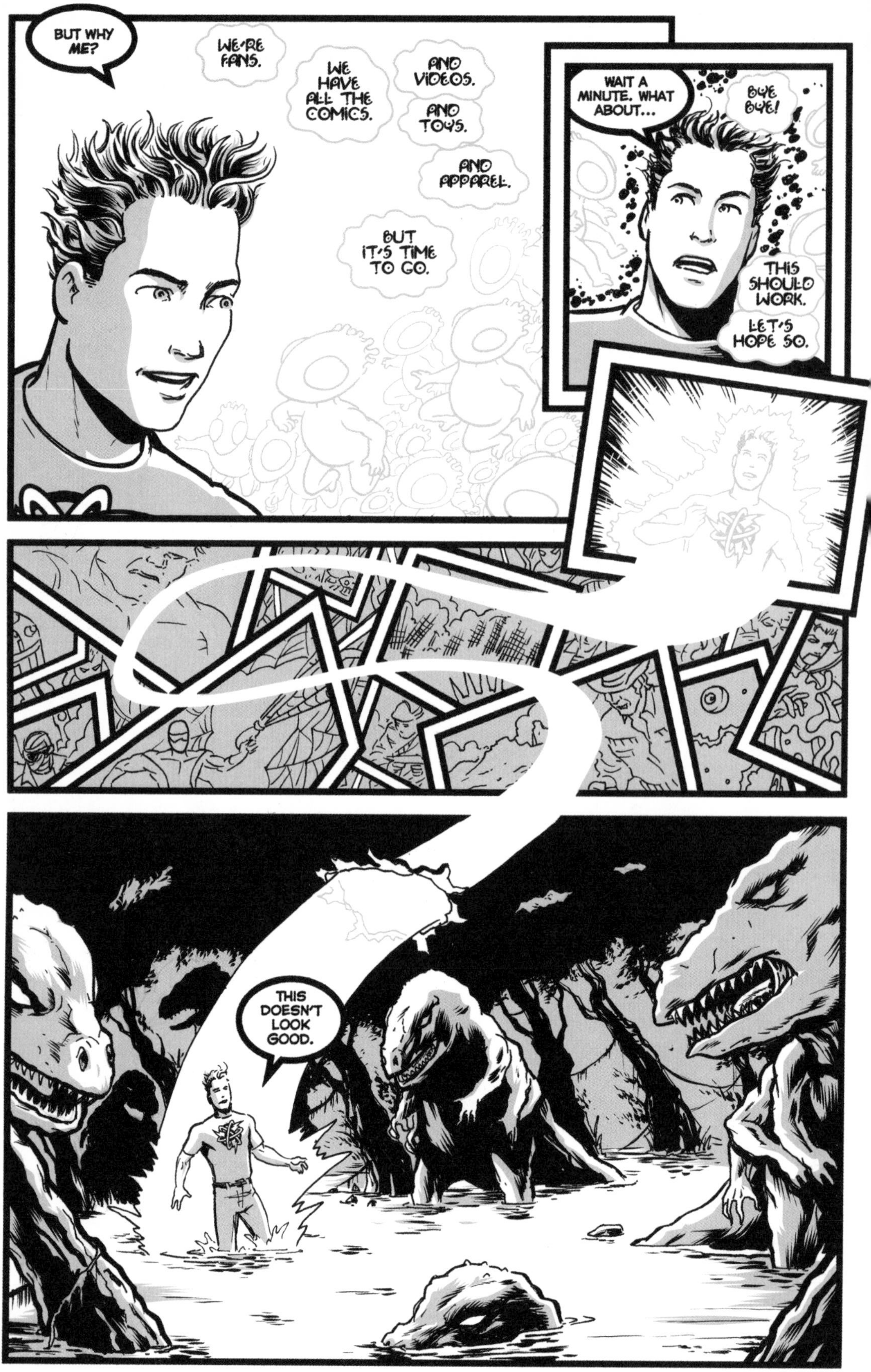
BUT WHY ME?
WE'RE FANS.
WE HAVE ALL THE COMICS.
AND VIDEOS.
AND TOYS.
AND APPAREL.
BUT IT'S TIME TO GO.
WAIT A MINUTE. WHAT ABOUT...
BYE BYE!
THIS SHOULD WORK.
LET'S HOPE SO.
THIS DOESN'T LOOK GOOD.

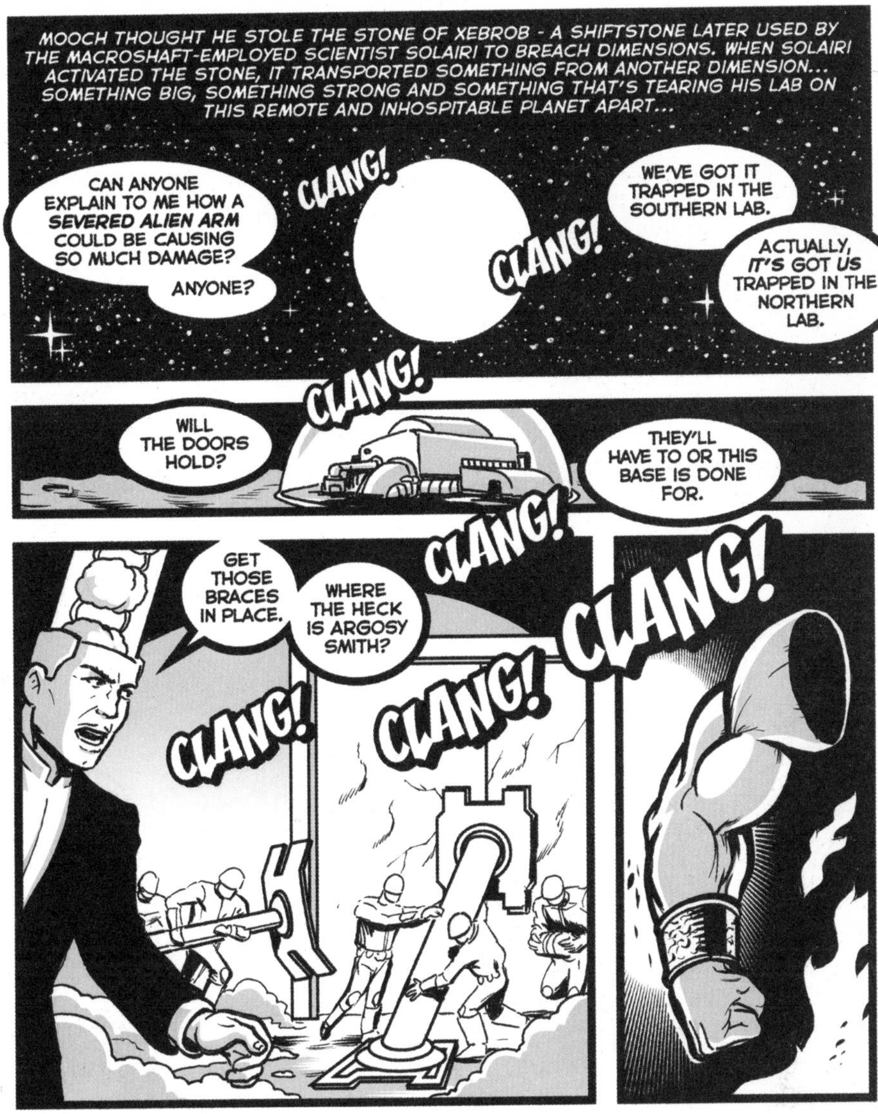
MOOCH THOUGHT HE STOLE THE STONE OF XEBROB - A SHIFTSTONE LATER USED BY THE MACROSHAFT-EMPLOYED SCIENTIST SOLAIRI TO BREACH DIMENSIONS. WHEN SOLAIRI ACTIVATED THE STONE, IT TRANSPORTED SOMETHING FROM ANOTHER DIMENSION... SOMETHING BIG, SOMETHING STRONG AND SOMETHING THAT'S TEARING HIS LAB ON THIS REMOTE AND INHOSPITABLE PLANET APART...
CAN ANYONE EXPLAIN TO ME HOW A SEVERED ALIEN ARM COULD BE CAUSING SO MUCH DAMAGE?
ANYONE?
CLANG!
CLANG!
WE'VE GOT IT TRAPPED IN THE SOUTHERN LAB.
ACTUALLY, IT'S GOT US TRAPPED IN THE NORTHERN LAB.
CLANG!
WILL THE DOORS HOLD?
THEY'LL HAVE TO OR THIS BASE IS DONE FOR.
CLANG!
GET THOSE BRACES IN PLACE.
WHERE THE HECK IS ARGOSY SMITH?
CLANG!
CLANG!
CLANG!
CLANG!

THE SECRET OF MOOCH'S LOOT: PART FOUR

ARMS CONTROL & NON-PROLIFERATION

WRITTEN AND ILLUSTRATED BY STEVE CONLEY

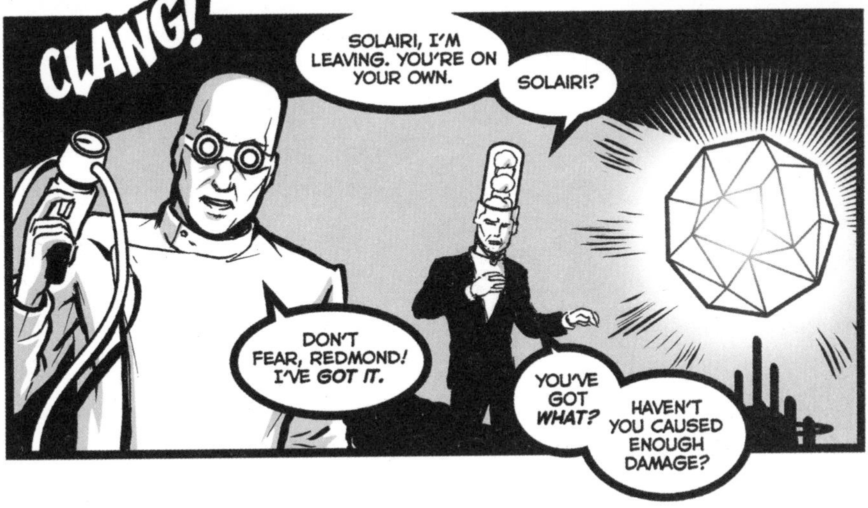
CLANG!
SOLAIRI, I'M LEAVING. YOU'RE ON YOUR OWN.
SOLAIRI?
DON'T FEAR, REDMOND! I'VE GOT IT.
YOU'VE GOT WHAT?
HAVEN'T YOU CAUSED ENOUGH DAMAGE?

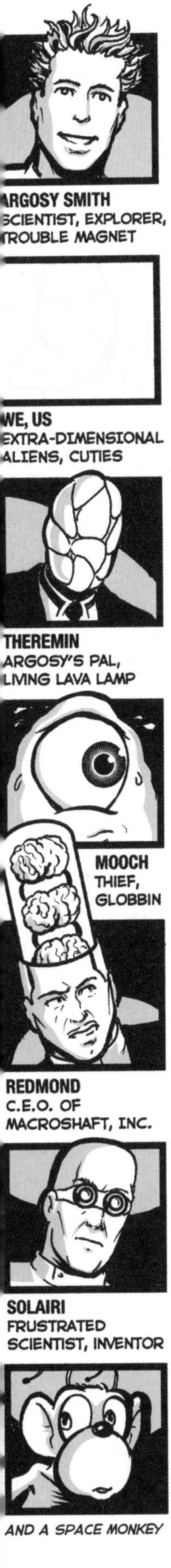
ARGOSY SMITH
SCIENTIST, EXPLORER, TROUBLE MAGNET
WE, US
EXTRA-DIMENSIONAL ALIENS, CUTIES
THEREMIN
ARGOSY'S PAL, LIVING LAVA LAMP
MOOCH
THIEF, GLOBBIN
REDMOND
C.E.O. OF MACROSHAFT, INC.
SOLAIRI
FRUSTRATED SCIENTIST, INVENTOR
AND A SPACE MONKEY

MEANWHILE-ISH...

ROARRRRRRR!!!

IT LOOKS LIKE WE TOOK A WRONG TURN SOMEWHERE.

SORRY, ARGOSY. OUR TRANSPORT BEAM MUST'VE MISSED THE EVIL MURDEN'S WORLD.

WHERE I CAN DESTROY HIS STOLEN SHIFTSTONE AND GET BACK HOME?

THAT'S WHAT WE HOPE. WE'RE SURE ANOTHER RIFT IS NEARBY.

YIKES!

I CERTAINLY HOPE SO!

THERE!

JUST IN TIME.

ROARRRRRRR!!!

OUT OF THE FRYING PAN...

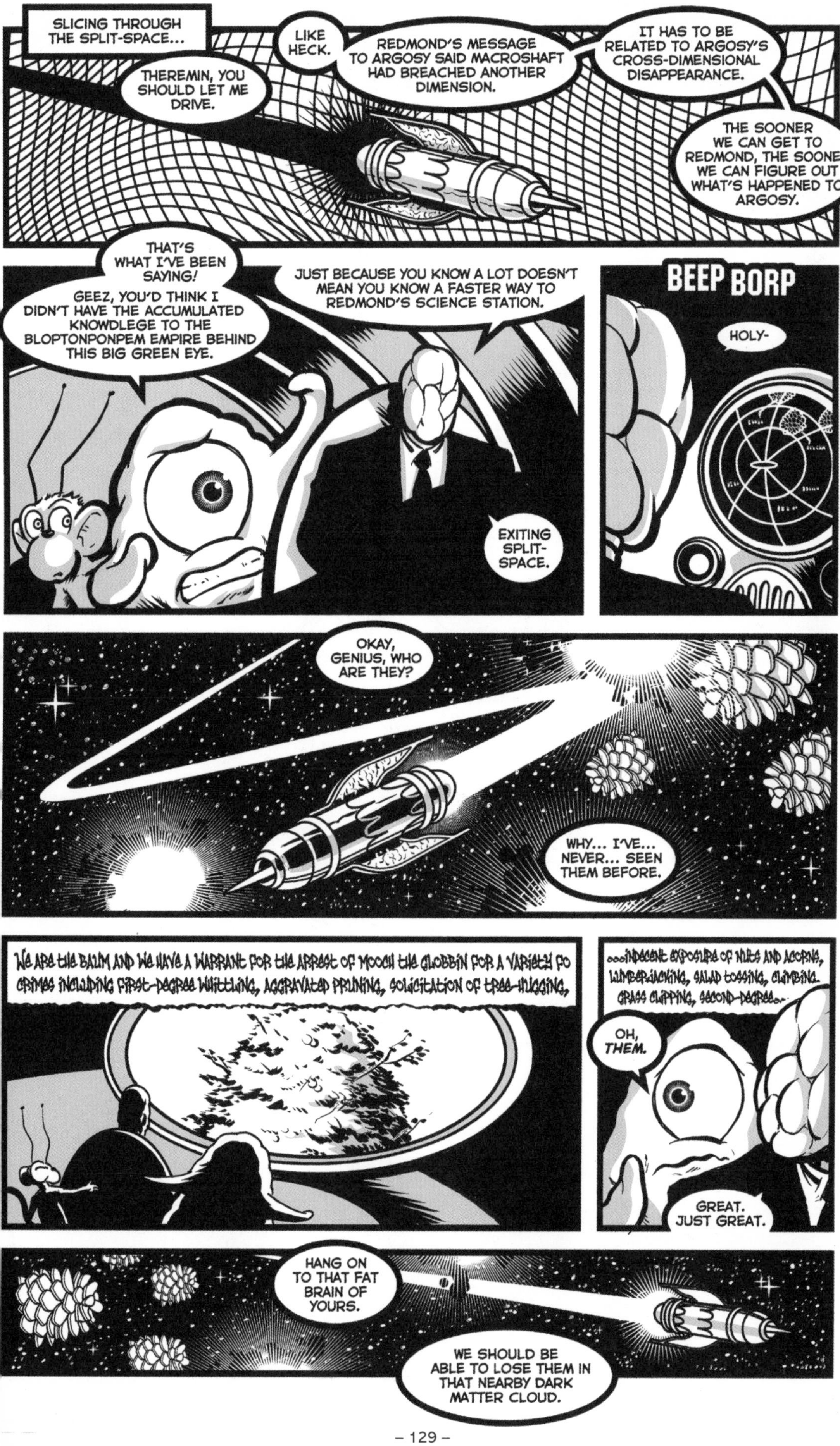

SLICING THROUGH THE SPLIT-SPACE...
THEREMIN, YOU SHOULD LET ME DRIVE.
LIKE HECK.
REDMOND'S MESSAGE TO ARGOSY SAID MACROSHAFT HAD BREACHED ANOTHER DIMENSION.
IT HAS TO BE RELATED TO ARGOSY'S CROSS-DIMENSIONAL DISAPPEARANCE.
THE SOONER WE CAN GET TO REDMOND, THE SOONER WE CAN FIGURE OUT WHAT'S HAPPENED TO ARGOSY.
THAT'S WHAT I'VE BEEN SAYING! GEEZ, YOU'D THINK I DIDN'T HAVE THE ACCUMULATED KNOWDLEGE TO THE BLOPTONPONPEM EMPIRE BEHIND THIS BIG GREEN EYE.
JUST BECAUSE YOU KNOW A LOT DOESN'T MEAN YOU KNOW A FASTER WAY TO REDMOND'S SCIENCE STATION.
EXITING SPLIT-SPACE.
BEEP BORP
HOLY-
OKAY, GENIUS, WHO ARE THEY?
WHY... I'VE... NEVER... SEEN THEM BEFORE.
WE ARE THE BAUM AND WE HAVE A WARRANT FOR THE ARREST OF MOOCH THE GLOBBIN FOR A VARIETY FO CRIMES INCLUDING FIRST-DEGREE WHITTLING, AGGRAVATED PRUNING, SOLICITATION OF TREE-HUGGING,
...INDECENT EXPOSURE OF NUTS AND ACORNS, LUMBERJACKING, SALAD TOSSING, CLIMBING. GRASS CLIPPING, SECOND-DEGREE...
OH, THEM.
GREAT. JUST GREAT.
HANG ON TO THAT FAT BRAIN OF YOURS.
WE SHOULD BE ABLE TO LOSE THEM IN THAT NEARBY DARK MATTER CLOUD.

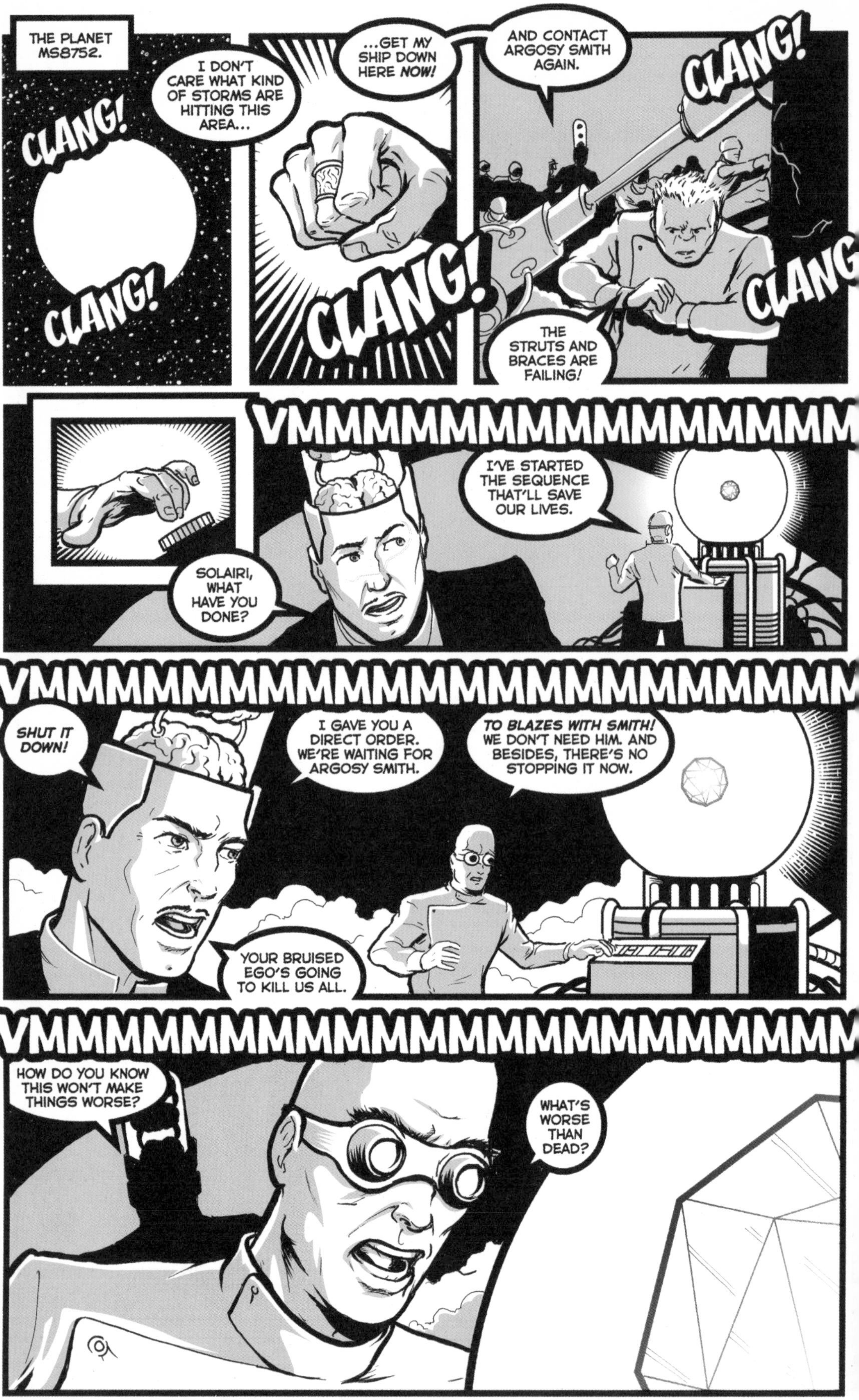
THE PLANET MS8752.
CLANG!
CLANG!
I DON'T CARE WHAT KIND OF STORMS ARE HITTING THIS AREA...
...GET MY SHIP DOWN HERE NOW!
CLANG!
AND CONTACT ARGOSY SMITH AGAIN.
CLANG!
CLANG
THE STRUTS AND BRACES ARE FAILING!
VMMMMMMMMMMMMMMMM
SOLAIRI, WHAT HAVE YOU DONE?
I'VE STARTED THE SEQUENCE THAT'LL SAVE OUR LIVES.
VMMMMMMMMMMMMMMMMMMMMM
SHUT IT DOWN!
I GAVE YOU A DIRECT ORDER. WE'RE WAITING FOR ARGOSY SMITH.
TO BLAZES WITH SMITH! WE DON'T NEED HIM. AND BESIDES, THERE'S NO STOPPING IT NOW.
YOUR BRUISED EGO'S GOING TO KILL US ALL.
VMMMMMMMMMMMMMMMMMMMMM
HOW DO YOU KNOW THIS WON'T MAKE THINGS WORSE?
WHAT'S WORSE THAN DEAD?

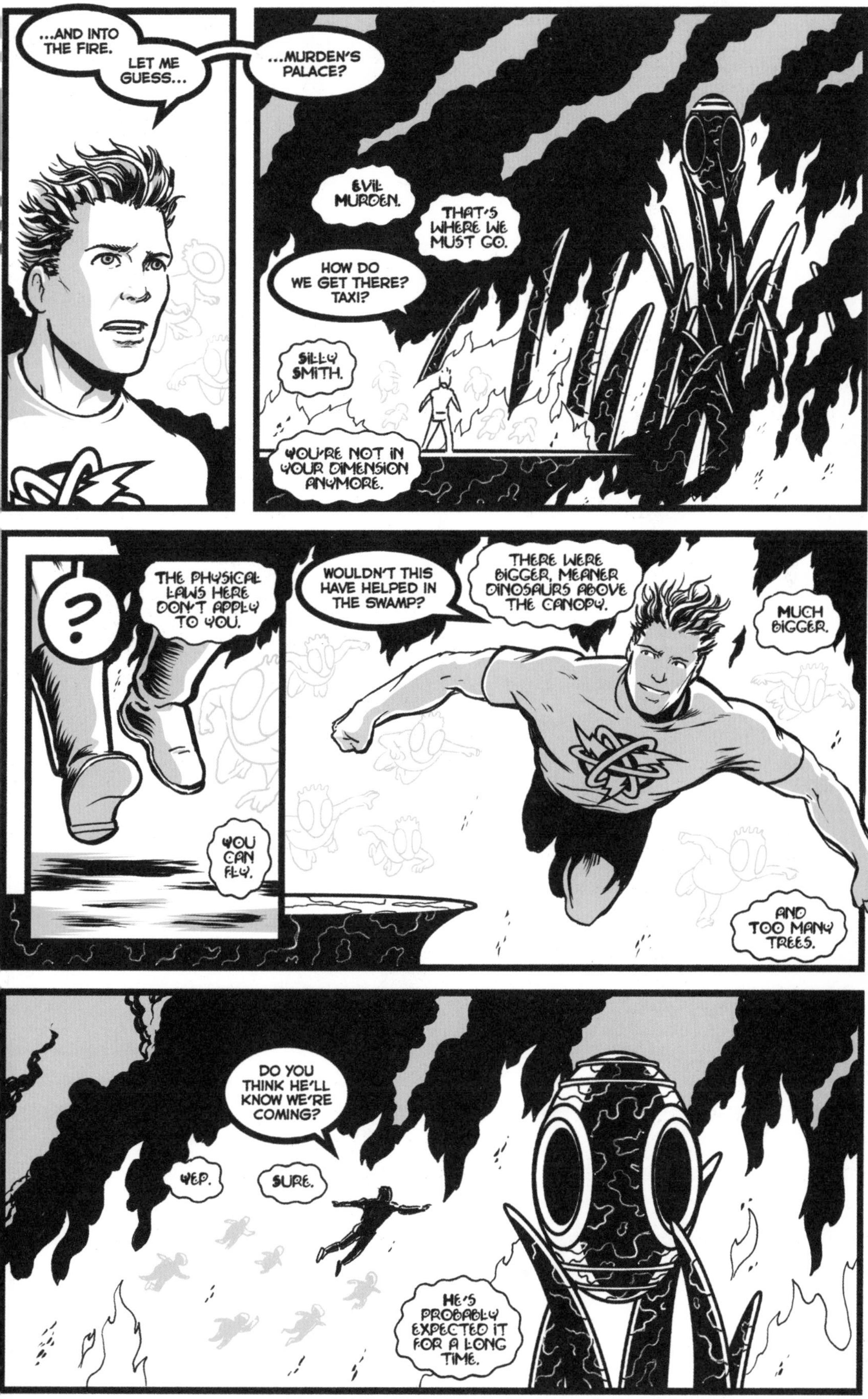
...AND INTO THE FIRE.
LET ME GUESS...
...MURDEN'S PALACE?
EVIL MURDEN.
THAT'S WHERE WE MUST GO.
HOW DO WE GET THERE? TAXI?
SILLY SMITH.
YOU'RE NOT IN YOUR DIMENSION ANYMORE.
?
THE PHYSICAL LAWS HERE DON'T APPLY TO YOU.
YOU CAN FLY.
WOULDN'T THIS HAVE HELPED IN THE SWAMP?
THERE WERE BIGGER, MEANER DINOSAURS ABOVE THE CANOPY.
MUCH BIGGER.
AND TOO MANY TREES.
DO YOU THINK HE'LL KNOW WE'RE COMING?
YEP.
SURE.
HE'S PROBABLY EXPECTED IT FOR A LONG TIME.

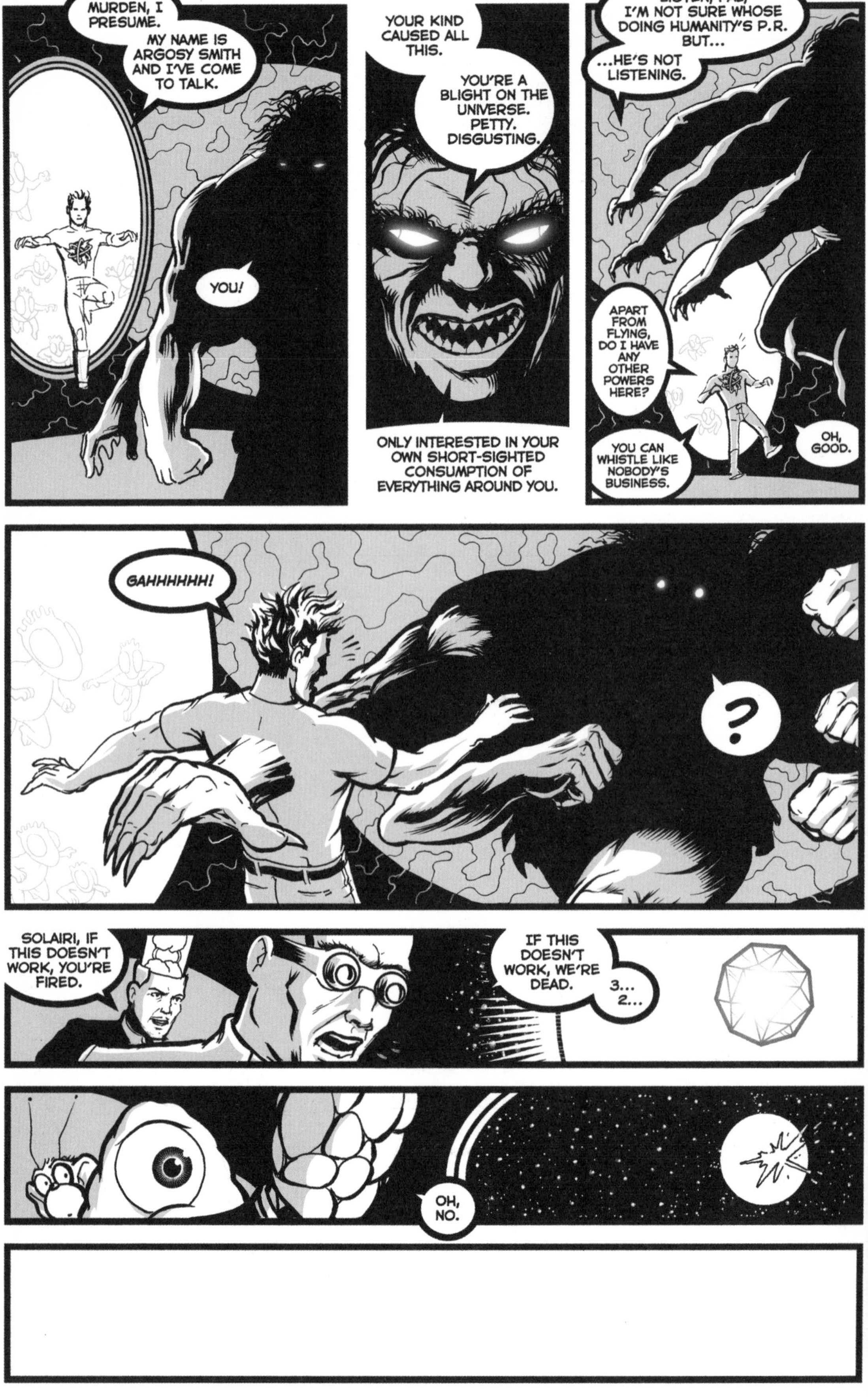
MURDEN, I PRESUME.
MY NAME IS ARGOSY SMITH AND I'VE COME TO TALK.
YOU!
YOUR KIND CAUSED ALL THIS.
YOU'RE A BLIGHT ON THE UNIVERSE. PETTY. DISGUSTING.
ONLY INTERESTED IN YOUR OWN SHORT-SIGHTED CONSUMPTION OF EVERYTHING AROUND YOU.
LISTEN, PAL, I'M NOT SURE WHOSE DOING HUMANITY'S P.R. BUT...
...HE'S NOT LISTENING.
APART FROM FLYING, DO I HAVE ANY OTHER POWERS HERE?
YOU CAN WHISTLE LIKE NOBODY'S BUSINESS.
OH, GOOD.
GAHHHHHH!
?
SOLAIRI, IF THIS DOESN'T WORK, YOU'RE FIRED.
IF THIS DOESN'T WORK, WE'RE DEAD.
3... 2...
OH, NO.

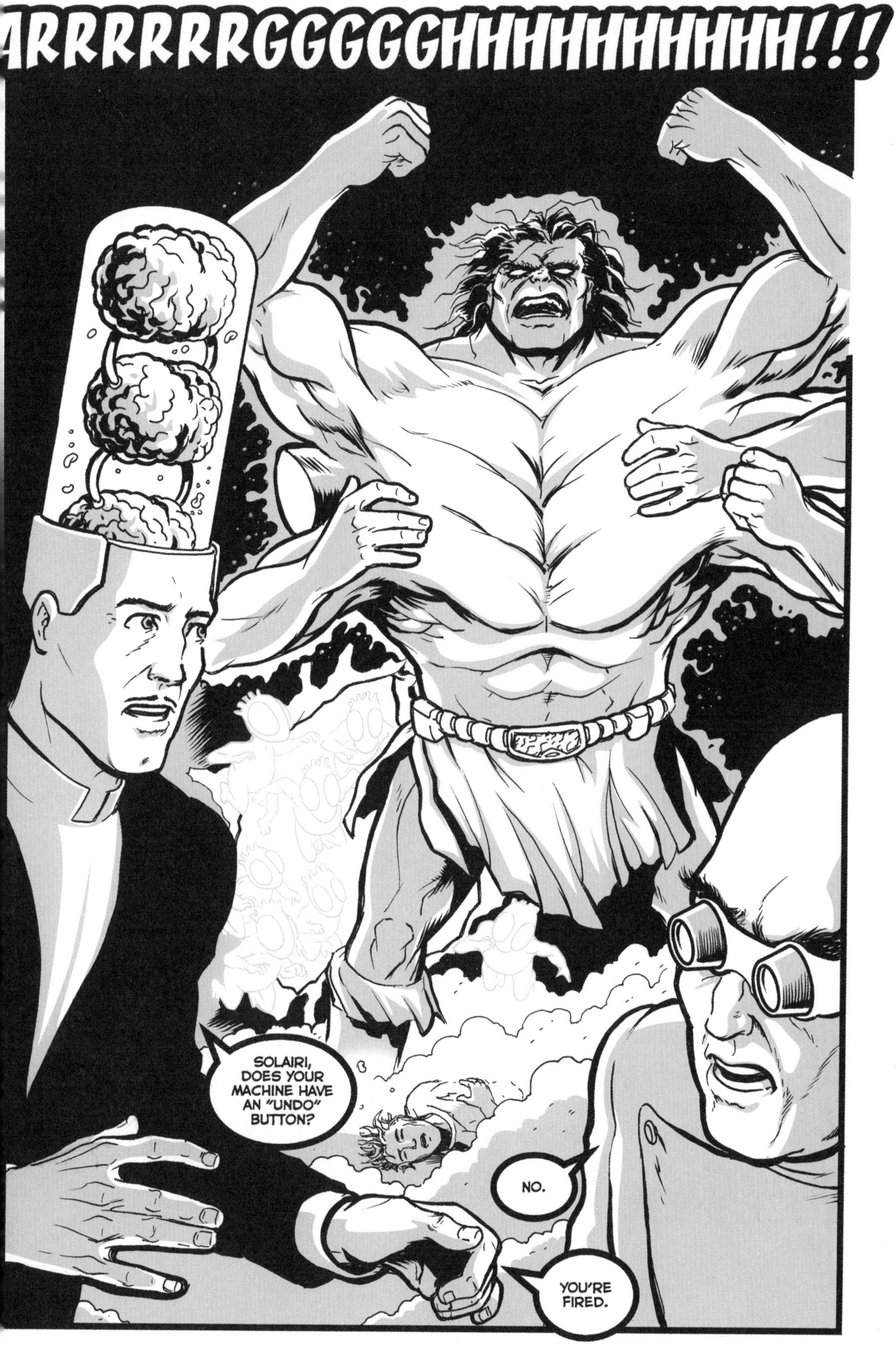
ARRRRRRRGGGGGHHHHHHHHHHHH!!!
SOLAIRI, DOES YOUR MACHINE HAVE AN "UNDO" BUTTON?
NO.
YOU'RE FIRED.

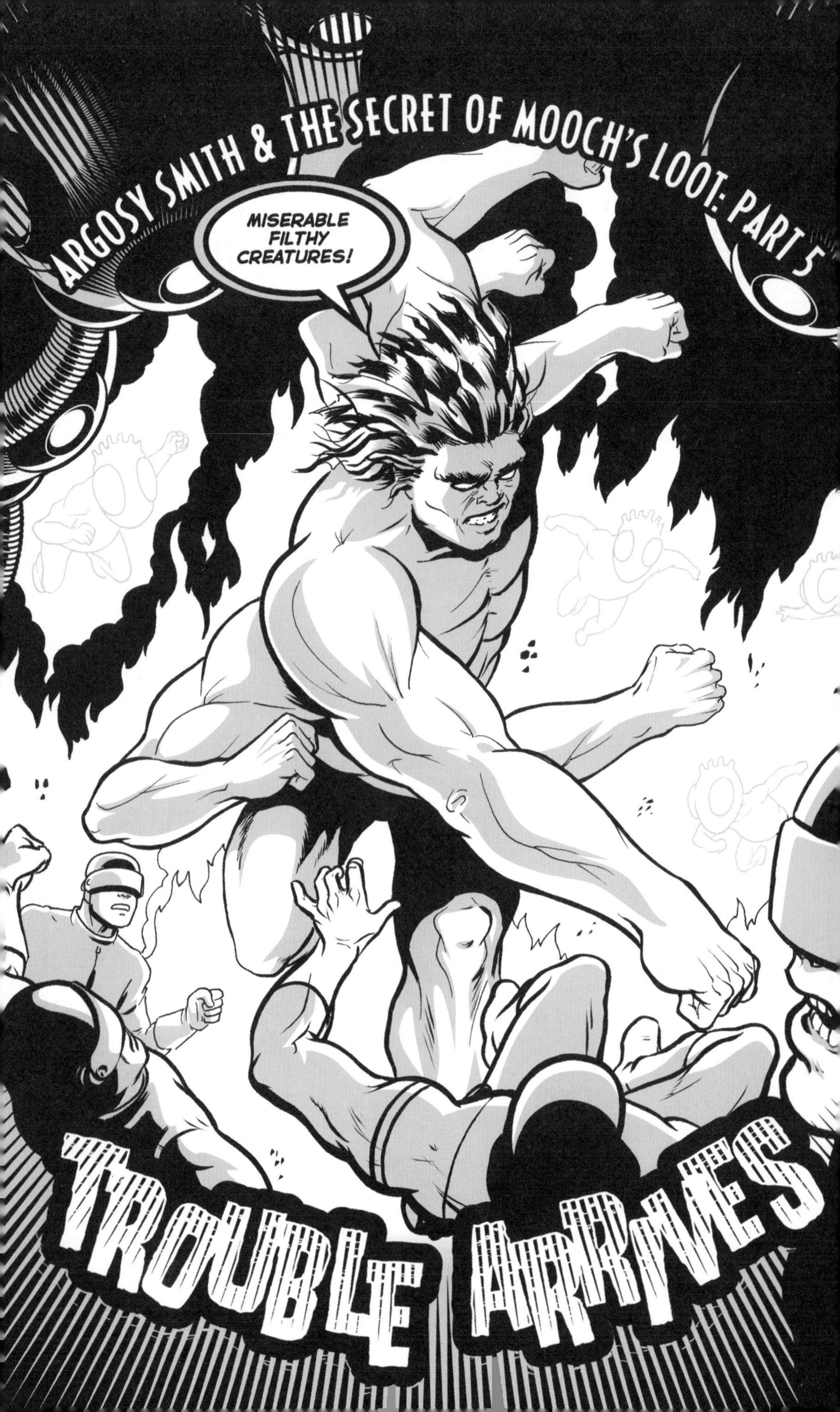

ARGOSY SMITH & THE SECRET OF MOOCH'S LOOT: PART 5
MISERABLE FILTHY CREATURES!
TROUBLE ARRIVES

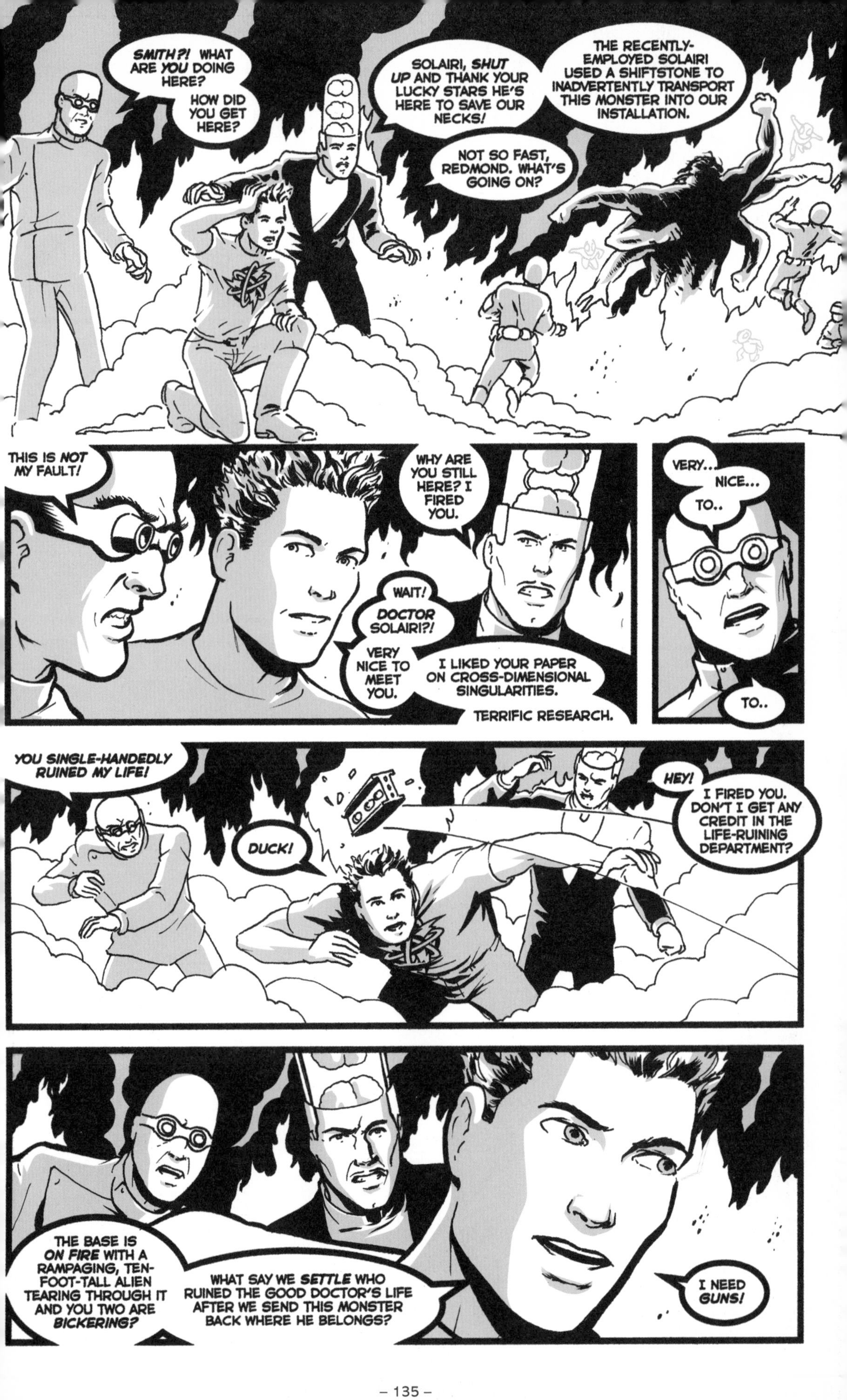
SMITH?! WHAT ARE YOU DOING HERE?
HOW DID YOU GET HERE?
SOLAIRI, SHUT UP AND THANK YOUR LUCKY STARS HE'S HERE TO SAVE OUR NECKS!
THE RECENTLY-EMPLOYED SOLAIRI USED A SHIFTSTONE TO INADVERTENTLY TRANSPORT THIS MONSTER INTO OUR INSTALLATION.
NOT SO FAST, REDMOND. WHAT'S GOING ON?
THIS IS NOT MY FAULT!
WHY ARE YOU STILL HERE? I FIRED YOU.
WAIT!
DOCTOR SOLAIRI?!
VERY NICE TO MEET YOU.
I LIKED YOUR PAPER ON CROSS-DIMENSIONAL SINGULARITIES.
TERRIFIC RESEARCH.
VERY... NICE... TO..
TO..
YOU SINGLE-HANDEDLY RUINED MY LIFE!
DUCK!
HEY!
I FIRED YOU. DON'T I GET ANY CREDIT IN THE LIFE-RUINING DEPARTMENT?
THE BASE IS ON FIRE WITH A RAMPAGING, TEN-FOOT-TALL ALIEN TEARING THROUGH IT AND YOU TWO ARE BICKERING?
WHAT SAY WE SETTLE WHO RUINED THE GOOD DOCTOR'S LIFE AFTER WE SEND THIS MONSTER BACK WHERE HE BELONGS?
I NEED GUNS!

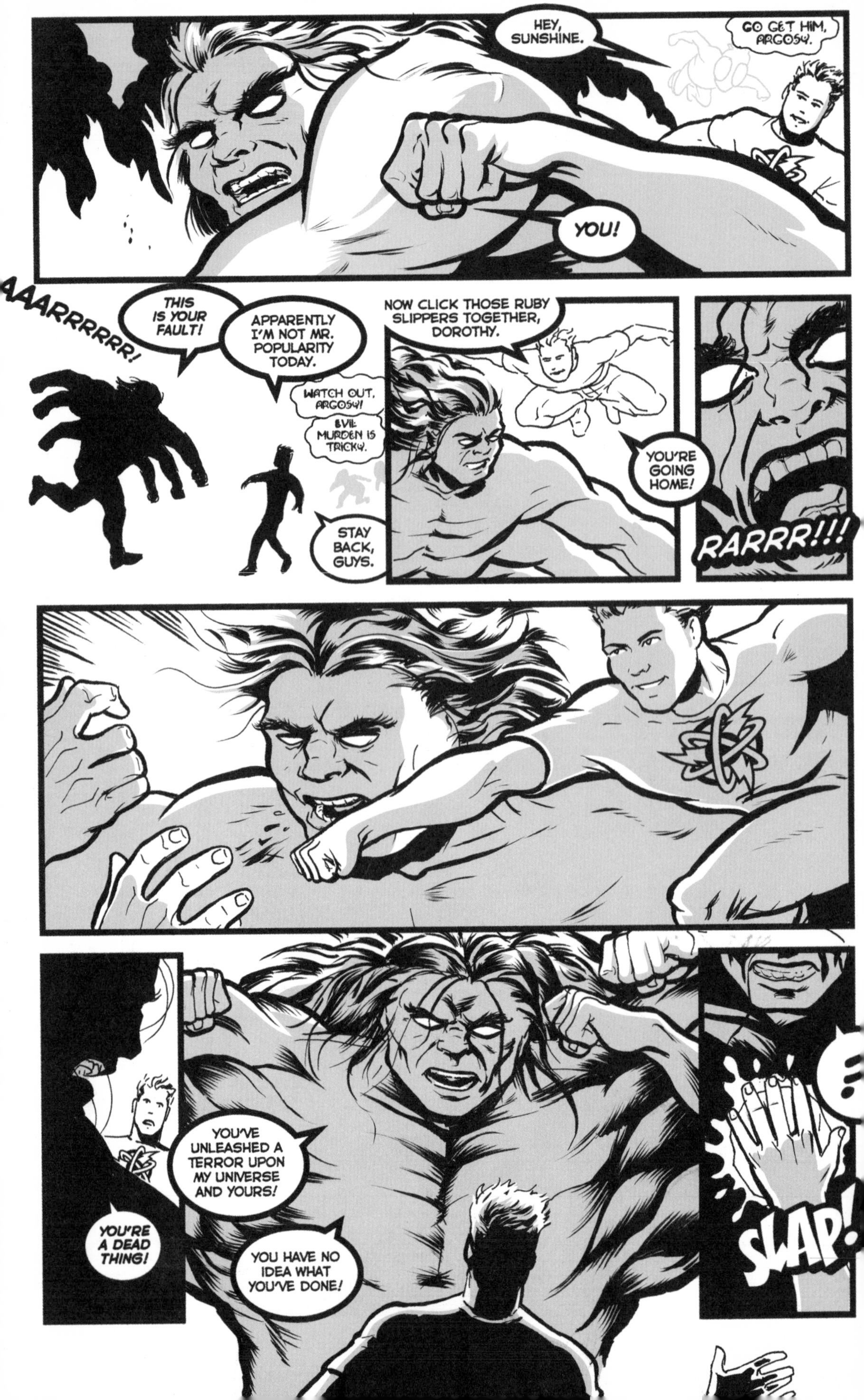
HEY, SUNSHINE.
GO GET HIM, ARGOSY.
YOU!
AAAARRRRRRR!
THIS IS YOUR FAULT!
APPARENTLY I'M NOT MR. POPULARITY TODAY.
WATCH OUT, ARGOSY!
EVIL MURDEN IS TRICKY.
STAY BACK, GUYS.
NOW CLICK THOSE RUBY SLIPPERS TOGETHER, DOROTHY.
YOU'RE GOING HOME!
RARRR!!!
YOU'RE A DEAD THING!
YOU'VE UNLEASHED A TERROR UPON MY UNIVERSE AND YOURS!
YOU HAVE NO IDEA WHAT YOU'VE DONE!
SLAP!

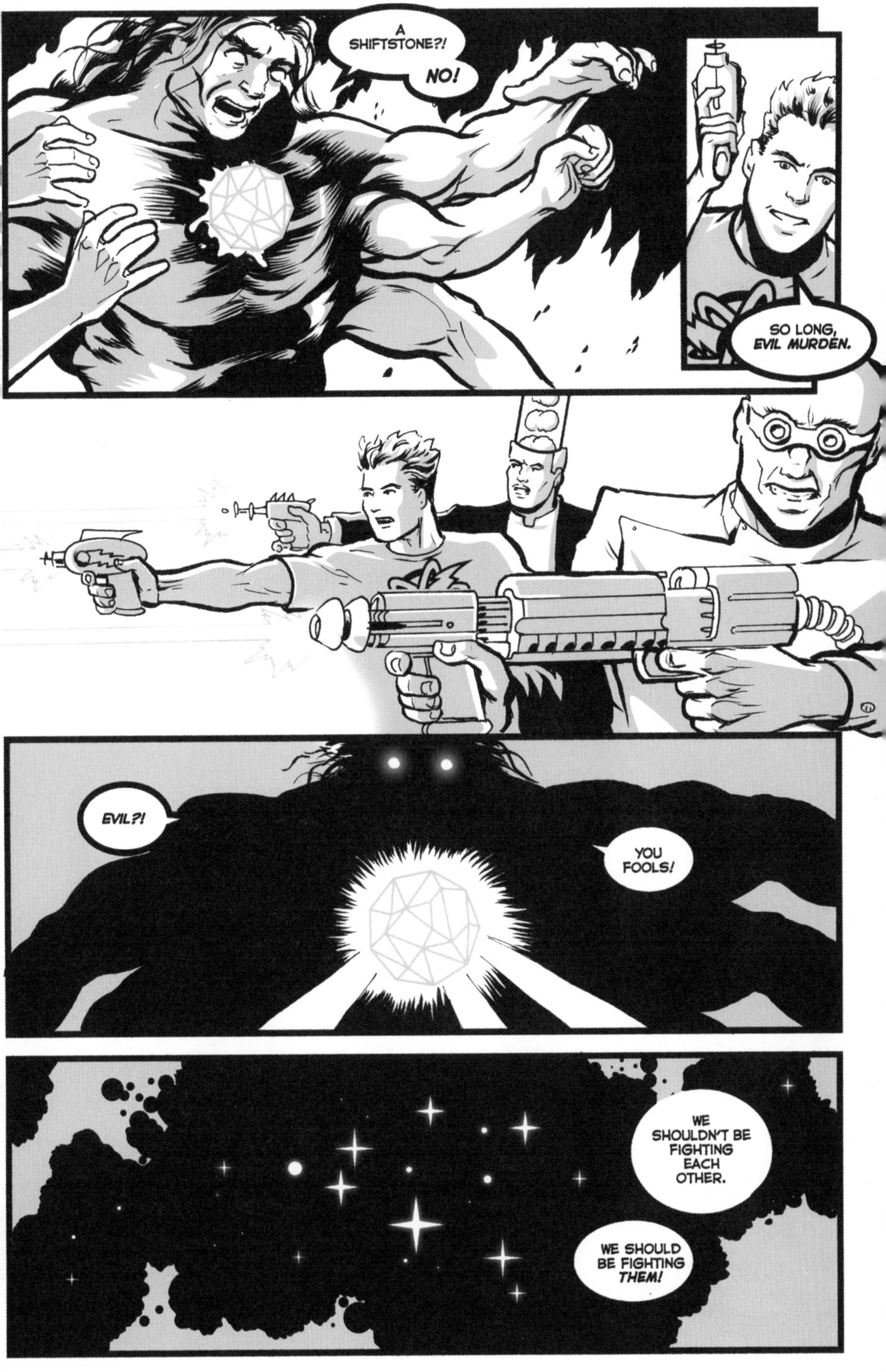
A SHIFTSTONE?!
NO!
SO LONG, EVIL MURDEN.
EVIL?!
YOU FOOLS!
WE SHOULDN'T BE FIGHTING EACH OTHER.
WE SHOULD BE FIGHTING THEM!

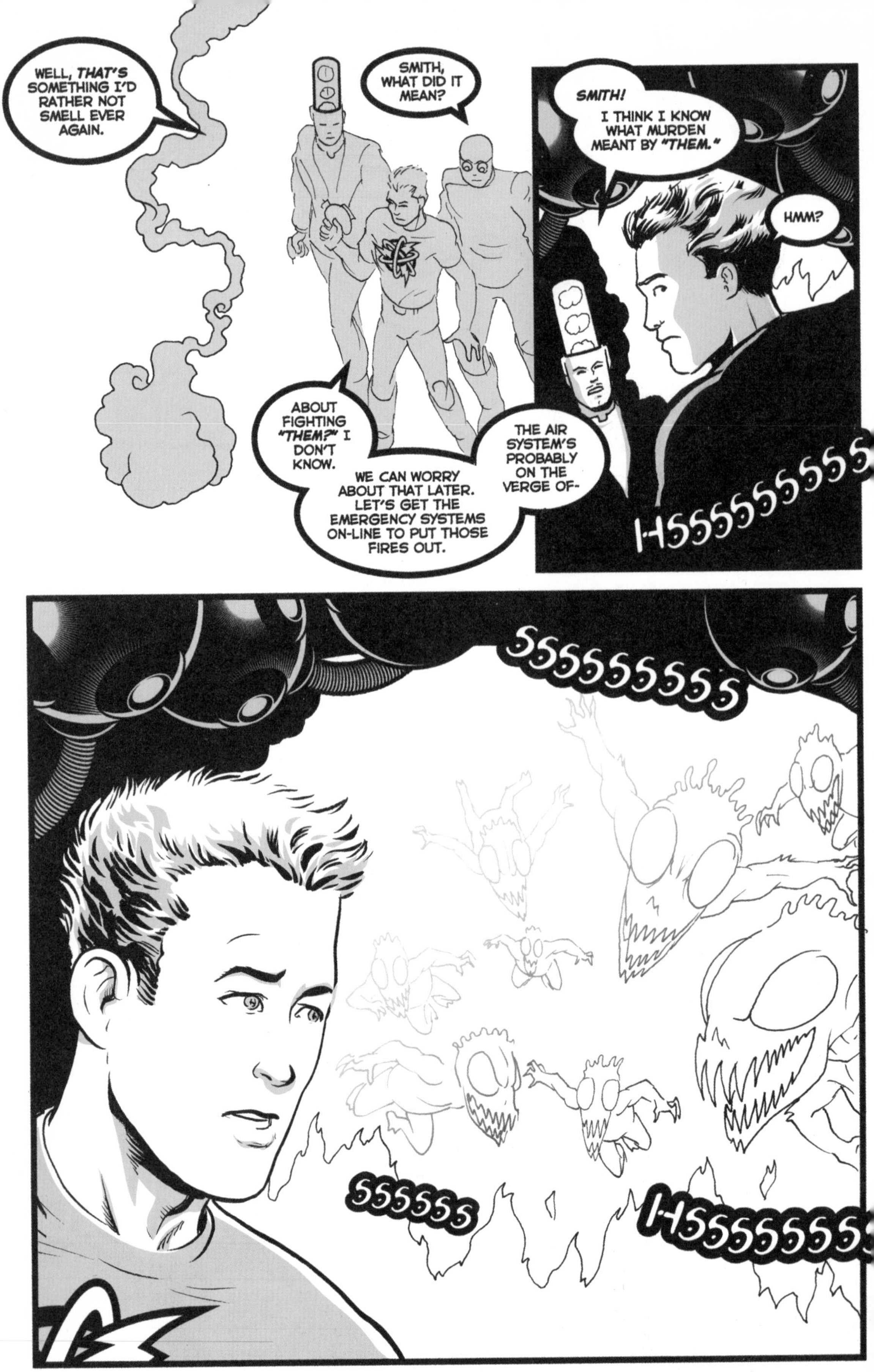
WELL, *THAT'S* SOMETHING I'D RATHER NOT SMELL EVER AGAIN.
SMITH, WHAT DID IT MEAN?
ABOUT FIGHTING *"THEM?"* I DON'T KNOW.
WE CAN WORRY ABOUT THAT LATER. LET'S GET THE EMERGENCY SYSTEMS ON-LINE TO PUT THOSE FIRES OUT.
THE AIR SYSTEM'S PROBABLY ON THE VERGE OF-
SMITH!
I THINK I KNOW WHAT MURDEN MEANT BY *"THEM."*
HMM?
HSSSSSSSSSS
SSSSSSSSSS
SSSSSS
HSSSSSSSSS

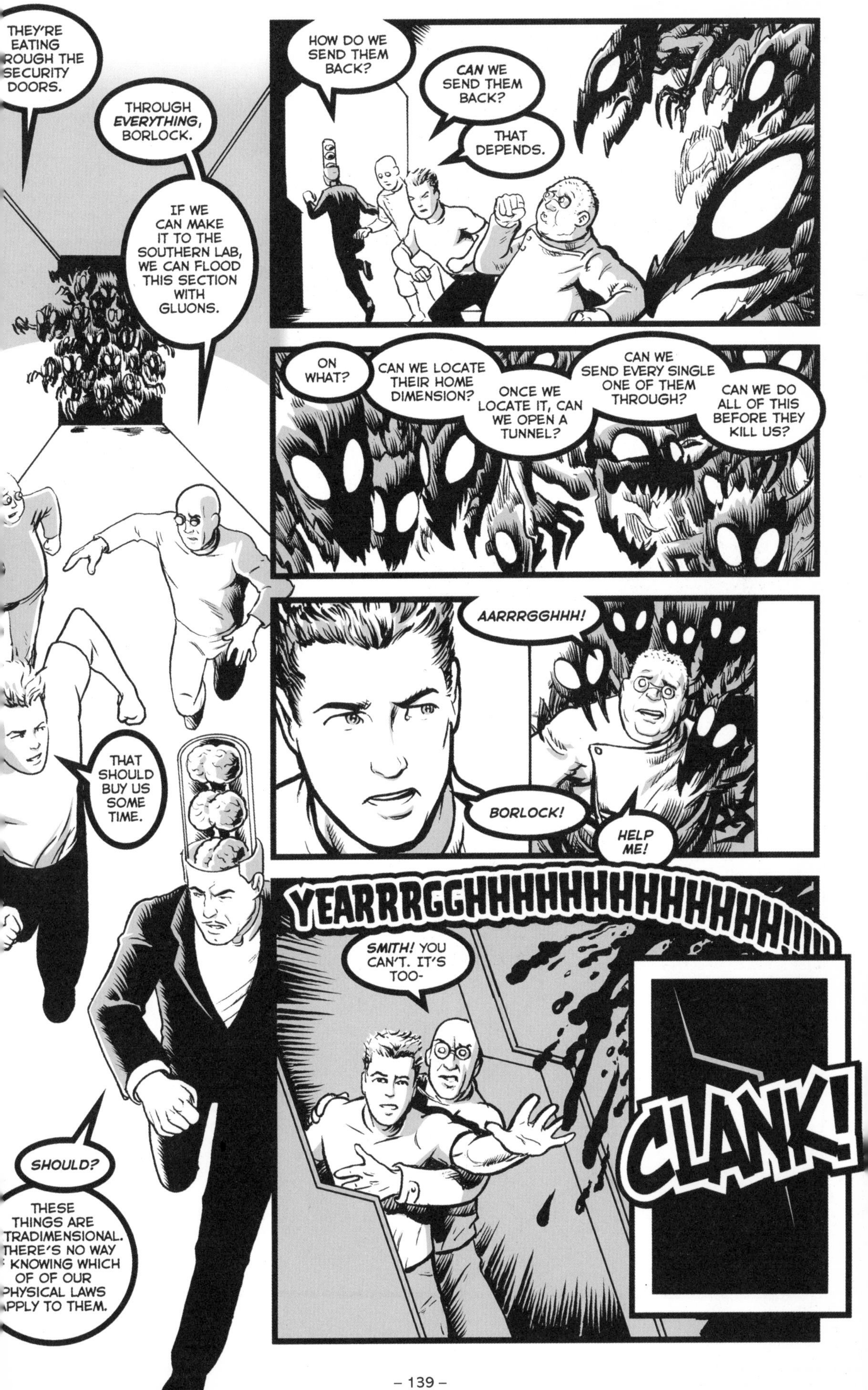
THEY'RE EATING ROUGH THE SECURITY DOORS.
THROUGH *EVERYTHING*, BORLOCK.
IF WE CAN MAKE IT TO THE SOUTHERN LAB, WE CAN FLOOD THIS SECTION WITH GLUONS.
HOW DO WE SEND THEM BACK?
CAN WE SEND THEM BACK?
THAT DEPENDS.
ON WHAT?
CAN WE LOCATE THEIR HOME DIMENSION?
ONCE WE LOCATE IT, CAN WE OPEN A TUNNEL?
CAN WE SEND EVERY SINGLE ONE OF THEM THROUGH?
CAN WE DO ALL OF THIS BEFORE THEY KILL US?
THAT SHOULD BUY US SOME TIME.
SHOULD?
THESE THINGS ARE TRADIMENSIONAL. THERE'S NO WAY KNOWING WHICH OF OF OUR PHYSICAL LAWS APPLY TO THEM.
AARRRGGHHH!
BORLOCK!
HELP ME!
YEARRRGGHHHHHHHHHHHHHH!!!!!
SMITH! YOU CAN'T. IT'S TOO-
CLANK!

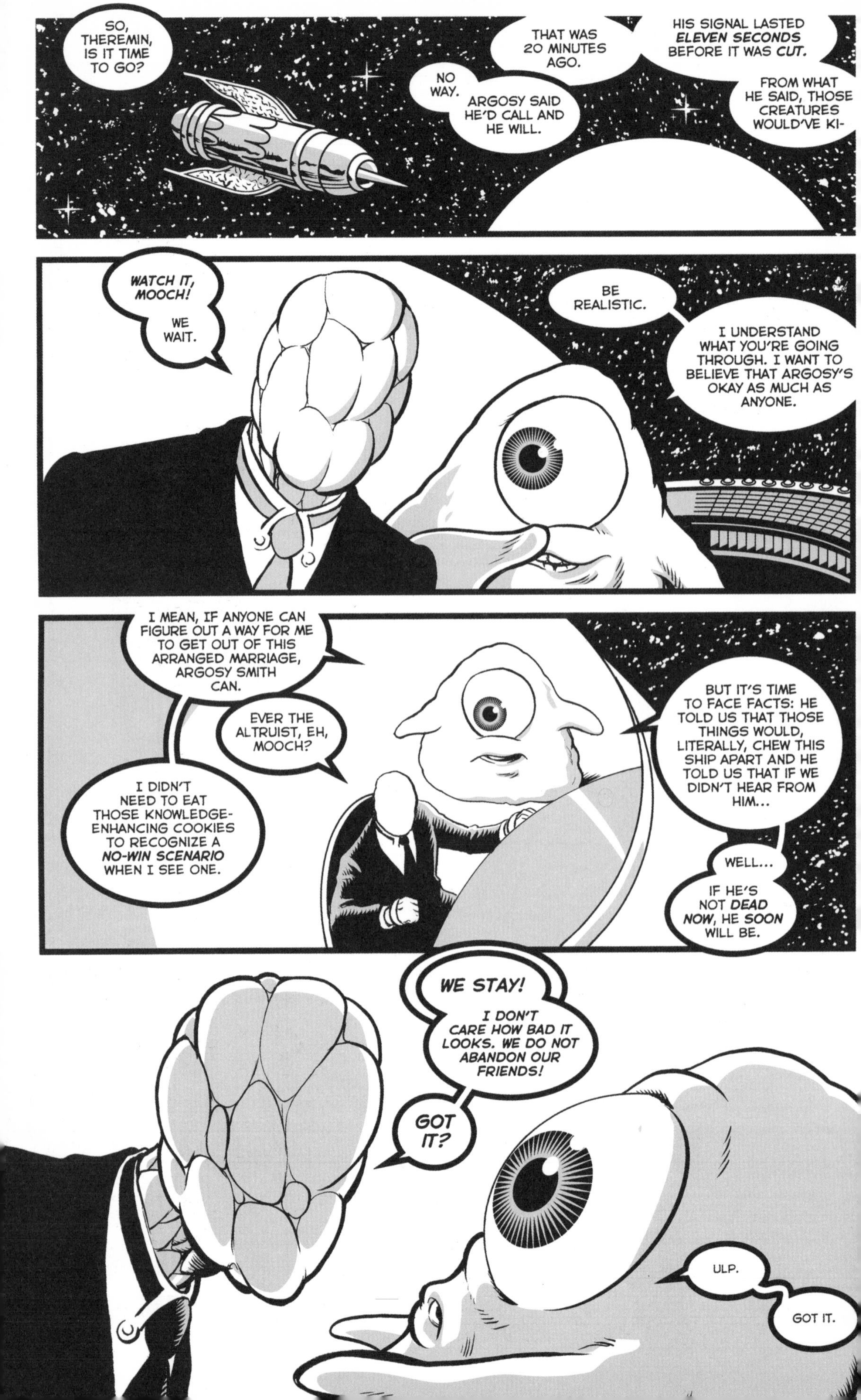
SO, THEREMIN, IS IT TIME TO GO?
NO WAY.
ARGOSY SAID HE'D CALL AND HE WILL.
THAT WAS 20 MINUTES AGO.
HIS SIGNAL LASTED ELEVEN SECONDS BEFORE IT WAS CUT.
FROM WHAT HE SAID, THOSE CREATURES WOULD'VE KI-
WATCH IT, MOOCH!
WE WAIT.
BE REALISTIC.
I UNDERSTAND WHAT YOU'RE GOING THROUGH. I WANT TO BELIEVE THAT ARGOSY'S OKAY AS MUCH AS ANYONE.
I MEAN, IF ANYONE CAN FIGURE OUT A WAY FOR ME TO GET OUT OF THIS ARRANGED MARRIAGE, ARGOSY SMITH CAN.
EVER THE ALTRUIST, EH, MOOCH?
I DIDN'T NEED TO EAT THOSE KNOWLEDGE-ENHANCING COOKIES TO RECOGNIZE A NO-WIN SCENARIO WHEN I SEE ONE.
BUT IT'S TIME TO FACE FACTS: HE TOLD US THAT THOSE THINGS WOULD, LITERALLY, CHEW THIS SHIP APART AND HE TOLD US THAT IF WE DIDN'T HEAR FROM HIM...
WELL...
IF HE'S NOT DEAD NOW, HE SOON WILL BE.
WE STAY!
I DON'T CARE HOW BAD IT LOOKS. WE DO NOT ABANDON OUR FRIENDS!
GOT IT?
ULP.
GOT IT.

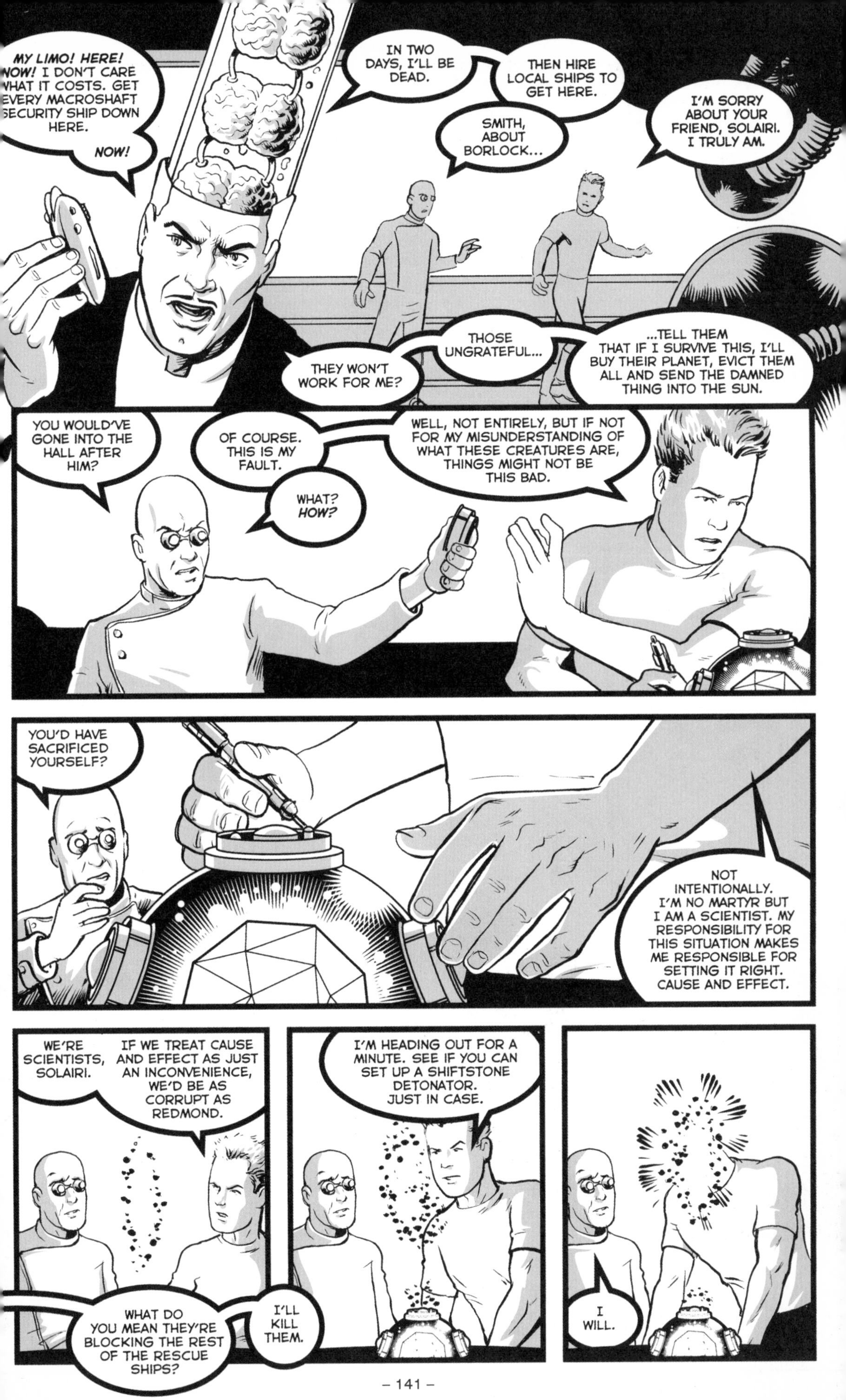
MY LIMO! HERE! NOW! I DON'T CARE WHAT IT COSTS. GET EVERY MACROSHAFT SECURITY SHIP DOWN HERE.
NOW!
IN TWO DAYS, I'LL BE DEAD.
THEN HIRE LOCAL SHIPS TO GET HERE.
SMITH, ABOUT BORLOCK...
I'M SORRY ABOUT YOUR FRIEND, SOLAIRI. I TRULY AM.
THEY WON'T WORK FOR ME?
THOSE UNGRATEFUL...
...TELL THEM THAT IF I SURVIVE THIS, I'LL BUY THEIR PLANET, EVICT THEM ALL AND SEND THE DAMNED THING INTO THE SUN.
YOU WOULD'VE GONE INTO THE HALL AFTER HIM?
OF COURSE. THIS IS MY FAULT.
WHAT? HOW?
WELL, NOT ENTIRELY, BUT IF NOT FOR MY MISUNDERSTANDING OF WHAT THESE CREATURES ARE, THINGS MIGHT NOT BE THIS BAD.
YOU'D HAVE SACRIFICED YOURSELF?
NOT INTENTIONALLY. I'M NO MARTYR BUT I AM A SCIENTIST. MY RESPONSIBILITY FOR THIS SITUATION MAKES ME RESPONSIBLE FOR SETTING IT RIGHT. CAUSE AND EFFECT.
WE'RE SCIENTISTS, SOLAIRI.
IF WE TREAT CAUSE AND EFFECT AS JUST AN INCONVENIENCE, WE'D BE AS CORRUPT AS REDMOND.
WHAT DO YOU MEAN THEY'RE BLOCKING THE REST OF THE RESCUE SHIPS?
I'LL KILL THEM.
I'M HEADING OUT FOR A MINUTE. SEE IF YOU CAN SET UP A SHIFTSTONE DETONATOR. JUST IN CASE.
I WILL.

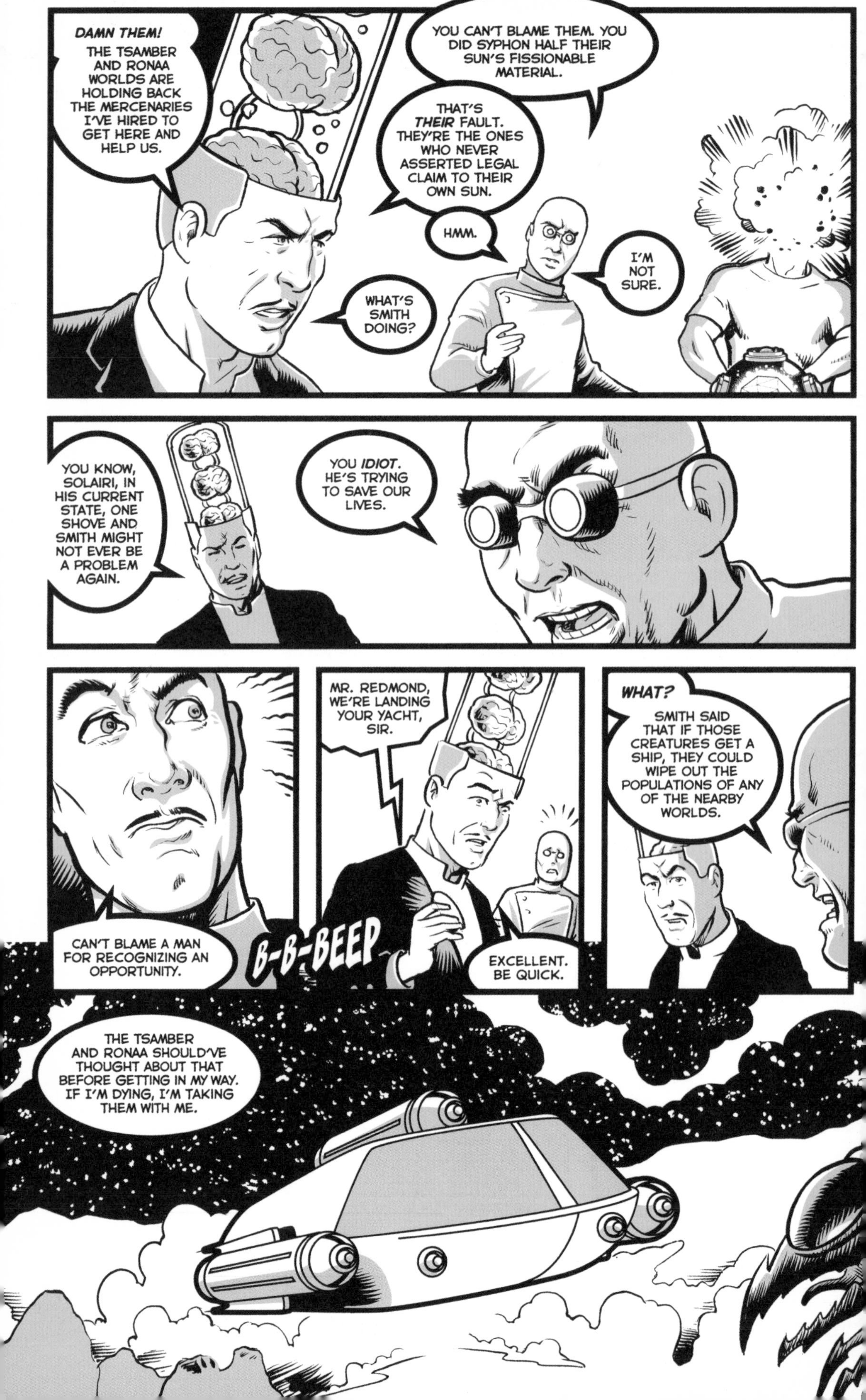
DAMN THEM!
THE TSAMBER AND RONAA WORLDS ARE HOLDING BACK THE MERCENARIES I'VE HIRED TO GET HERE AND HELP US.
YOU CAN'T BLAME THEM. YOU DID SYPHON HALF THEIR SUN'S FISSIONABLE MATERIAL.
THAT'S *THEIR* FAULT. THEY'RE THE ONES WHO NEVER ASSERTED LEGAL CLAIM TO THEIR OWN SUN.
HMM.
WHAT'S SMITH DOING?
I'M NOT SURE.
YOU KNOW, SOLAIRI, IN HIS CURRENT STATE, ONE SHOVE AND SMITH MIGHT NOT EVER BE A PROBLEM AGAIN.
YOU *IDIOT*. HE'S TRYING TO SAVE OUR LIVES.
CAN'T BLAME A MAN FOR RECOGNIZING AN OPPORTUNITY.
B-B-BEEP
MR. REDMOND, WE'RE LANDING YOUR YACHT, SIR.
EXCELLENT. BE QUICK.
WHAT?
SMITH SAID THAT IF THOSE CREATURES GET A SHIP, THEY COULD WIPE OUT THE POPULATIONS OF ANY OF THE NEARBY WORLDS.
THE TSAMBER AND RONAA SHOULD'VE THOUGHT ABOUT THAT BEFORE GETTING IN MY WAY. IF I'M DYING, I'M TAKING THEM WITH ME.

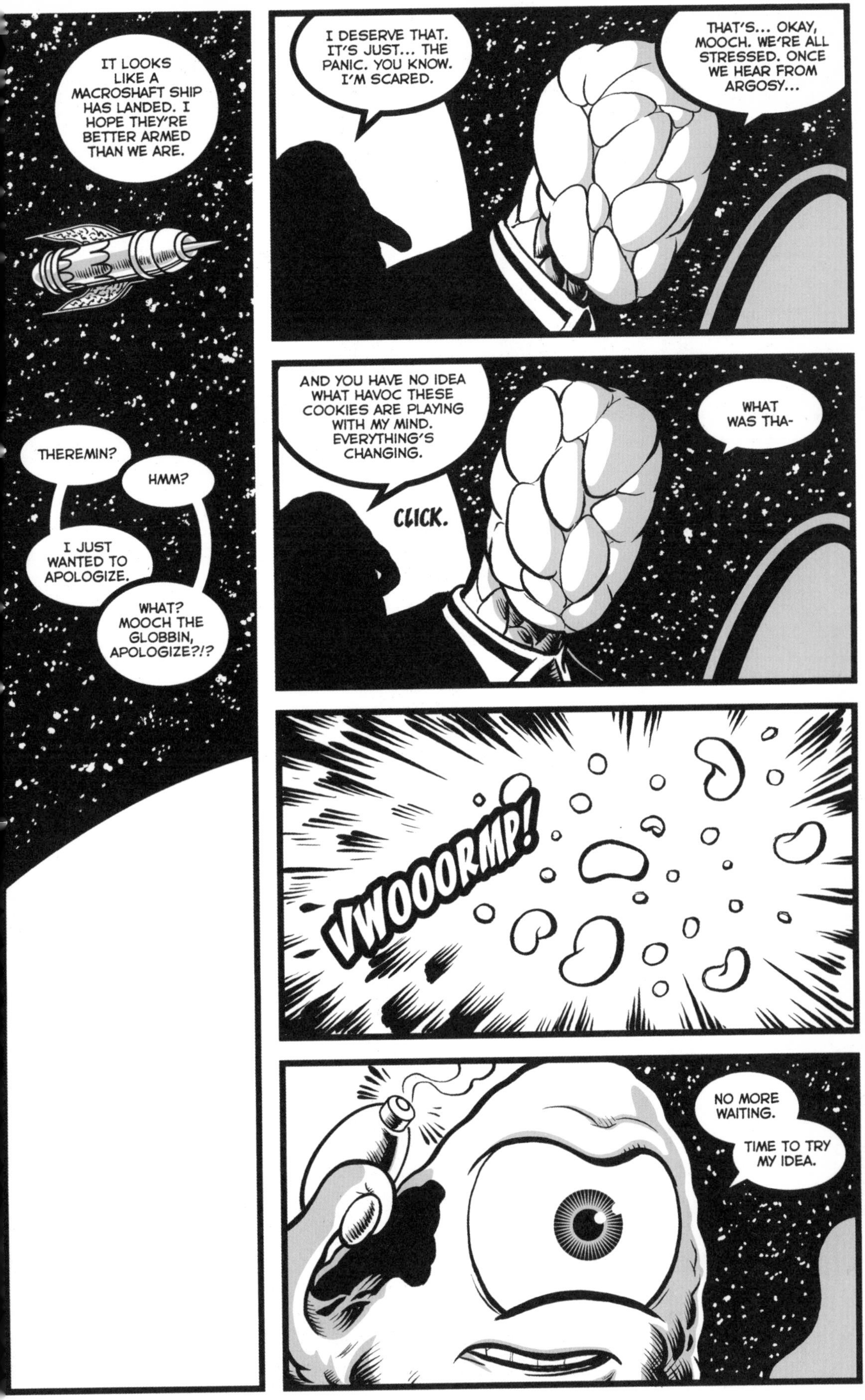
IT LOOKS LIKE A MACROSHAFT SHIP HAS LANDED. I HOPE THEY'RE BETTER ARMED THAN WE ARE.
THEREMIN?
HMM?
I JUST WANTED TO APOLOGIZE.
WHAT? MOOCH THE GLOBBIN, APOLOGIZE?!?
I DESERVE THAT. IT'S JUST... THE PANIC. YOU KNOW. I'M SCARED.
THAT'S... OKAY, MOOCH. WE'RE ALL STRESSED. ONCE WE HEAR FROM ARGOSY...
AND YOU HAVE NO IDEA WHAT HAVOC THESE COOKIES ARE PLAYING WITH MY MIND. EVERYTHING'S CHANGING.
CLICK.
WHAT WAS THA-
VWOOORMP!
NO MORE WAITING.
TIME TO TRY MY IDEA.

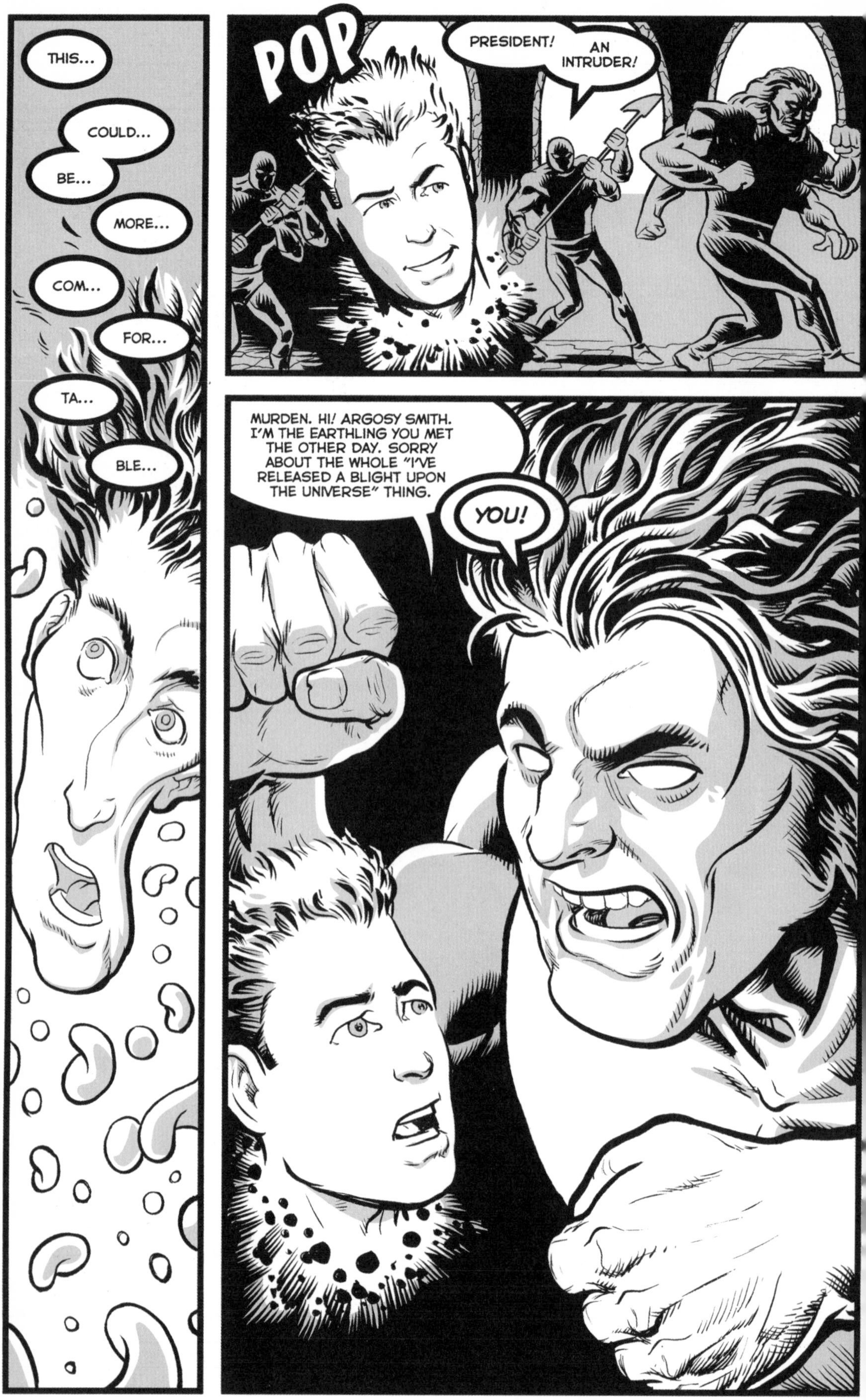
THIS...
COULD...
BE...
MORE...
COM...
FOR...
TA...
BLE...
POP
PRESIDENT!
AN INTRUDER!
MURDEN. HI! ARGOSY SMITH. I'M THE EARTHLING YOU MET THE OTHER DAY. SORRY ABOUT THE WHOLE "I'VE RELEASED A BLIGHT UPON THE UNIVERSE" THING.
YOU!

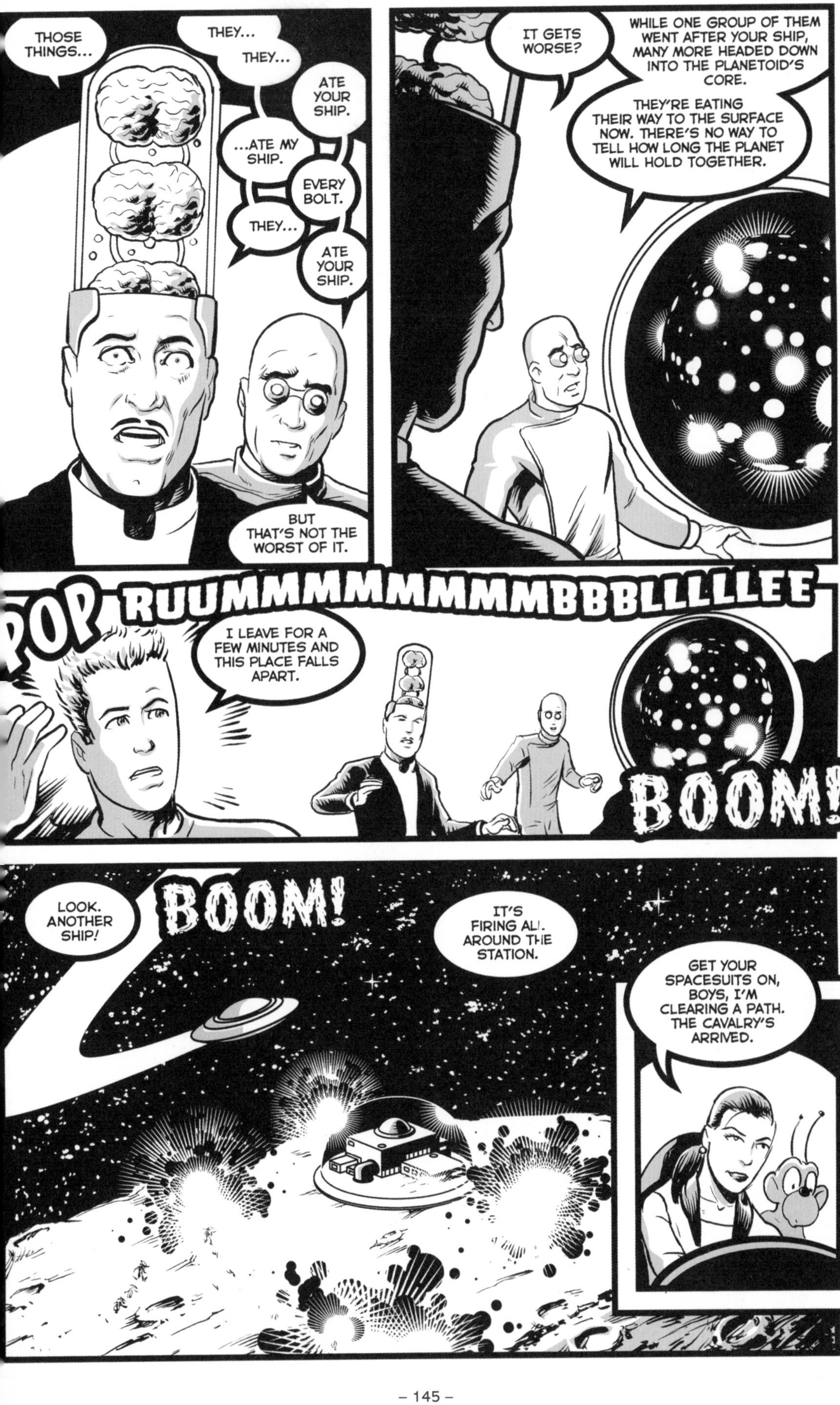
THOSE THINGS...
THEY...
THEY...
ATE YOUR SHIP.
...ATE MY SHIP.
EVERY BOLT.
THEY...
ATE YOUR SHIP.
BUT THAT'S NOT THE WORST OF IT.
IT GETS WORSE?
WHILE ONE GROUP OF THEM WENT AFTER YOUR SHIP, MANY MORE HEADED DOWN INTO THE PLANETOID'S CORE.
THEY'RE EATING THEIR WAY TO THE SURFACE NOW. THERE'S NO WAY TO TELL HOW LONG THE PLANET WILL HOLD TOGETHER.
POP
RUUMMMMMMMMMMBBBLLLLLEE
I LEAVE FOR A FEW MINUTES AND THIS PLACE FALLS APART.
BOOM!
LOOK. ANOTHER SHIP!
BOOM!
IT'S FIRING ALL AROUND THE STATION.
GET YOUR SPACESUITS ON, BOYS, I'M CLEARING A PATH. THE CAVALRY'S ARRIVED.

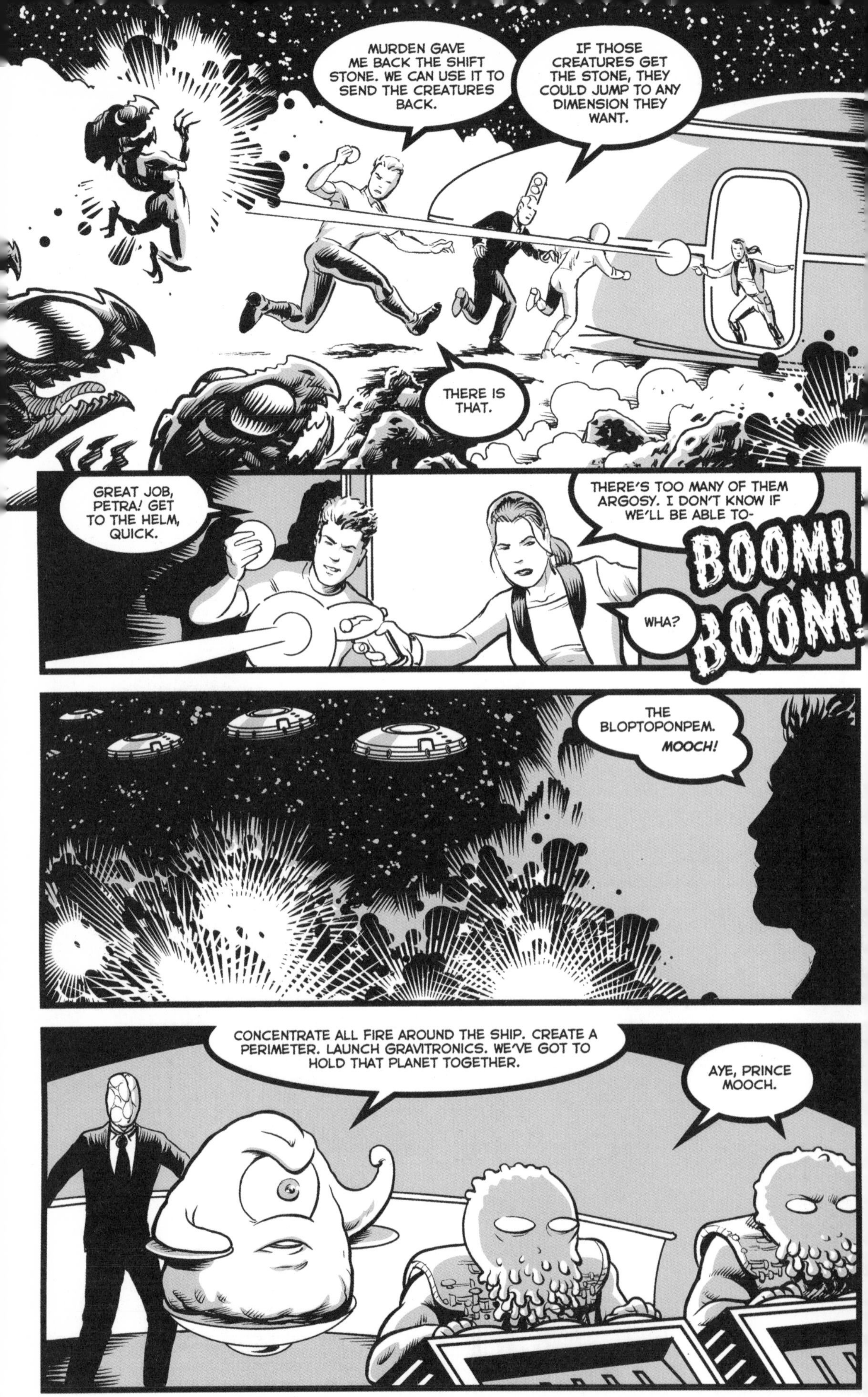
MURDEN GAVE ME BACK THE SHIFT STONE. WE CAN USE IT TO SEND THE CREATURES BACK.
IF THOSE CREATURES GET THE STONE, THEY COULD JUMP TO ANY DIMENSION THEY WANT.
THERE IS THAT.
GREAT JOB, PETRA! GET TO THE HELM, QUICK.
THERE'S TOO MANY OF THEM ARGOSY. I DON'T KNOW IF WE'LL BE ABLE TO-
BOOM! BOOM!
WHA?
THE BLOPTOPONPEM. MOOCH!
CONCENTRATE ALL FIRE AROUND THE SHIP. CREATE A PERIMETER. LAUNCH GRAVITRONICS. WE'VE GOT TO HOLD THAT PLANET TOGETHER.
AYE, PRINCE MOOCH.

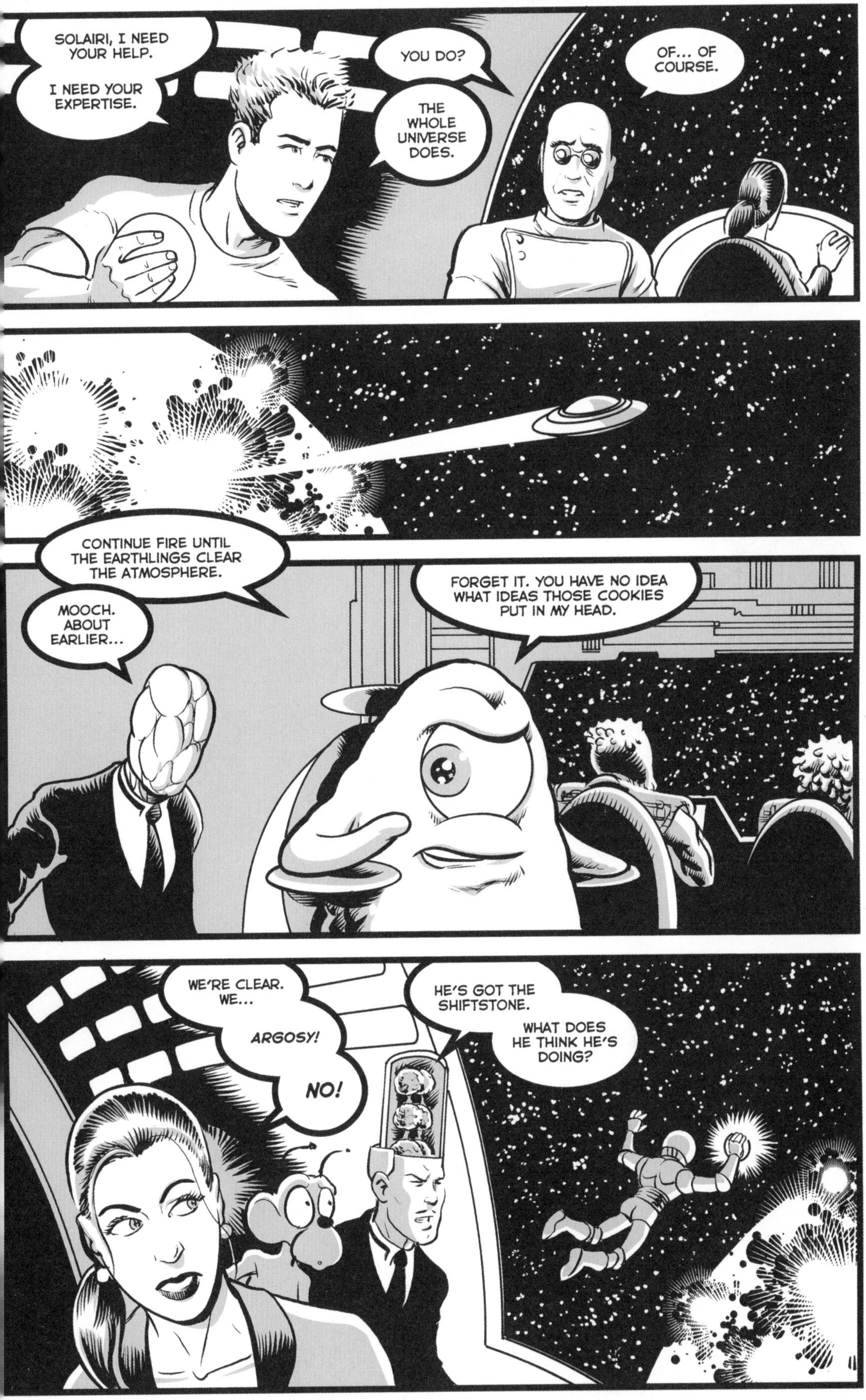
SOLAIRI, I NEED YOUR HELP.
I NEED YOUR EXPERTISE.
YOU DO?
THE WHOLE UNIVERSE DOES.
OF... OF COURSE.
CONTINUE FIRE UNTIL THE EARTHLINGS CLEAR THE ATMOSPHERE.
MOOCH. ABOUT EARLIER...
FORGET IT. YOU HAVE NO IDEA WHAT IDEAS THOSE COOKIES PUT IN MY HEAD.
WE'RE CLEAR. WE...
ARGOSY!
NO!
HE'S GOT THE SHIFTSTONE.
WHAT DOES HE THINK HE'S DOING?

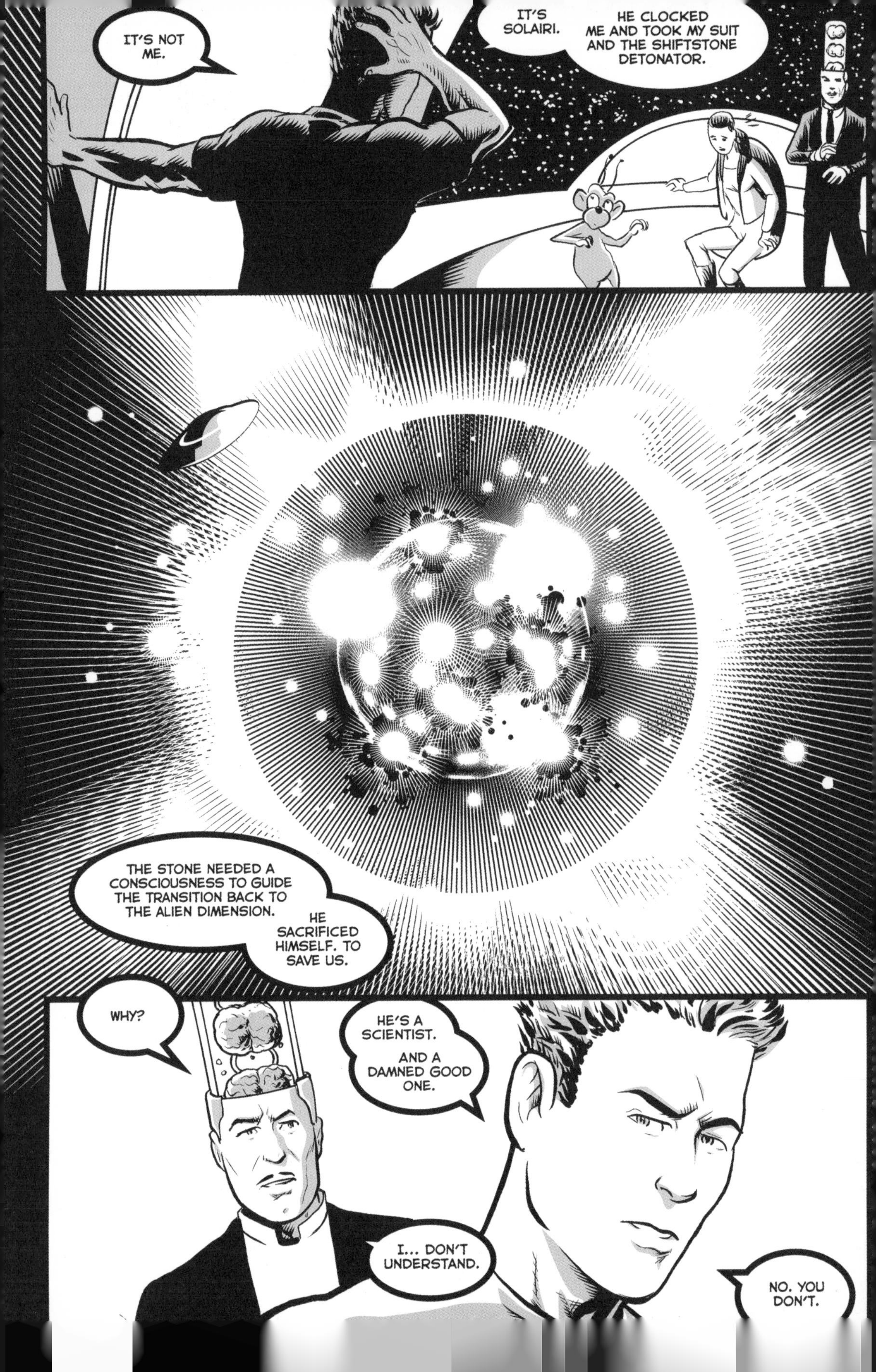
IT'S NOT ME.
IT'S SOLAIRI.
HE CLOCKED ME AND TOOK MY SUIT AND THE SHIFTSTONE DETONATOR.
THE STONE NEEDED A CONSCIOUSNESS TO GUIDE THE TRANSITION BACK TO THE ALIEN DIMENSION.
HE SACRIFICED HIMSELF. TO SAVE US.
WHY?
HE'S A SCIENTIST.
AND A DAMNED GOOD ONE.
I... DON'T UNDERSTAND.
NO. YOU DON'T.

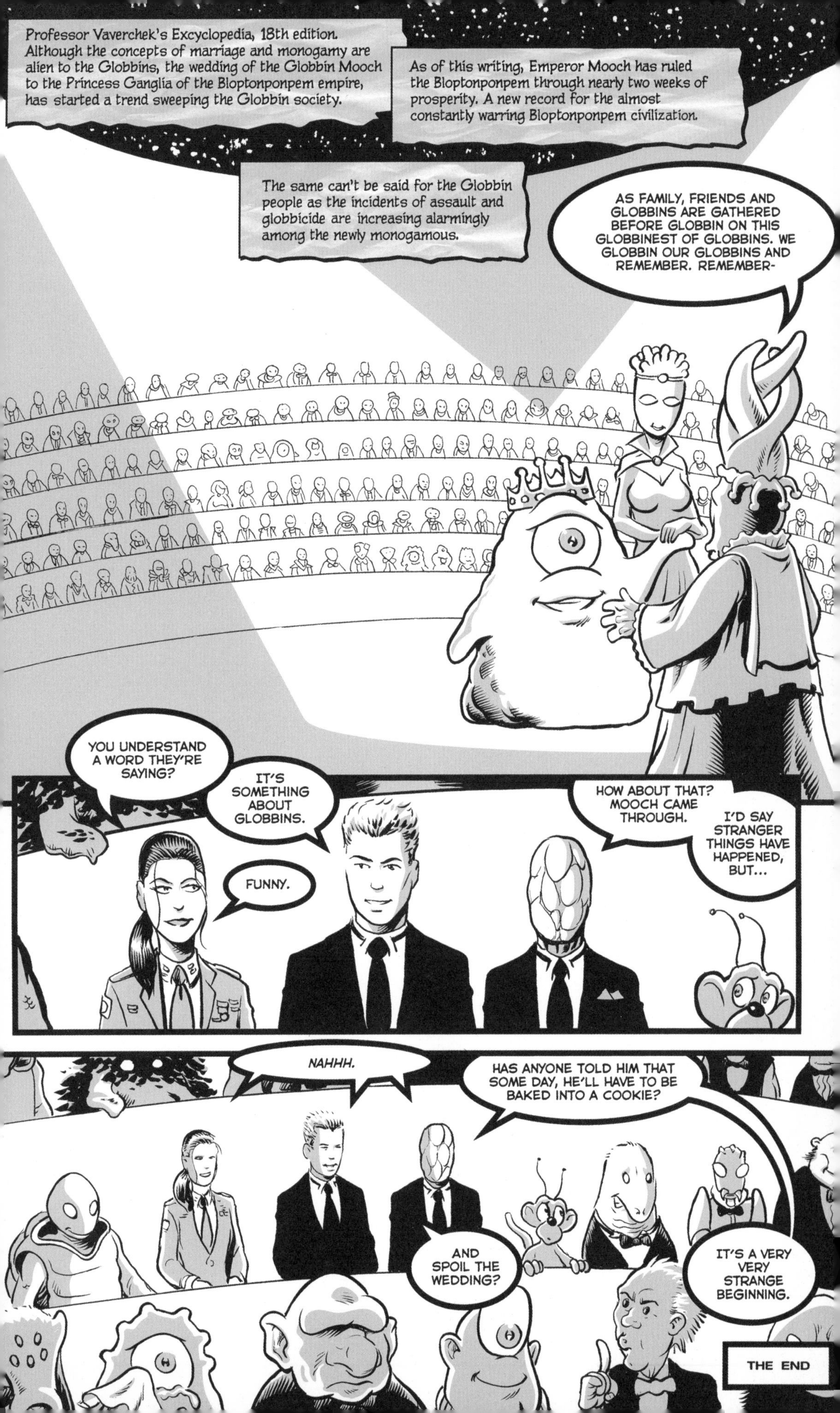

Professor Vaverchek's Excyclopedia, 18th edition. Although the concepts of marriage and monogamy are alien to the Globbins, the wedding of the Globbin Mooch to the Princess Ganglia of the Bloptonponpem empire, has started a trend sweeping the Globbin society.
As of this writing, Emperor Mooch has ruled the Bloptonponpem through nearly two weeks of prosperity. A new record for the almost constantly warring Bloptonponpem civilization.
The same can't be said for the Globbin people as the incidents of assault and globbicide are increasing alarmingly among the newly monogamous.
AS FAMILY, FRIENDS AND GLOBBINS ARE GATHERED BEFORE GLOBBIN ON THIS GLOBBINEST OF GLOBBINS. WE GLOBBIN OUR GLOBBINS AND REMEMBER. REMEMBER-
YOU UNDERSTAND A WORD THEY'RE SAYING?
IT'S SOMETHING ABOUT GLOBBINS.
FUNNY.
HOW ABOUT THAT? MOOCH CAME THROUGH.
I'D SAY STRANGER THINGS HAVE HAPPENED, BUT...
NAHHH.
HAS ANYONE TOLD HIM THAT SOME DAY, HE'LL HAVE TO BE BAKED INTO A COOKIE?
AND SPOIL THE WEDDING?
IT'S A VERY VERY STRANGE BEGINNING.
THE END

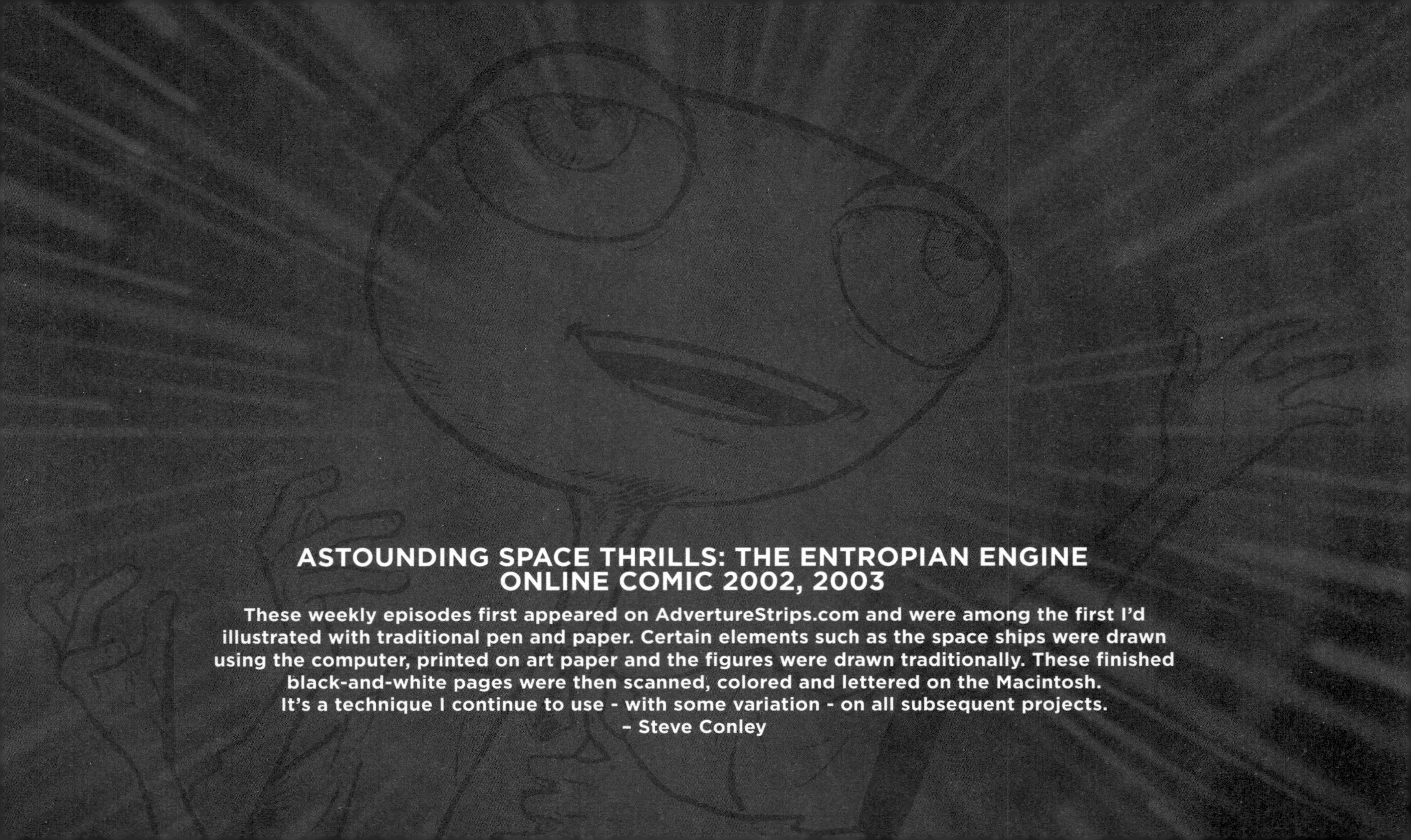

ASTOUNDING SPACE THRILLS: THE ENTROPIAN ENGINE ONLINE COMIC 2002, 2003

These weekly episodes first appeared on AdvertureStrips.com and were among the first I'd illustrated with traditional pen and paper. Certain elements such as the space ships were drawn using the computer, printed on art paper and the figures were drawn traditionally. These finished black-and-white pages were then scanned, colored and lettered on the Macintosh. It's a technique I continue to use - with some variation - on all subsequent projects.

– Steve Conley

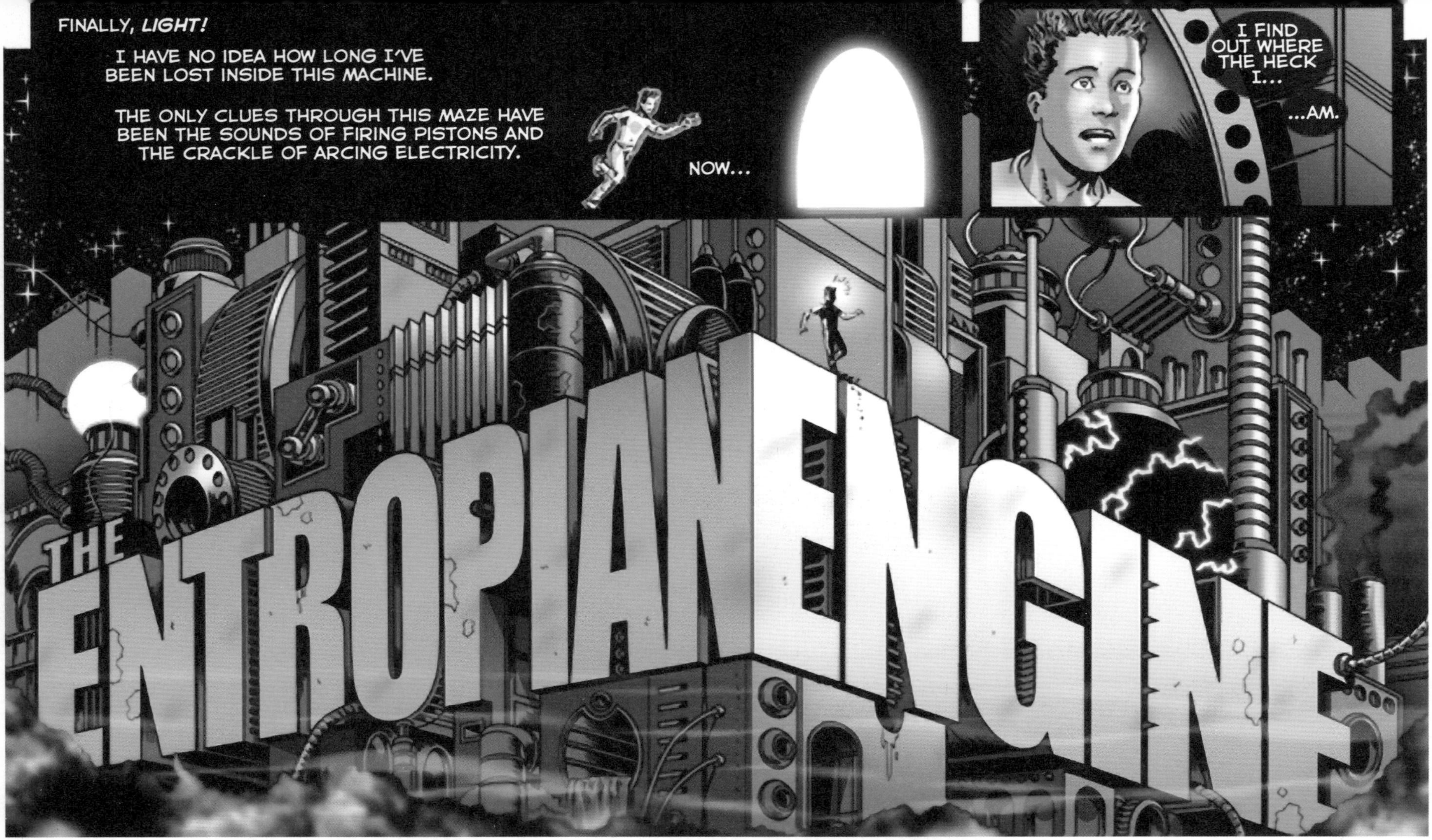
FINALLY, *LIGHT!*
I HAVE NO IDEA HOW LONG I'VE BEEN LOST INSIDE THIS MACHINE.
THE ONLY CLUES THROUGH THIS *MAZE* HAVE BEEN THE SOUNDS OF FIRING PISTONS AND THE CRACKLE OF ARCING ELECTRICITY.
NOW...
I FIND OUT WHERE THE HECK I...
...AM.
THE ENTROPIAN ENGINE

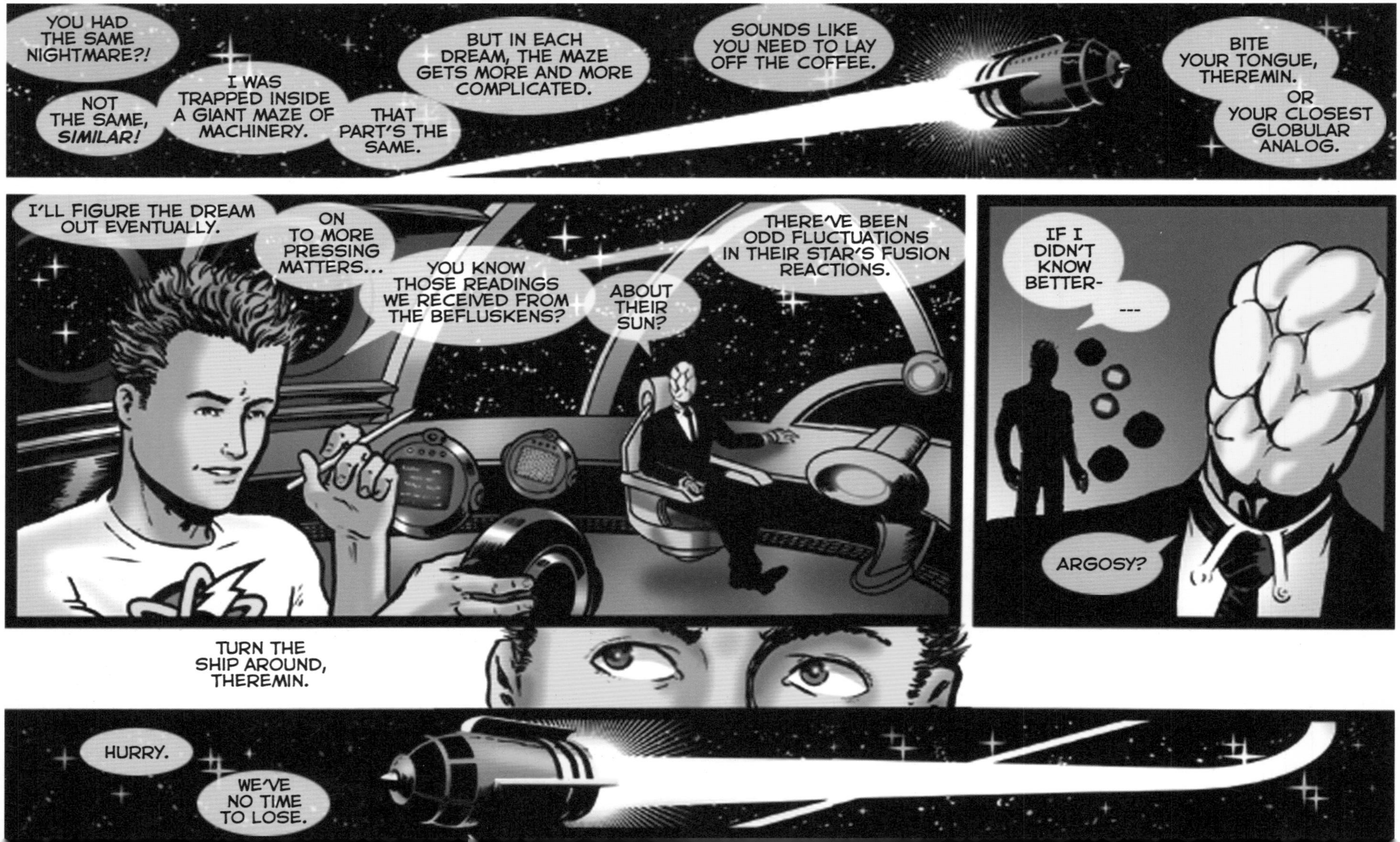
YOU HAD THE SAME NIGHTMARE?!
NOT THE SAME, *SIMILAR!*
I WAS TRAPPED INSIDE A GIANT MAZE OF *MACHINERY.*
THAT PART'S THE SAME.
BUT IN EACH DREAM, THE MAZE GETS *MORE* AND MORE COMPLICATED.
SOUNDS LIKE YOU NEED TO LAY OFF THE COFFEE.
BITE YOUR TONGUE, THEREMIN.
OR YOUR CLOSEST GLOBULAR ANALOG.
I'LL FIGURE THE DREAM OUT EVENTUALLY.
ON TO *MORE* PRESSING MATTERS...
YOU KNOW THOSE READINGS WE RECEIVED FROM THE BEFLUSKENS?
ABOUT THEIR SUN?
THERE'VE BEEN ODD FLUCTUATIONS IN THEIR STAR'S FUSION REACTIONS.
IF I DIDN'T KNOW BETTER-

ARGOSY?
TURN THE SHIP AROUND, THEREMIN.
HURRY.
WE'VE NO TIME TO LOSE.

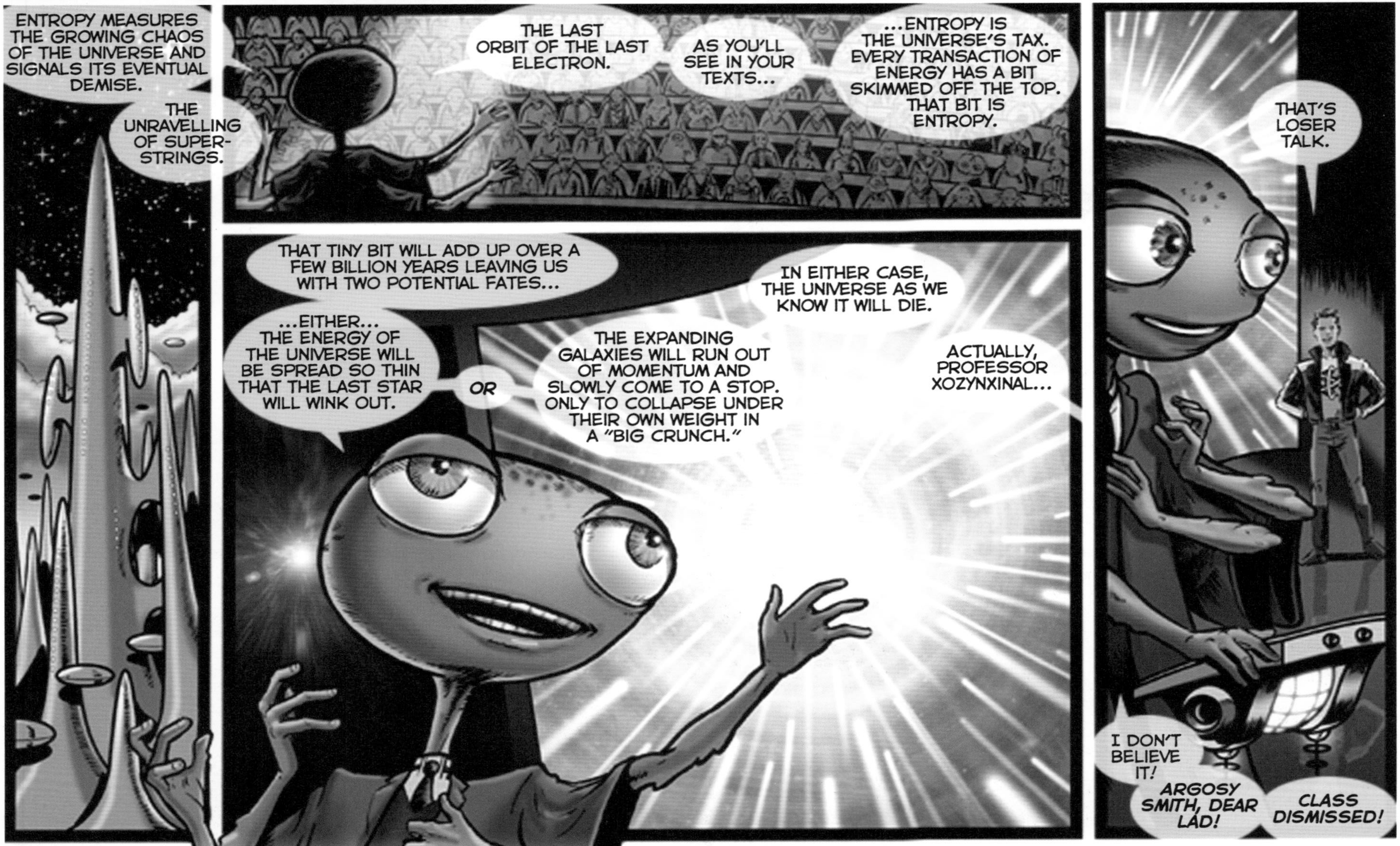
ENTROPY *MEASURES* THE GROWING CHAOS OF THE UNIVERSE AND SIGNALS ITS EVENTUAL DEMISE.
THE UNRAVELLING OF SUPER-STRINGS.
THE LAST ORBIT OF THE LAST ELECTRON.
AS YOU'LL SEE IN YOUR TEXTS...
...ENTROPY IS THE UNIVERSE'S TAX. EVERY TRANSACTION OF ENERGY HAS A BIT SKIMMED OFF THE TOP. THAT BIT IS ENTROPY.
THAT TINY BIT WILL ADD UP OVER A FEW BILLION YEARS LEAVING US WITH TWO POTENTIAL FATES...
...EITHER... THE ENERGY OF THE UNIVERSE WILL BE SPREAD SO THIN THAT THE LAST STAR WILL WINK OUT.
OR
THE EXPANDING GALAXIES WILL RUN OUT OF MOMENTUM AND SLOWLY COME TO A STOP. ONLY TO COLLAPSE UNDER THEIR OWN WEIGHT IN A "BIG CRUNCH."
IN EITHER CASE, THE UNIVERSE AS WE KNOW IT WILL DIE.
ACTUALLY, PROFESSOR XOZYNXINAL...
THAT'S LOSER TALK.
I DON'T BELIEVE IT!
ARGOSY SMITH, DEAR LAD!
CLASS DISMISSED!

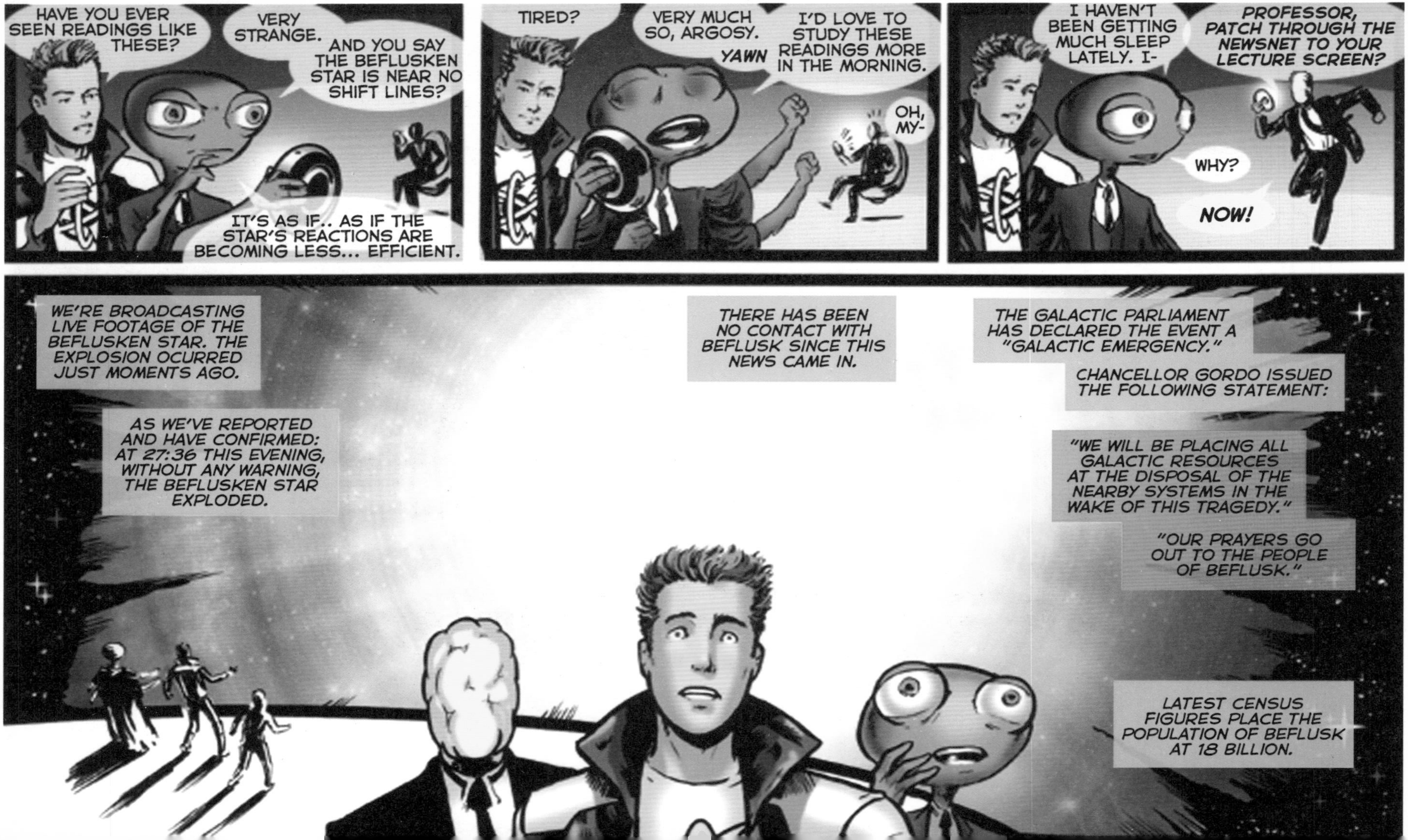
HAVE YOU EVER SEEN READINGS LIKE THESE?
VERY STRANGE.
AND YOU SAY THE BEFLUSKEN STAR IS NEAR NO SHIFT LINES?
IT'S AS IF.. AS IF THE STAR'S REACTIONS ARE BECOMING LESS... EFFICIENT.
TIRED?
VERY MUCH SO, ARGOSY.
YAWN
I'D LOVE TO STUDY THESE READINGS MORE IN THE MORNING.
OH, MY-
I HAVEN'T BEEN GETTING MUCH SLEEP LATELY. I-
PROFESSOR, PATCH THROUGH THE NEWSNET TO YOUR LECTURE SCREEN?
WHY?
NOW!
WE'RE BROADCASTING LIVE FOOTAGE OF THE BEFLUSKEN STAR. THE EXPLOSION OCURRED JUST MOMENTS AGO.
AS WE'VE REPORTED AND HAVE CONFIRMED: AT 27:36 THIS EVENING, WITHOUT ANY WARNING, THE BEFLUSKEN STAR EXPLODED.
THERE HAS BEEN NO CONTACT WITH BEFLUSK SINCE THIS NEWS CAME IN.
THE GALACTIC PARLIAMENT HAS DECLARED THE EVENT A "GALACTIC EMERGENCY."
CHANCELLOR GORDO ISSUED THE FOLLOWING STATEMENT:
"WE WILL BE PLACING ALL GALACTIC RESOURCES AT THE DISPOSAL OF THE NEARBY SYSTEMS IN THE WAKE OF THIS TRAGEDY."
"OUR PRAYERS GO OUT TO THE PEOPLE OF BEFLUSK."
LATEST CENSUS FIGURES PLACE THE POPULATION OF BEFLUSK AT 18 BILLION.

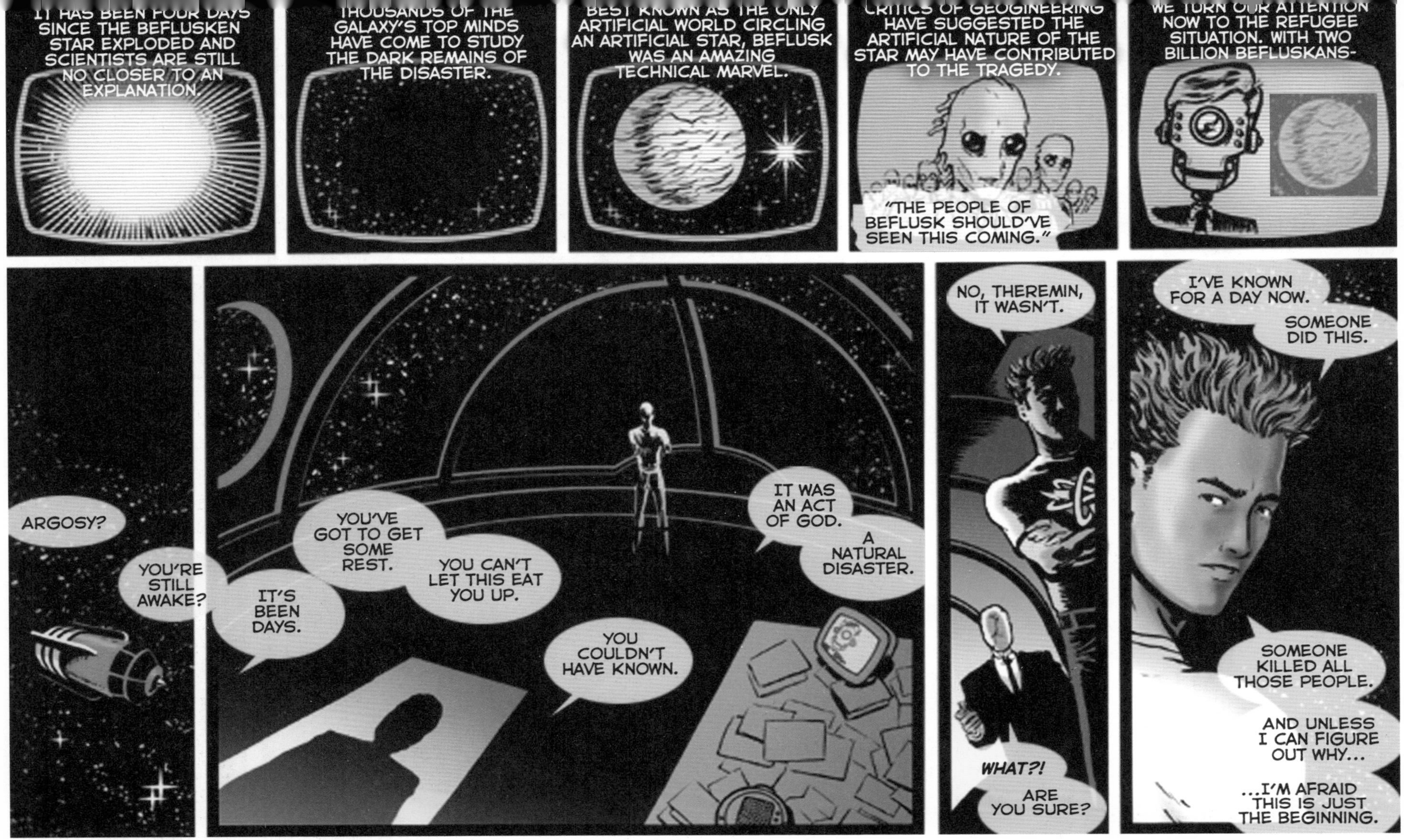
IT HAS BEEN FOUR DAYS SINCE THE BEFLUSKEN STAR EXPLODED AND SCIENTISTS ARE STILL NO CLOSER TO AN EXPLANATION.
THOUSANDS OF THE GALAXY'S TOP MINDS HAVE COME TO STUDY THE DARK REMAINS OF THE DISASTER.
BEST KNOWN AS THE ONLY ARTIFICIAL WORLD CIRCLING AN ARTIFICIAL STAR, BEFLUSK WAS AN AMAZING TECHNICAL MARVEL.
CRITICS OF GEOGINEERING HAVE SUGGESTED THE ARTIFICIAL NATURE OF THE STAR MAY HAVE CONTRIBUTED TO THE TRAGEDY.
"THE PEOPLE OF BEFLUSK SHOULD'VE SEEN THIS COMING."
WE TURN OUR ATTENTION NOW TO THE REFUGEE SITUATION. WITH TWO BILLION BEFLUSKANS-
ARGOSY?
YOU'RE STILL AWAKE?
IT'S BEEN DAYS.
YOU'VE GOT TO GET SOME REST.
YOU CAN'T LET THIS EAT YOU UP.
YOU COULDN'T HAVE KNOWN.
IT WAS AN ACT OF GOD.
A NATURAL DISASTER.
NO, THEREMIN, IT WASN'T.
WHAT?!
ARE YOU SURE?
I'VE KNOWN FOR A DAY NOW.
SOMEONE DID THIS.
SOMEONE KILLED ALL THOSE PEOPLE.
AND UNLESS I CAN FIGURE OUT WHY...
...I'M AFRAID THIS IS JUST THE BEGINNING.

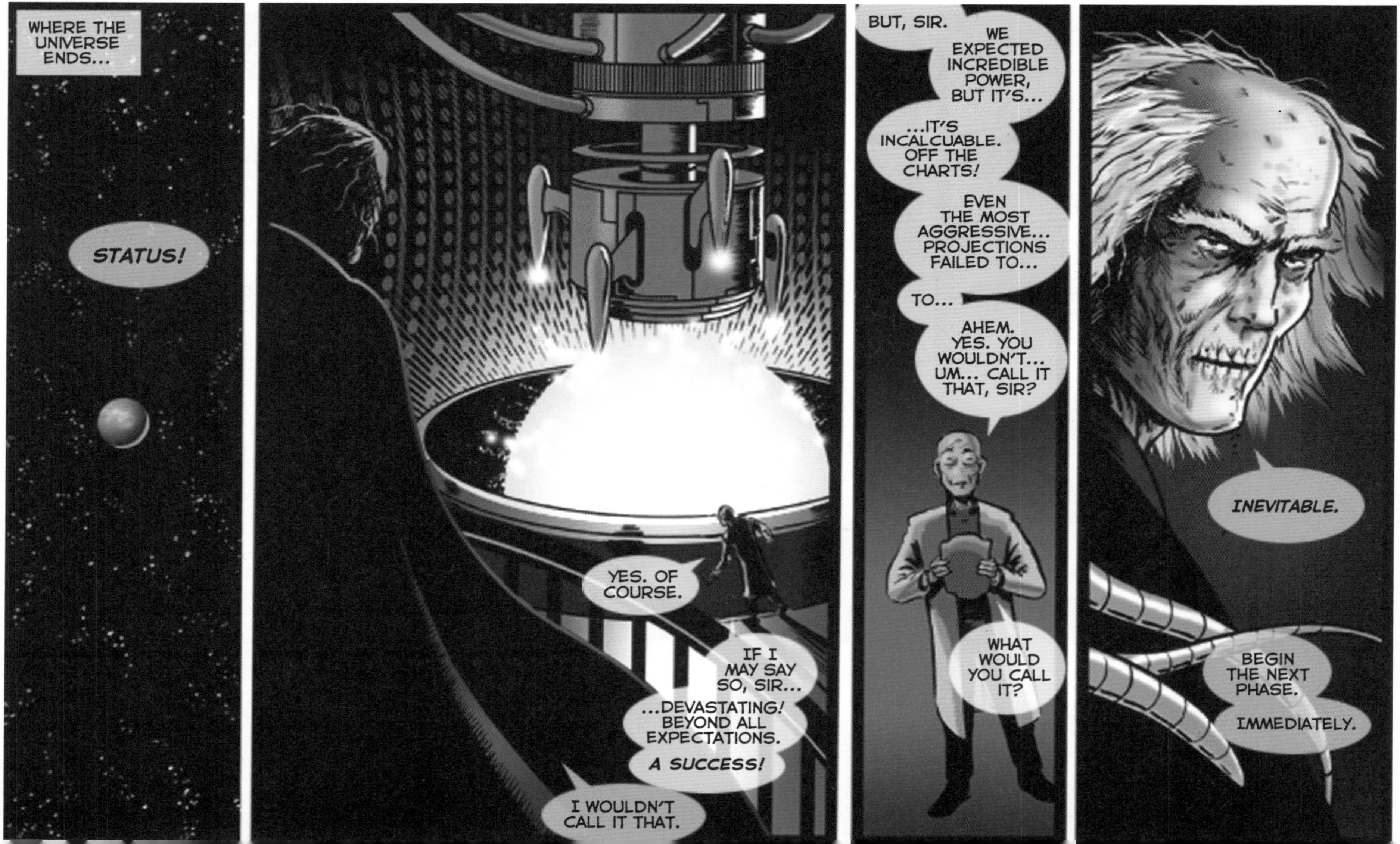
WHERE THE UNIVERSE ENDS...
STATUS!
YES. OF COURSE.
IF I MAY SAY SO, SIR...
...DEVASTATING! BEYOND ALL EXPECTATIONS.
A SUCCESS!
I WOULDN'T CALL IT THAT.
BUT, SIR.
WE EXPECTED INCREDIBLE POWER, BUT IT'S...
...IT'S INCALCUABLE. OFF THE CHARTS!
EVEN THE MOST AGGRESSIVE... PROJECTIONS FAILED TO...
TO...
AHEM. YES. YOU WOULDN'T... UM... CALL IT THAT, SIR?
WHAT WOULD YOU CALL IT?
INEVITABLE.
BEGIN THE NEXT PHASE.
IMMEDIATELY.

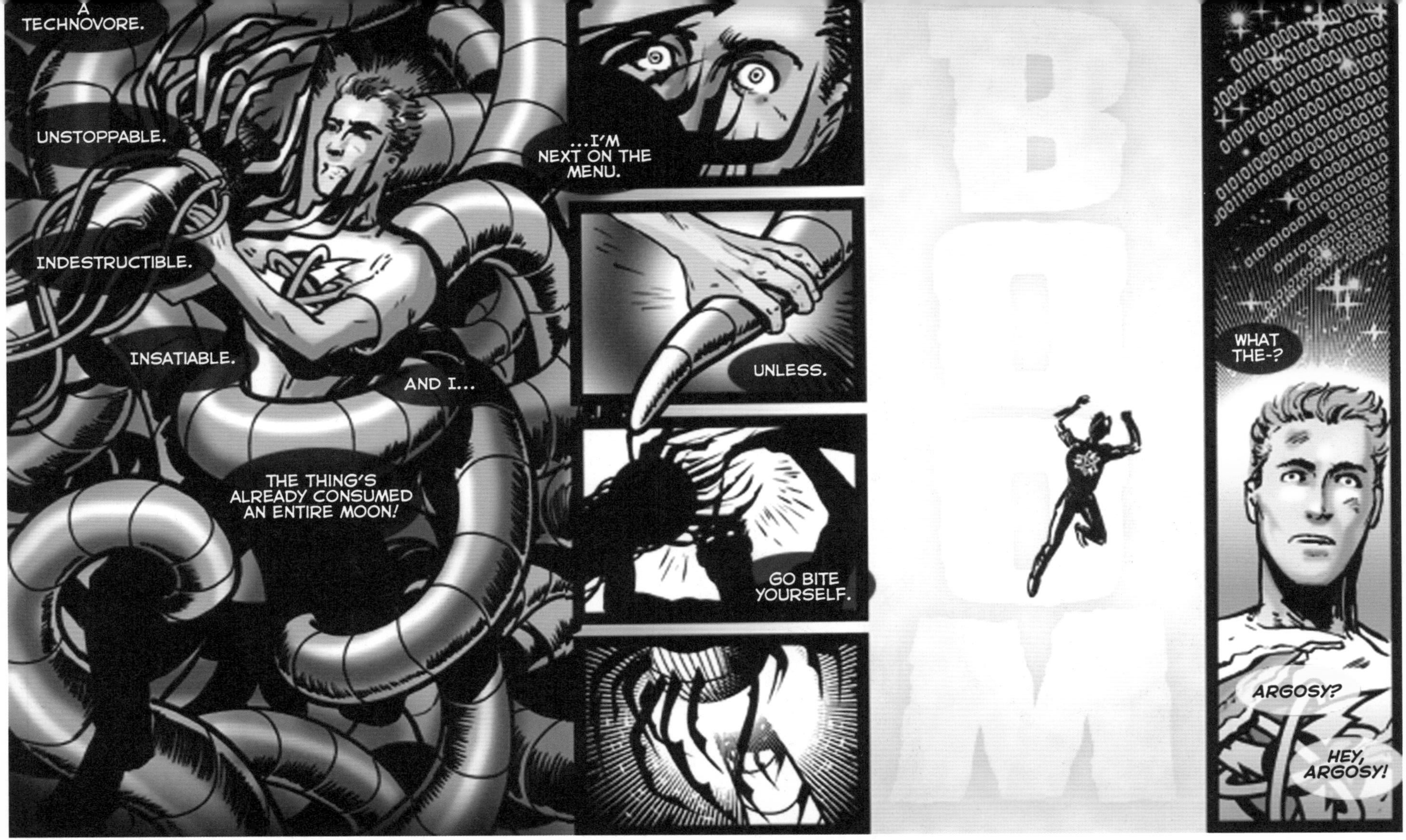
A TECHNOVORE.
UNSTOPPABLE.
INDESTRUCTIBLE.
INSATIABLE.
AND I...
THE THING'S ALREADY CONSUMED AN ENTIRE MOON!
...I'M NEXT ON THE MENU.
UNLESS.
GO BITE YOURSELF.
BOOM
WHAT THE-?
ARGOSY?
HEY, ARGOSY!

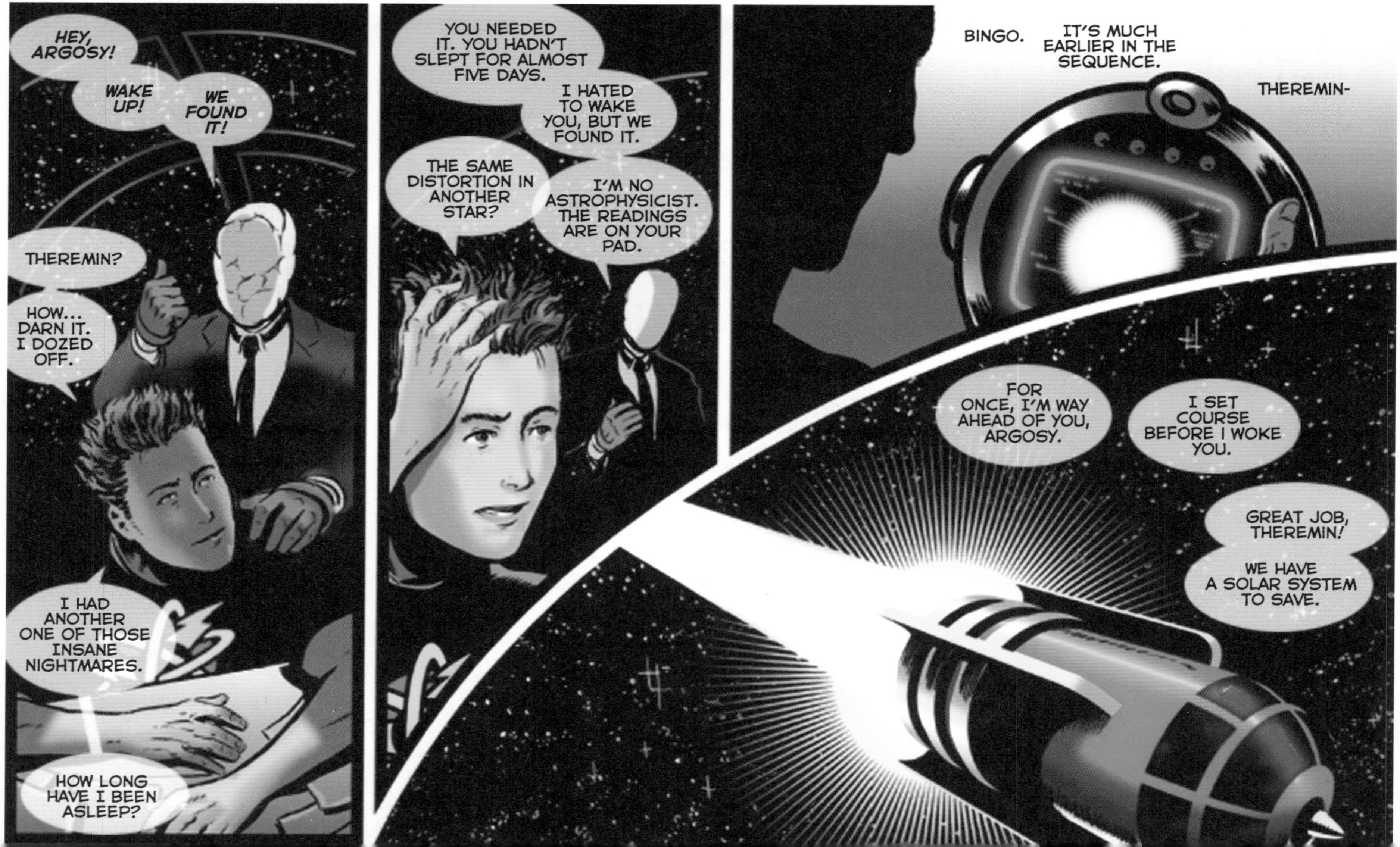
HEY, ARGOSY!
WAKE UP!
WE FOUND IT!
THEREMIN?
HOW... DARN IT. I DOZED OFF.
I HAD ANOTHER ONE OF THOSE INSANE NIGHTMARES.
HOW LONG HAVE I BEEN ASLEEP?
YOU NEEDED IT. YOU HADN'T SLEPT FOR ALMOST FIVE DAYS.
I HATED TO WAKE YOU, BUT WE FOUND IT.
THE SAME DISTORTION IN ANOTHER STAR?
I'M NO ASTROPHYSICIST. THE READINGS ARE ON YOUR PAD.
BINGO.
IT'S MUCH EARLIER IN THE SEQUENCE.
THEREMIN-
FOR ONCE, I'M WAY AHEAD OF YOU, ARGOSY.
I SET COURSE BEFORE I WOKE YOU.
GREAT JOB, THEREMIN!
WE HAVE A SOLAR SYSTEM TO SAVE.

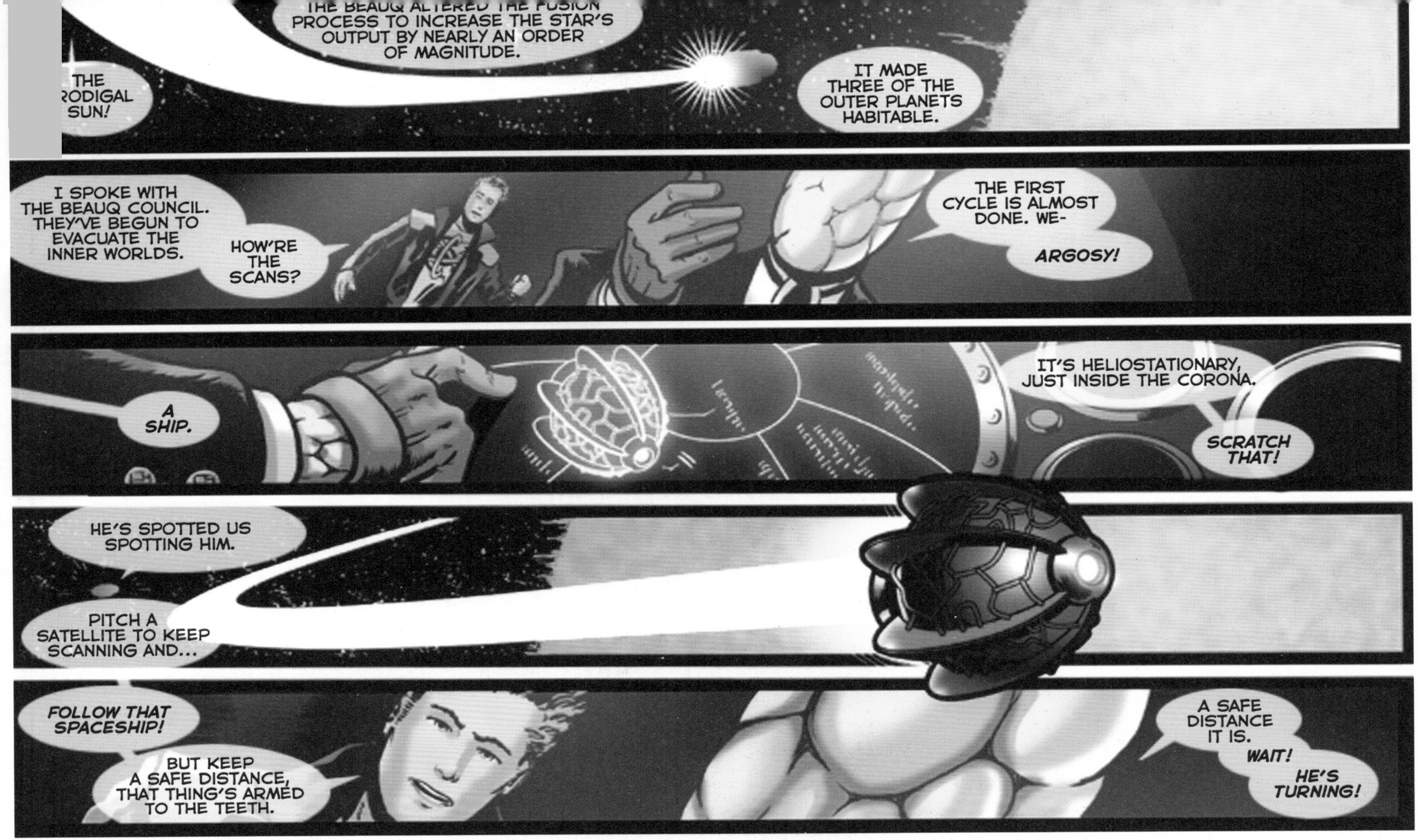
THE BEAUQ ALTERED THE FUSION PROCESS TO INCREASE THE STAR'S OUTPUT BY NEARLY AN ORDER OF MAGNITUDE.
RODIGAL SUN!
IT MADE THREE OF THE OUTER PLANETS HABITABLE.
I SPOKE WITH THE BEAUQ COUNCIL. THEY'VE BEGUN TO EVACUATE THE INNER WORLDS.
HOW'RE THE SCANS?
THE FIRST CYCLE IS ALMOST DONE. WE-
ARGOSY!
A SHIP.
IT'S HELIOSTATIONARY, JUST INSIDE THE CORONA.
SCRATCH THAT!
HE'S SPOTTED US SPOTTING HIM.
PITCH A SATELLITE TO KEEP SCANNING AND...
FOLLOW THAT SPACESHIP!
BUT KEEP A SAFE DISTANCE, THAT THING'S ARMED TO THE TEETH.
A SAFE DISTANCE IT IS.
WAIT!
HE'S TURNING!

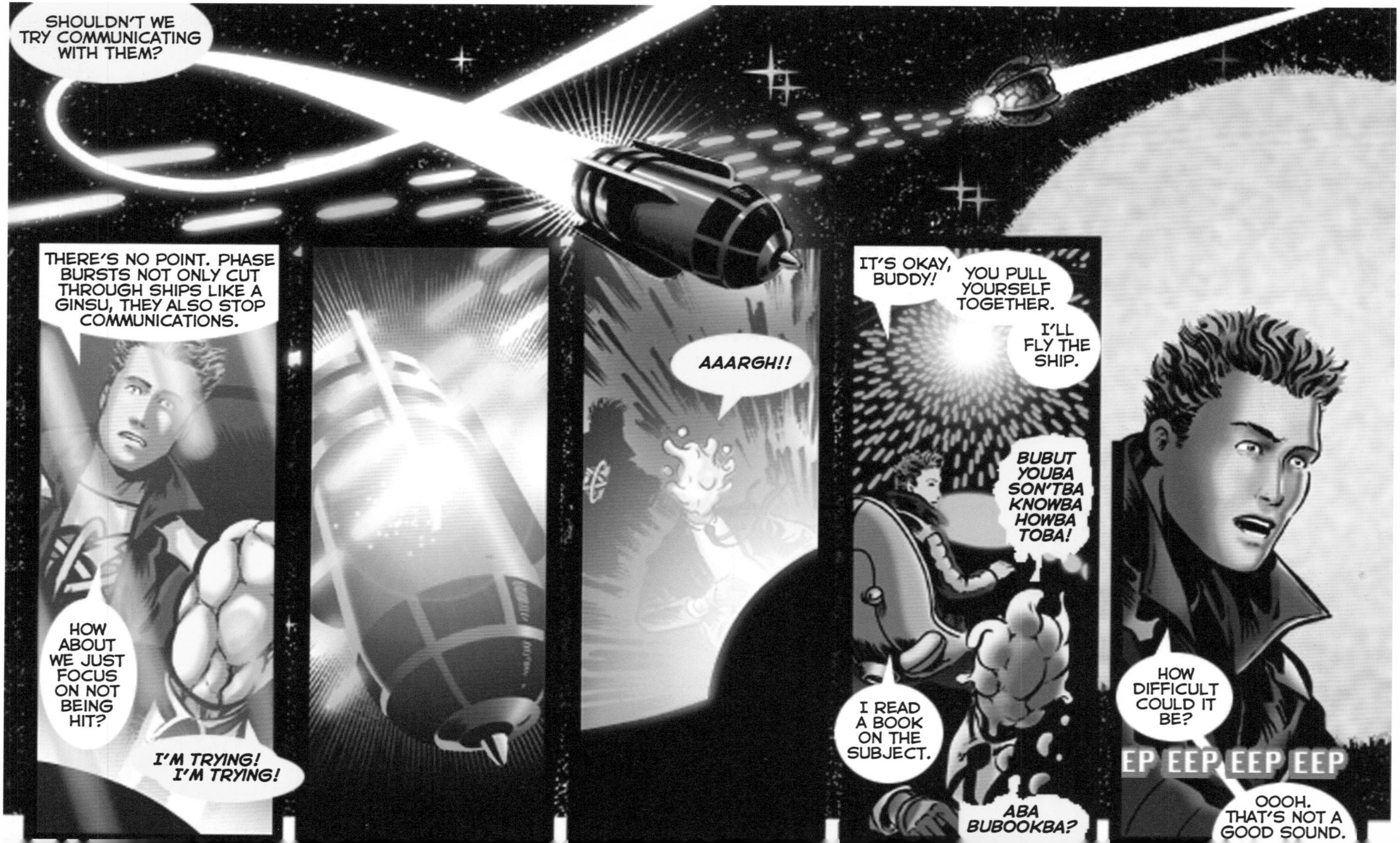
SHOULDN'T WE TRY COMMUNICATING WITH THEM?
THERE'S NO POINT. PHASE BURSTS NOT ONLY CUT THROUGH SHIPS LIKE A GINSU, THEY ALSO STOP COMMUNICATIONS.
HOW ABOUT WE JUST FOCUS ON NOT BEING HIT?
I'M TRYING! I'M TRYING!
AAARGH!!
IT'S OKAY, BUDDY!
YOU PULL YOURSELF TOGETHER.
I'LL FLY THE SHIP.
BUBUT YOUBA SON'TBA KNOWBA HOWBA TOBA!
I READ A BOOK ON THE SUBJECT.
ABA BUBOOKBA?
HOW DIFFICULT COULD IT BE?
EP EEP EEP EEP
OOOH. THAT'S NOT A GOOD SOUND.

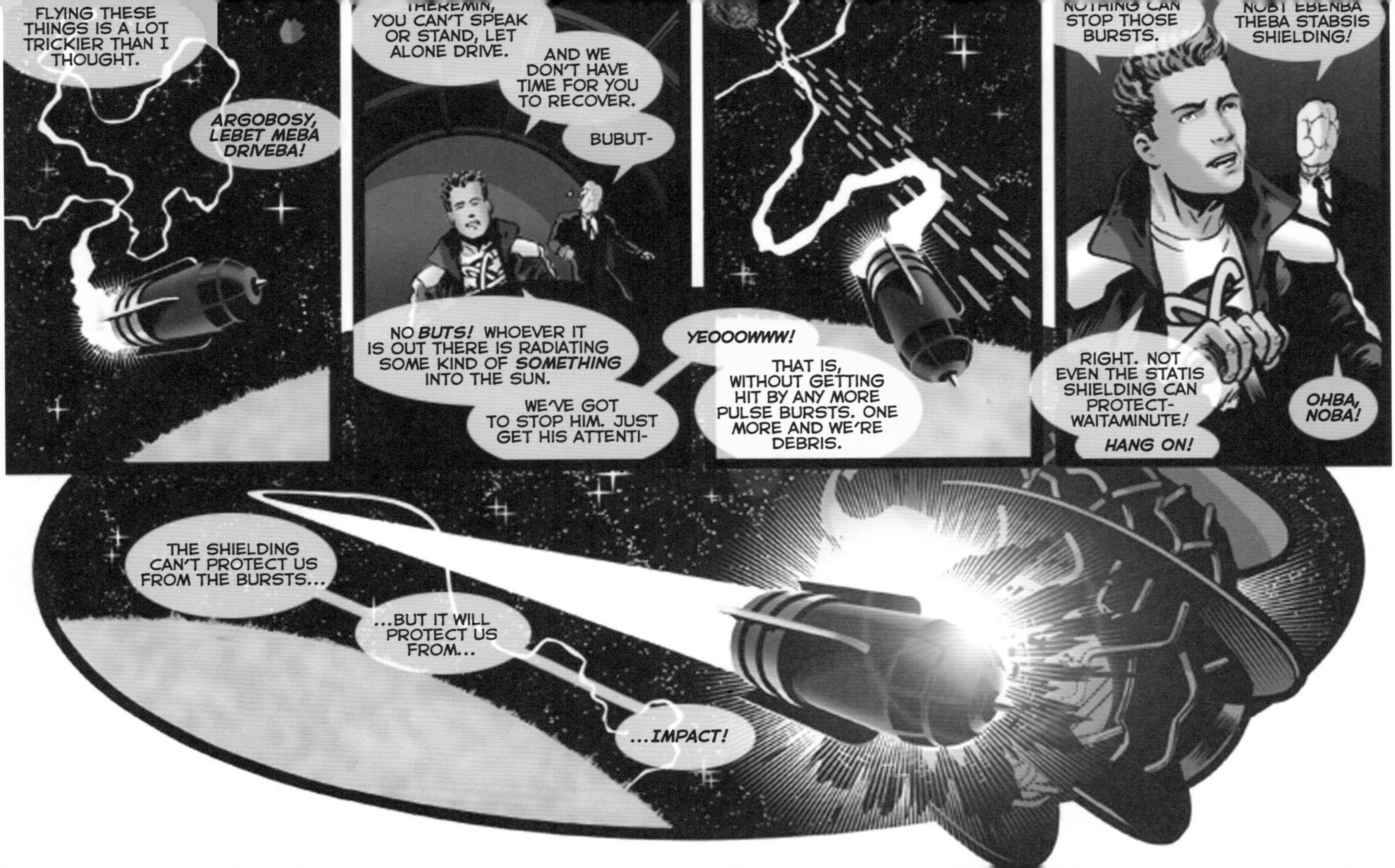

FLYING THESE THINGS IS A LOT TRICKIER THAN I THOUGHT.
ARGOBOSY, LEBET MEBA DRIVEBA!
THEREMIN, YOU CAN'T SPEAK OR STAND, LET ALONE DRIVE.
AND WE DON'T HAVE TIME FOR YOU TO RECOVER.
BUBUT-
NO BUTS! WHOEVER IT IS OUT THERE IS RADIATING SOME KIND OF SOMETHING INTO THE SUN.
WE'VE GOT TO STOP HIM. JUST GET HIS ATTENTI-
YEOOOWWW!
THAT IS, WITHOUT GETTING HIT BY ANY MORE PULSE BURSTS. ONE MORE AND WE'RE DEBRIS.
NOTHING CAN STOP THOSE BURSTS.
NOBI EBENBA THEBA STABSIS SHIELDING!
RIGHT. NOT EVEN THE STATIS SHIELDING CAN PROTECT-
WAITAMINUTE!
HANG ON!
OHBA, NOBA!
THE SHIELDING CAN'T PROTECT US FROM THE BURSTS...
...BUT IT WILL PROTECT US FROM...
...IMPACT!

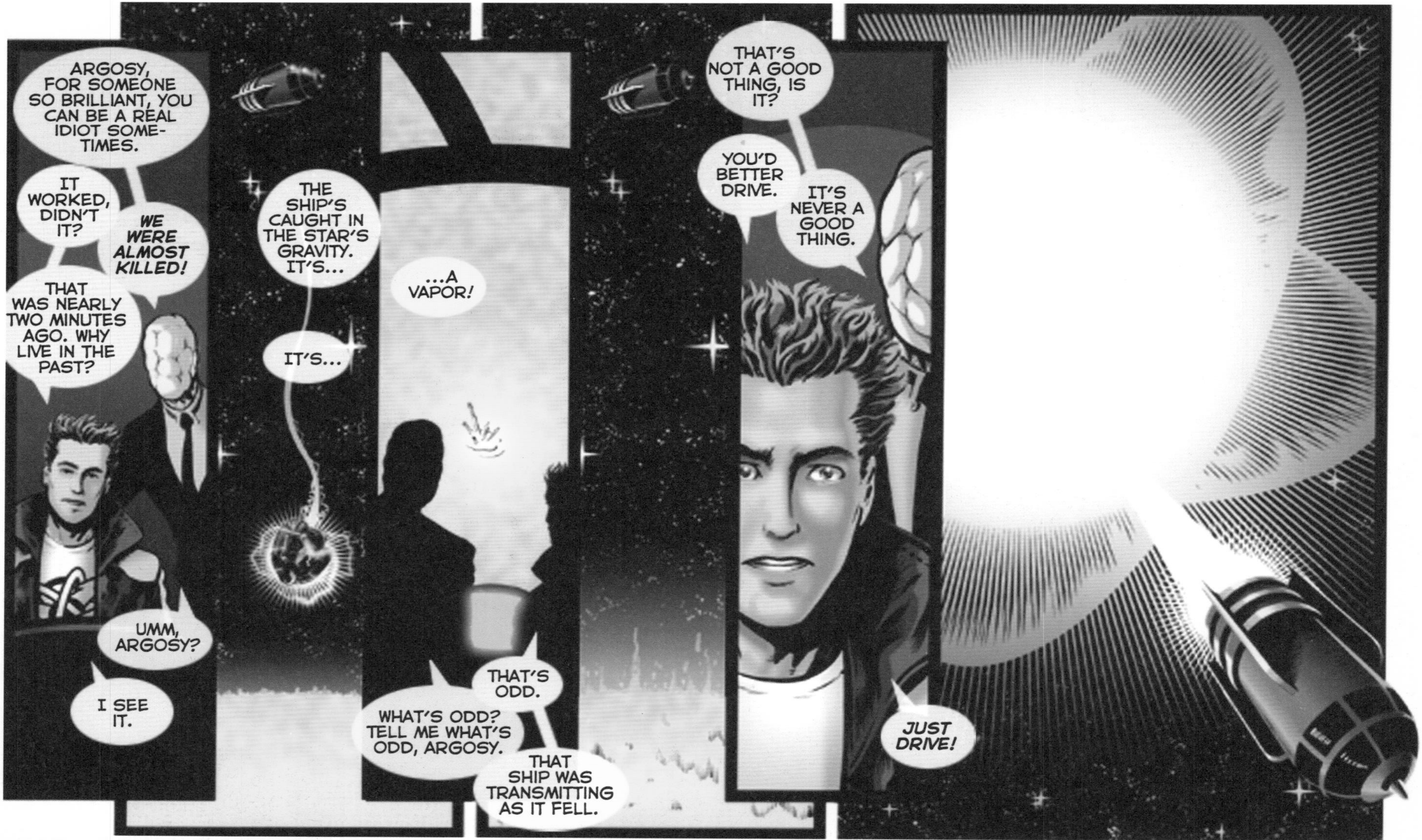
ARGOSY, FOR SOMEONE SO BRILLIANT, YOU CAN BE A REAL IDIOT SOME-TIMES.
IT WORKED, DIDN'T IT?
WE WERE ALMOST KILLED!
THAT WAS NEARLY TWO MINUTES AGO. WHY LIVE IN THE PAST?
UMM, ARGOSY?
I SEE IT.
THE SHIP'S CAUGHT IN THE STAR'S GRAVITY. IT'S...
IT'S...
...A VAPOR!
WHAT'S ODD? TELL ME WHAT'S ODD, ARGOSY.
THAT'S ODD.
THAT SHIP WAS TRANSMITTING AS IT FELL.
THAT'S NOT A GOOD THING, IS IT?
YOU'D BETTER DRIVE.
IT'S NEVER A GOOD THING.
JUST DRIVE!

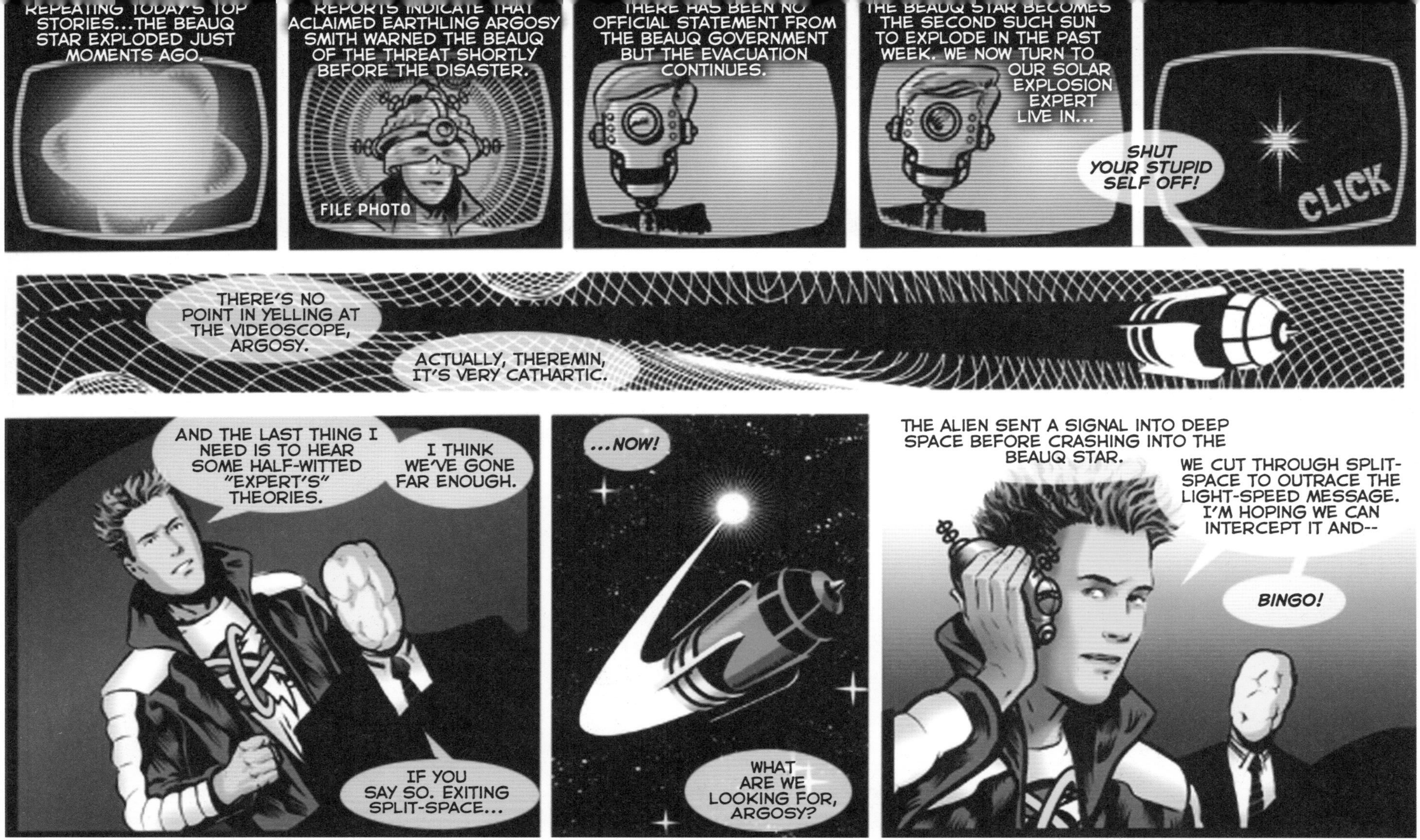
REPEATING TODAY'S TOP STORIES...THE BEAUQ STAR EXPLODED JUST MOMENTS AGO.
REPORTS INDICATE THAT ACLAIMED EARTHLING ARGOSY SMITH WARNED THE BEAUQ OF THE THREAT SHORTLY BEFORE THE DISASTER.
FILE PHOTO
THERE HAS BEEN NO OFFICIAL STATEMENT FROM THE BEAUQ GOVERNMENT BUT THE EVACUATION CONTINUES.
THE BEAUQ STAR BECOMES THE SECOND SUCH SUN TO EXPLODE IN THE PAST WEEK. WE NOW TURN TO OUR SOLAR EXPLOSION EXPERT LIVE IN...
SHUT YOUR STUPID SELF OFF!
CLICK
THERE'S NO POINT IN YELLING AT THE VIDEOSCOPE, ARGOSY.
ACTUALLY, THEREMIN, IT'S VERY CATHARTIC.
AND THE LAST THING I NEED IS TO HEAR SOME HALF-WITTED "EXPERT'S" THEORIES.
I THINK WE'VE GONE FAR ENOUGH.
IF YOU SAY SO. EXITING SPLIT-SPACE...
...NOW!
WHAT ARE WE LOOKING FOR, ARGOSY?
THE ALIEN SENT A SIGNAL INTO DEEP SPACE BEFORE CRASHING INTO THE BEAUQ STAR.
WE CUT THROUGH SPLIT-SPACE TO OUTRACE THE LIGHT-SPEED MESSAGE. I'M HOPING WE CAN INTERCEPT IT AND--
BINGO!

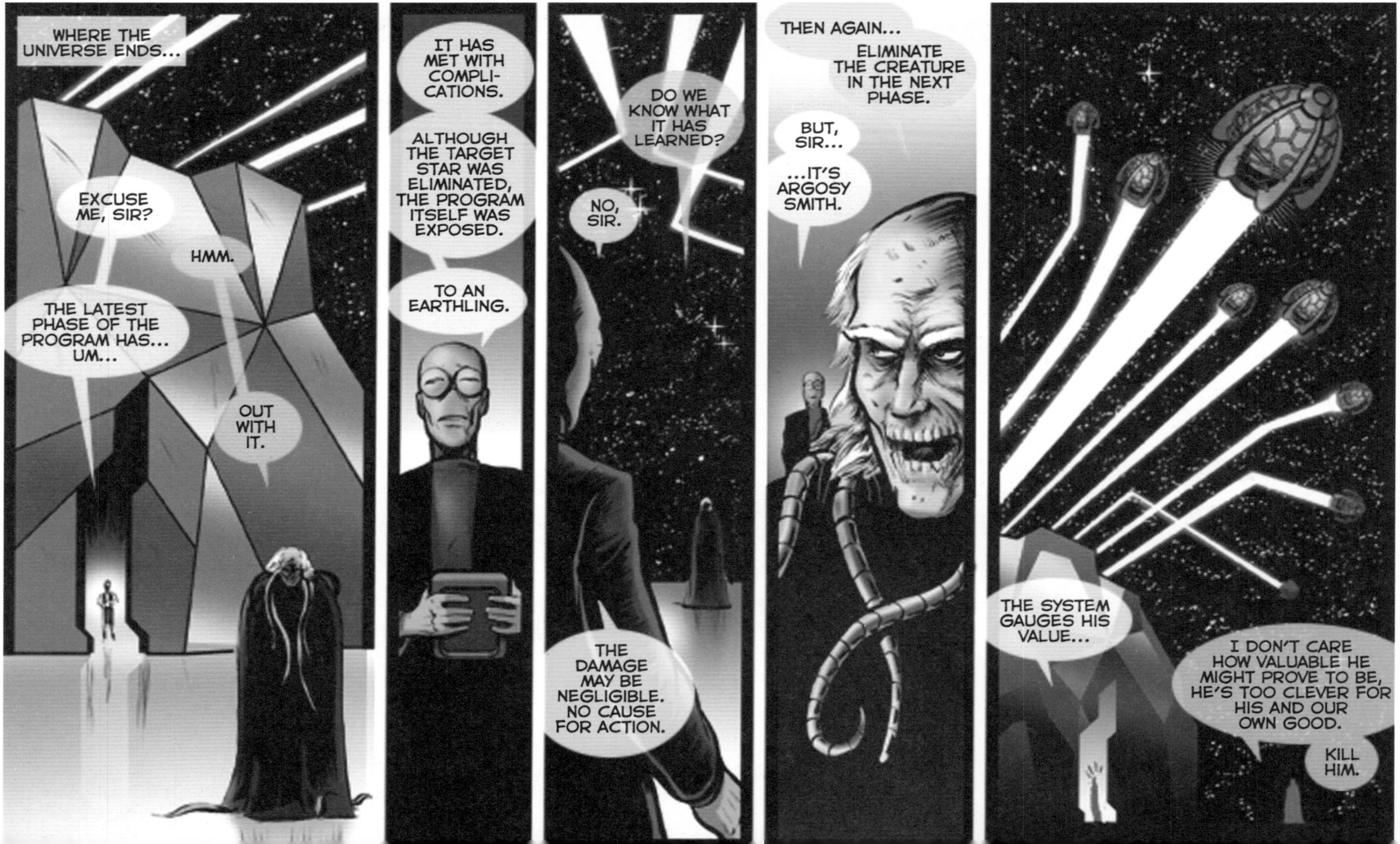
WHERE THE UNIVERSE ENDS...
EXCUSE ME, SIR?
HMM.
THE LATEST PHASE OF THE PROGRAM HAS... UM...
OUT WITH IT.
IT HAS MET WITH COMPLI-CATIONS.
ALTHOUGH THE TARGET STAR WAS ELIMINATED, THE PROGRAM ITSELF WAS EXPOSED.
TO AN EARTHLING.
DO WE KNOW WHAT IT HAS LEARNED?
NO, SIR.
THE DAMAGE MAY BE NEGLIGIBLE. NO CAUSE FOR ACTION.
THEN AGAIN...
ELIMINATE THE CREATURE IN THE NEXT PHASE.
BUT, SIR...
...IT'S ARGOSY SMITH.
THE SYSTEM GAUGES HIS VALUE...
I DON'T CARE HOW VALUABLE HE MIGHT PROVE TO BE, HE'S TOO CLEVER FOR HIS AND OUR OWN GOOD.
KILL HIM.

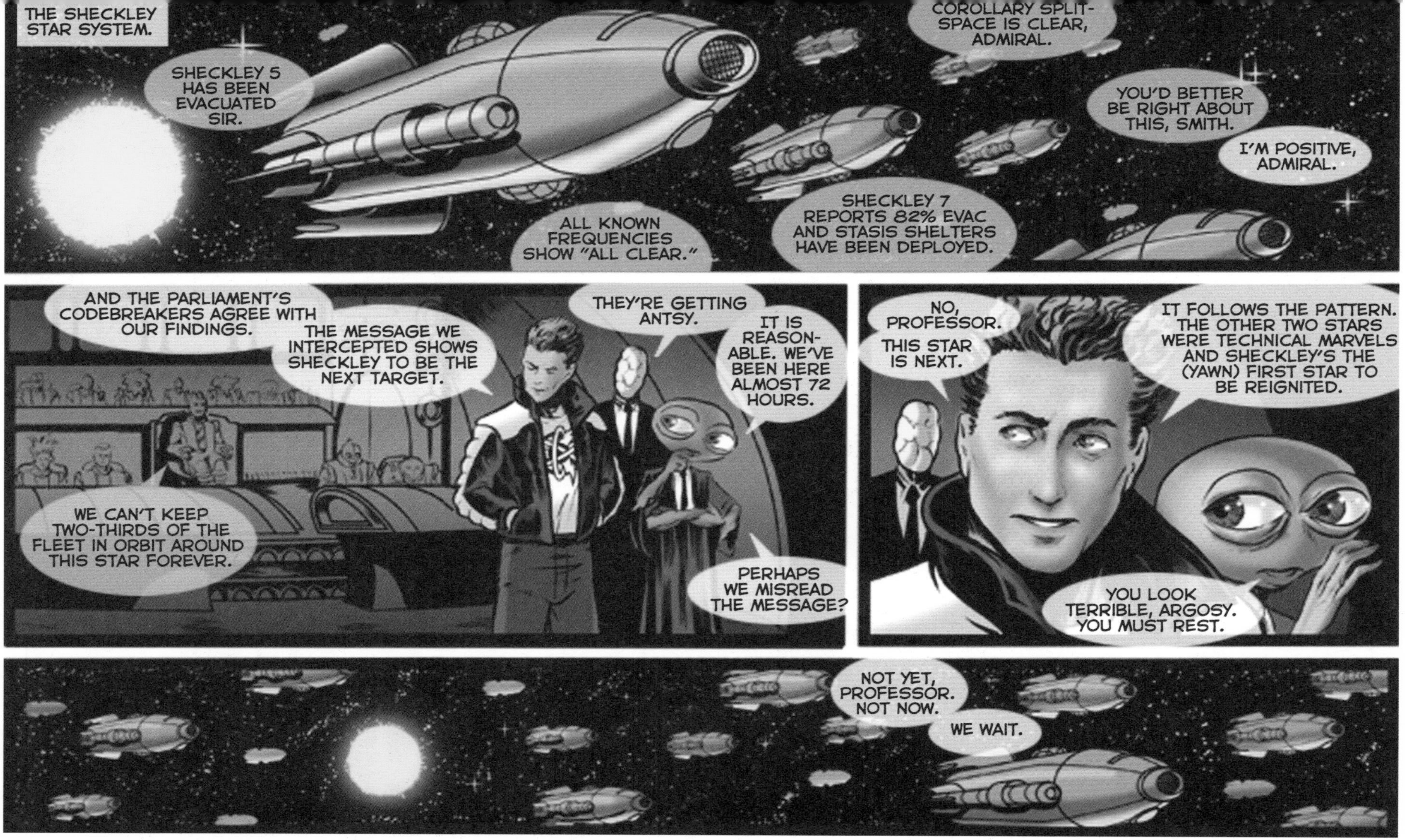
THE SHECKLEY STAR SYSTEM.
SHECKLEY 5 HAS BEEN EVACUATED SIR.
ALL KNOWN FREQUENCIES SHOW "ALL CLEAR."
SHECKLEY 7 REPORTS 82% EVAC AND STASIS SHELTERS HAVE BEEN DEPLOYED.
COROLLARY SPLIT-SPACE IS CLEAR, ADMIRAL.
YOU'D BETTER BE RIGHT ABOUT THIS, SMITH.
I'M POSITIVE, ADMIRAL.
AND THE PARLIAMENT'S CODEBREAKERS AGREE WITH OUR FINDINGS.
THE MESSAGE WE INTERCEPTED SHOWS SHECKLEY TO BE THE NEXT TARGET.
WE CAN'T KEEP TWO-THIRDS OF THE FLEET IN ORBIT AROUND THIS STAR FOREVER.
THEY'RE GETTING ANTSY.
IT IS REASON-ABLE. WE'VE BEEN HERE ALMOST 72 HOURS.
PERHAPS WE MISREAD THE MESSAGE?
NO, PROFESSOR.
THIS STAR IS NEXT.
IT FOLLOWS THE PATTERN. THE OTHER TWO STARS WERE TECHNICAL MARVELS AND SHECKLEY'S THE (YAWN) FIRST STAR TO BE REIGNITED.
YOU LOOK TERRIBLE, ARGOSY. YOU MUST REST.
NOT YET, PROFESSOR. NOT NOW.
WE WAIT.

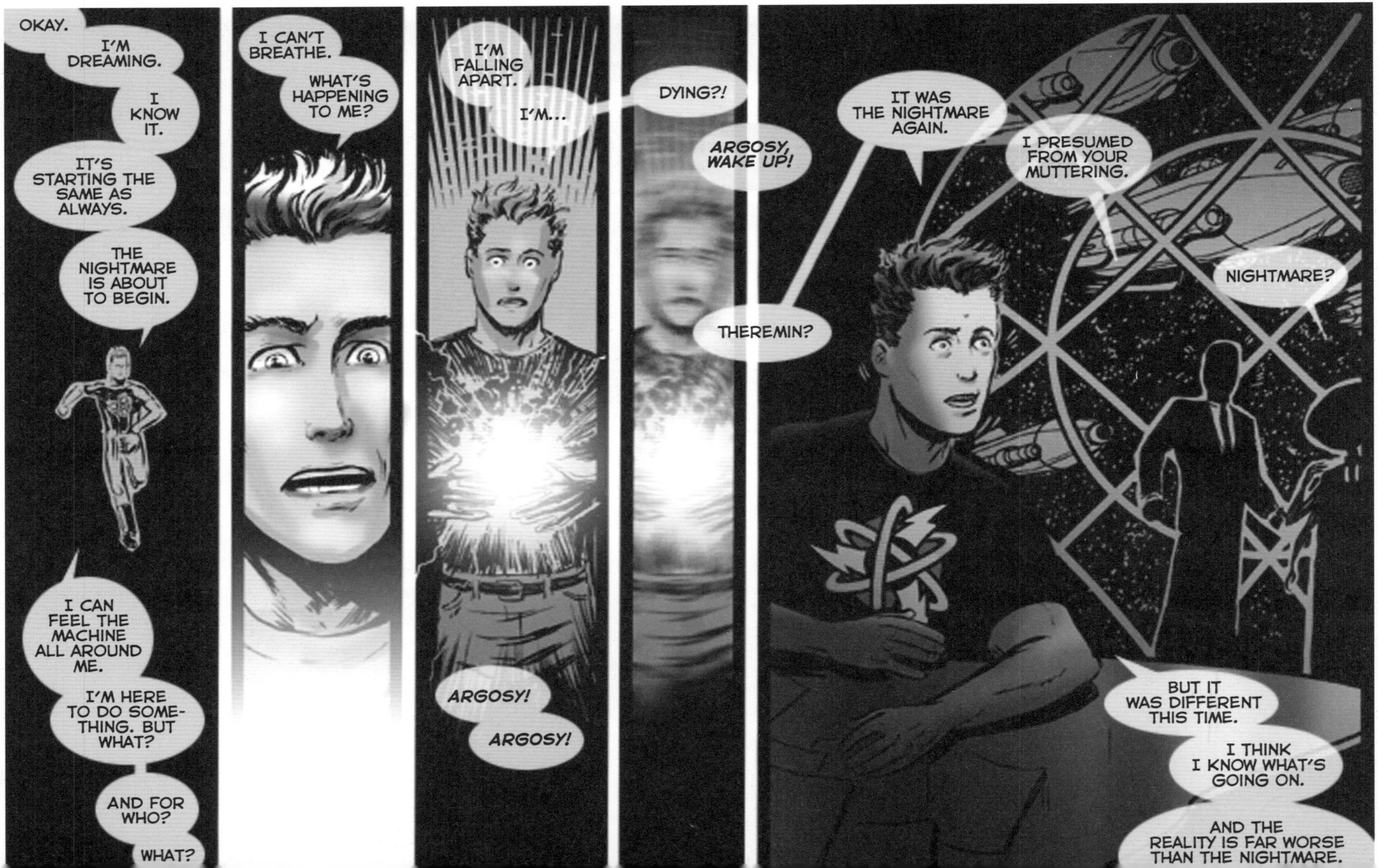
OKAY.
I'M DREAMING.
I KNOW IT.
IT'S STARTING THE SAME AS ALWAYS.
THE NIGHTMARE IS ABOUT TO BEGIN.
I CAN FEEL THE MACHINE ALL AROUND ME.
I'M HERE TO DO SOME-THING. BUT WHAT?
AND FOR WHO?
WHAT?
I CAN'T BREATHE.
WHAT'S HAPPENING TO ME?
I'M FALLING APART.
I'M...
DYING?!
ARGOSY!
ARGOSY!
ARGOSY, WAKE UP!
THEREMIN?
IT WAS THE NIGHTMARE AGAIN.
I PRESUMED FROM YOUR MUTTERING.
NIGHTMARE?
BUT IT WAS DIFFERENT THIS TIME.
I THINK I KNOW WHAT'S GOING ON.
AND THE REALITY IS FAR WORSE THAN THE NIGHTMARE.

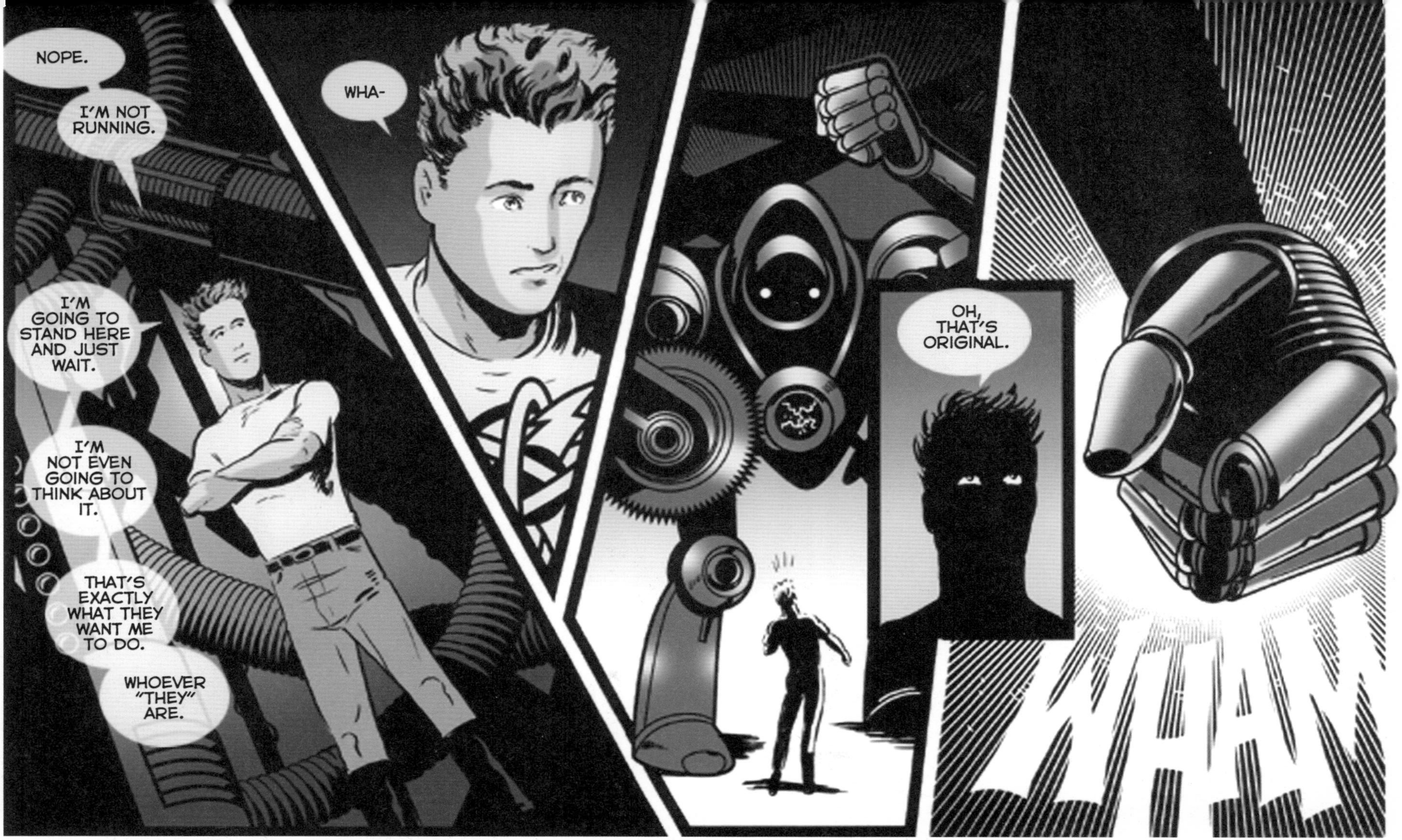
NOPE.
I'M NOT RUNNING.
I'M GOING TO STAND HERE AND JUST WAIT.
I'M NOT EVEN GOING TO THINK ABOUT IT.
THAT'S EXACTLY WHAT THEY WANT ME TO DO.
WHOEVER "THEY" ARE.
WHA-
OH, THAT'S ORIGINAL.
WHAM

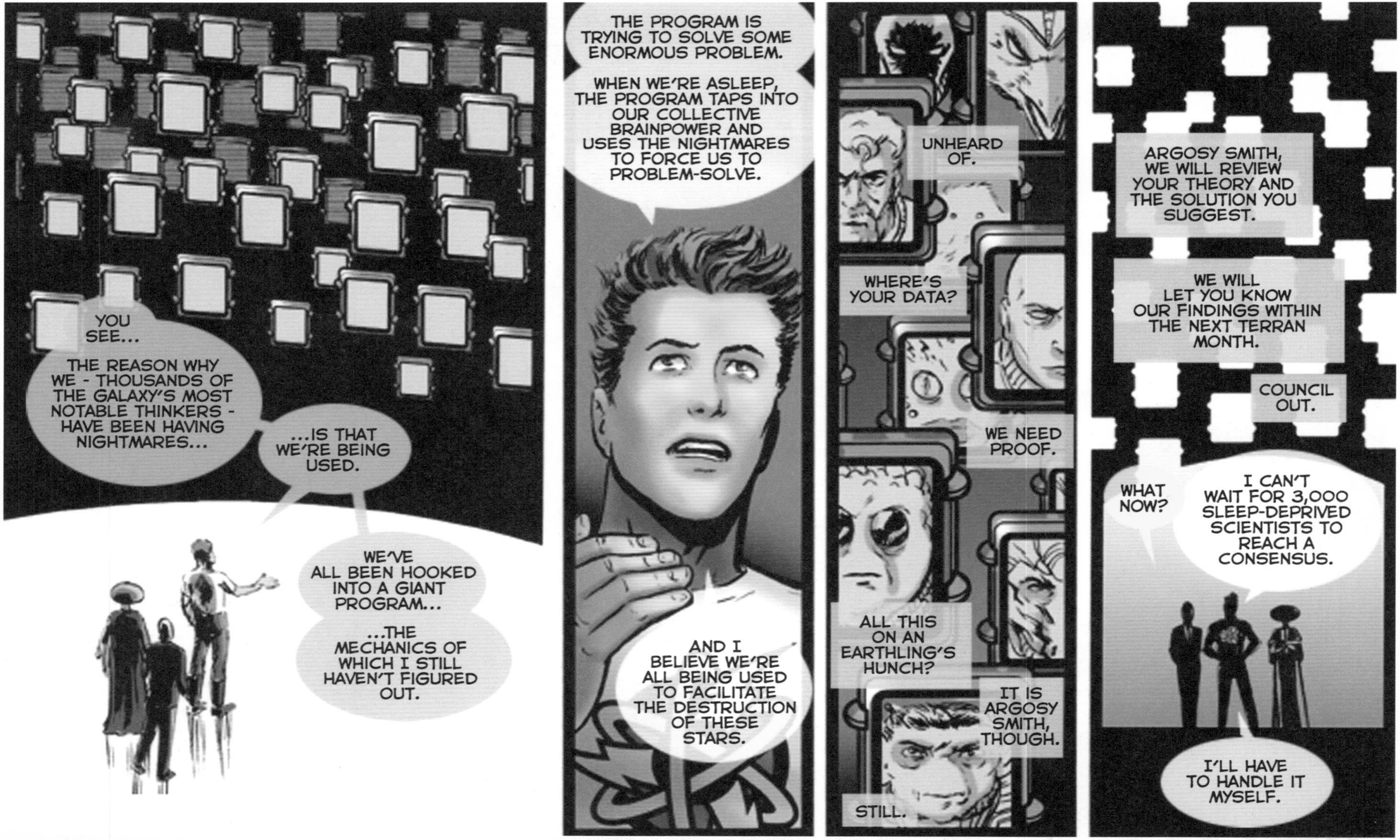
YOU SEE...
THE REASON WHY WE - THOUSANDS OF THE GALAXY'S MOST NOTABLE THINKERS - HAVE BEEN HAVING NIGHTMARES...
...IS THAT WE'RE BEING USED.
WE'VE ALL BEEN HOOKED INTO A GIANT PROGRAM...
...THE MECHANICS OF WHICH I STILL HAVEN'T FIGURED OUT.
THE PROGRAM IS TRYING TO SOLVE SOME ENORMOUS PROBLEM.
WHEN WE'RE ASLEEP, THE PROGRAM TAPS INTO OUR COLLECTIVE BRAINPOWER AND USES THE NIGHTMARES TO FORCE US TO PROBLEM-SOLVE.
AND I BELIEVE WE'RE ALL BEING USED TO FACILITATE THE DESTRUCTION OF THESE STARS.
UNHEARD OF.
WHERE'S YOUR DATA?
WE NEED PROOF.
ALL THIS ON AN EARTHLING'S HUNCH?
IT IS ARGOSY SMITH, THOUGH.
STILL.
ARGOSY SMITH, WE WILL REVIEW YOUR THEORY AND THE SOLUTION YOU SUGGEST.
WE WILL LET YOU KNOW OUR FINDINGS WITHIN THE NEXT TERRAN MONTH.
COUNCIL OUT.
WHAT NOW?
I CAN'T WAIT FOR 3,000 SLEEP-DEPRIVED SCIENTISTS TO REACH A CONSENSUS.
I'LL HAVE TO HANDLE IT MYSELF.

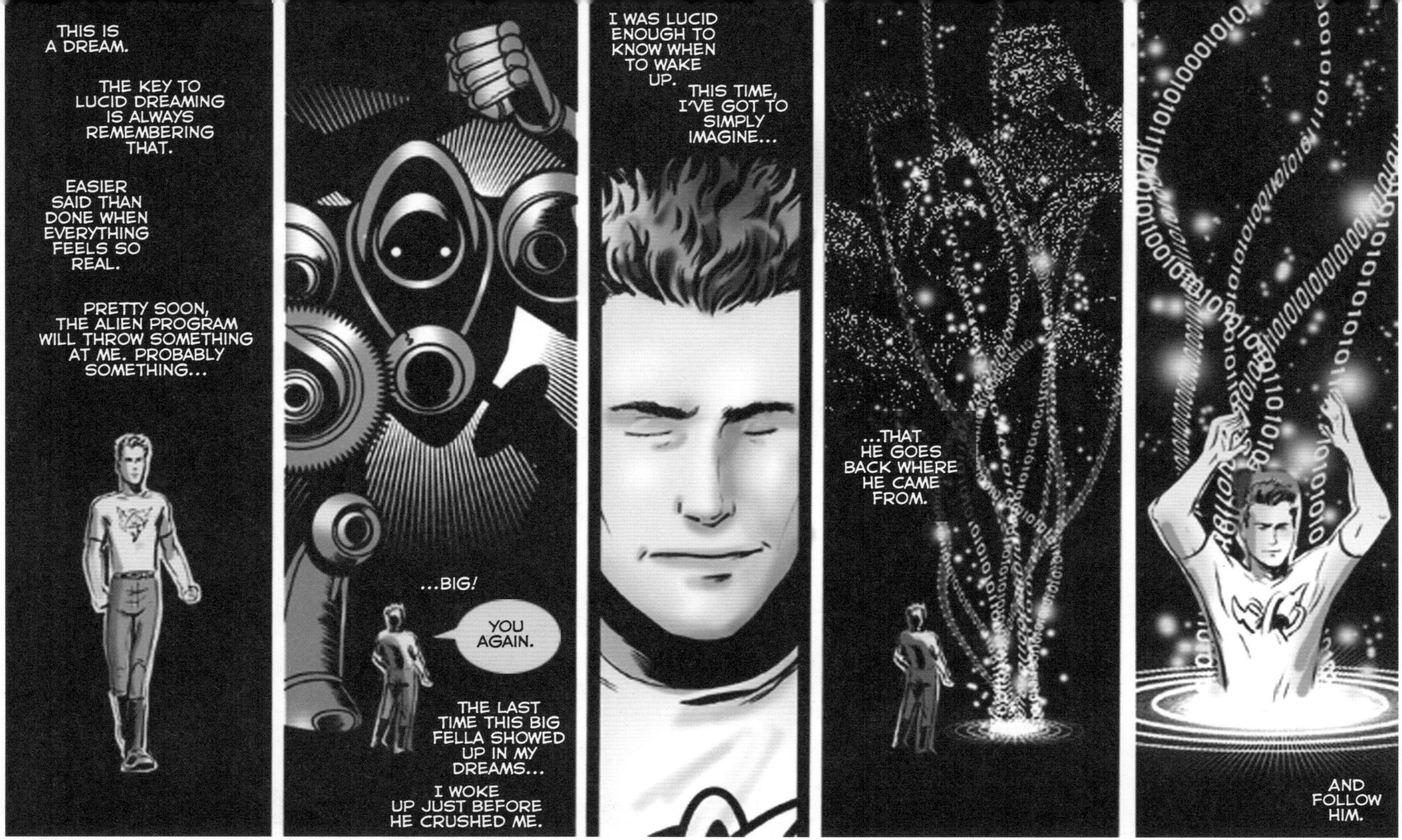
THIS IS A DREAM.
THE KEY TO LUCID DREAMING IS ALWAYS REMEMBERING THAT.
EASIER SAID THAN DONE WHEN EVERYTHING FEELS SO REAL.
PRETTY SOON, THE ALIEN PROGRAM WILL THROW SOMETHING AT ME. PROBABLY SOMETHING...
...BIG!
YOU AGAIN.
THE LAST TIME THIS BIG FELLA SHOWED UP IN MY DREAMS...
I WOKE UP JUST BEFORE HE CRUSHED ME.
I WAS LUCID ENOUGH TO KNOW WHEN TO WAKE UP.
THIS TIME, I'VE GOT TO SIMPLY IMAGINE...
...THAT HE GOES BACK WHERE HE CAME FROM.
AND FOLLOW HIM.

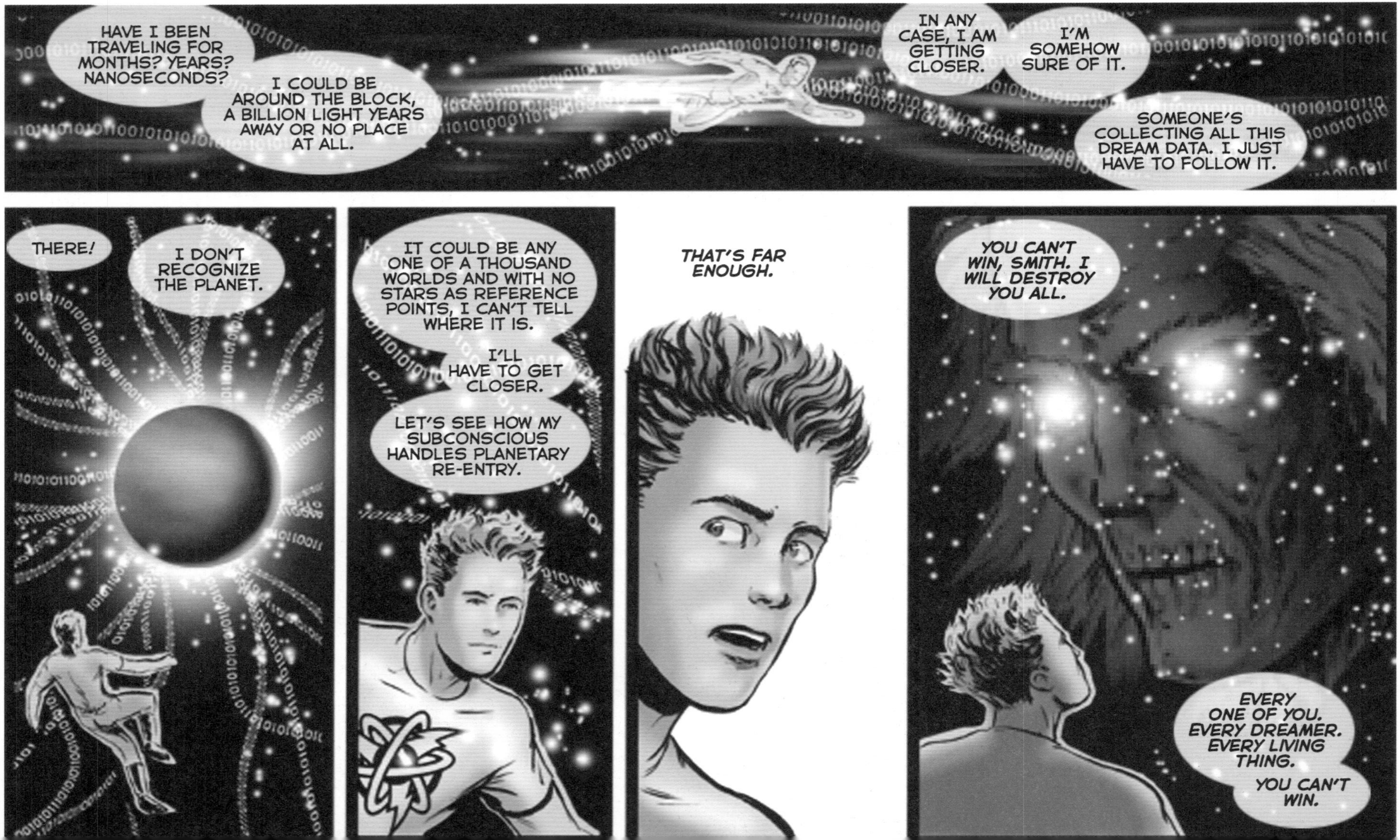

HAVE I BEEN TRAVELING FOR MONTHS? YEARS? NANOSECONDS?
I COULD BE AROUND THE BLOCK, A BILLION LIGHT YEARS AWAY OR NO PLACE AT ALL.
IN ANY CASE, I AM GETTING CLOSER.
I'M SOMEHOW SURE OF IT.
SOMEONE'S COLLECTING ALL THIS DREAM DATA. I JUST HAVE TO FOLLOW IT.
THERE!
I DON'T RECOGNIZE THE PLANET.
IT COULD BE ANY ONE OF A THOUSAND WORLDS AND WITH NO STARS AS REFERENCE POINTS, I CAN'T TELL WHERE IT IS.
I'LL HAVE TO GET CLOSER.
LET'S SEE HOW MY SUBCONSCIOUS HANDLES PLANETARY RE-ENTRY.
THAT'S FAR ENOUGH.
YOU CAN'T WIN, SMITH. I WILL DESTROY YOU ALL.
EVERY ONE OF YOU. EVERY DREAMER. EVERY LIVING THING.
YOU CAN'T WIN.

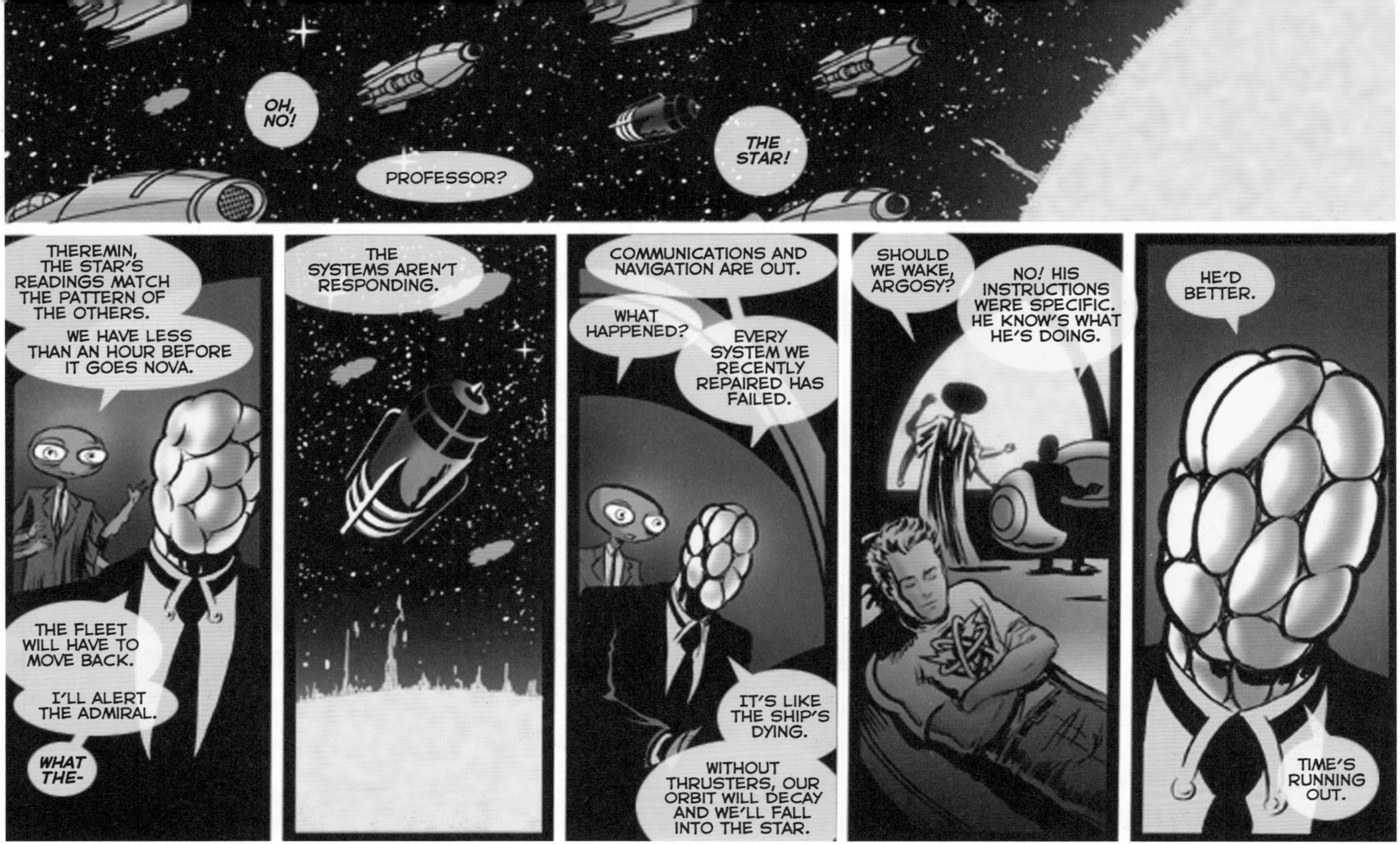
OH, NO!
PROFESSOR?
THE STAR!
THEREMIN, THE STAR'S READINGS MATCH THE PATTERN OF THE OTHERS.
WE HAVE LESS THAN AN HOUR BEFORE IT GOES NOVA.
THE FLEET WILL HAVE TO MOVE BACK.
I'LL ALERT THE ADMIRAL.
WHAT THE-
THE SYSTEMS AREN'T RESPONDING.
COMMUNICATIONS AND NAVIGATION ARE OUT.
WHAT HAPPENED?
EVERY SYSTEM WE RECENTLY REPAIRED HAS FAILED.
IT'S LIKE THE SHIP'S DYING.
WITHOUT THRUSTERS, OUR ORBIT WILL DECAY AND WE'LL FALL INTO THE STAR.
SHOULD WE WAKE, ARGOSY?
NO! HIS INSTRUCTIONS WERE SPECIFIC. HE KNOW'S WHAT HE'S DOING.
HE'D BETTER.
TIME'S RUNNING OUT.

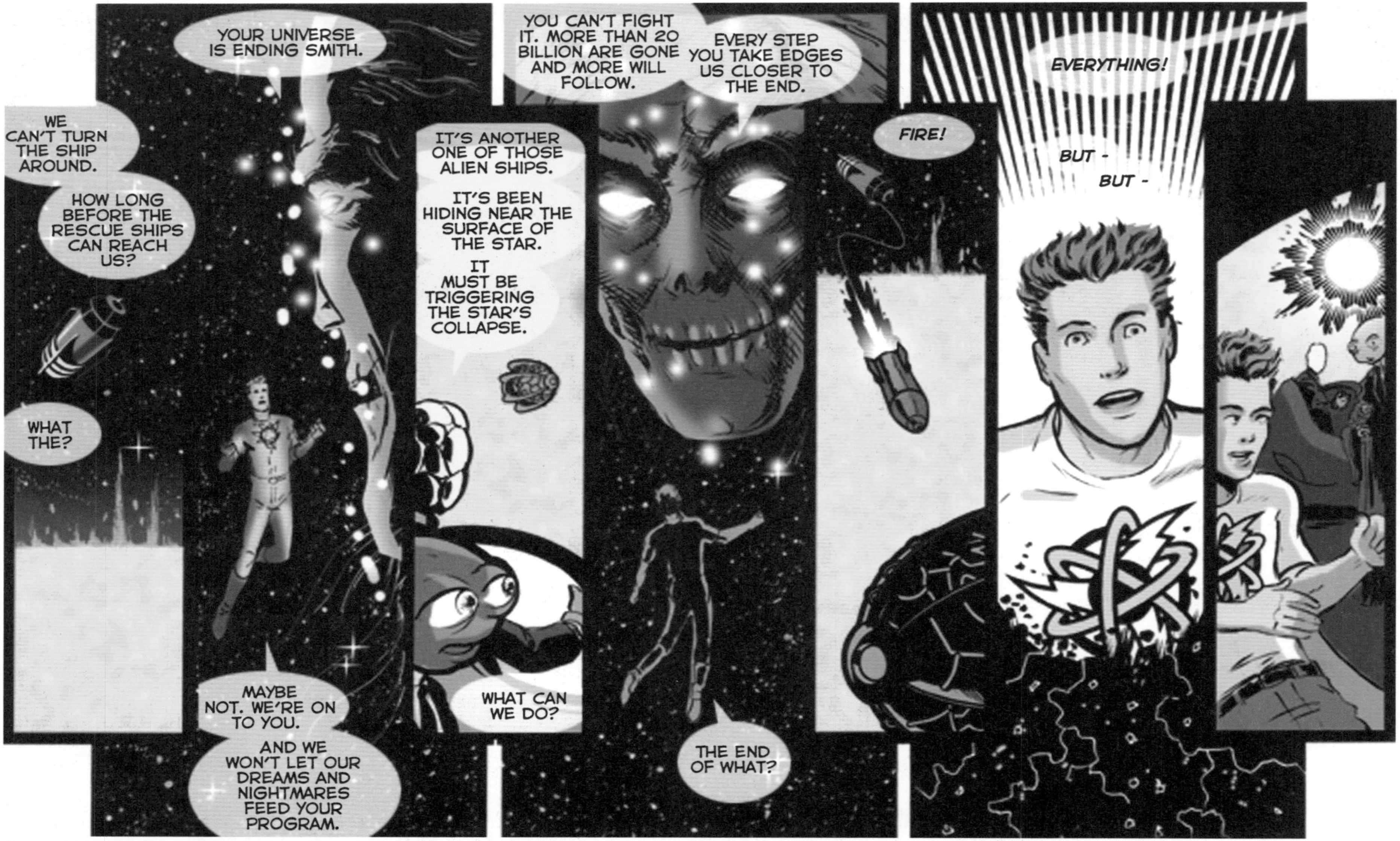

WE CAN'T TURN THE SHIP AROUND.
HOW LONG BEFORE THE RESCUE SHIPS CAN REACH US?
WHAT THE?
YOUR UNIVERSE IS ENDING SMITH.
MAYBE NOT. WE'RE ON TO YOU.
AND WE WON'T LET OUR DREAMS AND NIGHTMARES FEED YOUR PROGRAM.
IT'S ANOTHER ONE OF THOSE ALIEN SHIPS.
IT'S BEEN HIDING NEAR THE SURFACE OF THE STAR.
IT MUST BE TRIGGERING THE STAR'S COLLAPSE.
WHAT CAN WE DO?
YOU CAN'T FIGHT IT. MORE THAN 20 BILLION ARE GONE AND MORE WILL FOLLOW.
EVERY STEP YOU TAKE EDGES US CLOSER TO THE END.
THE END OF WHAT?
FIRE!
EVERYTHING!
BUT -
BUT -

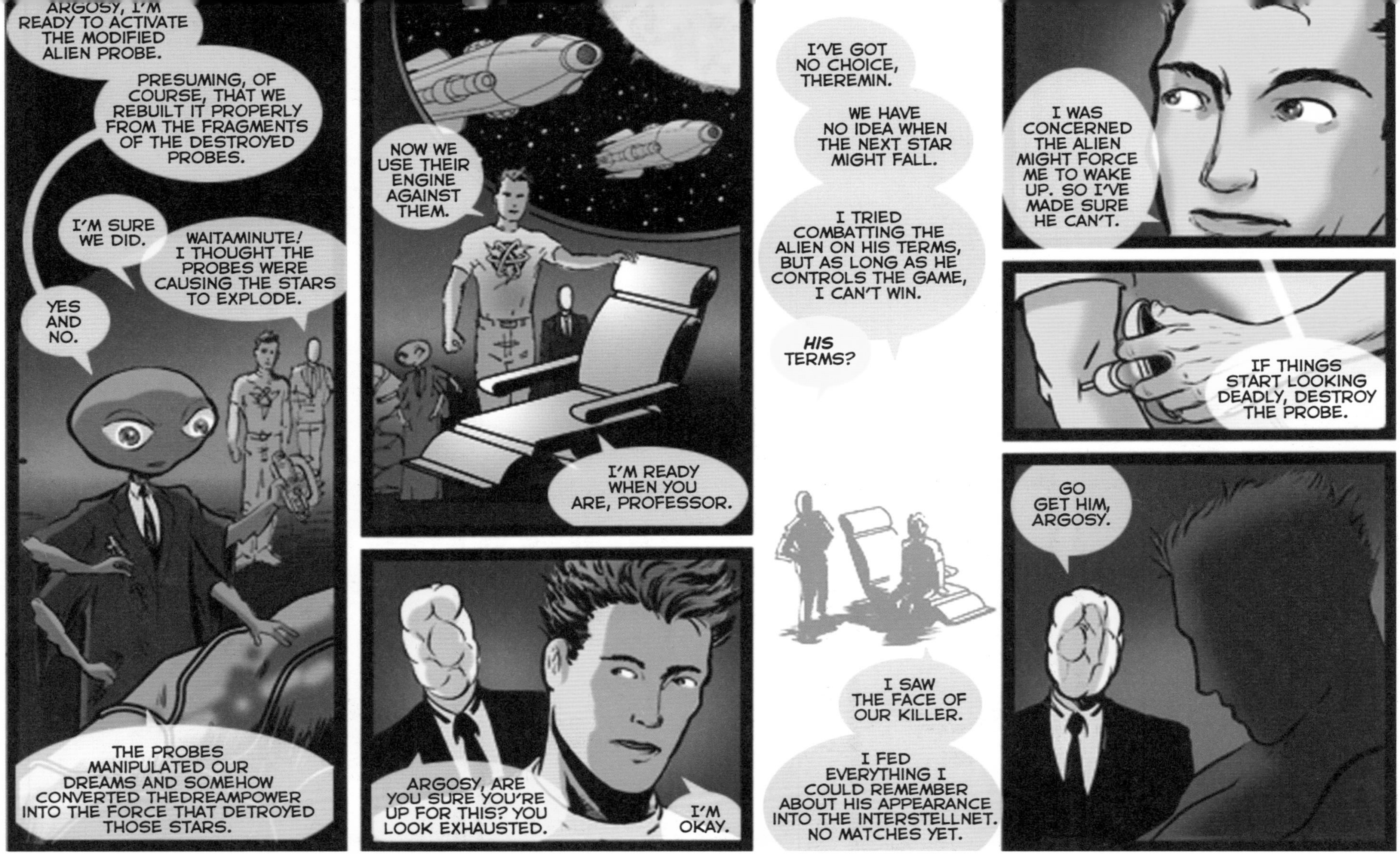
ARGOSY, I'M READY TO ACTIVATE THE MODIFIED ALIEN PROBE.
PRESUMING, OF COURSE, THAT WE REBUILT IT PROPERLY FROM THE FRAGMENTS OF THE DESTROYED PROBES.
I'M SURE WE DID.
WAITAMINUTE! I THOUGHT THE PROBES WERE CAUSING THE STARS TO EXPLODE.
YES AND NO.
THE PROBES MANIPULATED OUR DREAMS AND SOMEHOW CONVERTED THEDREAMPOWER INTO THE FORCE THAT DETROYED THOSE STARS.
NOW WE USE THEIR ENGINE AGAINST THEM.
I'M READY WHEN YOU ARE, PROFESSOR.
ARGOSY, ARE YOU SURE YOU'RE UP FOR THIS? YOU LOOK EXHAUSTED.
I'M OKAY.
I'VE GOT NO CHOICE, THEREMIN.
WE HAVE NO IDEA WHEN THE NEXT STAR MIGHT FALL.
I TRIED COMBATTING THE ALIEN ON HIS TERMS, BUT AS LONG AS HE CONTROLS THE GAME, I CAN'T WIN.
HIS TERMS?
I SAW THE FACE OF OUR KILLER.
I FED EVERYTHING I COULD REMEMBER ABOUT HIS APPEARANCE INTO THE INTERSTELLNET. NO MATCHES YET.
I WAS CONCERNED THE ALIEN MIGHT FORCE ME TO WAKE UP. SO I'VE MADE SURE HE CAN'T.
IF THINGS START LOOKING DEADLY, DESTROY THE PROBE.
GO GET HIM, ARGOSY.

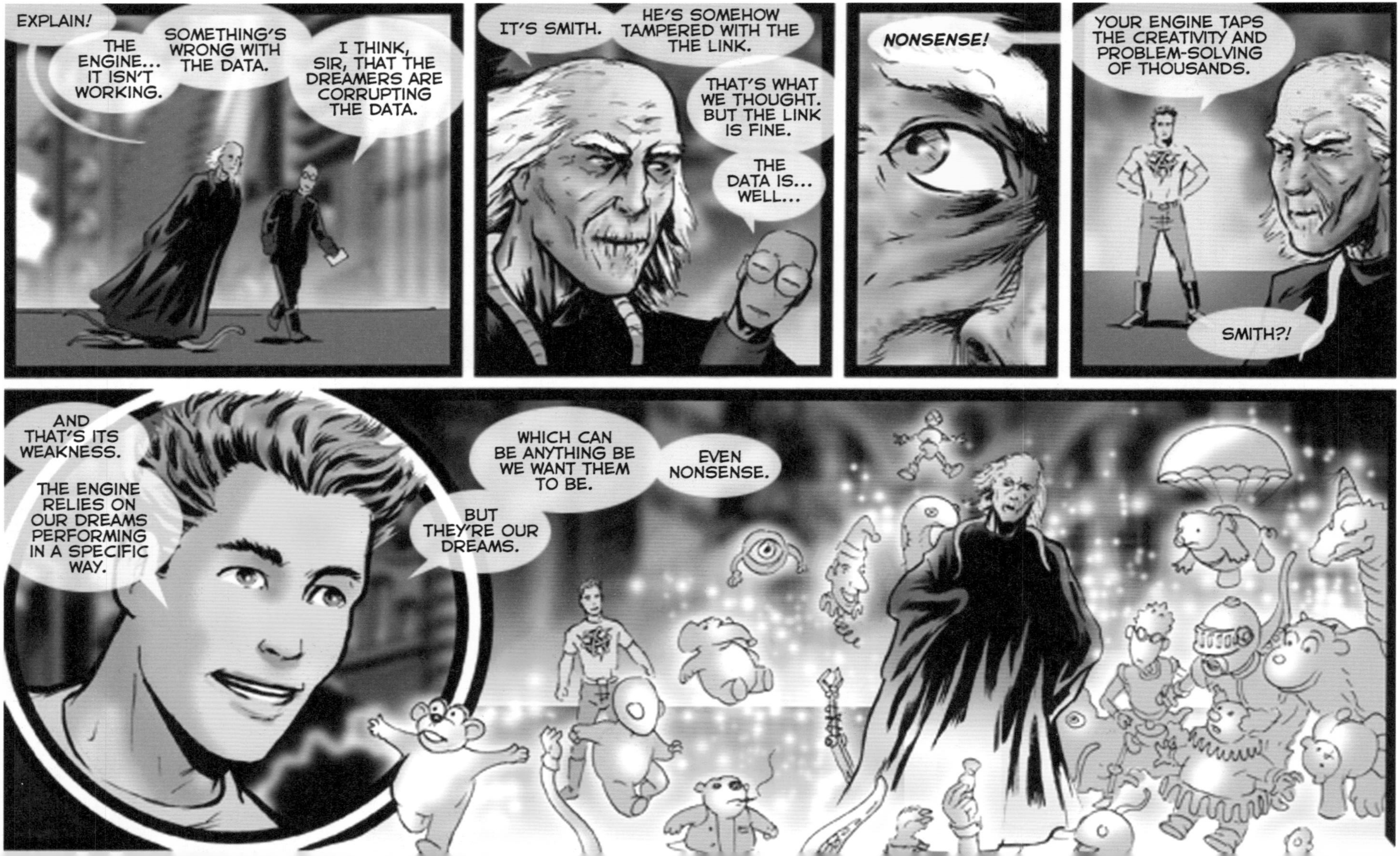
EXPLAIN!
THE ENGINE... IT ISN'T WORKING.
SOMETHING'S WRONG WITH THE DATA.
I THINK, SIR, THAT THE DREAMERS ARE CORRUPTING THE DATA.
IT'S SMITH.
HE'S SOMEHOW TAMPERED WITH THE THE LINK.
THAT'S WHAT WE THOUGHT. BUT THE LINK IS FINE.
THE DATA IS... WELL...
NONSENSE!
YOUR ENGINE TAPS THE CREATIVITY AND PROBLEM-SOLVING OF THOUSANDS.
SMITH?!
AND THAT'S ITS WEAKNESS.
THE ENGINE RELIES ON OUR DREAMS PERFORMING IN A SPECIFIC WAY.
BUT THEY'RE OUR DREAMS.
WHICH CAN BE ANYTHING BE WE WANT THEM TO BE.
EVEN NONSENSE.

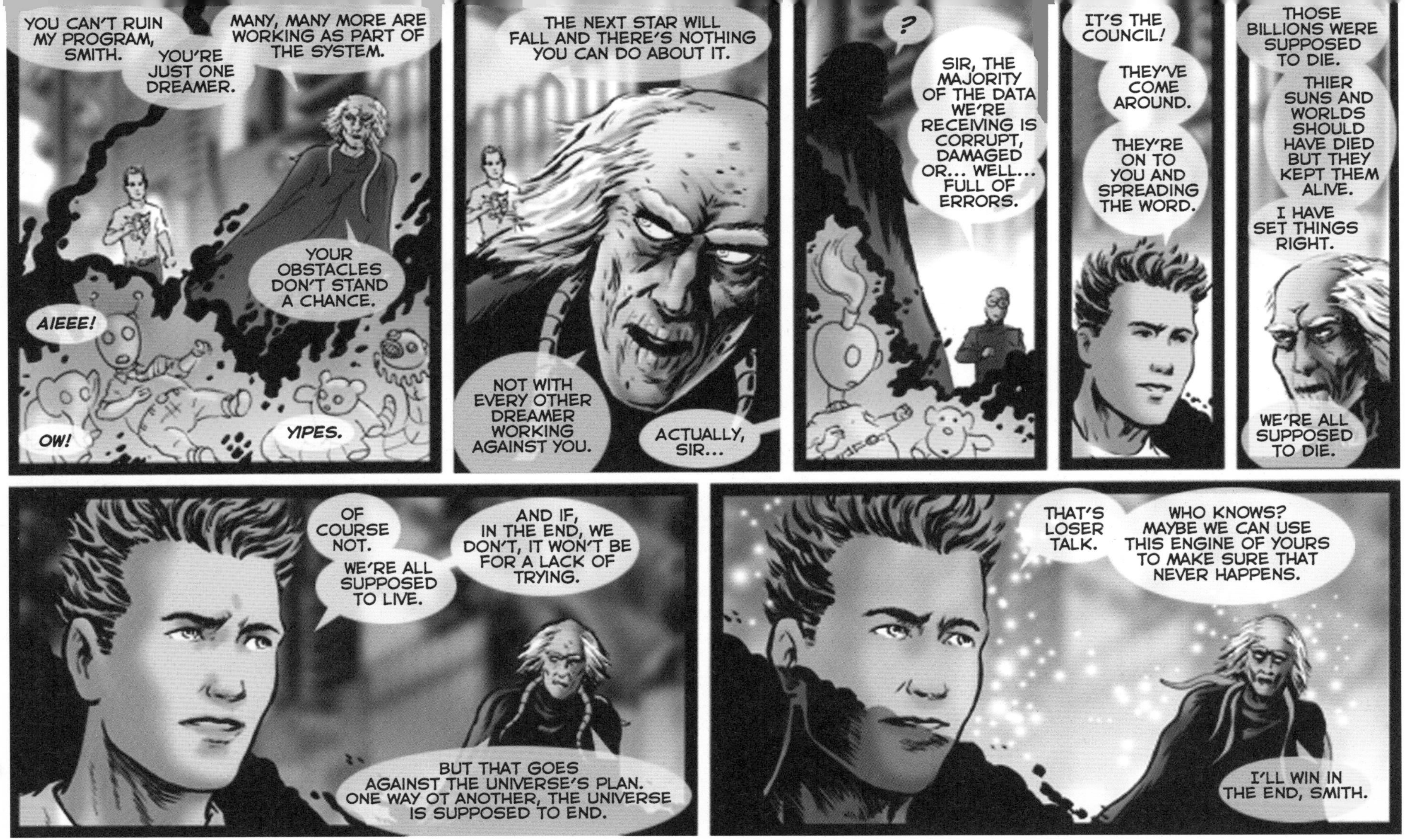

YOU CAN'T RUIN MY PROGRAM, SMITH.
YOU'RE JUST ONE DREAMER.
MANY, MANY MORE ARE WORKING AS PART OF THE SYSTEM.
YOUR OBSTACLES DON'T STAND A CHANCE.
AIEEE!
OW!
YIPES.
THE NEXT STAR WILL FALL AND THERE'S NOTHING YOU CAN DO ABOUT IT.
NOT WITH EVERY OTHER DREAMER WORKING AGAINST YOU.
ACTUALLY, SIR...
?
SIR, THE MAJORITY OF THE DATA WE'RE RECEIVING IS CORRUPT, DAMAGED OR... WELL... FULL OF ERRORS.
IT'S THE COUNCIL!
THEY'VE COME AROUND.
THEY'RE ON TO YOU AND SPREADING THE WORD.
THOSE BILLIONS WERE SUPPOSED TO DIE.
THIER SUNS AND WORLDS SHOULD HAVE DIED BUT THEY KEPT THEM ALIVE.
I HAVE SET THINGS RIGHT.
WE'RE ALL SUPPOSED TO DIE.
OF COURSE NOT.
WE'RE ALL SUPPOSED TO LIVE.
AND IF, IN THE END, WE DON'T, IT WON'T BE FOR A LACK OF TRYING.
BUT THAT GOES AGAINST THE UNIVERSE'S PLAN. ONE WAY OT ANOTHER, THE UNIVERSE IS SUPPOSED TO END.
THAT'S LOSER TALK.
WHO KNOWS? MAYBE WE CAN USE THIS ENGINE OF YOURS TO MAKE SURE THAT NEVER HAPPENS.
I'LL WIN IN THE END, SMITH.

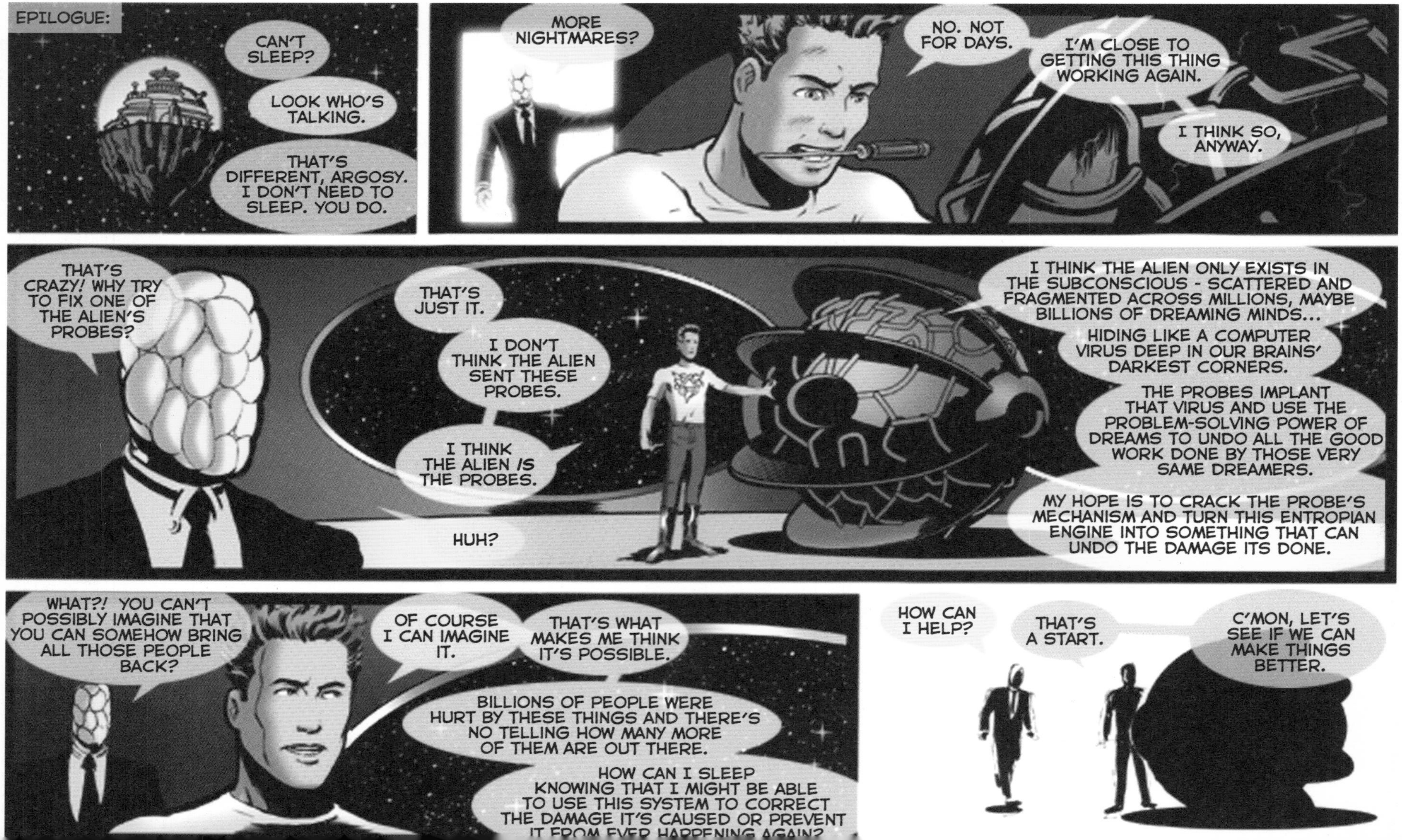
EPILOGUE:
CAN'T SLEEP?
LOOK WHO'S TALKING.
THAT'S DIFFERENT, ARGOSY. I DON'T NEED TO SLEEP. YOU DO.
MORE NIGHTMARES?
NO. NOT FOR DAYS.
I'M CLOSE TO GETTING THIS THING WORKING AGAIN.
I THINK SO, ANYWAY.
THAT'S CRAZY! WHY TRY TO FIX ONE OF THE ALIEN'S PROBES?
THAT'S JUST IT.
I DON'T THINK THE ALIEN SENT THESE PROBES.
I THINK THE ALIEN *IS* THE PROBES.
HUH?
I THINK THE ALIEN ONLY EXISTS IN THE SUBCONSCIOUS - SCATTERED AND FRAGMENTED ACROSS MILLIONS, MAYBE BILLIONS OF DREAMING MINDS...
HIDING LIKE A COMPUTER VIRUS DEEP IN OUR BRAINS' DARKEST CORNERS.
THE PROBES IMPLANT THAT VIRUS AND USE THE PROBLEM-SOLVING POWER OF DREAMS TO UNDO ALL THE GOOD WORK DONE BY THOSE VERY SAME DREAMERS.
MY HOPE IS TO CRACK THE PROBE'S MECHANISM AND TURN THIS ENTROPIAN ENGINE INTO SOMETHING THAT CAN UNDO THE DAMAGE ITS DONE.
WHAT?! YOU CAN'T POSSIBLY IMAGINE THAT YOU CAN SOMEHOW BRING ALL THOSE PEOPLE BACK?
OF COURSE I CAN IMAGINE IT.
THAT'S WHAT MAKES ME THINK IT'S POSSIBLE.
BILLIONS OF PEOPLE WERE HURT BY THESE THINGS AND THERE'S NO TELLING HOW MANY MORE OF THEM ARE OUT THERE.
HOW CAN I SLEEP KNOWING THAT I MIGHT BE ABLE TO USE THIS SYSTEM TO CORRECT THE DAMAGE IT'S CAUSED OR PREVENT
HOW CAN I HELP?
THAT'S A START.
C'MON, LET'S SEE IF WE CAN MAKE THINGS BETTER.

GALLERY

When I was putting *Astounding Space Thrills* together, my friend Steranko offered to collaborate on the first issue's cover. As anyone familiar with Steranko's legendary work in comics, pulp art and film design can attest, it was an offer I'd have been nuts to pass up.

Following that beautiful debut cover, I approached my favorite science fiction and fantasy illustrators to contribute subsequent covers and interior pin-up illustrations.

The following pages showcase just a few of the terrific pieces done for the series.

I'll remain forever grateful to these men for their dazzling work.

— Steve Conley, 2008

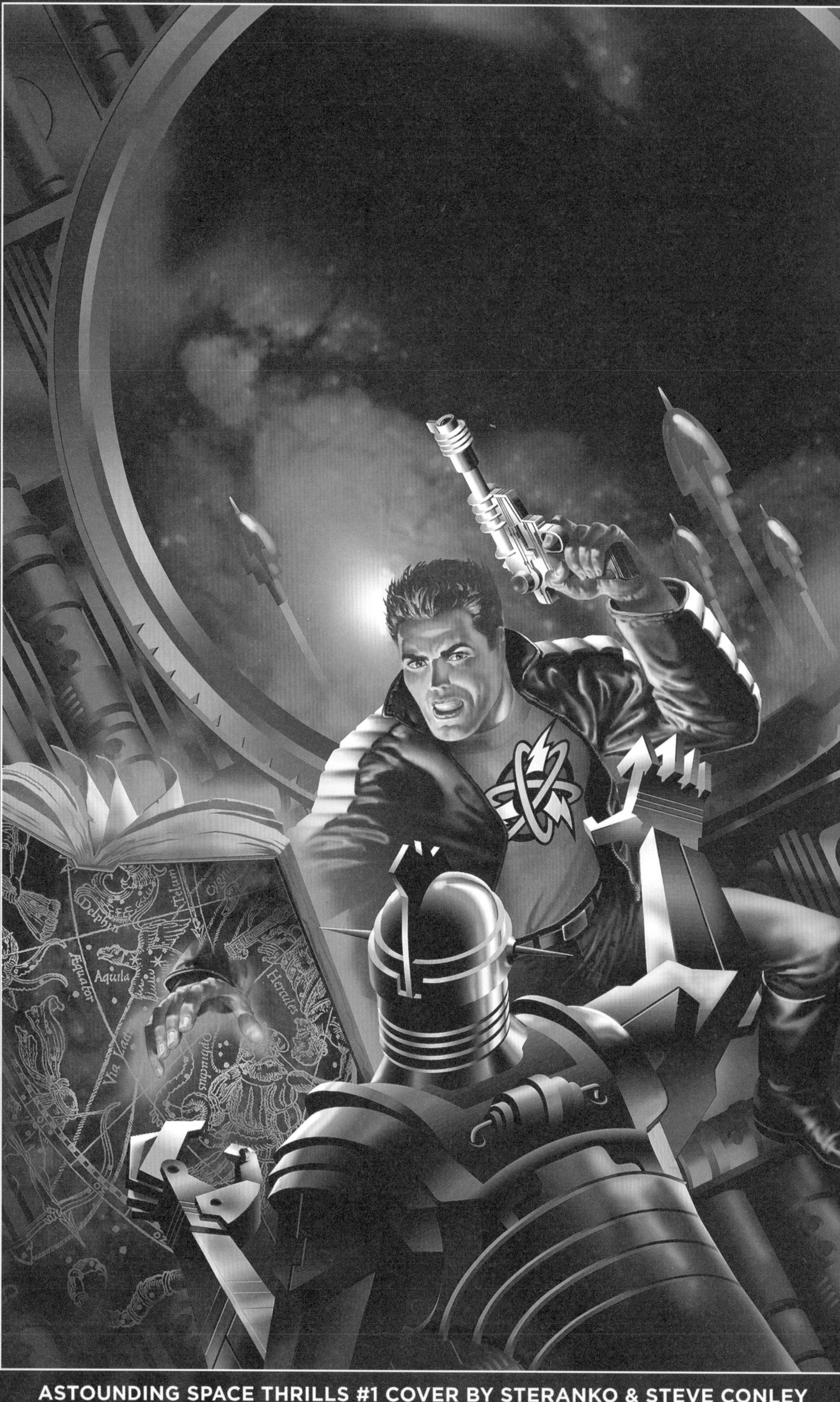

Delphin
Aquila
Aequator
Hercules

ASTOUNDING SPACE THRILLS #1 COVER BY STERANKO & STEVE CONLEY

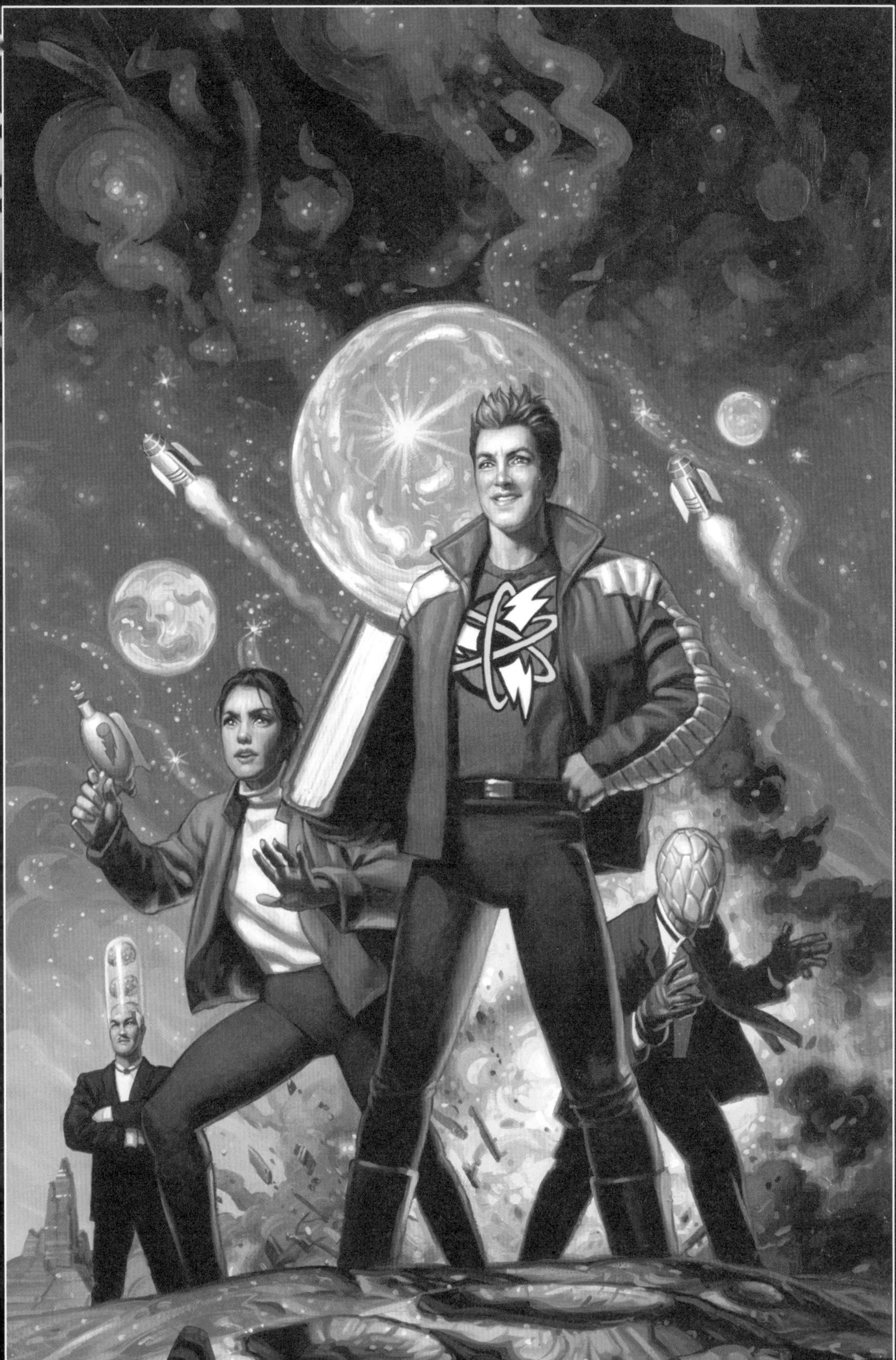
GREG & TIM HILDEBRANDT

ASTOUNDING SPACE THRILLS #2 COVER BY GREG & TIM HILDEBRANDT

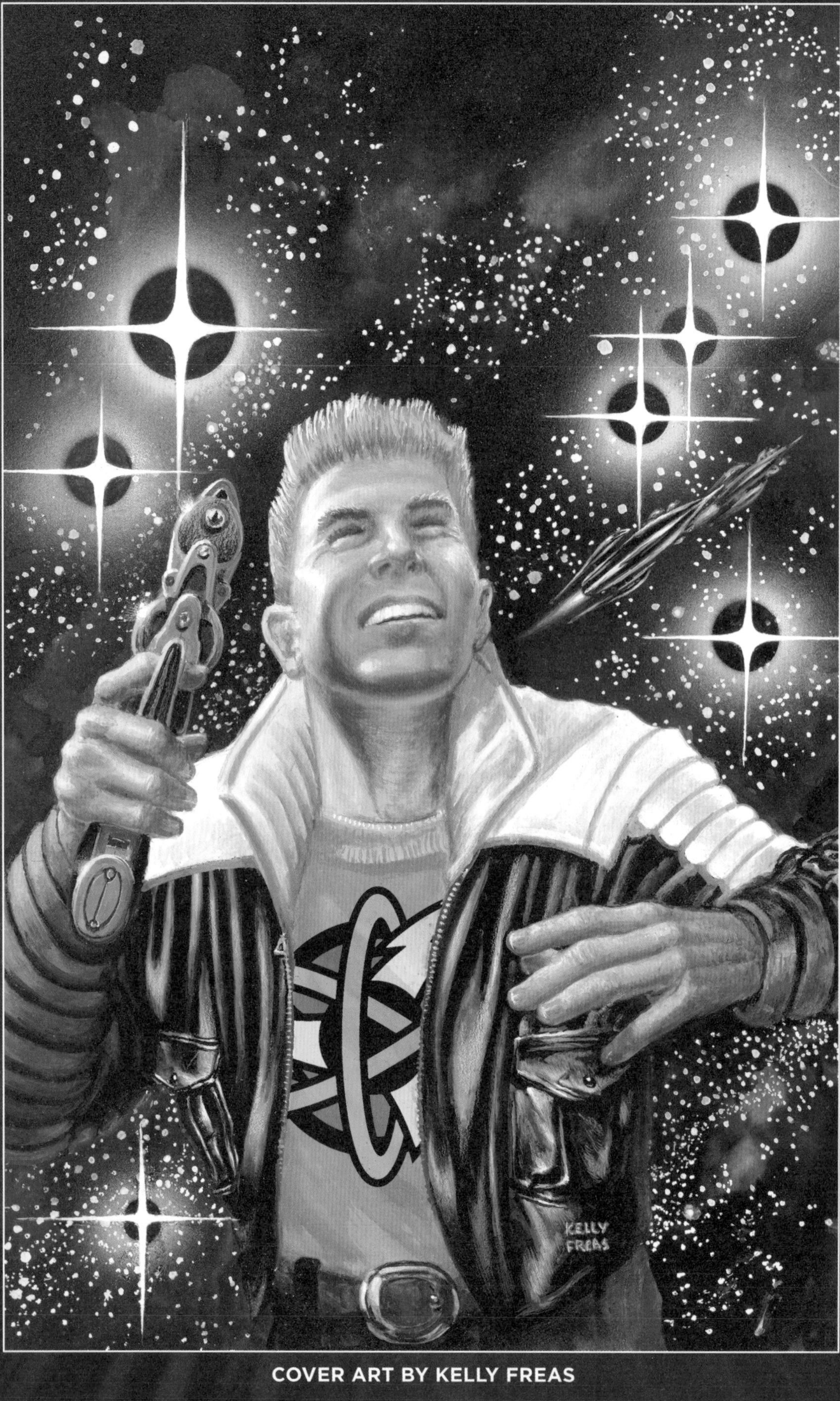
KELLY
FREAS
COVER ART BY KELLY FREAS

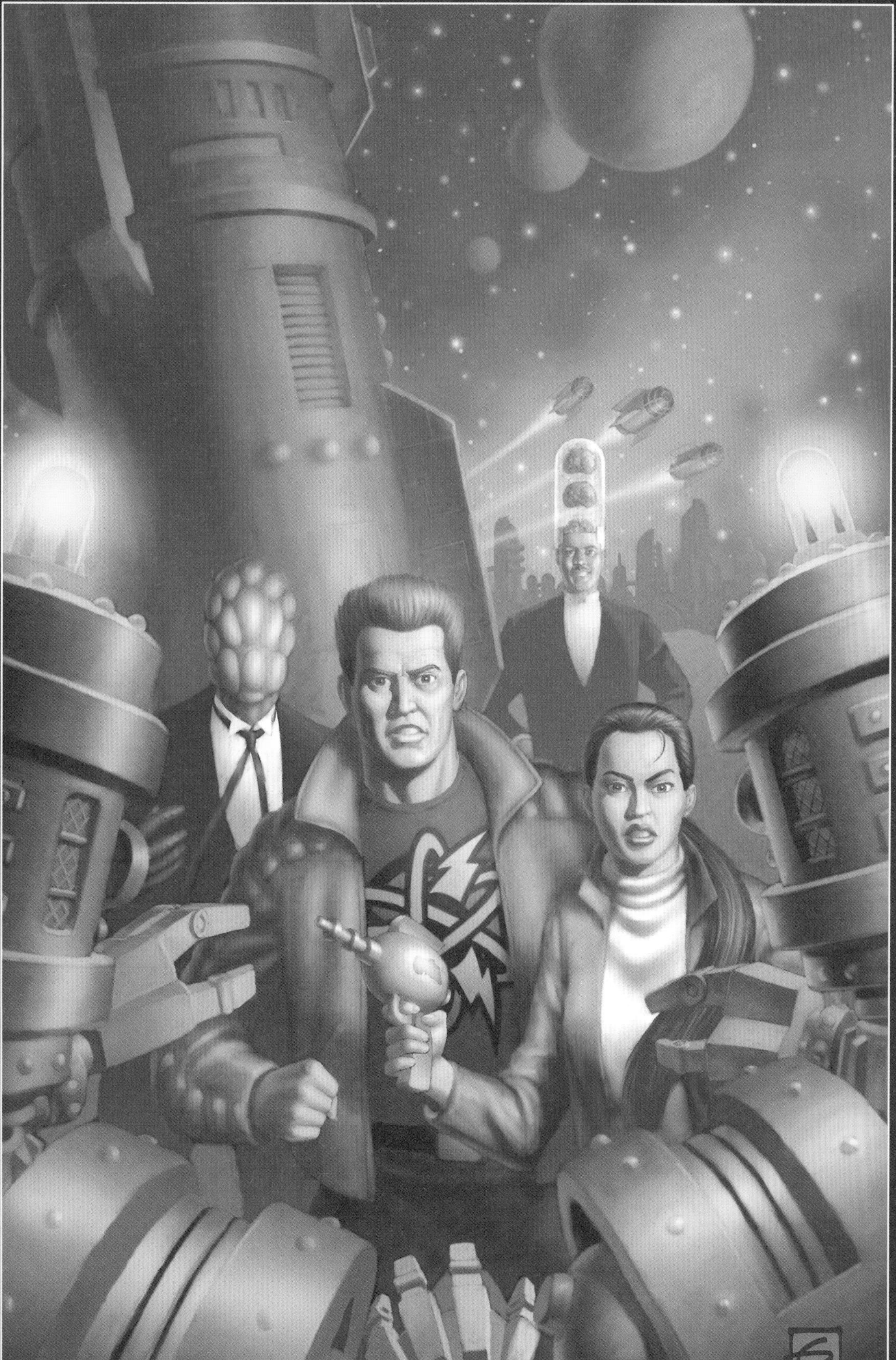

COVER ART BY DAVE GIBBONS

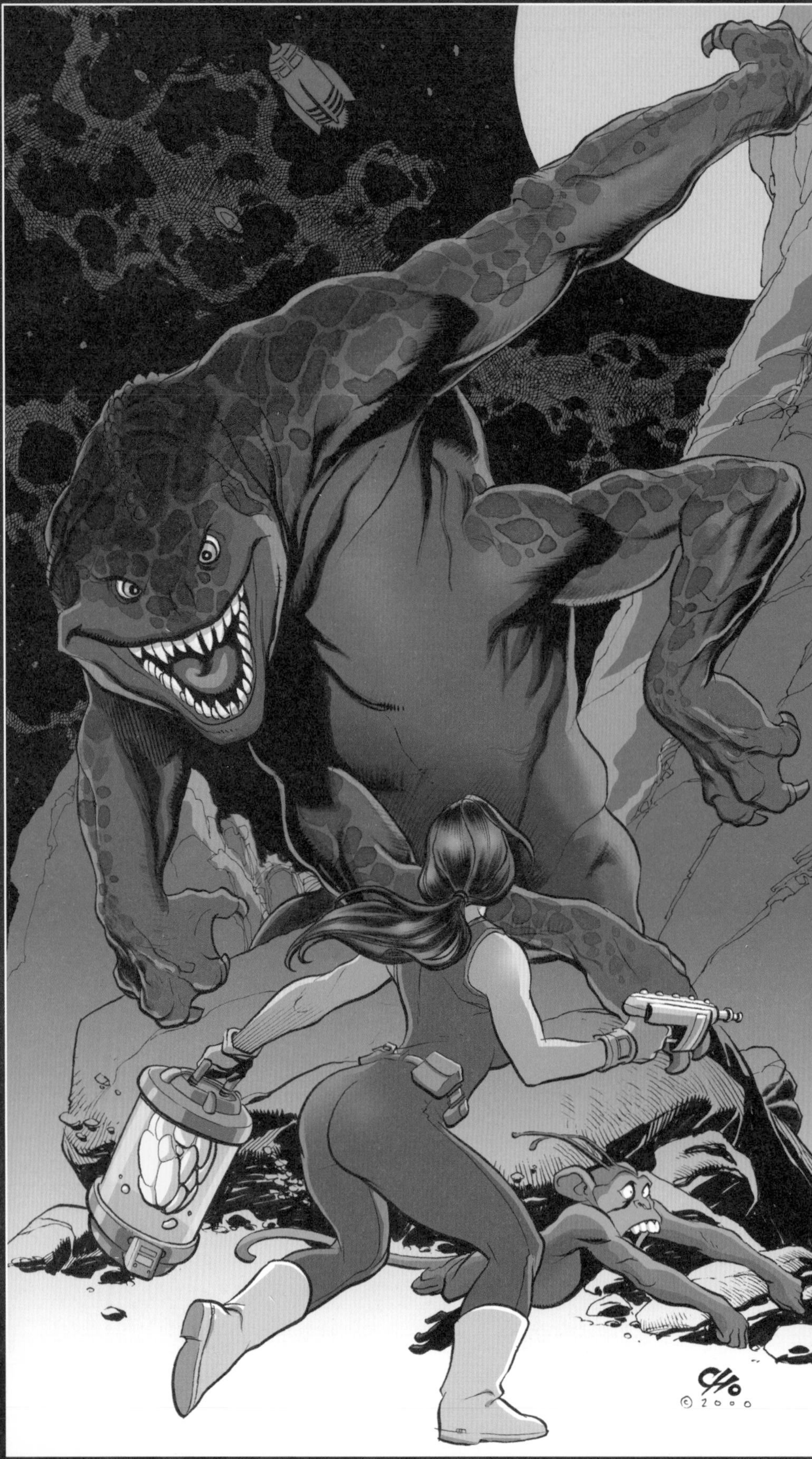
CHO
© 2000

PIN-UP BY FRANK CHO

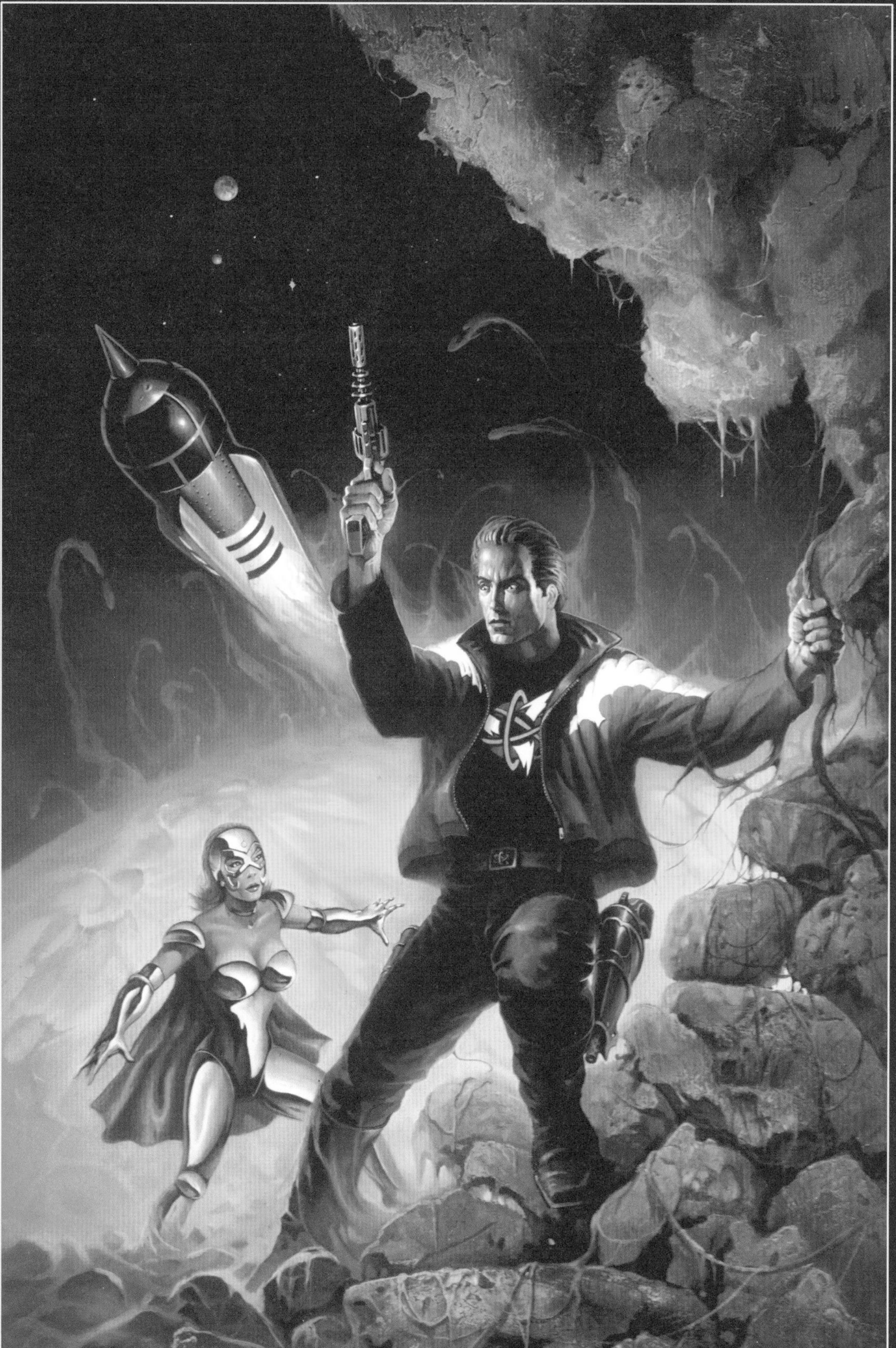

COVER ART BY KEN KELLY

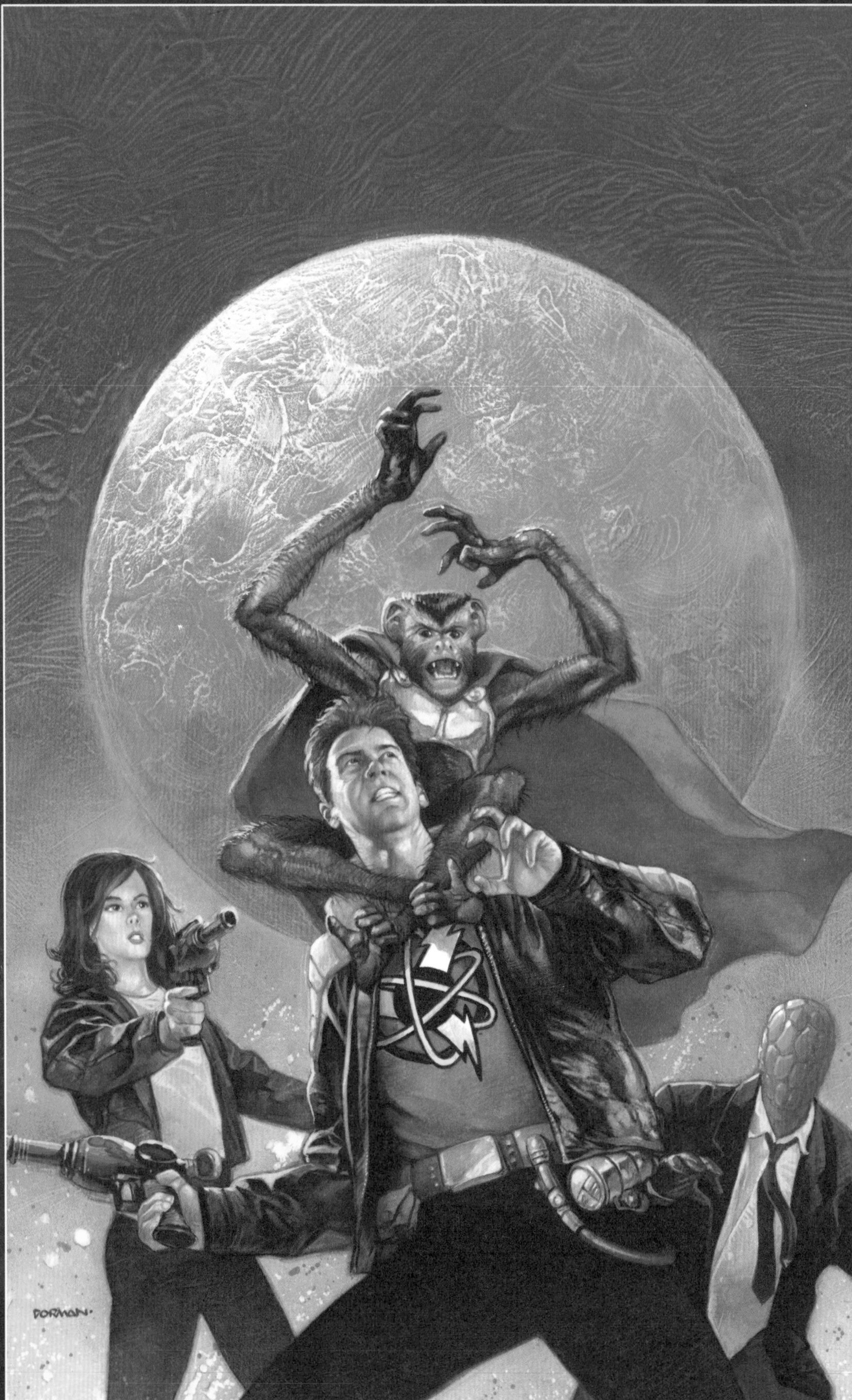
DORMAN

COVER ART BY DAVE DORMAN

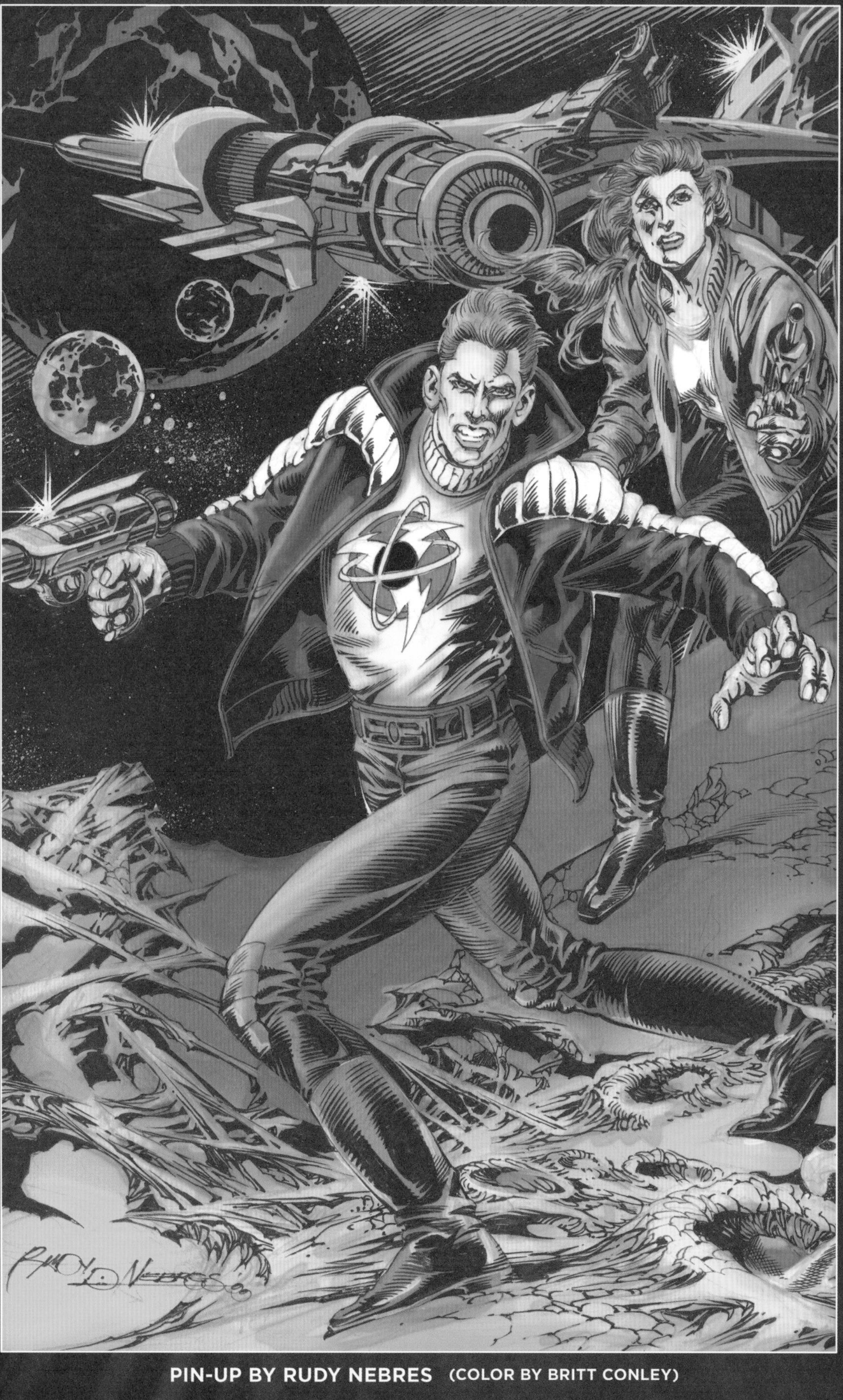

PIN-UP BY RUDY NEBRES (COLOR BY BRITT CONLEY)

The Lost Notes of

Astounding Space Thrills

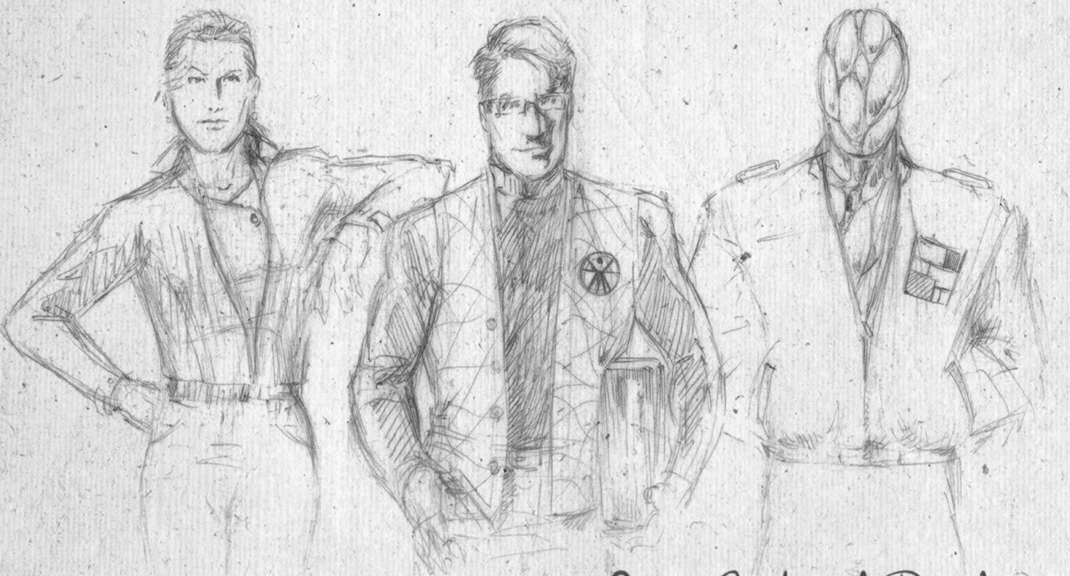

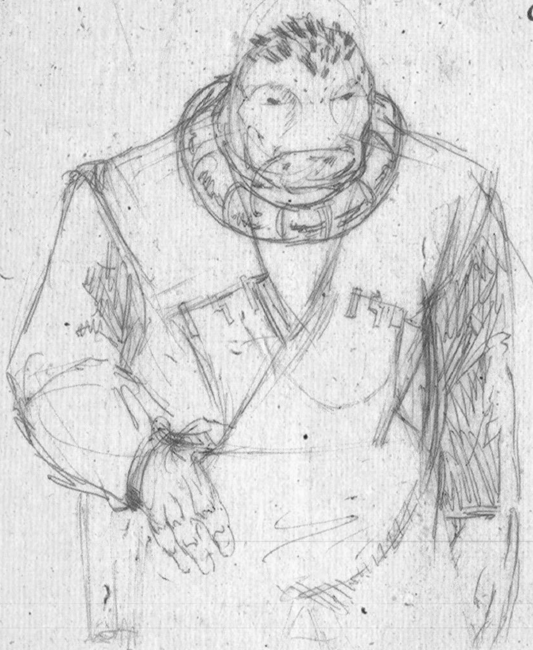

Petra, Tycho and David

Above are the first sketches of the characters in the Codex Reckoning. Argosy Smith was still going by the name Tycho Roswell. Theremin was named David (an ironic reference to the physical perfection of Michaelangelo's David in relation to what had happened to Theremin). Petra remained mostly unchanged. Note Argosy's original Leonardo-inspired logo and Theremin's Mondrian-inspired one.

The Hujno

The Hujno started as a more militaristic religious race. One concession to the packed first issue of Astounding Space Thrills was the loss of the "ring pipe." The Hujno would fill that ring around their necks with insects (Rasps) and breathe the gasses/wastes. It struck me as no weirder than burning leaves and inhaling the gasses for pleasure.

The Lost Notes of Astounding Space Thrills

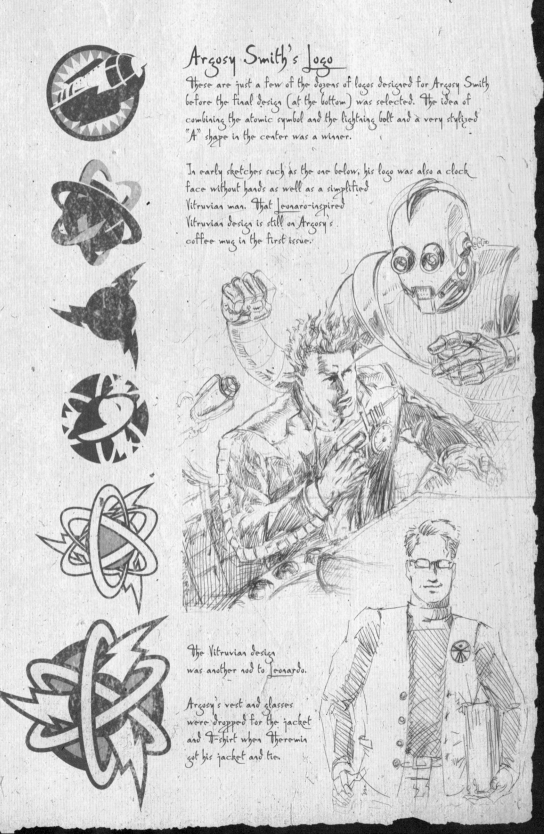

Argosy Smith's Logo

These are just a few of the dozens of logos designed for Argosy Smith before the final design (at the bottom) was selected. The idea of combining the atomic symbol and the lightning bolt and a very stylized "A" shape in the center was a winner.

In early sketches such as the one below, his logo was also a clock face without hands as well as a simplified Vitruvian man. That Leonaro-inspired Vitruvian design is still on Argosy's coffee mug in the first issue.

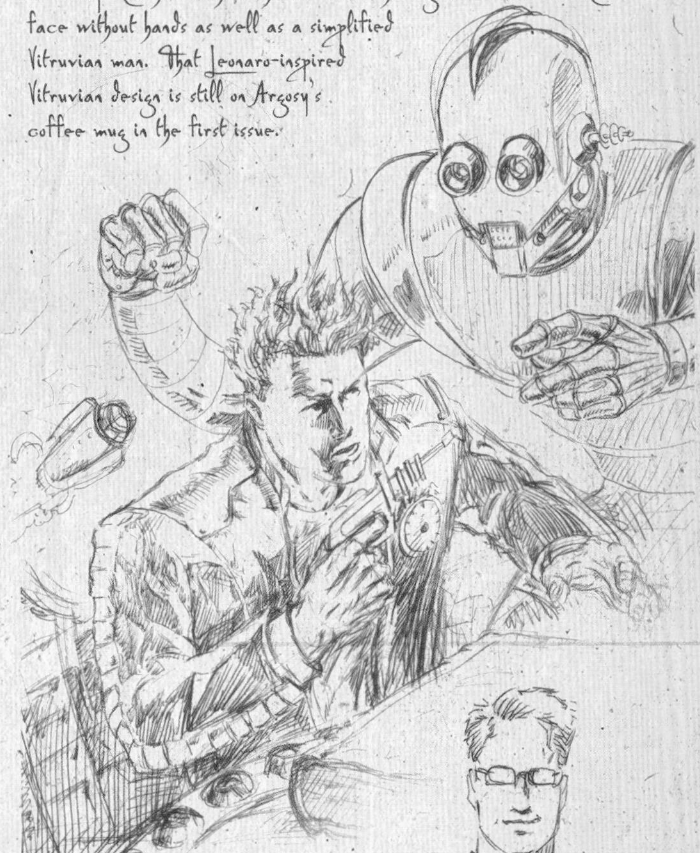

The Vitruvian design was another nod to Leonardo.

Argosy's vest and glasses were dropped for the jacket and T-shirt when Theremin got his jacket and tie.

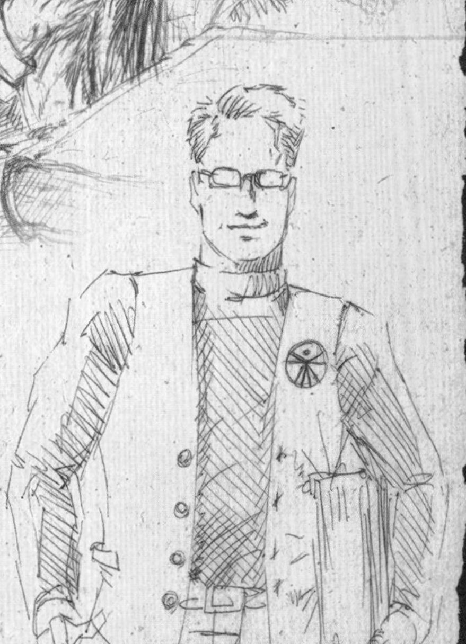

The Lost Notes of Astounding Space Thrills

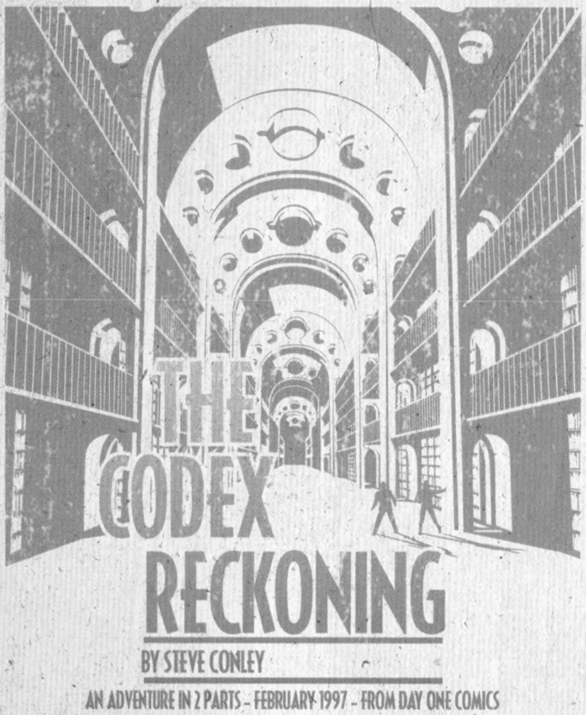
THE CODEX RECKONING
BY STEVE CONLEY
AN ADVENTURE IN 2 PARTS – FEBRUARY 1997 – FROM DAY ONE COMICS

The Codex Reckoning

Originally, the Astounding Space Thrills series was going to be a two-part mini-series called The Codex Reckoning.

The name was changed in the end because Astounding Space Thrills sounded like more fun.

That promo art shows the original view of the Faber 2B library. About ten pages of the Codex Reckoning - with Argosy, Theremin and Redomond (then named Baslik and without his additional brains) in their early forms.

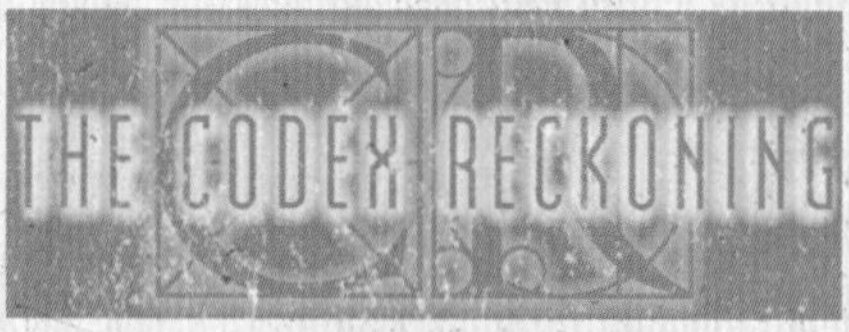
THE CODEX RECKONING

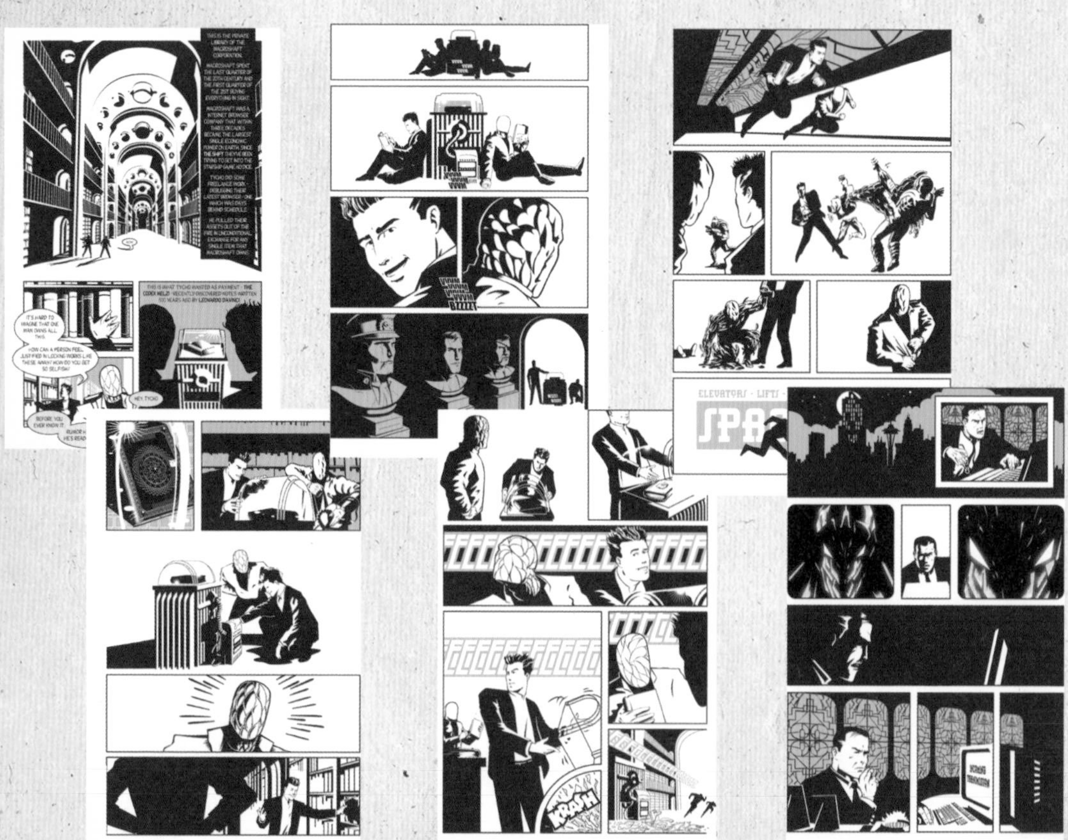
IT'S HARD TO IMAGINE THAT ONE MAN OWNS ALL THIS.
HOW CAN A PERSON FEEL JUSTIFIED IN LOCKING WORKS LIKE THESE AWAY? HOW DO YOU GET SO SELFISH?
HEY, TYCHO
BEFORE YOU EVER KNOW IT
ELEVATORS · LIFTS ·
KRASH

The Lost Notes of Astounding Space Thrills

Entropian splash page

This shows the process behind Steve's later works. Pages start as a rough sketch.

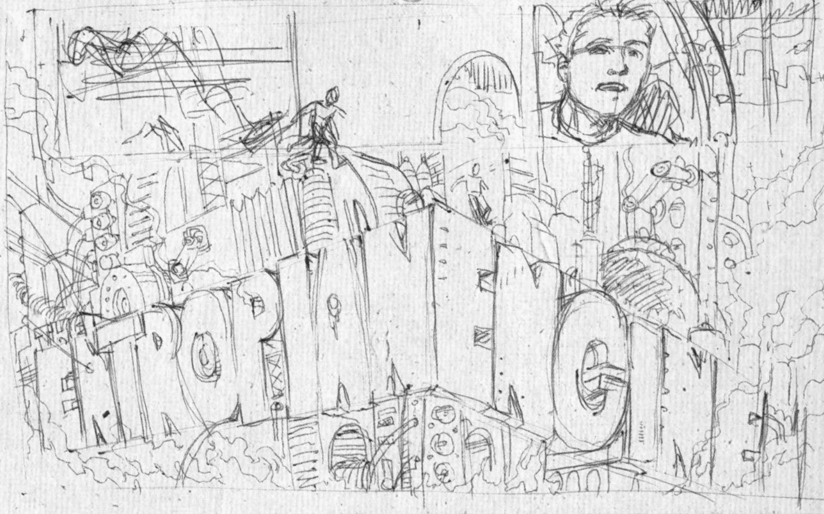

The rough is then tightened up and scanned into the computer.

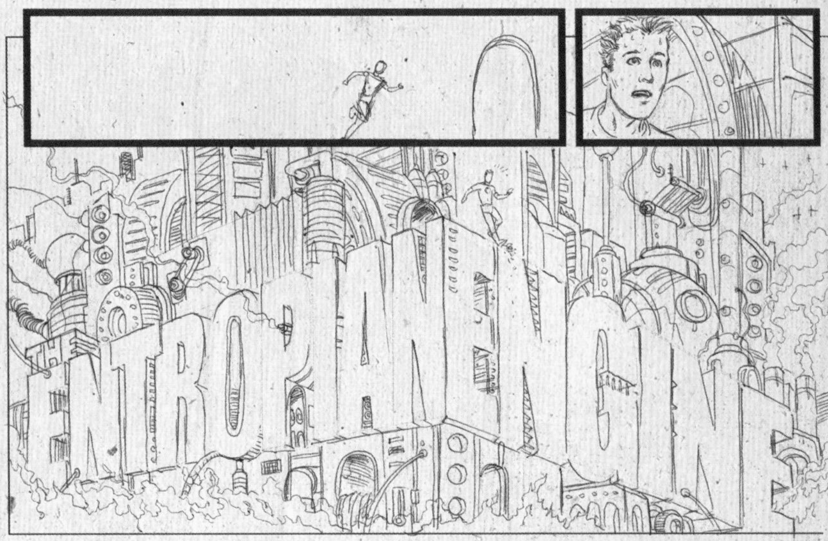
THE
ENTROPIAN ENGINE

The geometric elements (machines, architecture and panel borders) are drawn using the computer tools.

The image seen here is then printed on drawing paper and the figures, clouds and shadows are added using pen and ink.

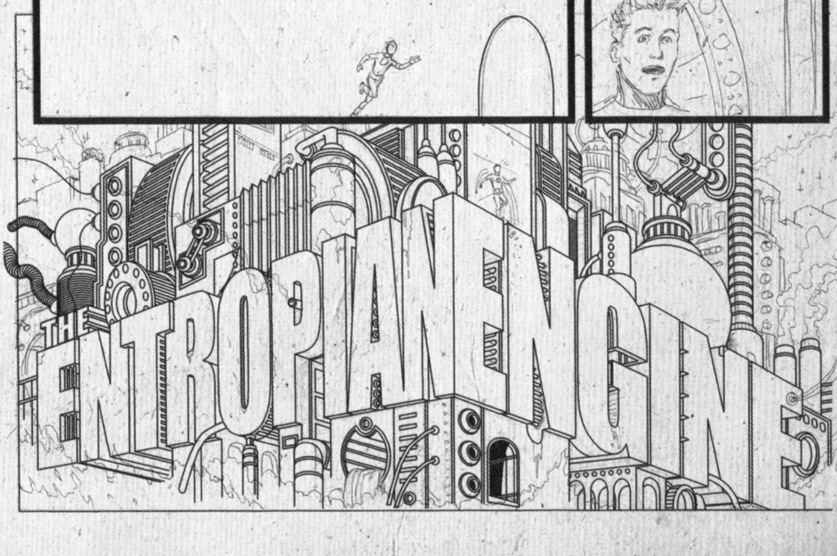
THE
ENTROPIAN ENGINE

The Lost Notes of Astounding Space Thrills

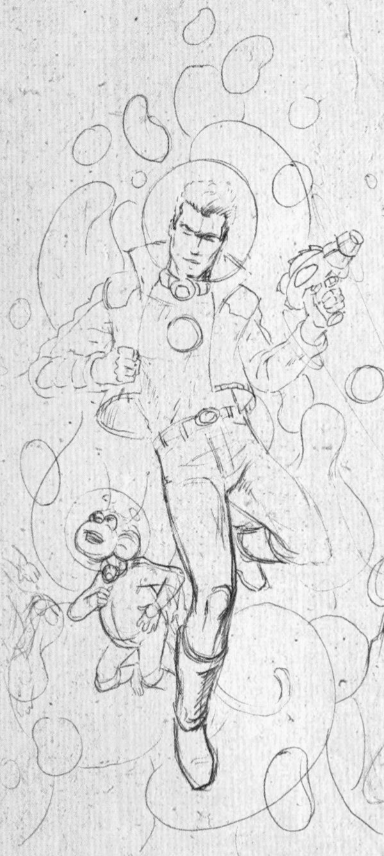

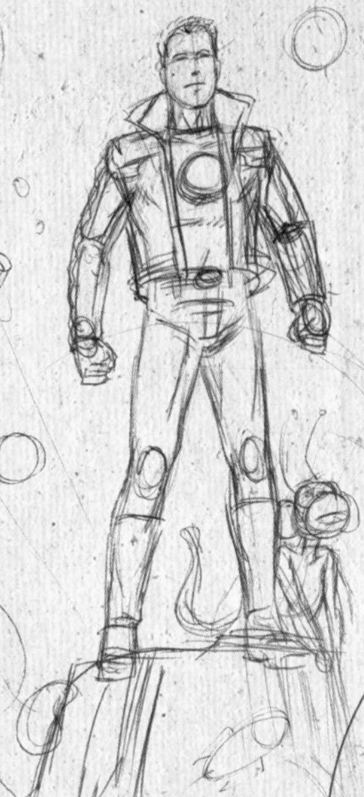

Sketches

Most of the sketches done here are done in ballpoint ink on paper. The final inked pieces are doone on 11 by 17 art paper.

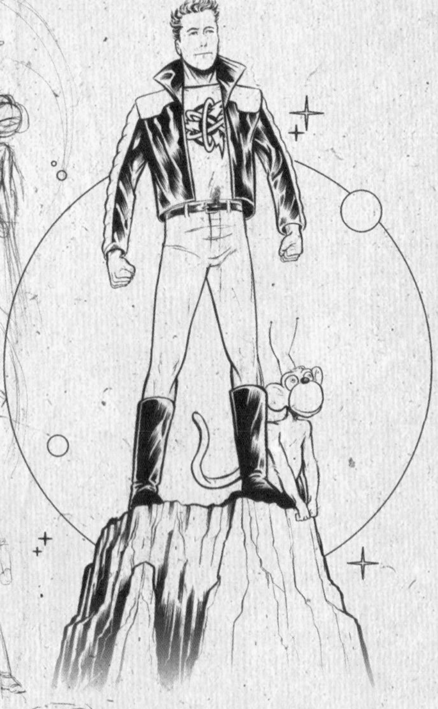

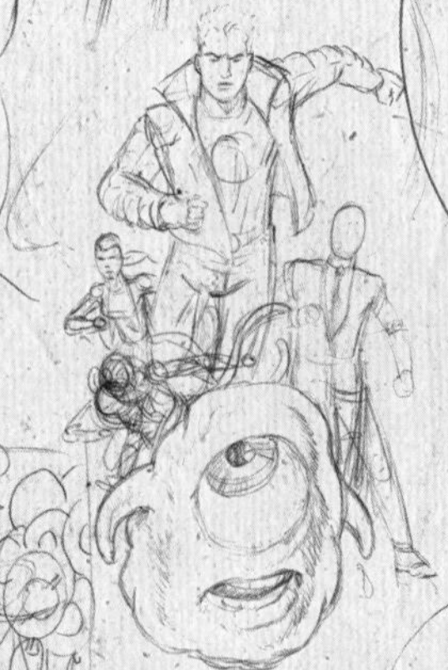

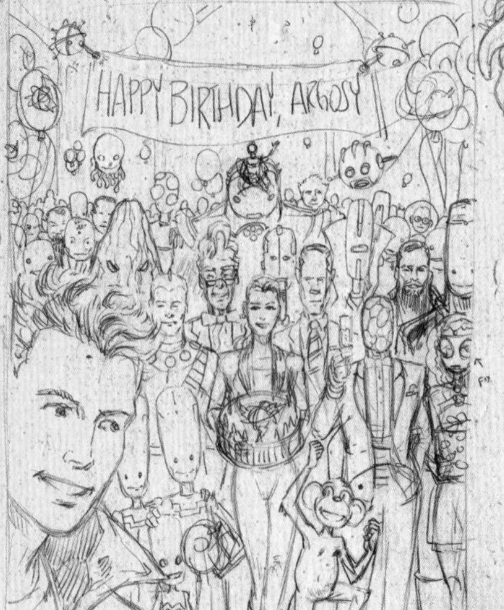
HAPPY BIRTHDAY, ARGOSY

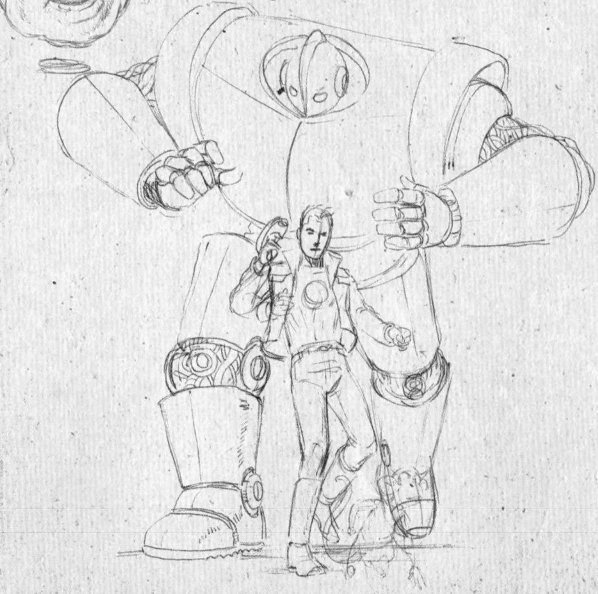

The Lost Notes of Astounding Space Thrills

Blip The Book of Little Independent Publishers included this 4-page preview in early 1998.
The inclusion of Tycho Brahe on the first page was a holdover from when Argosy's name was Tycho.

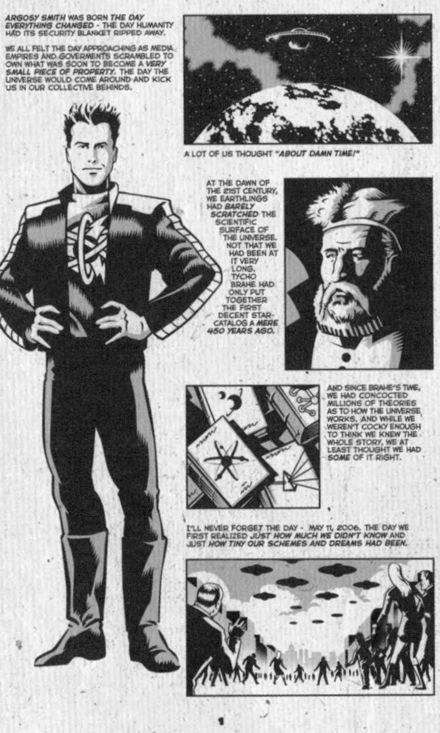
ARGOSY SMITH WAS BORN THE DAY EVERYTHING CHANGED - THE DAY HUMANITY HAD ITS SECURITY BLANKET RIPPED AWAY.
WE ALL FELT THE DAY APPROACHING AS MEDIA EMPIRES AND GOVERMENTS SCRAMBLED TO OWN WHAT WAS SOON TO BECOME A VERY SMALL PIECE OF PROPERTY. THE DAY THE UNIVERSE WOULD COME AROUND AND KICK US IN OUR COLLECTIVE BEHINDS.
A LOT OF US THOUGHT "ABOUT DAMN TIME!"
AT THE DAWN OF THE 21ST CENTURY, WE EARTHLINGS HAD BARELY SCRATCHED THE SCIENTIFIC SURFACE OF THE UNIVERSE. NOT THAT WE HAD BEEN AT IT VERY LONG. TYCHO BRAHE HAD ONLY PUT TOGETHER THE FIRST DECENT STAR-CATALOG A MERE 450 YEARS AGO.
AND SINCE BRAHE'S TIME, WE HAD CONCOCTED MILLIONS OF THEORIES AS TO HOW THE UNIVERSE WORKS. AND WHILE WE WEREN'T COCKY ENOUGH TO THINK WE KNEW THE WHOLE STORY, WE AT LEAST THOUGHT WE HAD SOME OF IT RIGHT.
I'LL NEVER FORGET THE DAY - MAY 11, 2006. THE DAY WE FIRST REALIZED JUST HOW MUCH WE DIDN'T KNOW AND JUST HOW TINY OUR SCHEMES AND DREAMS HAD BEEN.
1

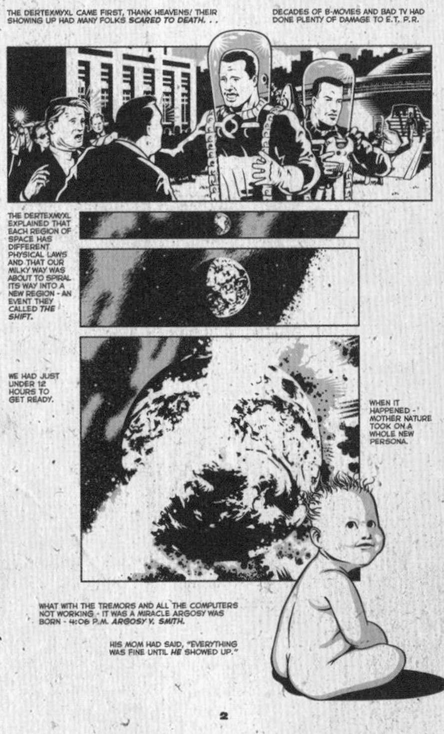
THE DERTEXMYXL CAME FIRST, THANK HEAVENS! THEIR SHOWING UP HAD MANY FOLKS SCARED TO DEATH. . .
DECADES OF B-MOVIES AND BAD TV HAD DONE PLENTY OF DAMAGE TO E.T. P.R.
THE DERTEXMYXL EXPLAINED THAT EACH REGION OF SPACE HAS DIFFERENT PHYSICAL LAWS AND THAT OUR MILKY WAY WAS ABOUT TO SPIRAL ITS WAY INTO A NEW REGION - AN EVENT THEY CALLED THE SHIFT.
WE HAD JUST UNDER 12 HOURS TO GET READY.
WHEN IT HAPPENED - MOTHER NATURE TOOK ON A WHOLE NEW PERSONA.
WHAT WITH THE TREMORS AND ALL THE COMPUTERS NOT WORKING - IT WAS A MIRACLE ARGOSY WAS BORN - 4:06 P.M. ARGOSY V. SMITH.
HIS MOM HAD SAID, "EVERYTHING WAS FINE UNTIL HE SHOWED UP."
2

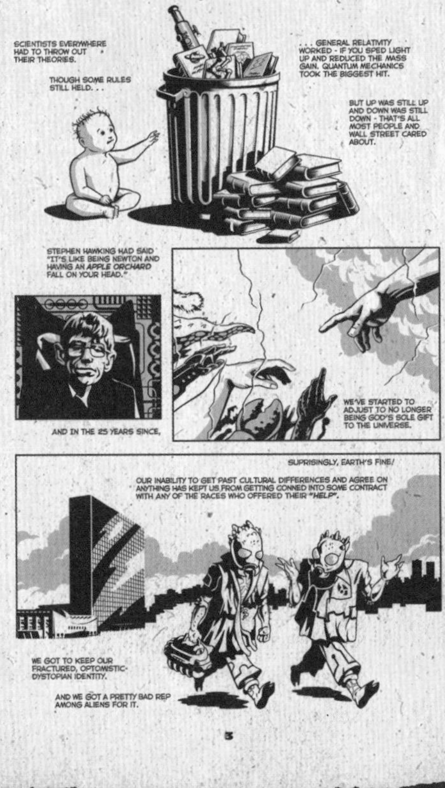
SCIENTISTS EVERYWHERE HAD TO THROW OUT THEIR THEORIES.
THOUGH SOME RULES STILL HELD. . .
. . . GENERAL RELATIVITY WORKED - IF YOU SPED LIGHT UP AND REDUCED THE MASS GAIN. QUANTUM MECHANICS TOOK THE BIGGEST HIT.
BUT UP WAS STILL UP AND DOWN WAS STILL DOWN - THAT'S ALL MOST PEOPLE AND WALL STREET CARED ABOUT.
STEPHEN HAWKING HAD SAID "IT'S LIKE BEING NEWTON AND HAVING AN APPLE ORCHARD FALL ON YOUR HEAD."
AND IN THE 25 YEARS SINCE,
WE'VE STARTED TO ADJUST TO NO LONGER BEING GOD'S SOLE GIFT TO THE UNIVERSE.
SUPRISINGLY, EARTH'S FINE!
OUR INABILITY TO GET PAST CULTURAL DIFFERENCES AND AGREE ON ANYTHING HAS KEPT US FROM GETTING CONNED INTO SOME CONTRACT WITH ANY OF THE RACES WHO OFFERED THEIR "HELP".
WE GOT TO KEEP OUR FRACTURED, OPTOMISTIC-DYSTOPIAN IDENTITY.
AND WE GOT A PRETTY BAD REP AMONG ALIENS FOR IT.
3

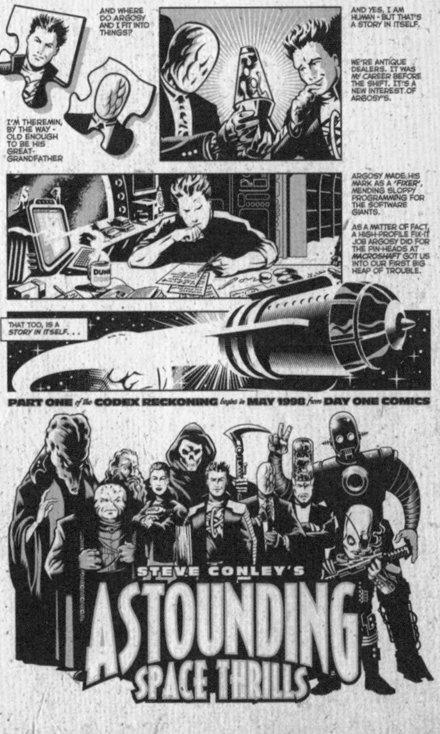
AND WHERE DO ARGOSY AND I FIT INTO THINGS?
I'M THEREMIN, BY THE WAY - OLD ENOUGH TO BE HIS GREAT-GRANDFATHER
AND YES, I AM HUMAN - BUT THAT'S A STORY IN ITSELF.
WE'RE ANTIQUE DEALERS. IT WAS MY CAREER BEFORE THE SHIFT. IT'S A NEW INTEREST OF ARGOSY'S.
ARGOSY MADE HIS MARK AS A 'FIXER', MENDING SLOPPY PROGRAMMING FOR THE SOFTWARE GIANTS.
AS A MATTER OF FACT, A HIGH-PROFILE FIX-IT JOB ARGOSY DID FOR THE PIN-HEADS AT MACROSHAFT GOT US INTO OUR FIRST BIG HEAP OF TROUBLE.
THAT TOO, IS A STORY IN ITSELF. . .
PART ONE of the CODEX RECKONING begins in MAY 1998 from DAY ONE COMICS
STEVE CONLEY'S
ASTOUNDING
SPACE THRILLS

ABOUT THE AUTHOR

Eisner nominated and Eagle Award-winner Steve Conley is a cartoonist, self-publisher, and online pioneer. He has written and illustrated his online and printed comics series *Astounding Space Thrills* since 1998, and has run the award-winning design studio Conley Interactive since 1996.

Steve co-created, with cartoonist Rick Veitch, COMICON.com, a popular community and daily comics news site found at www.comicon.com.

In 2004, he was a judge for the Eisner Awards, the Academy Awards for the comic book field. He wrote the proposal for the inclusion of web comics in the awards and thanks to his fellow judges, internet comics shared the stage with their printed counterparts for the first time.

He was Executive Director of the Small Press Expo, North America's Premier Independent Cartooning and Comics Arts Festival, from 2004-2005. He's taught cartooning as part of enrichment programs at a number of Virginia elementary schools and taught web and digital design at Northern Virginia Community College.

In addition to *Astounding Space Thrills*, Steve illustrated *Star Trek: Year Four* for IDW Publishing and *Michael Chabon Presents: The Amazing Adventures of the Escapist* for Dark Horse Comics.

Steve Conley lives in Arlington, Virginia, with his wife Britt.